Sparking Creativity

MW01069774

Blending popular culture and design theory, framed by a decade of scholarly research, this book highlights how play and humor fuel innovation. Now, more than ever, we are in need of creative solutions to global problems, but creative skills and abilities decline over time without intervention and practice.

Sparking Creativity provides empirically supported methods for embracing the often-trivialized domains of play and humor to increase our creativity. It shows that topical examples, such as *Seinfeld's* humor, the *Apples to Apples* board game, and the *Adventure Time* cartoon series, are more closely related to innovation than you might first think. The book is organized into five main parts, each containing short, engaging subsections and informative, playful, and colorful illustrations to demonstrate concepts.

Written in a humorous and accessible style, this book is aimed toward creative-minded entrepreneurs, designers, engineers, industry leaders, parents, educators, and students. It encourages a playful approach throughout a design process to produce truly innovative solutions.

Barry Kudrowitz, PhD, is a professor of product design and department head in the College of Design at the University of Minnesota, USA. There, he founded and directed the product design program from 2011–2021. Kudrowitz received his PhD from the Mechanical Engineering Department at the Massachusetts Institute of Technology (MIT), studying humor, creativity, and idea generation. Kudrowitz is interested in how creativity is perceived, evaluated, and learned. He has years of experience working with the toy industry and has taught toy design for over a decade. Kudrowitz co-designed a Nerf toy, an elevator simulator that was in operation at the International Spy Museum in Washington, D.C., and a ketchup-dispensing robot that was featured on the *Martha Stewart Show*. He is also the associate editor of the *International Journal of Food Design*.

"From Amy Klobachur's use of a comb to eat her salad to the invention of the Squatty Potty, from The Little Mermaid to Ru Paul's Drag Race, from robots that poop ketchup to Green Eggs and Ham, this playful, smart and engaging book by designer Barry Kudrowitz takes us on a twisty path to surprising and unfamiliar places as it helps to explore the nature of human creativity, how we can enhance it, and what ways we can use it to improve the quality of our lives. This is the ideal book to get your juices flowing."

Henry Jenkins, *Civic Imagination Project,*
University of Southern California, USA

"I once did a cartoon where a dad says to his young kid, 'Go out at play, Norman. It's your job.' It's a joke based on the idea that work and play are antithetical. Barry Kudrowitz has written a book that shows they mustn't be if we want the creative solutions our 21st-century workplace demands. He makes a compelling case for work being more like play and vice-versa to maximize the benefits of both."

Bob Mankoff, *former Cartoon Editor of* The New Yorker *Magazine, USA*

"It is not easy to write a serious book about creativity and innovation that is not to be read too seriously. But Kudrowitz does just that through a prolific use of playful design, humor, inspiring quotes and rigorous research. The book is filled with Silly Ideas, Shitty Robots and Poop Ice Cream – both the title of Chapter 10 and also examples of ways in which real innovation can spring forth from ideas, products, and designs that are fun, fanciful, and surprising. Kudrowitz writes, 'Things that seem silly at first may actually be innovative in the future.' And so an academic book that makes you laugh out loud might turn out to be a transformative approach to understanding the origins of and possibilities for creativity in our lives."

Steven J. Tepper, *Dean, Director and Foundation Professor,*
Herberger Institute for Design and the Arts, USA

"The beauty of humor is that it resolves tensions between opposites, aka as a pleasurable relief. In a world full of societal challenges, characterized by conflicts and polarities, we cannot underestimate the need for humor to spur innovation and creative solutions, connecting the non-obvious. Kudrowitz's incredibly rich and entertaining book demonstrates how we can design ourselves playfully out of any crisis. Meanwhile, you learn what is so great about very old Dutch cheese and our children's farms..."

Paul Hekkert, *Professor of Design,*
Delft University of Technology, The Netherlands

"Barry Kudrowitz has conducted years of rigorous, experimental studies on fostering creativity in designers, and he makes those results come alive in a playful, engaging way in Sparking Creativity. This book is a must for anyone who wants to unlock their own creativity, or teach others how to be more creative, using research-backed, yet accessible strategies. Barry will make you seriously creative!"

Maria Yang, *Associate Dean of Engineering, MIT, USA*

"This book provides great suggestions for using playful and humor-related experiences to enhance creative thinking and promote innovative actions. Readers from many professional fields can benefit from exploring its many ideas for fostering effective and wide-ranging actions to address contemporary issues and problems that need creative solutions."

Doris Bergen, *Distinguished Professor of Educational Psychology Emerita,*
Miami University, USA

Sparking Creativity

How Play and Humor Fuel Innovation and Design

Barry Kudrowitz

Routledge
Taylor & Francis Group

LONDON AND NEW YORK

Designed Cover Image: Barry Kudrowitz

First published 2023
by Routledge
4 Park Square, Milton Park, Abingdon, Oxon OX14 4RN

and by Routledge
605 Third Avenue, New York, NY 10158

Routledge is an imprint of the Taylor & Francis Group, an informa business

British Library Cataloguing-in-Publication Data
A catalogue record for this book is available from the British Library

Library of Congress Cataloging-in-Publication Data
Names: Kudrowitz, Barry, author.
Title: Sparking creativity : how play and humor fuel innovation and design /
Barry Kudrowitz.
Description: Abingdon, Oxon ; New York : Routledge, 2023. |
Includes bibliographical references and index.
Subjects: LCSH: Creative ability. | Design. | Wit and humor. | Play.
Classification: LCC BF408 .K8255 2023 (print) | LCC BF408 (ebook) |
DDC 153.3/5—dc23/eng/20230119
LC record available at https://lccn.loc.gov/2022049689
LC ebook record available at https://lccn.loc.gov/2022049690

ISBN: 978-1-032-23220-1 (hbk)
ISBN: 978-1-032-23215-7 (pbk)
ISBN: 978-1-003-27629-6 (ebk)

DOI: 10.4324/9781003276296

Typeset in Corbel
by codeMantra

Contents

Figures

A JOURNEY MAP OF
BIOGRAPHY AND ACKNOWLEDGEMENTS

I WAS RAISED IN BOCA RATON, FLORIDA
IN A CREATIVE AND LOVING FAMILY
WITH MY YOUNGER BROTHER. HI JON.
MY MOTHER WAS A TEACHER AND
MY FATHER WAS A PINSTRIPER
AND ENTREPRENEUR OF SORT.

I ATTRIBUTE MY SENSE OF PLAY AND HUMOR
TO MY GRANDFATHER, HARRY...
AND MY EXTENDED FAMILY IN NY AND NJ...
MY ARTISTIC INTERESTS TO MY FATHER, LARRY...
MY LOVE OF TEACHING TO MY MOTHER, SHARON...
AND MY LOVE OF PERFORMANCE AND THEATRE
TO MY GRANDMOTHER, GLORIA.

THEY ARE ALL VERY PROUD
THAT I WROTE A BOOK!

BOCARATON

ORLANDO

AS A KID, I LOVED MAKING THINGS
AND SPECIFICALLY CREATING
EXPERIENCES FOR PEOPLE.
WITH THE DREAM OF BECOMING AN
IMAGINEER FOR DISNEY, I STUDIED
MECHANICAL ENGINEERING AT THE
UNIVERSITY OF CENTRAL FLORIDA IN
ORLANDO.

MY PROFESSOR, ERIC PETERSEN,
ENCOURAGED ME TO GO TO GRADUATE
SCHOOL AND APPLY TO MIT.

AT MIT, I STUDIED UNDER
PROFESSOR DAVID WALLACE IN THE
MECHANICAL ENGINEERING DEPT.
MY PHD WORK WAS LATER ADVISED
ALSO BY PROFS. WOODIE FLOWERS,
MARIA YANG, DORIS BERGEN, AND
NICOLA SENIN.

DAVID WALLACE, BILL FIENUP,
AND I WORKED TOGETHER ON A
HASBRO SPONSORED RESEARCH
PROJECT TO DEVELOP NEW
PROJECTILE TOYS FOR
SUPERSOAKER AND NERF. THIS
WORK BECOME OUR MASTER'S
THESIS BUT ALSO LED TO THE
NERF ATOM BLASTER AND AN
MIT CLASS CALLED
TOY PRODUCT DESIGN.

DAVID SHOWED ME THAT
TEACHING IS DESIGNING AN
IMMERSIVE EXPERIENCE.
HE ALSO SHOWED ME THE VALUE
OF INDUSTRIAL DESIGN AND
ENCOURAGED ME TO STUDY
ABROAD AT TU DELFT.

MIT

DAVID

AT TU DELFT IN THE NETHERLANDS, I LEARNED FOUNDATIONAL INDUSTRIAL DESIGN SKILLS.
I ALSO WORKED CLOSELY WITH PROFS. GEKE LUDDEN, RICK SCHIFFERSTEIN, AND PAUL HEKKERT IN THE ID STUDIOLAB ON RESEARCH RELATED TO SURPRISE AND HUMOR IN PRODUCTS. THEY TAUGHT ME HOW TO CONDUCT EXPERIMENTAL STUDIES AND WHAT RESEARCH IN A DESIGN SCHOOL CAN BE. THIS WORK SET THE FOUNDATION FOR WHAT EVENTUALLY BECAME MY PHD RESEARCH ON IMPROVISATIONAL COMEDY AND CREATIVITY.

AFTER RETURNING TO MIT TO FINISH MY PHD, I WAS A TEACHING ASSISTANT AND RESEARCH ASSISTANT WITH MY FUTURE WIFE, MONICA. SHE IS MY GREATEST INSPIRATION AND FRIEND.

TOGETHER WE LIVED WITH SIX OTHER GRADUATE STUDENTS IN A HOUSE THAT WE CALLED LOPEZ. WE BECAME A FAMILY OF FRIENDS. STEVE, TERESA, TONY, SUNGYON, MONICA, AND I SUPPORTED EACH OTHER THROUGH LIFE.

MONICA AND I MOVED TO MINNEAPOLIS WHERE I DEVELOPED THE PRODUCT DESIGN PROGRAM AT THE UNIVERSITY OF MINNESOTA COLLEGE OF DESIGN WITH THE HELP OF SOME FANTASTIC COLLEAGUES LIKE CHRIS, TEJAS, CARLYE, JIM, BECKY, TREVOR, SUE, ANDREW, AMANDA, AND TOM. MUCH OF THE CONTENT OF THIS BOOK WAS DEVELOPED FOR CLASSES AND WHILE ON SABBATICAL.

AFTER ELEVEN YEARS OF DIRECTING THE UMN PRODUCT DESIGN PROGRAM, I BECAME A DEPARTMENT HEAD.

MY INSPIRATION NOW COMES FROM OUR TWO CHILDREN, POPPY AND SAGE.
THIS BOOK IS DEDICATED TO YOU. I HOPE YOU STAY AS PLAYFUL, SILLY, AND CURIOUS AS YOU ARE NOW. I HOPE YOU ENJOY THE FUN PICTURES IN THIS BOOK, AND, WHEN YOU ARE OLDER, MAYBE YOU WILL ENJOY THE WORDS TOO.

I LOVE YOU ALL.
THANK YOU FOR MAKING ME WHO I AM, SUPPORTING ME, AND INSPIRING THE CONTENT OF THIS BOOK.

INTRODUCTION

Hi, my name is Barry and I study creativity and innovation. I'd like to play a short game with you. It really won't take that long. For this activity, you will need something to write with and something to keep time. I've provided some lines on the page for you to write on, but if writing in a book is sacrilege to you or maybe this isn't even your book (yet), you can always play this game on a separate sheet of paper.

On the following page, I would like you to list as many uses that you can think of for a paper clip. Set your timer for three minutes. Please don't cheat! You will be referencing your responses later in this book. Are you ready? Begin!

DOI: 10.4324/9781003276296-1

So, what you just did was actually a creativity assessment called the *Alternative Uses Test* or *Unusual Uses Test* and it is a measure of *divergent thinking ability* (Guilford, 1956). In other words, this was a test of your ability to think in a variety of different directions when given a certain prompt. So how did you do? Well, there is a relatively easy means of scoring this test. It simply involves counting the number of uses that you wrote down. Let's do that now.

In my research, I have found that the more alternative uses that you generate, the more likely you are to uncover alternative uses that other people think are creative (Kudrowitz & Dippo, 2013). In another similar study, I asked people to generate creative product ideas (specifically for toasters, umbrellas, and toothbrushes) and, in that study, the results were the same. Those who generated more product ideas had more product ideas that others thought were creative (Kudrowitz & Wallace, 2013).

In the latter study, I was testing different groups of individuals including students, non-experts, professional designers, and professional engineers. The unexpected finding was that the group of people who had the most creative product ideas (the individuals circled in Figure 0.1) had no connection to the product industry whatsoever. This highly creative group of people were professional improvisational (improv) comedians (Kudrowitz & Wallace, 2010). *Improv comedians were generating more creative consumer product ideas than professional product designers.*

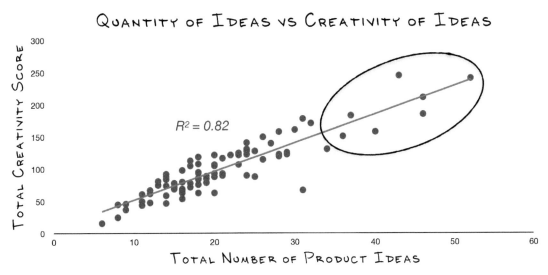

Figure 0.1 A visual of the relationship between creativity scores and quantity of ideas in the Kudrowitz & Wallace (2012) product idea generation study. The dots represent individual participants in the study including designers, engineers, and students. The circled dots were professional improvisational comedians.

If you have seen the television show *Whose Line is it Anyway?,* you may be familiar with the game called "props." In this game, the performers (improv comedians) are asked to come up with alternative uses for an assortment of random physical objects. This is the Alternative Uses Test presented as a physical challenge. Improvisational comedians are very good at divergent thinking, and you will see in Part IV how improvisational training builds these skills.

There is a second demographic of people who are equally good at divergent thinking. Any guesses who this might be?

Children!

Children are great at taking an object and turning that object into a variety of different things. The cardboard box axiom is that children are often more engaged with the packaging than the toy that came inside. For those of you who have had the pleasure of watching children play, you may notice that toys and objects are often used in ways that are not intended or expected.

In one study, Land and Jarman took a group of 1600 children and gave them a creativity assessment like the one you just completed. In this study, there was a score for which the individual was determined to be an expert. Out of the 1600 children, almost all of them (98%) were experts at divergent thinking (Land & Jarman, 1992). An interesting thing about this study was that it was longitudinal, meaning that they took the same group of children, and they tested them again five years later. And five years later, only 32% of them were experts at divergent thinking. And five years later, only 10%. And then they took a group of 200,000 adults, and out of this group of adults, only 2% were experts at divergent thinking.

So how did you do on that paper clip Alternative Uses Test? Perhaps not as well as you think you did. We will look at some detailed data on this in Part I as we discuss creativity assessment methods.

The good news is that almost all of us *were* capable of being creative at one time (at least as measured by this assessment of divergent thinking). The bad news is that somewhere along the way, we lost this ability. Creativity expert, Sir Ken Robinson, says that "we are educating people out of their creativity capacities" (Robinson, 2006). This is beyond reducing time for recess and the arts in primary and secondary school. We are taught that we shouldn't mess up. Because if we mess up, we will get bad grades. And we don't want bad grades, do we? So, *don't do things differently from how you are taught!*

Moving beyond secondary school, what do universities look for in applicants? In the United States, it is typically GPA, SAT, and ACT scores. Where is the assessment of creativity in those standardized tests? And does that even matter in the admission process? Studies found *no* relationship between creativity measures and the SAT, and *inverse* relationships between creative measures and both the ACT and high school class rank (Kaufman, 2015; McCarthy & Blake, 2017). We are actively penalizing the creative students and we need to rethink our selection process in higher education.

In the United States, "since 1990, even as IQ scores have risen, creative thinking scores have significantly decreased. The decrease for kindergartners through third graders was the most significant" (Kim, 2011). The American educational system is trending toward rote memorization and standardized testing, while play, art, and creativity appear to be reduced (Bronson & Merryman, 2010). This is a major concern as we are in desperate need of new creative solutions to national and international problems of technical, social, and environmental nature. Creativity is a core competency that industry values (Nussbaum et al., 2005). Industry wants employees to have knowledge in a field, but also to have the creative skills to bring change, address problems, and innovate. If society needs creative solutions and industry wants creative leaders, how can we innovate if we are stifling our creative abilities?

This is when I put on my clown nose and say...*You know children and comedians are pretty creative.* Come join me on an empirically supported adventure into the magical world of play and humor to uncover how these whimsical domains spark creativity, innovation, and design. And how they can do the same for you.

References

Bronson, P., & Merryman, S. (2010, July 10). The creativity crisis. *Newsweek*.

Guilford, J. P. (1956). The structure of intellect. *Psychological Bulletin, 53*(4), 267–293.

Kaufman, S. B. (2015). Does college admissions criteria capture creativity? *Scientific American*.

Kim, K. H. (2011). The creativity crisis: The decrease in creative thinking scores on the Torrance tests of creative thinking. *Creativity Research Journal, 23*(4), 285–295.

Kudrowitz, B., & Dippo, C. (2013). When does a paper clip become a sundial? Exploring the progression of novelty in the alternative uses test. *Journal of Integrated Design and Process Science: Special Issue on Applications and Theory of Computational Creativity, 17*(4), 3–18.

Kudrowitz, B., & Wallace, D. (2010, October). Improvisational comedy and product design ideation: Making non-obvious connections between seemingly unrelated things. *International Conference on Design and Emotion*, Chicago, Illinois, USA.

Kudrowitz, B. M., & Wallace D. R. (2013). Assessing the quality of ideas from prolific, early-stage product ideation. *Journal of Engineering Design, 24*(2), 120–139.

Land, G., & Jarman, B. (1992). *Breakpoint and beyond: Mastering the future today*. HarperCollins Publishers.

McCarthy, C., & Blake, S. (2017). Is this going to be on the test? No child left creative. *SRATE Journal, 26*(2), 25–31.

Nussbaum, B., Berner, R., & Brady, D. (2005, August 1). Get creative! How to build innovative companies. *Bloomberg BuisnessWeek*.

Robinson, K. (Presenter). (2006, February). Do schools kill creativity? *TED2006*.

Part I

Creativity, Play, and Humor

1

THE FOUR REQUISITES OF A CREATIVE PERSON, DR. MOMEN'S CLOTHING DRYER, AND *CAPTAIN PLANET*

The first step in learning how we can be more creative and innovative is to better understand what we mean by *creativity* and what it means to be a creative person. In academic literature, there are typically four factors that contribute to your individual creativity. This four-part model is in line with creativity expert Dr. Teresa Amabile's *Componential Model of Creativity* (1996); however, I'm going to take this in a *Captain Planet* direction (or maybe I should say "Captain Creativity").

The first creative factor is appropriate **cognitive skills and knowledge**. To have ideas, you need to have some intelligence and knowledge of a domain. Aside from *serendipitous* examples, you are unlikely to discover a cure for a disease without knowing anything about the disease, you are unlikely to produce a creative meal without having cooked before, and you are unlikely to compose a creative song without knowing anything about music. In addition to your knowledge of a specific domain, there is also general intelligence. Ellis Paul Torrance and Joy Paul Guilford (1967) were the first to suggest the *Threshold Hypothesis*, illustrated in Figure 1.1. This theory proposes a positive correlation between low intelligence scores and low creativity scores, and a diminishing

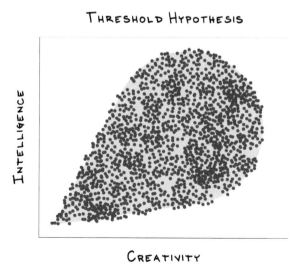

Figure 1.1 An illustration of the Threshold Hypothesis in which creativity and intelligence are correlated at low intelligence, and the correlation disappears as intelligence increases.

DOI: 10.4324/9781003276296-3

correlation as intelligence increases. In other words, if you are "not smart," you are not going to be creative; *however*, being smart doesn't necessarily mean you are also going to be creative.

This brings us to the second factor (or set of factors) that contributes to your creativity: your **personality, mood, and mindset**. This is often the factor that most people equate with creativity. The person wearing the fluorescent space-cat-with-laser-beam-eyes shirt must be creative, right? There are a handful of personality traits, mindsets, and moods that correlate with creativity. Some of the personality traits that are important for creativity are: tolerance for ambiguity, openness to experience, novelty-seeking, curiosity, extraversion, unconventional values, independence of judgment, preference for challenge/complexity, self-confidence, and propensity for risk taking (Russ, 2003).

Let's take a moment to introspect. Are you the type of person who is open to tasting something that you haven't tasted before? Are you seeking out interesting new restaurants, and when at restaurants, do you always try new dishes? Are you the type of person that enjoys going to new places? If you answered yes to these, you are likely a novelty-seeking person that is open to new experiences. *Openness to experience* is the personality factor that most strongly and consistently correlates with creativity (Puryear et al., 2017). Another personality trait, *novelty-seeking*, correlates with both *openness to experience* and standard tests of creativity (Gocłowska et al., 2019). It seems that being open to new things and seeking out new things is the essence of the creative personality. This type of person would be open to: alternative solutions, trying new ways of doing things, looking for ways to improve something, exploring options, and, in general, seeking out inspiration. You may say, "that sounds too extraverted for me!" As it turns out, *extraversion* is the second most strongly correlated personality trait linked to creativity (Puryear et al., 2017). Lastly, in line with the subject of this book, research has shown that *positive affect* including *happiness* (Pannells & Claxton, 2008), *playfulness* (Russ & Grossman-McKee, 1990; Wyver & Spence, 1990; Russ et al., 1999), and *sense of humor* (Humke & Scheafer, 1996) are positively correlated with creativity.

Some of these traits and moods may seem obvious, but there are a few less obvious traits that correlate with creativity. *Conscientiousness* (or wanting to do a task well and carefully), for example, is sometimes correlated with creativity, specifically when the creative measure involves achievement or production as opposed to simply coming up with ideas. Some people would assume perhaps the opposite trait would be affiliated with creativity (being a messy, reckless, risk-taker); however, innovative people may actually be more risk averse (Toh & Miller, 2016). It takes creativity to determine that you have had a creative idea, but it also takes creativity to determine which ideas to pursue, which ideas to save for later, and which ideas to discard. Or, in other words, parodying Kenny Rogers' *The Gambler* (Schlitz, 1976): you have to know when to hold [ideas], know when to fold [ideas], know when to walk away [from ideas], and know when to run [from ideas]. Although creativity is typically associated with positive personality traits, creativity has also been correlated with a few negative traits including *dishonesty* (Gino & Ariely, 2012) and *arrogance* (Silvia et al., 2011). You dishonest creative types know who you are, but you are also probably too arrogant to admit it.

Alright, so let's assume you meet some basic threshold of intelligence, *and* you are generally open to experience (with maybe a dash of extraversion and conscientiousness). There are still two more factors that contribute to your creativity. A third factor is **intrinsic motivation and interest**. You may have all the cognitive abilities to be creative, but the prompt, situation, or challenge may not be of any interest to you! At least 15 studies to date have shown intrinsic motivation and creativity to be strongly correlated (de Jesus et al., 2013). In my own research, an individual's interest in a topic was significantly correlated with the originality of their responses in real-world design challenges (Tran et al., 2022). In other words, you are more likely to be creative if you find the subject matter engaging.

These first three factors start to overlap and blur together as you are likely more knowledgeable about a topic you are interested in, *and* you are likely more open to experiences related to a topic you are interested in. Assuming all three of these factors are present, a final *external* factor that contributes to your creative ability is your **environment**.

There are a variety of studies that explore specific physical environmental factors on creative performance. Here are a few fun ones:

- You can be more creative if you spend time outside in a natural setting (Atchley et al., 2012; Ferraro, 2015; Yu & Hsieh, 2020).
- You can be more creative in a blue-colored room (Mehta & Zhu, 2009).
- You can be more creative in a room with ceilings that are perceived to be tall (Meyers-Levy & Zhu, 2007).
- You can be more creative in a space with plants, bright lights, and windows (Ceylan et al., 2008).

Looking at this list of creative environmental characteristics, it's quite possible that they are all related in that we tend to be more creative when we don't feel constrained by an indoor structure.

There are also more general and abstract elements to an environment suitable for creativity. For example, are you in an environment where creativity is *encouraged and valued*? Do you have *time* to try new things and explore? Is there *space* for you to experiment and test ideas? Do you have access to the necessary *tools* and *materials*?

Using a *Captain Planet* parody: when your creative-componential-powers combine (*knowledge, creative mindset, motivation, environment*), the power is yours to change the world!

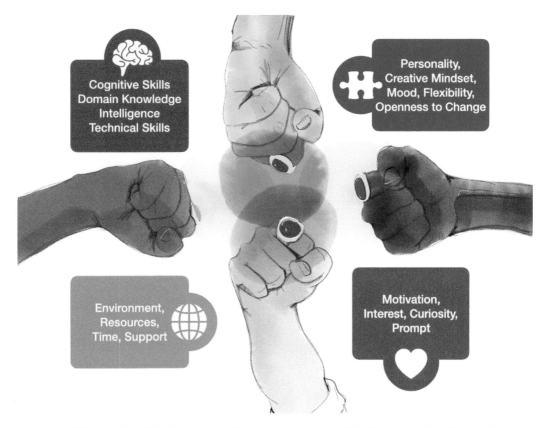

Figure 1.2 "Captain Creativity": A Captain Planet parody model of the four requisites of a creative person (knowledge, creative mindset, motivation, environment).

Let's apply this four-point "Captain Creativity" framework to a real "Planeteer." Dr. Ayyoub Momen invented new way of drying clothes (Pepitone, 2016). The impetus of his idea was the fact that clothing dryers are one of the most energy-intensive appliances in the home. Dr. Momen was both *knowledgeable* about this issue and was also intrinsically *motivated* to reduce energy consumption. He also had the *creative mindset* to question this current established means of drying clothes and consider if there are better ways of doing the same task. Additionally, he had prior *knowledge* of other means of evaporating water, including ultrasonic vibration, like the mechanism inside humidifiers. It was then his curious and conscientious *personality* that questioned if it were possible to use something like a low-power ultrasonic humidifier to evaporate the water out of clothing. His years of training and *knowledge* of science and engineering allowed him to evaluate the feasibility of this concept. He was also fortunate to have the supportive work *environment* at the Oak Ridge National Laboratory to allow the time and resources to test the idea.

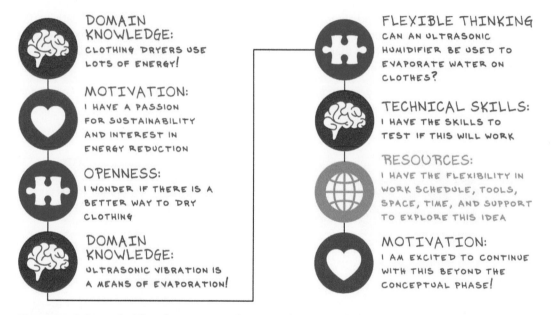

Figure 1.3 A theoretical flowchart representing a creative process behind Dr. Momen's clothing dryer invention.

Dr. Momen found that this method can dry clothes in half the time using 7–16 times less energy than a standard clothing dryer, and without heating up the clothing or producing lint (Pepitone, 2016; Peng et al., 2017). If this type of clothing dryer replaced the current technology, it could save billions of dollars yearly on energy—in addition to the positive environmental impact (which was the original *motivation*).

In this chapter, we covered some general prerequisites for creativity, but what does it mean to be creative? For that, we should look at how we measure and evaluate creativity. There are a variety of assessments of creativity (you already experienced one of them in the Introduction) and I'll discuss a few more in the following chapters.

References

Amabile, T. M. (1996). *Creativity in context: Update to "the social psychology of creativity."* Westview Press.

Atchley, R. A., Strayer, D. L., & Atchley, P. (2012). Creativity in the wild: Improving creative reasoning through immersion in natural settings. *PLoS ONE, 7*(12), e51474.

Ceylan, C., Dul, J., & Aytac, S. (2008). Can the office environment stimulate a manager's creativity? *Human Factors and Ergonomics in Manufacturing & Service Industries, 18*(6), 589–602.

de Jesus, S. N., Rus, C. L., Lens, W., & Imaginário, S. (2013). Intrinsic motivation and creativity related to product: A meta-analysis of the studies published between 1990–2010. *Creativity Research Journal, 25*(1), 80–84.

Ferraro, F. (2015). Enhancement of convergent creativity following a multiday wilderness experience. *Ecopsychology, 7*(1), 7–11.

Gino, F., & Ariely, D. (2012). The dark side of creativity: Original thinkers can be more dishonest. *Journal of Personality and Social Psychology, 102*(3), 445–459.

Gocłowska, M. A., Ritter, S. M., Elliot, A. J., & Baas, M. (2019). Novelty seeking is linked to openness and extraversion, and can lead to greater creative performance. *Journal of personality, 87*(2), 252–266.

Guilford, J. P. (1967). *The nature of human intelligence.* McGraw-Hill Book Co.

Humke, C., & Schaefer, C. E. (1996). Sense of humor and creativity. *Perceptual and Motor Skills, 82*(2), 544–546.

Mehta, R., & Zhu, R. J. (2009). Blue or Red? Exploring the effect of color on cognitive task. Performances. *Science, 323*(5918), 1226–1229.

Meyers-Levy, J., & Zhu, R. J. (2007). The influence of ceiling height: The effect of priming on the type of processing that people use. *Journal of Consumer Research, 34*, 174–186.

Pannells, T. C., & Claxton, A. F. (2008). Happiness, creative ideation, and locus of control. *Creativity Research Journal, 20*(1), 67–71.

Peng, C., Momen, A. M., & Moghaddam, S. (2017). An energy-efficient method for direct-contact ultrasonic cloth drying. *Energy, 138*, 133–138.

Pepitone, J. (2016, June 21). This ultrasonic dryer will dry your clothes in half the time. *CNN Money.*

Puryear, J. S., Kettler, T., & Rinn, A. N. (2017). Relationships of personality to differential conceptions of creativity: A systematic review. *Psychology of Aesthetics, Creativity, and the Arts, 11*(1), 59–68.

Russ, S. W. (2003). Play and creativity: Developmental issues. *Scandinavian Journal of Educational Research, 47*(3), 291–303.

Russ, S. W., & Grossman-McKee, A. (1990). Affective expression in children's fantasy play, primary process thinking on the Rorschach, and divergent thinking. *Journal of Personality Assessment, 54*(3–4), 756–771.

Russ, S. W., Robins, A. L., & Christiano, B. A. (1999). Pretend play: Longitudinal prediction of creativity and affect in fantasy in children. *Creativity Research Journal, 12*(2), 129–139.

Schlitz, D. A. (1976). The Gambler [Recorded by K. Rogers]. On *The Gambler* [Vinyl]. New York, NY: United Artists Records. (1978).

Silvia, P. J., Kaufman, J. C., Reiter-Palmon, R., & Wigert, B. (2011). Cantankerous creativity: Honesty–Humility, Agreeableness, and the HEXACO structure of creative achievement. *Personality and Individual Differences, 51*(5), 687–689.

Toh, C. A., & Miller, S. R. (2016). Choosing creativity: the role of individual risk and ambiguity aversion on creative concept selection in engineering design. *Research in Engineering Design, 27*, 195–219.

Tran, K., Kudrowitz, B., & Koutstaal, W. (2022). Fostering creative minds: what predicts and boosts design competence in the classroom? *International Journal of Technology and Design Education, 32*(1), 585–616.

Wyver, S. R., & Spence, S. H. (1999). Play and divergent problem solving: Evidence supporting a reciprocal relationship. *Early Education and Development, 10*(4), 419–444.

Yu, C. P., & Hsieh, H. (2020). Beyond restorative benefits: Evaluating the effect of forest therapy on creativity. *Urban Forestry & Urban Greening, 51*, 126670.

2

DIVERGENT THINKING, ROCKET RACOON, AND *SCRIBBLENAUTS*

In the Introduction, you did an example of the *Alternative Uses Test* (if you skipped it, go back and do it now as we will continuously reference your data). This test was developed by J.P. Guilford in 1967 as part of a theory called the *Structure of Intellect*. He was the first person to propose evaluating the creativity of people with a pen and paper psychometric assessment (Guilford, 1956). His test was originally called the *Unusual Uses Test*, and, over the years, others have adapted versions of it.

In the test, subjects are asked to think of as many unconventional uses for a simple object (e.g., a brick, a newspaper). In theory, a creative person can think of a variety of different ideas when given a certain starting point. Guilford calls this ability *spontaneous flexibility*, but it can also be referred to as *divergent thinking*. There are a few other creative terms related to this concept. For example: *lateral thinking*, a process promoted by Edward de Bono (1970), involves viewing a problem or concept through different lenses to obtain non-obvious solutions. This involves divergent thinking to break away from the expected or traditional path. Another related term is "*Thinking Outside of the Box.*" An inverse phenomenon is called *functional fixedness*, which is the state of *not* being able to see an object beyond its traditional uses. To have more than one response on this Alternative Uses Test, you need to break free of any functional fixedness associated with the traditional uses of the paperclip.

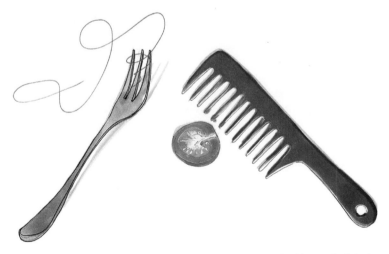

Figure 2.1 Examples of breaking functional fixedness and divergent thinking: a fork being used as a comb by *The Little Mermaid* and a comb allegedly being used as a fork by Senator Amy Klobuchar.

DOI: 10.4324/9781003276296-4

During the 2020 US presidential election, presidential candidate and Minnesota State Senator, Amy Klobuchar, was criticized for allegedly eating a salad with a comb when she did not have a fork (Flegenheimer & Ember, 2019). This is divergent thinking and breaking functional fixedness in practice! It should be a celebrated problem-solving ability (especially for a presidential candidate). Interestingly, the exact inverse exemplum occurs in Disney's *Little Mermaid* with "the Dinglehopper" (i.e., fork) where Scuttle (the seagull) explains to Ariel (the mermaid) how the fork is used by humans to "straighten their hair out," which Ariel later demonstrates (also to criticism).

No matter what terms you use to describe this ability, divergent thinking has been shown to be moderately predictive of creative ability and it remains widely used as a creativity assessment (Furnham et al., 2008; Runco & Acar, 2012; Beaty & Silvia, 2012).

Popular culture also tends to associate divergent thinking ability with creativity. Protagonists of television shows *MacGyver* and *Burn Notice* as well as Marvel's Tinkerer and Rocket Racoon are celebrated for solving a wide range of situational problems using common objects in unusual manners. The verb "MacGyver" has become part of the American English lexicon to mean "improvise with existing resources" to find a non-obvious solution to a problem.

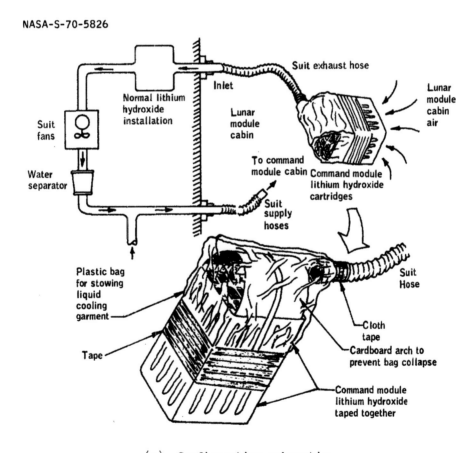

NASA-S-70-5826

(a) Configuration schematic.

Figure 6.7-1.- Supplemental carbon dioxide removal system.

Figure 2.2 Figure from NASA's Apollo 13 Mission Report (1970) showing the "MacGyvered" carbon dioxide removal system that saved the lives of the astronauts onboard.

A non-fiction "MacGyvering" occurred on the Apollo 13 mission when an oxygen tank exploded, and the crew had to relocate to a lunar module for the trip home. This lunar module, unfortunately, was not designed for more than two astronauts and it began to quickly fill with dangerous levels of carbon dioxide (Patel, 2014). The crew could only use items on board (including the stereotypical MacGyvering essential: duct tape) to retrofit a square peg (new carbon dioxide scrubber) into a round hole (ventilation system). A schematic of this MacGyvered solution is shown in Figure 2.2 taken from the Apollo 13 Mission Report (1970). The story was so suspenseful and creative that it became a key plot element of the *Apollo 13* movie.

There are a couple of experimental tests of functional fixedness that also double as measures of creativity as they relate to divergent thinking, lateral thinking, and thinking outside the box. The most popular of these tests is Karl Duncker's (1945) *Candle Problem* that involves giving a participant a candle, a box of thumbtacks, and a book of matches. The participant is asked to attach the candle to the wall such that it does not drip onto a table below when lit. If you have not seen this problem before, how would you solve it?

Common "incorrect" responses involve attempting to use the tacks to secure the candle to the wall directly or using the matches to melt the candle to the wall. An elegant solution involves removing the tacks from the box, tacking the box to the wall, and putting the candle in the box.

To get to this solution, it requires the individual to view the tack box as something other than a container to hold tacks. It requires the individual to think like MacGyver (or Rocket Raccoon or Amy Klobuchar) and separate the objects from their traditional functions. You have to literally think of the tacks as being "outside of the box" to come up with this solution. An interesting finding in Duncker's study was that participants were twice as likely to see the box as a potential candlestick holder if the box was presented without the thumbtacks inside (1945). This is an example of an *insight problem.* Insight problems are not able to be solved systematically or in a structured conventional manner and require you to engage in flexible thinking (Gilhooly & Murphy, 2005). These problems require a shift in perspective to come to a solution.

Figure 2.3 An illustrated representation of the visual supplement from the Duncker Candle Problem.

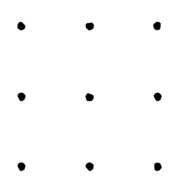

Figure 2.4 The Nine Dots Puzzle is an example of an insight problem.

A common insight problem is the *Nine Dots Puzzle* in which nine dots are presented as in Figure 2.4 and one is tasked with connecting all nine dots using four straight lines without lifting the writing implement from the paper.

If you have not seen this before, all solutions require drawing lines that extend outside of the perceived box created by the grid of dots. Some attribute the saying "thinking outside the box" to *this* puzzle (Boyd, 2014). Like the Duncker Candle Problem, participants are more likely to solve the puzzle if they are presented with a hint—in this case, that the lines need to go outside the "box" (Lung & Dominowski, 1985). In insight problems, such as the Candle Problem and the Nine Dots, the moment the shift in perspective occurs, a solution suddenly presents itself and there is an *Aha! moment* (to be discussed further in the next chapter).

You may recall from the previous chapter that *intrinsic* motivation fuels creativity, however *extrinsic* motivation does not. Another study looked at the Candle Problem and found that subjects who were told that they would receive a cash reward for solving the puzzle performed *worse* than those who were told that they were simply helping with an experiment (Glucksberg, 1962).

If the Candle Stick problem seemed fun to you, there is a video game called *Scribblenauts* that rewards divergent thinking of this nature. Like in the real world, there are many ways of solving a problem and *Scribblenauts* encourages players to search for these alternative solutions. One problem-solving technique is to *look for another solution* because there can be *more than one right answer*. Often in games and in life, we are told there is *one* right way of doing something or there is a *best* way of doing something. In the game of *Scribblenauts*, there are dozens (or maybe hundreds) of ways of solving a problem. The gameplay is simple: a challenge is presented (e.g., get cat down from tree) and you can type anything, and it will appear to help you complete the task (e.g., ladder, chainsaw, boomerang, jetpack, firehose). As Mark Twain said in *A Connecticut Yankee in King Arthur's Court* (1889), there is "more than one way to skin a cat." In this specific case, there is more than one way to safely get a cat out of a tree (while keeping its skin intact).

If you are concerned that maybe you are not great at divergent thinking, there are some tools that help facilitate this critical element of creativity. A *mind map* is one technique that helps organize and visualize one's thoughts and ideas in a non-linear, network-structured representation (Buzan, 1974). In a mind map, one starts with a central concept (such as a paperclip) and radially adds related topics to that central concept with lines (i.e., branches). By branching outward away from the central concept through linked associations, the process forces you to diverge. If you have three minutes to spare, try doing the paperclip Alternative Uses Test again, but this time do it with a mind map instead of a list—you may think of a wider variety of ideas (Leeds & Kudrowitz, 2016). As association making is so critical to creativity and humor, I will address mind mapping again in Chapter 28. For now, to get meta with this topic, here is a mind map *about* divergent thinking *demonstrating* divergent thinking. Interestingly, an inverted pentagram seems to have emerged. This was not intentional, but just in case, maybe do not recite any spells with this page open.

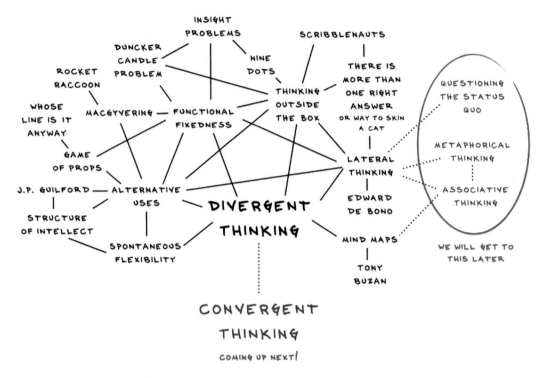

Figure 2.5 A mind map of divergent thinking illustrating divergent thinking.

References

Beaty, R. E., & Silvia, P. J. (2012). Why do ideas get more creative across time? An executive interpretation of the serial order effect in divergent thinking tasks. *Psychology of Aesthetics, Creativity, and the Arts, 6*(4), 309–319.

Boyd, D. (2014, February 6). Thinking outside the box: A misguided idea. *Psychology Today.*

Buzan, T. (1974). *Use your head.* BBC Books.

De Bono, E. (1970). *Lateral thinking: A textbook of creativity.* Ward Lock Educational.

Duncker, K. (1945). On problem-solving. *Psychological Monographs, 58*(5), i–113.

Flegenheimer, M., & Ember, S. (2019, February 22). How Amy Klobuchar treats her staff. *The New York Times.*

Furnham, A., Batey, M., Anand, K., & Manfield, J. (2008). Personality, hypomania, intelligence and creativity. *Personality and Individual Differences, 44*(5), 1060–1069.

Gilhooly, K. J., & Murphy, P. (2005). Differentiating insight from non-insight problems. *Thinking & Reasoning, 11*(3), 279–302.

Glucksberg, S. (1962). The influence of strength of drive on functional fixedness and perceptual recognition. *Journal of Experimental Psychology, 63*(1), 36–41.

Guilford, J. P. (1956). The structure of intellect. *Psychological Bulletin, 53*(4), 267–293.

Leeds, A., & Kudrowitz, B. (2016). Exploring how novel ideas are generated in mind maps. *Proceedings of the 4th International Conference on Design Creativity, ICDC 2016*, Atlanta, Georgia, USA.

Lung, C. T., & Dominowski, R. L. (1985). Effects of strategy instructions and practice on nine-dot problem solving. *Journal of Experimental Psychology: Learning, Memory, and Cognition, 11*(4), 804–811.

Mission Evaluation Team. (1970). *Apollo 13 Mission Report* (Report No. MSC-02680). National Aeronautics and Space Administration (NASA).

Patel, N. (2014, October 8). The greatest space hack ever. *Popular Science.*

Runco, M. A., & Acar. S. (2012). Divergent thinking as an indicator of creative potential. *Creativity Research Journal, 24*(1), 66–75.

Twain, M. (1889). *A Connecticut Yankee in King Arthur's court.* Charles L. Webster & Co.

3

CONVERGENT THINKING, BUNNY SCISSORS, AND SHERLOCK HOLMES

Divergent thinking is only one piece of creativity. You can imagine that going on and on in all different directions is not very helpful unless you can ultimately bring it back to some original problem or impetus. Creativity also requires *convergent thinking*. Convergent thinking is congruent with the *Associative Theory of Creativity* by Sarnoff Mednick (1962). This theory is quite simple:

Creativity is about making non-obvious connections between seemingly unrelated things.

Variations of this theory emerged around the same time. Koestler's *Bisociative Theory* (1964) describes any creative act to involve "the bringing together of previously separate areas of knowledge and experience." Cartier describes a similar theory in his work:

> There is only one way in which a person ever acquires a new idea: that is, by the combination or association of two or more ideas [they] already [have] into a new juxtaposition, in such a manner as to discover a relationship among them of which [they were] not previously aware (1963).

Let's look at an example of the Associative Theory of Creativity. Cyrus McCormick was an American inventor, and sometime between 1830 and 1840, he developed the first mechanical reaper (patented in 1834). This is a device that gets pulled by horses through a wheat field and mechanically cuts and bales the stalks. For those young city folk, this is like *Frank the Combine* from Disney's *Cars*. The idea for the mechanical reaper emerged by making the connection that shears are used for hair and wheat stalks look like large hairs (Hoorn, 2014). Therefore, giant shears might be used to cut wheat.

Figure 3.1 An illustration of the non-obvious connection between cutting hair and cutting wheat that may have resulted in the invention of the mechanical reaper.

DOI: 10.4324/9781003276296-5

It may seem obvious *now* to use a large shearing mechanism to cut wheat, but that is not how wheat was harvested prior to this invention. Since the dawn of agriculture, people were harvesting grain by walking down a field and swinging a giant blade (a scythe) and someone else would follow behind them tying the cut crop into bales. They were like a bunch of grim reapers in a field, but *slightly* less grim. McCormick revolutionized agriculture and allowed farmers to harvest much more grain in a fraction of the time. As fewer farmers were needed to provide food for the entire country, this invention allowed America to shift from predominately agriculture-based industries (90% in 1831) to the diverse world of industries we live in today.

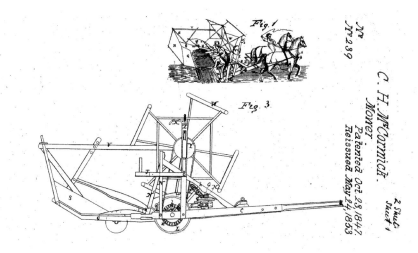

Figure 3.2 A page from one of McCormick's reissued patents (USRE 239) related to the mechanical reaper (1853).

More recently (circa 2009), a designer made the connection that shears look somewhat like bunny ears and made a pair of bunny scissors. The pair I own looks something like that in Figure 3.3.

Figure 3.3 Illustration of a playfully designed pair of bunny scissors.

These are very different examples. One concept is primarily about function while the other is primarily about form. One is quite serious and revolutionary, while the other is more playful and incremental. However, they are both examples of the Associative Theory of Creativity. They are both about making non-obvious connections between shears and some seemingly unrelated other thing. The clothing dryer invention in Chapter 1 could also be viewed as a result of a non-obvious connection (between a clothing dryer and an ultrasonic humidifier).

In the past, scientists associated the *right hemisphere of the brain* with creative processes and the left hemisphere with logical processes. Current research shows that the entire brain is important for creativity, but there are some recent studies that are bringing the right hemisphere back into the spotlight (Aberg, 2017). There seems to be some benefit when information enters first through the left eye/right brain when working on insight problems (Bowden & Jung-Beeman, 1998). Another study found that participants squeezing a ball with their left hand/right brain had higher creativity scores (Goldstein et al., 2010). Similarly, another study found that left-handed people in general had higher creativity scores (Abbasi et al., 2011).

There are fMRI studies that investigate what happens in the brain when novel connections are made, specifically between unrelated words (Mashal et al., 2007). This process of convergent thinking with words is termed *verbal creativity*, and it takes place in the *right posterior superior*

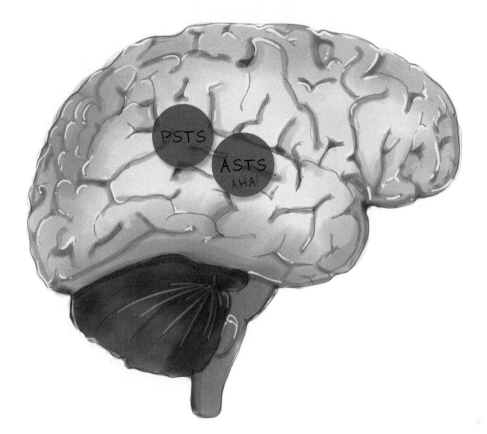

Figure 3.4 A representation of the brain viewed from the right side showing general locations of the posterior superior temporal sulcus (PSTS) and the anterior superior temporal sulcus (ASTS), aka "The Aha Zone".

temporal sulcus (PSTS) shown in Figure 3.4 (Flaherty, 2005; Mashal et al., 2007; Pobric et al., 2008). Verbal creativity is the basis of creative thought according to Koestler (1964) and Mednick (1962) as well as the basis of *wit* and *humor comprehension* according to others (Suls, 1972; Cundall, 2007), which we will explore in Chapter 4. Adjacent to the PSTS is the *right anterior superior temporal sulcus* (ASTS), which was found to be active in the *"Aha!" experience* occurring immediately after making distant connections (Bowden & Jung-Beeman, 2003).

That *Aha! moment* of sudden realization is called the *moment of insight* or the *Eureka Effect.* It occurs when you have some seemingly unsolvable problem or contradiction in mind and, due to some reframing or realization (through lateral thinking, flexible thinking, or thinking outside of the box), a non-obvious connection is made. The first highway centerline was invented by Edward Hines in 1911 in Michigan when a moment of insight was allegedly sparked by a milk wagon leaking a white trail down the road (Laskow, 2014). A few years later in California, Dr. June McCarroll had the same moment of insight when she noticed that cars stayed to their side when the road had an unintentional middle "line" created by widening the street from 8 feet to 16 (Rasmussen, 2003). Non-obvious connections can come from very different sources of inspiration (e.g., a leaking milk wagon or a visual artifact of road expansion) yet result in the same idea.

When someone solves the Duncker Candle Stick problem in the prior chapter, that is the moment of insight. Whenever you figured out the *twist ending* in *The Sixth Sense*, that was the moment of insight. That twist ending is the non-obvious connection. A good twist in a movie requires that connection to remain unlinked as long as possible such that the viewer remains engaged in a state of actively trying to make sense of the puzzle until the moment when a clue (or blatant solution) is provided that resolves the incongruity(s). At that point, the viewer is then rewarded for solving the puzzle with *dopamine*. In movies and books, twist endings are like false creativity on the part of the viewer: the creators provide the solution to the viewer in such as a way that makes the viewer feel as if they solved the puzzle themselves. Arriving at the punch line to a joke on your own is different from being told the punch line, and, similarly, creating a joke is different from understanding a joke (more on jokes in Part IV).

The *Aha! moment* is a byproduct of convergent thinking. This convergent thinking process is like building a mind map via divergent thinking and suddenly you realize that two nodes on your mind map connect in an unexpected way. The more nodes you have to work with, the more opportunities for non-obvious connections and new solutions. This is related to the threshold hypothesis of Chapter 1 in which people with greater knowledge (or nodes) have greater potential for creativity than those with fewer nodes. But again, having a large quantity of nodes or breadth of knowledge doesn't necessarily equate to being creative.

In the prior chapter, I referenced some popular fictional characters celebrated for divergent thinking (e.g., MacGyver). *Sherlock Holmes* (and modern derivations like *House MD*) is the iconic fictional character celebrated for convergent thinking (i.e., solving problems by making non-obvious connections between many bits of seemingly unrelated things). Contrary to how the novels present Sherlock—a master of "deductive" reasoning—he is more like a master of "abductive" reasoning. *Deductive reasoning* does not create new knowledge, it only draws out what we already know by seeking out information that supports an initial hypothesis. This top-down method of gathering information to justify an existing hypothesis is not very Sherlock (or Dr. House). *Inductive reasoning* starts with general observations and uses them to develop a general principle with some element of probability. Although Sherlock starts with observations, he also uses them to develop a functional hypothesis for the situation and not simply generalizations about the world. The third method of inferential reasoning, *abduction*, is the closest to Sherlock's method (Carson, 2009) as well as convergent thinking. *Abductive reasoning* makes a probable conclusion from a set of collected observations. With abductive reasoning, the major premise is evident (e.g., a character in the story is dead), but the minor premise and conclusions are only probable.

Let's go back to that divergent thinking mind map from the prior chapter and build some convergent thinking into it...with convergent thinking.

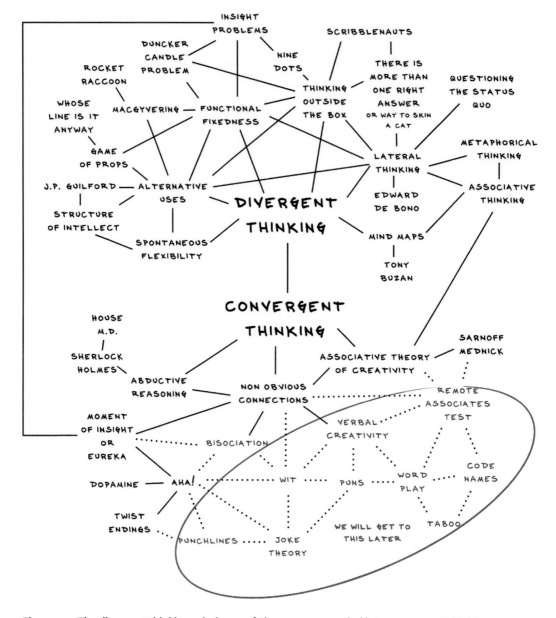

Figure 3.5 The divergent thinking mind map of Figure 2.5 expanded into convergent thinking.

References

Abbasi, M., Shahbazzadegan, B., & Samadzadeh, M. (2011). Survey of relationship between creativity and lateral dominance in guidance school students. *Procedia - Social and Behavioral Sciences, 28*, 293–299.

Aberg, K. C., Doell, K. C., & Schwartz, S. (2017). The "Creative Right Brain" revisited: Individual creativity and associative priming in the right hemisphere relate to hemispheric asymmetries in reward brain function. *Cerebral Cortex, 27*(10), 4946–4959.

Bowden, E. M., & Jung-Beeman, M. (1998). Getting the right idea: Semantic activation in the right hemisphere may help solve insight problems. *Psychological Science, 9*(6), 435–440.

Bowden, E. M., & Jung-Beeman, M. (2003). Aha! - Insight experience correlates with solution activation in the right hemisphere. *Psychonomic Bulletin & Review, 10*(3), 730–737.

Carson, D. (2009). The abduction of Sherlock Holmes. *International Journal of Police Science & Management, 11*(2), 193–202.

Cartier, F. A. (1963). Three misconceptions of communication. *ETC: A Review of General Semantic, 20*(2), 135–145.

Cundall, M. K. (2007). Humor and the limits of incongruity. *Creativity Research Journal, 19*(2–3), 203–211.

Flaherty, A. W. (2005). Frontotemporal and dopaminergic control of idea generation and creative drive. *Journal of Comparative Neurology, 493*(1), 147–153.

Goldstein, A., Revivo, K., Kreitler, M., & Metuki, N. (2010). Unilateral muscle contractions enhance creative thinking. *Psychonomic Bulletin & Review, 17*, 895–899.

Hoorn, J. (2014). *Creative confluence.* John Benjamins Publishing Company.

Koestler, A. (1964). *The act of creation.* Macmillan.

Laskow, S. (2014, November 5). Thank cyclists, not drivers, for early road improvements. *The Atlantic.*

Mashal, N., Faust, M., Hendler, T., & Jung-Beeman, M. (2007). An fMRI investigation of the neural correlates underlying the processing of novel metaphoric expressions. *Brain and Language, 100*(2), 115–126.

McCormick, C. H. (1853). Mower. *USRE 239.* Washington, DC: U.S. Patent and Trademark Office.

Mednick, S. A. (1962). The associative basis of the creative process. *Psychological Review, 69*, 220–232.

Pobric, G., Mashal, N., Faust, M., & Lavidor, M. (2008). The role of the right cerebral hemisphere in processing novel metaphoric expressions: A transcranial magnetic stimulation study. *Journal of Cognitive Neuroscience, 20*(1), 170–181.

Rasmussen, C. (2003, October 12). 'Doc June' Drew the line on safety. *Los Angeles Times.*

Suls, J. M. (1972). A two-stage model for the appreciation of jokes and cartoons: An information-processing analysis. In J. H. Goldstein, & P. E. McGhee (Eds.), *The psychology of humor* (pp. 81–100). Academic Press.

4
VERBAL CREATIVITY, *CODE NAMES,* AND PUNS

The *Remote Associates Test (RAT)* is a test of creativity that specifically targets convergent thinking ability. It was developed along with the *Associative Theory of Creativity* by Sarnoff Mednick (1962). This test involves finding a connective link between a set of three seemingly unrelated words (a triad) that have a mutually remote association. Here is an example of a RAT triad: **tap, rain**, and **floor**. You would be required to find a single word that can be added to each of these three words, either before or after, to turn each word into a known compound word or phrase. Before you read ahead, take a moment to try to solve this puzzle.

For the given example, the word "dance" connects with the three words to form: tap dance, rain dance, and dance floor.

In some of the original studies, the RAT was found to correlate negatively with GPA (Mednick, 1962), positively with brainstorming productivity (Forbach & Evans, 1981), and positively with other convergent thinking tests (Taft & Rossiter, 1966). In my recent work, we found that the RAT has a weak and nonsignificant correlation with creative performance on real-world design challenges (Tran et al., 2022). One reason for this dissonance is that the RAT requires a deep understanding of language and knowledge of random bits of cultural information. It is almost equal parts trivia and creativity. For example, non-native speakers of the test's language are at a disadvantage not only because they may not be familiar with certain compound words, but also because they may not be familiar with the select cultural references required to solve the puzzle. For example, in the triad: **cottage, curds**, and **cake**, to come to the solution of "cheese," one would need to be famil-iar with *all* of these three specific foods: cottage cheese, cheese curds, and cheesecake (Wang & Kudrowitz, 2016). The RAT also has only one "correct" response whereas divergent thinking as-sessments and real-world challenges often have many viable responses.

You may have noticed by now that the titles of the chapters of this book are a set of three seem-ingly unrelated things. This is a nod to the RAT. Ideally, as you read each chapter, you will realize how those three seemingly unrelated things are connected. In the context of the theme of this book, the RAT was found to positively correlate with both humor comprehension (Rouff, 1975) and humor production (Treadwell, 1970; Brodzinsky & Rubien, 1976; Sitton & Pierce, 2004). This relationship seems reasonable given that both making sense of a joke and creating a joke involve making connections between seemingly unrelated words. We will explore this relationship further in Part IV.

DOI: 10.4324/9781003276296-6

While you were reading the RAT triads (e.g., Tap Rain Floor), you may have found yourself *playing* along—perhaps it reminded you of a board game or a TV gameshow. These types of word puzzles appear often in games. Let's explore a few specific games that exploit this cognitive process in a playful way.

Code Names was developed in 2015 by Czech game designer Vladimír Chvátil. The premise of the game is to get your partner/team to guess as many of your team's word cards as possible from an array of word cards on a playing area by crafting a one-word hint. In the RAT, you are finding one word that connects three other words. In this game, you could theoretically identify one word that links two to nine words in a single play. To add to the challenge, there are words in the playing area that you *don't* want your partner/team to guess and so you must find a word that relates to as many of your own cards *without* relating to any of the other team's cards. Figure 4.1 is an abstracted and hypothetical example of a Codenames array that a guessing teammate would see on the playing area. If I gave you the hint word "break," which of the cards in this array would you think I was referring to? Which connections come to you first?

In this game, the hint giver is alternating between divergent and convergent thinking, while simultaneously considering their partner/team's knowledge, interests and thought process. The guesser is then playing an interesting game of reverse RAT in which they are given the solution and must figure out which of the many words can be connected.

I've been discussing divergent thinking and convergent thinking as if they are completely unrelated processes when most of these creativity assessments, creative problem-solving, and games like *Code Names* requires a bit of both. Let's look at one other board game as a way of putting both processes in context.

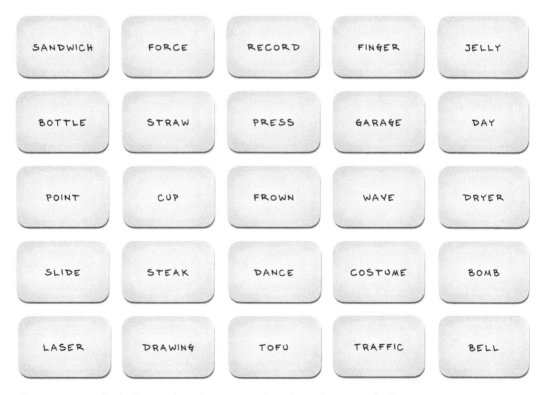

Figure 4.1 Hypothetical example and representation of a *Code Names* playing array.

The game *Taboo* is about getting your partner to say a certain keyword without using a list of words that are commonly associated with that word. For example, Player 1 would try to get Player 2 to say the word "toaster" without using the words: bread, appliance, or heat. Player 1, in this case, is the clue giver and is engaging in divergent thinking. This person is trying to envision everything that can possibly be related to toasters; they are making a mind map like the one in Figure 4.2. In this case, the central concept is a toaster, and the player is making associations around it such as bread, kitchen, breakfast, heating, etc. The creative challenge for Player 1 is to broaden their mind map to find associated words and phrases that are not the obvious ones on the card.

Meanwhile, Player 2 is engaging in a very different creative process: convergent thinking. Player 2 is hearing a string of seemingly unrelated words and phrases (such as "food pops out of it," "don't put it in the bathtub," and "it browns items") and is trying to find the word that connects them all, just like in the RAT. When Player 2 finds the connection, they come to some realization and have an *Aha! Moment*.

As the game of *Taboo* progresses, players rotate from being the clue giver to the guesser—switching from a state of rapid convergent thinking to rapid divergent thinking. This creative game play is also present in the board games *Catch Phrase* and *So Clover!* as well as the *Pyramid* and *Password* television game shows. However, unlike these other games, *Taboo* forces people to think "outside the box" or "think laterally" by removing the obvious responses. The game mechanic of *Taboo* is basically telling players: "there are lots of ways of solving this word puzzle, try finding a non-obvious connection."

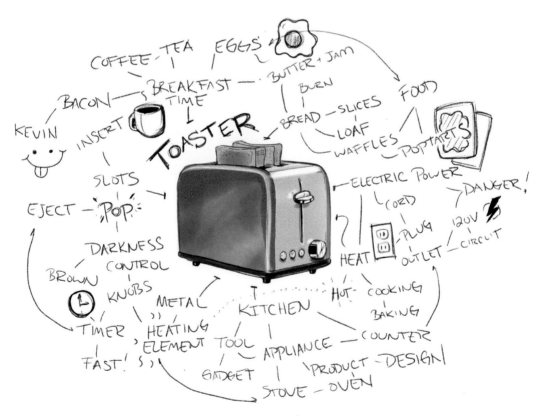

Figure 4.2 A toaster mind map.

Based on these games, it is clear how verbal creativity can be playful (i.e., *word games/word play*), but verbal creativity can also be humorous (i.e., *play on words*). The *pun* is one specific type of play-on-words that is connected to humor and creativity. The *pun* or *paronomasia* exploits the multiple meanings of a word or similar sounding words for comedic effect. Author and journalist, Arthur Koestler, developed a theory of creativity called *bisociation*, which is described as "the perceiving of a situation or idea in two self-consistent but habitually incompatible frames of reference" at the same time (1964). Or, in other words, the simultaneous association of a concept within two fields that are ordinarily unrelated. The pun is the simplest and most powerful form of *bisociation*. As Koestler describes it, a pun is "the bisociation of a single phonetic form with two meanings—two strings of thought tied together by an acoustic knot" (1964).

In the prior *Code Names* example, the clue giver is going through a similar process that someone thinking of a pun may go through. They are trying to find a word that can relate to multiple different things in different contexts while keeping the sound of the word the same. For example, the word "break" can mean "to crack" (as in a cup, a finger, or a camel's back), but it can also mean to stop, to rest, or a specific dance. To "humorize" this example, here is a break-related pun:

I have a brake fluid addiction, but it's OK because I can stop at any time.

In this pun, the phrase "stop at any time" or simply the word "stop" is what Koestler calls the "link" or the concept/word/situation that is bisociated on two intersecting mental "planes." On one "plane," as Koestler would call it, there is a tiny narrative in which the narrator has an addiction to brake fluid and the narrator uses a common saying that they can "stop at any time" to justify their addiction. In this context or narrative plane, the word "stop" simply takes on the meaning "to quit." Simultaneously, there is a separate plane with another tiny narrative, in which the narrator is again drinking brake fluid, but in this narrative plane, the narrator justifies this unusual behavior by declaring that they can "stop at any time" where "stop" takes on the meaning "brake like a vehicle." If the narrator chose to use the word "quit" or "brake" instead of the word "stop," there would be no bisociation, no pun, and the result would be one of two weird, but not necessarily funny, stories. This is illustrated in the left diagram of Figure 4.3.

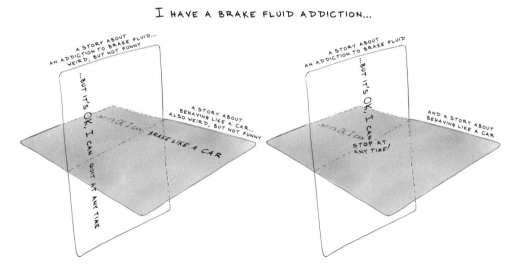

Figure 4.3 An illustration of bisociation—two unrelated narratives (the first image) can bisociate and form a pun by connecting via a key word or phrase (the second image).

For this pun to work, the link phrase "stop at any time" allows the narrative of these two incompatible frames of reference to intersect (illustrated in the diagram on the right of Figure 4.3). The result, when realizing the connection, is a moment of insight that can be humorous and cathartic or what Koestler calls "a simultaneous vibration on two different wavelengths" (1964).

Puns are more than just playing with words—they are playing with ideas. If you attend a *pun slam* you can see an improvised competitive display of *wit* where individuals are given a prompt or theme and participants must speak on the topic and deliver as many puns as they can in a prescribed amount of time. The judges' runway commentary in *RuPaul's Drag Race* and RuPaul's final decisions in each episode are a form of pun slam (O'Keeffe, 2018). A person who can uncover these interesting links or "simultaneous vibrations" across incompatible frames of reference has enormous wit. *Wit*, not simply meaning "being funny," but rather a more sophisticated ability to connect knowledge from seemingly unrelated domains. Uncovering links across different frames of reference is not just for excelling at verbal creativity like pun slams or Codenames; it goes beyond humor and is the source of all creative breakthroughs in science, engineering, art, design, and beyond. As you will see in Part IV, the domains of humor and creativity have a "simultaneous vibration."

References

Brodzinsky, D. M., & Rubien, J. (1976). Humor production as a function of sex of subject, creativity, and cartoon content. *Journal of Consulting and Clinical Psychology, 44*(4), 597–600.

Forbach, G. B., & Evans, R. G. (1981). The remote associates test as a predictor of productivity in brainstorming groups. *Applied Psychological Measurement, 5*(3), 333–339.

Koestler, A. (1964). *The act of creation*. Macmillan.

Mednick, S.A. (1962). The associative basis of the creative process. *Psychological Review, 69*, 220–232.

O'Keeffe, K. (2018, May 22). An encyclopedia of all 271 RuPuns from 'RuPaul's Drag Race'. *Huffington Post.*

Rouff, L. L. (1975). Creativity and sense of humor. *Psychological Reports, 37*(3), 1022.

Sitton, S. C., & Pierce, E. R. (2004). Synesthesia, creativity and puns. *Psychological Reports, 95*(2), 577–580.

Taft, R., & Rossiter, J. R. (1966). The remote associates test: Divergent or convergent thinking? *Psychological Reports, 19*(3), 1313–1314.

Tran, K., Kudrowitz, B., & Koutstaal, W. (2022). Fostering creative minds: What predicts and boosts design competence in the classroom? *International Journal of Technology and Design Education, 32*(1), 585–616.

Treadwell, Y. (1970). Humor and Creativity. *Psychological Reports, 26*(1), 55–58.

Wang, X. G., & Kudrowitz B. (2016, November). Language ability in creativity assessment. *Proceedings of the 4th International Conference on Design Creativity, ICDC 2016*, Atlanta, Georgia, USA.

5
FLUENCY, ORIGINALITY, AND *FAMILY FEUD*

In Chapters 2–4, we explored divergent and convergent thinking and focused primarily on verbal assessments like the Alternative Uses Test and the Remote Associates Test. Let's look at creativity through a different lens, and, in this case, with a more visual approach. In Figure 5.1, there are 30 circles. Using the shapes, make as many creative images as you can in three minutes. Once you have a timer ready, you may begin.

DOI: 10.4324/9781003276296-7

Figure 5.1 30 circles.

We will get back to these circles in a moment, but first I want to reintroduce Ellis Paul Torrance. You may remember him from the "Threshold Hypothesis" discussed in Chapter 1; however, he is perhaps more known for his *Torrance Test of Creative Thinking (TTCT)*. This assessment involves a series of verbal and non-verbal (figural) tasks to test a variety of different creative abilities (1966). His tests have been used extensively with children and adults as well as in longitudinal studies. He was the first to attempt to develop a more *holistic* creativity assessment. Although some of the test is derived from Guilford (1956), the TTCT looks at more than just divergent thinking (e.g., Alternative Uses Test) or convergent thinking (e.g., Remote Associates Test). Specifically, his test divides creativity into four main components (Torrance, 1974):

1) Fluency—the production of many ideas
2) Originality—the production of ideas that are not obvious or statistically frequent
3) Flexibility—the production of a wide variety of ideas
4) Elaboration—the embellishment of ideas

Depending on which variation of the test you take, there may be different types of questions that are scored on these four criteria. Some components of the TTCT include: formulating questions that arise from a provided scenario; listing ways to change a toy to add play value; turning a set of ambiguous markings into a picture that tells a story; and, based on Guilford's Alternative Uses Test, listing unusual uses for an object (Sternberg & Lubart, 1999). A common component of the TTCT involves providing a set of simple shapes (such as a set of circles) and the subject is asked to draw different objects using those shapes. Just as Torrance borrowed elements from Guilford, others borrowed elements from Torrance. This figural creativity test (specifically with circles) has been adapted/borrowed and called by different names such as the "circle game" or "30 circles." Let's use your drawings in the 30 circles, in addition to your results from the Introduction's Alternative Uses Test, to discuss the four criteria that Torrance uses to evaluate creativity.

Fluency is a fancy word for *quantity of ideas*. So, in the case of the Alternative Uses Test, fluency is the count of the number of listed uses. In the case of the 30 circles, you would count the number of (non-redundant) ideas you came up with. This is not necessarily the number of circles you used. For example, if you made a face by combining two circles (e.g., Figure 5.2), that would technically count as only *one idea* (however, Torrance gives you bonus points later for combining circles in that manner). Quantity, unlike other aspects of creativity, is objective and easy to measure. It also tends to correlate with other aspects of creativity such as novelty (Kudrowitz & Wallace, 2013).

Linus Pauling, a theoretical chemist and biologist and two-time Nobel Prize recipient says, "you aren't going to have good ideas unless you have lots of ideas" (Richter, 1977). Research, including several of my own studies, has supported this statement with strong correlations between the total number of ideas and the total number of good ideas (Diehl & Stroebe, 1987; Paulus et al., 2011; Kudrowitz & Dippo, 2013; Kudrowitz & Wallace, 2013). One could argue that individuals who

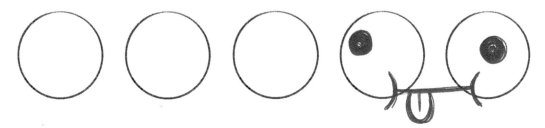

Figure 5.2 Example of combining circles to make one idea—one derpy face.

are uninhibited when expressing ideas will produce many ideas and their output should be less restrained and thus more creative. It could also be argued that individuals that produce a lot of ideas are better at divergent thinking and will therefore have more creative ideas. As Mednick says: "The greater number of associations that an individual has to the requisite elements of a problem, the greater the probability of [them] reaching a creative solution" (1962).

The *Serial Order Theory* best explains why quantity breeds creativity. Christensen, Guilford, and Wilson found that when subjects are instructed to generate ideas, the ideas become more original, novel, and remote the longer they spend on the task (1957). *The first ideas you think of are the same ideas everyone thinks of* and, as you develop more ideas, they become more and more unique (Van Der Lugt, 2001; Goldschmidt & Tatsa, 2005, Kudrowitz & Dippo, 2013, Leeds & Kudrowitz, 2016). Alex Osborn, the founder of the Brainstorming method, agrees: "quantity breeds quality in ideation" and that "early ideas are unlikely to be the best ideas generated during an ideation session" (Osborn, 1963). We tend to get attached to the first ideas we think of and then we get upset when we find out they already exist. The way to remedy this is to push yourself to come up with lots of ideas and not immediately pursue the first (seemingly) good idea you think of. "At first, creative and uncreative people tend to give similar responses in a similar order. However, creative people continue to respond at a steady rate, whereas uncreative people run out of responses" (Martindale, 1989).

Let's look at your 30 Circles and paperclip Alternative Uses Test responses. How many responses did you come up with? How common are your *first* few? How common the *latter* ones? For the Alternative Uses Test, did you write "pick a lock" and "hold paper together"? In the 30 Circles, did you turn one of the first circles into a sun or a face?

In a study of 293 participants from different ages and backgrounds taking the paperclip Alternative Uses Test, I found that professionals, on average, came up with 10 responses total while students had an average of 8 responses. On average, a participant would list 9 responses *before* arriving at what we determined to be highly novel responses. Participants that did not reach 9 responses in the study were likely to have fewer, if any, highly novel responses (Kudrowitz & Dippo, 2013). We observed a *Long Tail Effect*: On average, the first response someone lists was found in approximately 50% of other participants' responses. With subsequent responses, the novelty of those responses increased.

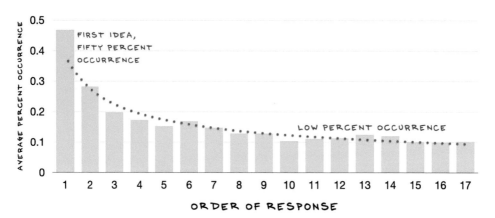

Figure 5.3 The long tail effect of the Kudrowitz and Dippo study (2013). The term "percent occurrence" is another way of saying how common an idea was among the entire group of participants. The first response listed had a 50% occurrence on average while ideas after the ninth had less than a 10% occurrence on average.

Originality is the uniqueness or novelty of the ideas as measured by how uncommon the idea is compared with data from the sample population. Originality is what most people equate with creativity, and it is the only consistent requirement across creativity research studies (Kudrowitz & Wallace, 2013). An idea can't be creative if it is not original! *Or can it?* It's not so much that originality is subjective, but rather that *originality is relative*. How many times have you had an idea that you thought was unique and you shared it with your colleagues, and they thought it was unique too, but when you looked online, you found out that someone else already developed the idea. It's not that the idea is *not* creative or *not* original. The idea was clearly original *to you* and *to your colleagues*; however, it just wasn't *original to a society*.

The perception of creativity and originality is culture or society dependent. According to Margaret Boden, there is said to exist two levels of originality: original to the individual and original in history (2004). "A case can be made that each and every one of us is creative to the extent that we discover things new to us [ourselves]" (Lieberman, 1977). Others have added a third classification that lies between these two realms: original to a situation or society (Sosa & Gero, 2003). In many industries, *original to a society* is what matters most (and perhaps it is even preferable over original to history as that implies the concept has been tested and proven). The terms "*mini-c,*" "*little-c,*" and "*big-C*" are related to this idea in that there are little creative acts at a personal level (i.e., mini-c), things a local group may find creative (i.e., little-c or "everyday creativity"), and then things that are creative to history (i.e., big-C) (Beghetto & Kaufman, 2007). Polling a section of the population online is a means of evaluating the size of your "c."

In creativity tests like these, the means of scoring originality is based on comparing your responses to those from a survey of the general population. This is a lot like the game show *Family Feud* (or the board game *Outburst*) in which a sample population of 100 people are polled with a certain question and their responses make up the most common answers. However, in *Family Feud* or *Outburst*, the objective of the game is to be as *uncreative* as possible and try to guess the most *common* responses. *Family Feud* and *Outburst* reward *unoriginality* whereas, in these creativity assessments, such as the TTCT, the goal is to think of the ideas that very few people think of.

Let's turn to your responses for the Alternative Uses Test. In our study (Kudrowitz & Dippo, 2013), we tested 293 people and determined the most common 26 responses (these are the uses that at least 10% of the participants had listed). This is like the big "*Survey says!?*" reveal on *Family Feud*, but I'm giving you all the answers. Just like on the *Family Feud* board, these answers are provided in order of most common to least common with some showing the percent occurrence (high percent occurrence = very common). Antithetical to *Family Feud*, the more responses you have that are *not* on this list, the better. Having uncommon ideas gives you a higher originality score and thus a higher creativity score. Let's see how you did. How many responses did you have that are *not* listed in Figure 5.4?

If most of your ideas were on this list, that's OK! There are still two more dimensions of creativity according to Torrance (1974) that we will discuss in Chapter 6.

Figure 5.4 A *Family Feud* inspired board showing the top 26 most common alternative uses for a paperclip from the Kudrowitz and Dippo study (2013). The uses are ranked from most common with a 77% occurrence (top left) to the less common (bottom right).

References

Beghetto, R. A., & Kaufman, J. C. (2007). Toward a broader conception of creativity: A case for "mini-c" creativity. *Psychology of Aesthetics, Creativity, and the Arts, 1*(2), 73–79.

Boden, M. (2004). *The creative mind: Myths and mechanisms*. Routledge.

Christensen, P. R., Guilford, J. P., & Wilson, R. C. (1957). Relations of creative responses to working time and instructions. *Journal of Experimental Psychology, 53*(2), 82–88.

Diehl, M., & Stroebe, W. (1987). Productivity loss in brainstorming groups: Toward the solution of a riddle. *Journal of Personality and Social Psychology, 53*(3), 497–509.

Goldschmidt, G., & Tatsa, D. (2005). How good are good ideas? Correlates of design creativity. *Design Studies, 26*(6), 593–611.

Guilford, J. P. (1956). The structure of intellect. *Psychological Bulletin, 53*(4), 267–293.

Kudrowitz, B., & Dippo, C. (2013). When does a paper clip become a sundial? Exploring the progression of novelty in the alternative uses test. *Journal of Integrated Design and Process Science: Special Issue on Applications and Theory of Computational Creativity, 17*(4), 3–18.

Kudrowitz, B. M., & Wallace D. R. (2013). Assessing the quality of ideas from prolific, early-stage product ideation. *Journal of Engineering Design, 24*(2), 120–139.

Leeds, A., & Kudrowitz, B. (2016). Exploring how novel ideas are generated in mind maps. *Proceedings of the 4th International Conference on Design Creativity, ICDC 2016*, Atlanta, Georgia, USA.

Lieberman, J. N. (1977). *Playfulness: Its relationship to imagination and creativity* (A. J. Edwards, Ed.). Academic Press.

Martindale, C. (1989). Personality, situation, and creativity. In J. A. Glover, R. R. Ronning, & C. R. Reynolds (Eds.), *Handbook of creativity* (pp. 211–232). Plenum Press.

Mednick, S. A. (1962). The associative basis of the creative process. *Psychological Review, 69*, 220–232.

Osborn, A. F. (1963). *Applied imagination; principles and procedures of creative problem-solving.* Scribner.

Paulus, P., Kohn, N., & Arditti, L. (2011). Effects of the quantity and quality instructions on brainstorming. *The Journal of Creative Behavior, 45*(1), 38–46.

Richter, R. (1977). *Linus Pauling, crusading scientist.* [Radio broadcast]. WGBH-Boston.

Sosa, R., & Gero, J. S. (2003). Design and change: A model of situated creativity. In C. Bento, A. Cardosa, & J. S. Gero (Eds.), *Approaches to creativity in artificial intelligence and cognitive science, IJCAI03* (pp. 25–34). Acapulco, Mexico.

Sternberg, R. J., & Lubart, T. I. (1999). The concept of creativity: Prospects and paradigms. In R. J. Sternberg (Ed.), *Handbook of creativity* (pp. 3–15). Cambridge University Press.

Torrance, E. P. (1974). *The Torrance tests of creative thinking: Norms-technical manual.* Personal Press.

Van Der Lugt, R. (2001). Relating the quality of the idea generation process to the quality of the resulting design ideas. In A. Folkeson, K. Gralen, M. Norell & U. Sellgren (Eds.), *Proceedings of 14th International Conference on Engineering Design Society,* Stockholm, Sweden.

6

FLEXIBILITY, ELABORATION, AND
SCATTERGORIES

In Chapter 5, we discussed two of the more common measures of creativity: fluency and original-ity. In this chapter, we will cover two of the less common measures: flexibility and elaboration.

Flexibility is the number of different categories or themes that appear in a set of ideas. This metric strongly maps to divergent thinking ability. Someone with low flexibility will come up with ideas that are all very similar to each other and do not explore different domains. Low flexibility is equiv-alent to having only one branch on a mind map and putting all time and effort into growing leaves onto that one branch. In the 30 Circles test, if you transformed all the circles into a set of different faces or a set of different sport balls, these would be examples of low flexibility (and low divergent thinking). In the paperclip Alternative Uses Test from the Introduction, if all your ideas simply in-volve clipping different things together, this would show low flexibility. As there are a multitude of different ways of categorizing responses, there are different ways of scoring flexibility.

One way of scoring flexibility on this paperclip Alternative Uses Test is by looking at the way you *manipulated* the paperclip to complete a function. In my research, we were able to classify all pa-perclip uses into one of eight general manipulations or treatments, which are listed from most common to least common (Kudrowitz & Dippo, 2013):

1) As a *clip*, it can hold items together with a clamping force.
2) As a *loop*, it can be a ring for linking things together or hanging something.
3) Extending out an end as a *pick*, it can be used as a pointed tool to pry, poke, press, prod, puncture, etc.
4) Extending it out fully into a straight *rod*, it can be used as a dowel, bearing, pivot, pin, etc.
5) As a malleable metal *wire*, it can be formed into different thin wire shapes.
6) As a small flat metal object, it can be simply a *token* like a spacer or a guitar pick.
7) As a metal material, it can be melted and transformed or used simply for its *material* properties.
8) It can represent *abstract* concepts like currency or an icon.

Figure 6.1 shows iconic representations of these eight high-level treatments of a paperclip. How many of these *categories* did you use in your set of responses?

This is only one means of evaluating flexibility of responses—one that is based on how the object is manipulated. Another means could be classifying the uses by their theme (i.e., is it used for cleaning, decorating, or repairing). Regardless of the lens through which you want to view the responses, Torrance would argue that a creative person would produce responses across a variety

DOI: 10.4324/9781003276296-8

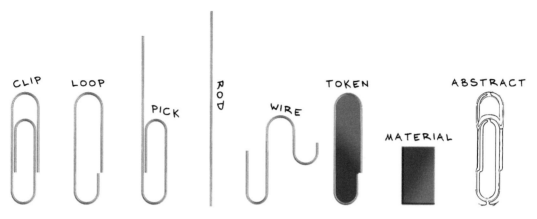

Figure 6.1 Seven paperclip treatments for classification of alternative uses.

of different manipulations or themes (1974). A creative person would be more flexible with the subject matter viewing it from different perspectives as opposed to maintaining a fixated or blinkered path (or branch, if we are viewing this as a mind map). Of course, creativity and novelty can and will likely emerge at some point along that blinkered path. Even Bubba's shrimp preparation monologue from *Forest Gump* starts with the more common shrimp preparations (BBQ, boil, bake) and ends with a few less common preparations (e.g., shrimp burger) (Zemeckis, 1994). This is why Torrance has multiple metrics for creativity assessment (1974). The problem with being fixated is that the paper clip can only be used for clipping things, the tack box can only be used to hold tacks, and you may miss opportunities or potential creative solutions. Low flexibility makes it difficult to solve insight problems.

This method in which flexibility is scored can also be viewed as an idea generation technique. By starting with the many treatments or properties of an object (clip, loop, pick, etc.), one can then list ideas under each treatment forcing a diverse assortment of ideas. This is like some idea generation tools such as *Morphological Analysis* or *Attribute Listing* in which something is broken down into its constituent elements and those elements are used to generate idea variations.

The final metric that Torrance uses in evaluating creativity is ***Elaboration*** (1974). This is measured by the number of details provided in the responses. For example, if you turned a circle into a bowling ball, it may only have a couple of details, but if you turned it into a bowling ball and also drew the bowling alley with a set of pins at the end, this would have a great number of *extraneous* details for the same general concept (i.e., a circle can be a bowling ball). Although the elaboration adds context and realism, that precious time you spent drawing the bowling alley could have gone into developing *other* ideas. If you recall from prior chapters, the more ideas you have, the more likely you are going to have creative ideas. So, differing with Torrance, my research shows that elaboration can be helpful in clarifying the novelty of ideas, *but only to some degree*. Elaboration may *impair* creativity in that it takes away time from generating a large quantity of ideas, and therefore limits the *overall* originality and flexibility in the set of ideas (Dippo & Kudrowitz, 2015). My studies have shown that elaboration is generally inversely related to the other measures of creativity (fluency, originality, and flexibility). A *few* details are helpful (and often required) to explain the uniqueness of an idea. After all, anything that is new and surprising will naturally require some level of elaboration (Gernert, 2007). However, after two extraneous details (on average), participants' overall creativity scores tend to decrease (Dippo & Kudrowitz, 2015).

LUDWIG MIES VAN DER ROHE
"LESS IS MORE"

RAYMOND LOEWY
"MOST ADVANCED YET ACCEPTABLLE"

DIETER RAMS
"LESS, BUT BETTER"

HOMER SIMPSON
"PUT A HORN HERE, HERE AND HERE..."

Figure 6.2 Famous designers' quotes on simplicity and representative illustrations of their design work including: The Neue Nationalgalerie (1968) by Ludwig Mies van der Rohe, the Streamlined Pencil Sharpener (1934) by Raymond Loewy, Pocket Radio (model T3) (1958) by Dieter Rams, and The Homer (Martin & Archer, 1991) by Homer Simpson.

I wrote a paper on this phenomenon and used hypocritical self-referential humor in the title: "The Effects of Elaboration in Creativity Tests as it Pertains to Overall Scores and How it Might Prevent a Person from Thinking of Creative Ideas During the Early Stages of Brainstorming and Idea Generation." The reviewers didn't get the joke: "The title needs to be significantly shorter. I suggest removing any unnecessarily/redundant terms." At least they agreed with the general premise of the article in that *more* is sometimes *less*.

There are a handful of sayings/theories that advocate for simple and minimal solutions. Starting with the oldest and most general: philosopher William of Ockham (or Occam) suggested that when competing hypotheses are presented, the one with fewer assumptions should always be selected, as it is less likely to be proven incorrect (Gernert, 2007). This philosophy is called *Occam's Razor* and is paraphrased to be "the simplest solution is the best solution." The slightly offensive variation of Occam's Razor is "*Keep it Simple Stupid*" or *KISS* coined by Lockheed engineer, Clarence Leonard "Kelly" Johnson. In the design world, architect Ludwig Mies van der Rohe coined the term *Less is More* which implies that minimal design is better than overdesigning. This philosophy was promoted again by German industrial designer, Dieter Rams, as one of his ten principles of "good design": *Good Design is as Little Design as Possible* (Rams, 2011). This can be clearly seen in his work at Braun in the 1950s. Another industrial designer, Raymond Loewy, introduced the concept of *Most Advanced Yet Acceptable*, which states that design solutions should be the most advanced option from an aesthetic standpoint without going so far that they get in the way of solving the problem at hand (Hekkert et al., 2003). [Richard] Buckminster Fuller, inventor of the geodesic dome, promoted a variation of these design philosophies for engineering contexts with the saying of *do more with less* (Aaseng, 1986).

All these sayings can be connected back to Thomas Aquinas: "If a thing can be done adequately by means of one, it is superfluous to do it by means of several; for we observe that nature does not employ two instruments [if] one suffices" (1945). A creative solution (just like a well-written joke or pun) is one that can serve its purpose without any extraneous bits. ***There is creativity in restraint.*** Just as all these famous philosophers, engineers, and designers would agree with Thomas Aquinas, they would all disagree with "The Car Built for Homer." This infamous concept car also known as "The Homer" was designed by Homer Simpson and included an elaborate assortment of features such as two bubble domes, three horns, gigantic cup holders, tail fins, and ornaments (Martin & Archer, 1991).

Now that we have addressed the four primary metrics that make up the Torrance evaluation: Fluency, Originality, Flexibility, and Elaboration, we are ready to play the game of *Scattergories*! To excel at this game, you need to flex all four of these abilities.

In the game of *Scattergories*, players are given three minutes and a random letter of the alphabet and must list unique examples of items beginning with that letter that also fit into a set of provided categories. For example, if the letter for the round was "G," Player 1 could write "glue stick" under the category "School Supplies" or "Gremlin" under the category "Fictional Characters." Players score points by having the greatest number of responses (*fluency*), but you can only get points for those responses if they are *original*. For each round, players must come up with 12 responses for 12 different categories in a limited amount of time and so you need to balance quantity and novelty. It's easy to simply list the first thing you can think of for each topic; it's harder to come up with a novel response for each topic that the other players are not thinking about.

The way originality is scored in this game is a mini version of how originality is scored in creativity assessments: it is based on a poll of popular responses. If any two players in the game have written the same response to a category, those responses are invalidated and crossed out. To get points, you need to think of a response that no one else presented.

Figure 6.3 An illustration of a representative *Scattergories* playbook.

As I noted in Chapter 5, *the first ideas you think of are the same ideas everyone thinks of*, and thus not novel nor creative. *Scattergories* discourages players from writing "elephant" or "eagle" for the category "Animals" with a given letter "E." Instead, the game rewards players who think of the less common, more novel: egret, emu, and earthworm.

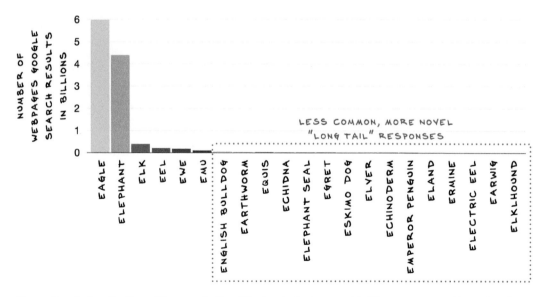

Figure 6.4 A visualization of the popularity of "animals that start with E" as represented by a Google search webpage result count from 2021. The head of the graph are likely the common responses that most people think of first. The "long tail" is populated by a long series of less common items, which represents the more novel, creative responses like egret and earwig.

Flexibility is also important in this game as it forces you to shift categories 12 times in one round. You can only afford a short time on one category before having to think of original responses for a completely unrelated category. In a mind map, this is like forcing you to make 12 unique branches in three minutes.

Lastly, *elaboration* is valued in the game as bonus points are provided for responses that have multiple words all starting with the same letter. For example, if the letter was "G" and the category was "Fictional Characters," Guardians of the Galaxy, Gonzo the Great, Godric Gryffindor, Green Goblin, Gandalf the Grey, and Gorilla Grodd would each get 2 points for using two G's. Grim Grinning Ghosts would get 3 points!

Scattergories is so similar to a creativity test, that has been used *as* a creativity test in at least two academic studies (Markman et al., 2007; Rios et al., 2018).

In Chapters 1–6, we explored what it means to be creative and how creativity is assessed. In the next two chapters, we will explore what we can do to *improve* our creative abilities.

References

Aaseng, N. (1986). *More with less: The future world of Buckminster Fuller.* Lerner Pub Group.

Aquinas, T. (1945). *Basic writings of St. Thomas Aquinas.* Random House.

Dippo, C., & Kudrowitz, B. (2015). The effects of elaboration in creativity tests as it pertains to overall scores and how it might prevent a person from thinking of creative ideas during the early stages of brainstorming and idea generation. *ASME Proceedings of the 27th International Conference on Design Theory and Methodology,* Boston, Massachusetts, USA.

Gernert, D. (2007). Ockham's Razor and its improper use. *Journal of Scientific Exploration, 21*(1), 136–139.

Hekkert, P., Snelders, D., & van Wieringen, P. C. (2003). 'Most advanced, yet acceptable': Typicality and novelty as joint predictors of aesthetic preference in industrial design. *British Journal of Psychology, 94*(1), 111–124.

Kudrowitz, B. & Dippo, C. (2013). When does a paper clip become a sundial? Exploring the progression of novelty in the alternative uses test. *Journal of Integrated Design and Process Science: Special Issue on Applications and Theory of Computational Creativity, 17*(4), 3–18.

Markman, K. D., Lindberg, M. J., Kray, L. J., & Galinsky, A. D. (2007). Implications of counterfactual structure for creative generation and analytical problem solving. *Personality and Social Psychology Bulletin, 33,* 312–324.

Martin, J. (Writer), & Archer, W. M. (Director). (1991, February 21). Oh brother, where art thou? [Television series episode]. In M. Groening (Producer), *The Simpsons,* Fox.

Rams, D. (2009). Ten principles of good design. In K. Ueki-Polet & K. Klemp (Eds.), *Less and more: The design ethos of Dieter Rams* (pp. 584–592). Gestalten.

Rios, K., Markman, K. D., Schroeder, J., & Dyczewski, E. A. (2014). A (creative) portrait of the uncertain individual: Self-uncertainty and individualism enhance creative generation. *Personality and Social Psychology Bulletin, 40*(8), 1050–1062.

Torrance, E. P. (1974). *The Torrance tests of creative thinking: Norms-technical manual.* Personal Press.

Zemeckis, R. (Director). (1994). *Forrest Gump* [Film]. The Tisch Company.

7

INSPIRATION, DA VINCI'S NOTEBOOKS, AND *RUPAUL'S DRAG RACE*

Can you be more creative?

In short, yes!

In long, these next two chapters:

My research has shown that almost anyone can improve their creative abilities through practicing design methods, specifically those described in this book based on play and humor (*wink*). In a longitudinal study (Tran et al., 2022), nearly all students (*N* = 98) in my undergraduate course, *Creative Design Methods,* significantly improved their creative design abilities as measured by pre and post ecologically valid industry-provided design challenges as well as creativity assessments like the Torrance Test and Alternative Uses. In this study, the improvement occurred regardless of initial creative abilities, major of study, or personality characteristics. Furthermore, one of the key findings of this study was that *those who improved their creative abilities the most, were those with the lowest creativity scores prior to training.*

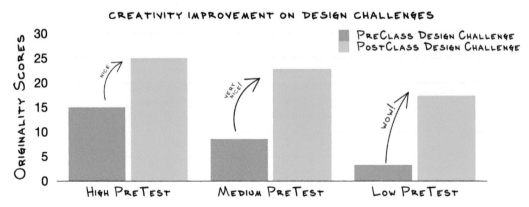

Figure 7.1 Creative improvement from students (*N* = 98) on real-world design challenges given as a pre-test prior to training and post-test after training. The student data is presented as a function of the relative standing of the participants' design challenge originality scores at pre-test (high, medium, low). The data shown is the average originality scores at pre-test and post-test for each group. These widely shared gains in design challenge performance were not confined to the originality dimension of creativity and a similar approach using a "value" measurement found similar results (Tran et al., 2022).

DOI: 10.4324/9781003276296-9

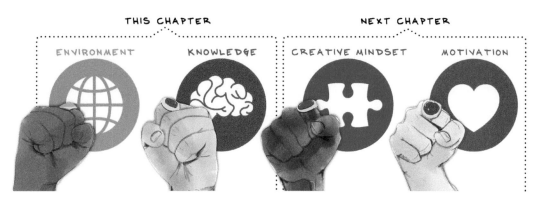

Figure 7.2 The "Captain Creativity" framework divided for discussion across this chapter and the following chapter.

Aside from reading this book or enrolling in a creativity class, there are other tools and techniques that have shown to increase your creative abilities. In the prior chapters, I discussed some interesting environmental factors that increase creativity (e.g., blue rooms, high ceilings, plants, natural light) and a few right brain/left brain studies (i.e., reading a problem with your right eye shut). This chapter discusses a selection of other creative correlates for being a more creative person related to environment and knowledge.

If creativity is about making non-obvious connections, one path toward being more creative is getting better at connection making (the next chapter), alternatively, another path would be expanding your number of nodes (knowledge/skills). I'm going to tie this back to two traits that we discussed in Chapter 1 about what makes a creative personality/mindset: openness to experience and novelty-seeking. If these traits describe you, you are more likely to collect a variety of interesting bits of information as you go through life. You are going to be constantly open to *inspiration*. Those bits of random information may not be useful in the moment, but they get filed away in some memory bank of trivia night fodder just waiting for the right moment to poke their head out during problem-solving and idea generation. This is why *notebooks* are so important. Notebooks help us keep track of all these interesting nuggets that cross our path. It's not just me stressing the importance of design notebooks, it's also the author of the most famous design notebooks in history. The following quote is taken from *the notebooks of Leonardo da Vinci* with my paraphrasing following each line (1970):

"When you have well learnt perspective and have by heart the parts and forms of objects,"

[Once you can draw well enough...]

"You must go about, and constantly, as you go, observe, note and consider the circumstances and behavior of men in talking, quarreling or laughing or fighting together: the action of the men themselves and the actions of the bystanders, who separate them or who look on"

[Get out into the world, study, and interact with real people.]

"And take a note of them with slight strokes thus, in a little book which you should always carry with you."

[Always have a design notebook on hand to make notes and sketches.]

"And it should be of tinted paper, that it may not be rubbed out, but change the old [when full] for a new one; since these things should not be rubbed out but preserved with great care;"

[Don't erase stuff and don't throw anything away.]

"For the forms, and positions of objects are so infinite that the memory is incapable of retaining them,"

[You never know when any of the little details will come in handy. Our minds can't keep track of everything.]

"Wherefore keep these [sketches] as your guides and masters."

[Actually use those notes to help you design and innovate.]

In one of da Vinci's notebooks, the *Codex Leicester*, he explores fluid dynamics and the motion of water in rivers and canals—illustrating (among many other topics) how waves are created by wind, how turbulence occurs at the intersection of rivers, and how vortices form and revolve (Kemp, 2019). He then goes on to explore the flow of blood as a fluid within the body, pulling from the knowledge of how bodies of water move on land. He was interested in how the heart's aortic valve functions; specifically, the mechanism of how it closes. He predicted that the motion of the blood flowing through the aortic valve created revolving vortices at the valve exit—like water exiting a pipe or a river. These vortices develop within the small pockets (i.e., the sinus of Valsalva or aortic sinuses) on the exit side of the valve and they inflate like tiny parachutes that then close the valve to prevent blood reflux (Gharib et al., 2002). The astonishing part of this theory is that it came 450 years before modern science was able to confirm it. It is because of da Vinci's documentation, attention to details, and interest in a variety of different disciplines that he was able to make these interesting, non-obvious connections.

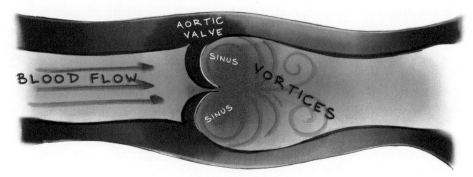

Figure 7.3 A representation of da Vinci's aortic valve sketch from the Codex Leicester showing how the vortices that form within the sinuses of the value cause it to close and prevent blood reflux.

Da Vinci is the best-known example (and perhaps an inspiration behind the term) of a *renaissance [person]* or someone who excels at many different things (in the case of da Vinci: painting, engineering, science, philosophy, anatomy, biology). This type of person may also be called a *polymath*. A related and more recent term is a *"T-shaped" person*, which describes someone who has a strong background in one specific discipline with working knowledge in a variety of other fields. This concept evolved to introduce other "shapes" of people (X, I, π, M, comb); with areas of deep skills equating to the number of appendages on the shape or letter (Vojak, 2013; Bredin et al., 2017; van Veenendaal, 2020). In any case, the important item here is that holding knowledge, skills, and interest in a *variety of domains* is helpful for creativity.

The Emmy-winning, *RuPaul's Drag Race*, is a polymath reality competition show. Unlike other competitions in which strong contestants require skills in just one specific field (such as cooking or fashion), *RuPaul's Drag Race* requires contestants to have skills across a wide range of disciplines. Challenges on the show are related to sewing, modeling, acting, singing, songwriting, lip-syncing, comedy-writing, interviewing, dancing, choreography, puppetry, product design, advertising, celebrity impersonation, hair styling, make-up, critique, and more. The contestants on the show also happen to be very talented drag queens. Most contestants are strong at some skills and weak at others, and this is what makes the show more unique and engaging. The show encourages contestants to push themselves to get help from others, try new things, and to develop their weaker skills. As RuPaul says, "we challenge them to go beyond their own limited perception of themself... the real challenge is for them to be willing to die and become reborn" (Winfrey, 2018). The show takes T-shaped or π-shaped contestants, and they transform into M-shaped or comb-shaped performers with depth in a variety of domains (Vojak, 2013; Bredin et al., 2017; van Veenendaal, 2020).

I have a da Vinci/RuPaul theory: people who are generally creative (i.e., having all the Captain Creativity rings except the red/domain knowledge one) can apply that creativity across domains as they learn new skills. RuPaul describes a similar theory while encouraging a contestant who did not view themself as a "comedy queen":

> ...what you do with your make-up, what you do when you're lip-syncing, apply that to comedy... that is true for everyone... if you can apply what you know really well in another area to this area which you think you may not know, you got something.
>
> (Winfrey, 2018)

This theory includes shifting between art and science domains as one learns the fundamentals of new disciplines, much like da Vinci. When we think of people who are creative in multiple domains, we often think of *EGOT* winners or "triple threat" performers who can create across a spectrum of *arts*. There are many examples of what happens when creative people cross between arts and sciences and into new disciplines. Here are three examples of early–mid-1900s polymaths:

Paul Winchell is most known as a ventriloquist, comedian, television star, and voice actor (Tigger from *Winnie the Pooh*, Dick Dastardly, Gargamel from the *Smurfs*). He also filed 30 patents, was the inventor of one of the first mechanical artificial hearts and developed a process for cultivating tilapia in small villages in Africa (Variety Staff, 2005).

Hedy Lamarr was a film star of the 1930s with over 30 films. She started her own production company, published a best-selling autobiography, and was the inspiration for *Catwoman* and *Snow White*. She was also a highly prolific inventor of technologies related to electronics and communication. One of her inventions and patents for sending secure military transmissions involved pulling inspiration and technology from player pianos—another example of crossing disciplines (Burnett, 2018). Her work set the foundation for technologies including: "Wi-Fi, Bluetooth, GPS, cordless phones and cell phones" (Field, 2018). She also designed a fluorescent dog collar and tissue box concept (Burnett, 2018).

Zeppo Marx was the youngest of the slapstick comedy group, *The Marx Brothers*. He left the entertainment industry to start a product development company, Marman Products. He had multiple patents and inventions including a cardiac pulse rate monitor with a smart watch that detects pulse rate changes and signals an alarm. He also invented the electric heating pad (Greenfield, 2010).

In all three of these examples, these individuals have creative achievements *both* in the entertainment/arts domain *and* in the engineering/technology domain. Additionally, their work spans across a variety of seemingly unrelated topics (e.g., tilapia + mechanical hearts, military transmission + dog colors, pulse monitors + heating pads).

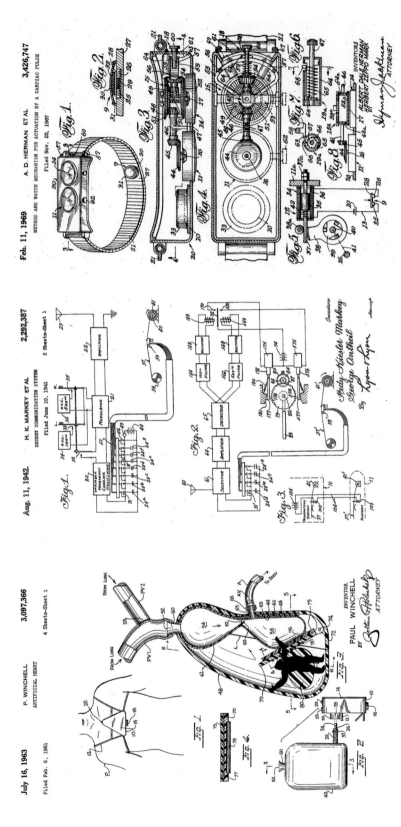

Figure 7.4 Front page of patents from Paul Winchell (Artificial Heart) (1963), Hedy Markey [Lamarr] (Secret Communication System) (1942), and [Herbert] Zeppo Marx (Method and Watch Mechanism for Actuation by a Cardiac Pulse) (1969).

In Steven Johnson's book, "Where Good Ideas Come From," he discusses several topics related to creativity and idea generation including *Liquid Networks* (2010). The more that diverse people and concepts collide, the greater chance of non-obvious connections and revelations. *Cafe culture* was a contributing factor of the enlightenment because it created a healthy venue for knowledge and concept sharing. European cafes were and still are a meeting place for people to share ideas, meet different people, and foster intellectual growth (Hughes, 1991). Some companies have embraced this concept and extended their *"water-cooler space"* (i.e., informal natural gathering spaces) to increase the likelihood of interesting knowledge collisions. The rise of *co-working spaces* is also a form of expanding this cafe culture. In a sense, you can be more creative simply by physically being around more people and thus more information and more inspiration.

> A city that was ten times larger than its neighbor is 17 times more innovative...a metropolis that is 50x bigger was 130x more innovative...a resident in a town of five million was 3x more creative than the average resident of town of hundred thousand.
>
> (Johnson, 2010)

King (2012) argues for having at least 50 people in your social network for creative inspiration with a good balance of familiarity (i.e., *Q-score*). If you have too many close friends in your network, you reduce your "openness to fresh ideas," but if you have too few close friends, you are not "sufficiently connected to let ideas flow" (King, 2012).

This is perhaps a latent factor that explains the correlation between *extroversion* and creativity. Bobbi Brown credits her successful cosmetic empire to "talking to everyone" including strangers (Clifford, 2017). As she describes it in an interview:

> 'I was in the elevator of my New York apartment and I said to the girl in the elevator, *hi, what do you do? She said, I work at a lab in Long Island City.* I'm like, *can I have your card?* And that's [the lab] where I made the lipstick...I was at a party and I introduced myself to the woman that was throwing the party and I said, *what do you do?* She said, *I'm a cosmetics buyer at Bergdorfs.* So, I said, *oh, I've got this line of lipsticks.'*
>
> (Clifford, 2017)

This is why extroverts are "more creative." They make connections and not just between a random set of three words on the RAT—they make connections with other people. It's not so much about having an outgoing personality, it's more about being in situations for bumping into opportunities and knowledge. As Steven Johnson says, the most productive tool for generating good ideas is "an environment where new combinations can occur, where information can spill over from one project to another" (Johnson, 2010).

There are tools that facilitate inspiration and inspiration management. One form of this is an *idea wallet*, which is a physical or digital, visual or written list of things you find interesting. This could be kept in a design notebook (as recommended by da Vinci) or in a digital form. One web-based form of an idea wallet is *Pinterest*. Pinterest is an online social platform for inspiration collection, organization, and sharing. As you explore the internet, you can easily pin (or collect) any visual inspiration from any webpage and organize it in your personal account. This account can be shared with different collaborators. Pinterest and similar online social tools like *TikTok* can serve as inspiration and as a digital social idea wallet (King, 2012; Linder et al., 2014). *TikTok* also promotes building on ideas and sharing original content and not simply posting existing content. These tools enable someone to expand their knowledge of a domain and collect interesting observations that may serve as future "guides and masters" (as per da Vinci, 1970).

To be more creative, you don't necessarily have to move to a larger city, talk to strangers in elevators, use Pinterest, and work in a co-working space (*although all these things may help!*). The important thread between these items is physically getting out into the world and *trying* to be inspired and learn new things.

References

Bredin, K., Enberg, C., Niss, C., & Söderlund, J. (2017). *Knowledge integration at work. Managing knowledge integration across boundaries.* Oxford University Press.

Burnett, E. (2018, April 13). But here's the thing about: Hedy Lamarr. *The Folding Chair History.*

Clifford, C. (2017, June 11). How self-made millionaire Bobbi Brown built a cosmetics empire by talking to everyone she met in elevators, at the park, at parties. *CNBC.*

Da Vinci, L. (1970). *The notebooks of Leonardo da Vinci* (J. P. Richter, Trans). Dover Publications. (Original translation published in 1883).

Field, S. (2018, February 28). Hedy Lamarr: The incredible mind behind secure WiFi, GPS And Bluetooth. *Forbes.*

Gharib, M., Kremers, D., Koochesfahani, M., & Kemp, M. (2002). Leonardo's vision of flow visualization. *Experiments in Fluids, 33,* 219–223.

Greenfield, R. (2010, October 8). Celebrity invention: Zeppo Marx's Heart Rate Monitor and Heating Pad. *The Atlantic.*

Herman, A. D., & Marx, H. Z. (1969). *U.S. Patent No. 3,426,747.* Washington, DC: U.S. Patent and Trademark Office.

Hughes, R. (1991). *The shock of the new.* Knopf.

Johnson, S. (2010). *Where good ideas come from: The natural history of innovation.* Riverhead Books.

Kemp, M. (2019). Leonardo da Vinci's laboratory: Studies in flow. *Nature, 571,* 322–323.

King, Z. (2012, May 26). The Goldilocks network. *New Scientist.*

Linder, R., Snodgrass, C., & Kerne, A. (2014, April). Everyday ideation: All of my ideas are on Pinterest. In *Proceedings of the SIGCHI conference on human factors in computing systems* (pp. 2411–2420).

Markey, H. K., & George, A. (1942). Secret communication system. *U.S. Patent No. 2,292,387.* Washington, DC: U.S. Patent and Trademark Office.

Tran, K., Kudrowitz, B., & Koutstaal, W. (2022). Fostering creative minds: What predicts and boosts design competence in the classroom? *International Journal of Technology and Design Education, 32*(1), 585–616.

Van Veenendaal, E. (2020). *The T-Shaped Tester.* erikvanveenendaal.nl.

Variety Staff. (2005, June 26). Paul Winchell. *Variety.*

Vojak, B. A. (2013). Flatland: Its π-shaped inhabitants. *On the Epistemology of Innovation: How Breakthrough Innovators Connect the Dots,* no. 21.

Winchell, P. (1963). Artificial Heart. *U.S. Patent No. 3,097,366.* Washington, DC: U.S. Patent and Trademark Office.

Winfrey, O. (2018). Oprah talks to RuPaul about life, liberty and the pursuit of fabulous. *O Magazine.*

8

DIFFUSING FOCUS, SHOWER THOUGHTS, AND (A FEW) PSYCHOACTIVE DRUGS

Chapter 7 discussed some tools for creativity based on knowledge and environment. This chapter will discuss some ways of being more creative related to motivation and creative mindset.

Diffusing Focus

The ability to *diffuse focus* seems to be important for creative thinking. The more bits of information that you can attend to, the more potential for analogies to discover (Mendelsohn, 1976; Martindale, 1989). In a related study, students who had a difficult time screening out irrelevant stimuli were seven times more likely to be considered an "eminent creative achiever" (Carson et al., 2003). Our environment also plays a role in our ability to diffuse focus. "Noise-free environments end up being too sterile and predictable in their output. The best innovation labs are always a little contaminated" (Johnson, 2010).

As we will discuss in Part III, people in a *positive mood* are better at solving insight problems. Studies show that positive mood diffuses your focus and makes you more sensitive to detecting alternative solutions (Subramaniam et al., 2009). Regularly playing video games, for example, has been found to enhance one's ability to diffuse focus and detect changes in the environment, thereby increasing the capacity to process different bits of information simultaneously (Green & Bavelier, 2003). In contrast, people who are overly focused are going to be weaker at insight problem-solving and convergent-thinking tasks. If you think about the Nine Dots puzzle (Chapter 2), to get to a solution, you can't focus on the dots forming a ridged box. Often creative people are perceived to be "bad students" when they have a difficult time focusing and are more distractible. Many highly successful creative leaders were deemed "failures" in school and/or dropped out.

> **Thomas Edison** attended public school for a total of just 12 weeks where he was labeled a hyperactive child, prone to distraction (Biography.com Editors, 2014b).

> **Pablo Picasso** dropped out of the Royal Academy of San Fernando. He was frustrated with the focus on classical subjects and techniques. He would skip class and roam the streets (Biography.com Editors, 2014a).

> **Lucille Ball** dropped out of high school to attend the John Murray Anderson School for the Dramatic Arts at which she was viewed as a failure (Norwood, 2017).

> **Albert Einstein** hated the strict protocols and rote learning of school, and he flunked the entrance exam to Zurich Polytechnic (Strauss, 2016).

DOI: 10.4324/9781003276296-10

John Lennon was expelled from Liverpool College of Art after a few years because of distracting behavior (Jonze, 2013).

It seems as if going to school doesn't make sense if you want to be a creative leader! Let's address this with the Captain Creativity framework (*knowledge, motivation, creative mindset, environment*). School is *intended* to be a place for acquiring knowledge and domain-specific skills (or at least *learning how to learn*). But if you are already a self-taught expert (e.g., Bill Gates) or highly skilled at something (e.g., Pablo Picasso), you may not need formal schooling, and classes may seem like busy work. School is *intended* to help you discover your interests and passions, but if you already know what you are passionate about (e.g., John Lennon) you don't need school to further motivate you. School is *intended* to help open your mind and provide creative toolsets, but that may not always be the case, and sometimes school may end up being rote learning (e.g., Albert Einstein). School is *intended* to provide a supportive environment, time, and resources for you to pursue creative endeavors; however, it may also take time (and money) away from pursing your passion (e.g., Kanye West) (Jones, 2018).

It seems as if I have gotten a bit off topic...what were we discussing again?

Oh yes, *diffusing focus*. Let's move on...

Incubation

One good way to diffuse focus is by *taking breaks*. When applied to creative problem-solving, this is called *incubation*. The theory of incubation is that when your brain takes a break, it lets go of any false organizing assumptions about the problem that it has been trying to use to solve it. Taking that break (regardless of how long it may be) allows your mind to wander and explore alternative and distant means of finding a solution (Segal, 2004). As Don Draper in *Mad Men* explained it: "Just think about it deeply. Then forget it, and an idea will jump up in your face" (Weiner et al., 2007). Incubation theory is the basis of the phenomena of taking a stroll to solve a problem. Research shows that walking a labyrinth helps with creative problem-solving (Sellers & Moss, 2016). Even the simple act of closing your eyes improves both convergent- and divergent-thinking abilities (Ritter et al., 2018).

Have you ever forgotten something important that you wanted to say to someone only to recall it later...when walking away? Or perhaps you get to your car after a meeting and ruminate on how you wish you said something differently. Or maybe you thought of the perfect comeback for an earlier argument when you were about to go to sleep. In French, there is a phrase for this: *L'esprit de l'escalier,* which translates to "*stairwell wit.*" In Yiddish, there is an equivalent term, *trepverter,* which translates to "staircase words." Both terms describe the difficulty of recalling something in the moment and having the words arrive too late to use them, but only after going through a process of walking down a set of stairs (i.e., having an incubation period).

Incubation theory also supports the phenomenon of waking up from a nap with an *Aha! Moment*. It is suggested to keep a notebook on your nightstand for this reason ("...always carry with you..." – da Vinci). Incubation is also why we have some of our best ideas in the shower or bath. It is why Oscar-winning screenwriter, Aaron Sorkin, takes *6–8 showers a day*:

> I have a shower at home, I have a shower at the office. It's a do over. It's a reset. If it's not going well, if I can't think of anything, I get in the shower, I take a shower, I put on different clothes, and try again. On a really bad day, I'll be incredibly clean.
>
> (Galloway, 2016).

In the shower, our brain enters a routine bathing mode, and it allows us to relax and look at things from a different perspective to make interesting connections. These are called *shower thoughts*.

Comedian Mitch Hedberg is known for his unique *shower thoughts* or interesting non-obvious perspectives on everyday things. Here is an example of a Mitch Hedberg joke: "…waffles are like pancakes with syrup traps. A waffle says to the syrup 'hold on, you ain't going anywhere…'" (2003). As we are talking about *stairwell wit,* here is a witty Mitch Hedberg joke about stairs: "I like an escalator, because an escalator can never break, it can only become stairs. There would never be an 'Escalator Temporarily Out of Order' sign, only an 'Escalator Temporarily Stairs. Sorry for the convenience'" (1999). These are both examples of interesting ways of viewing common things. They involve diffusing focus and looking at everyday things through a somewhat relaxed and distorted lens.

You may say, Barry, "I'm no Sherlock, but you have been weaving between a bunch of topics like distorted focus, video games, dropping out of school, John Lennon, waffles and syrup, etc. and my abductive reasoning is suggesting that you are going to talk about…"

Psychoactive Drugs

Although it is often theorized/suggested/suspected that (some) drugs increase creativity, there are surprisingly *few* studies on the topic because of two very important reasons: (1) evaluating creativity is complicated and (2) drug studies are complicated. As this could be a book topic on its own, I am going to focus on just a few drugs commonly assumed to be related to creativity: caffeine, alcohol, marijuana/cannabis, and psychedelics. Before we get into this, I must state that I am not encouraging drug use.

Let's start with the most legal and most widely consumed psychotropic drug in the world, *caffeine,* with 85% of the US consuming at least one caffeinated beverage daily (Mitchell et al., 2014). One of the most recent and rigorous studies on the relationship between creativity and caffeine found that one cup of coffee (220 mg of caffeine) improved problem-solving ability (as measured by convergent thinking in a RAT-like assessment). They also found that caffeine helped participants solve problems faster and that it improved mood (which indirectly impacts creative abilities). On the other hand, they also found that there was no significant impact (positive or negative) on divergent-thinking abilities or creative idea generation as measured by an abbreviated Torrance Test (Zabelina & Sivia, 2020). As expected, caffeine helps you focus and thus connect bits of information in front of you, but if your goal is to *diffuse focus,* think divergently, and let your mind wander, caffeine may not be useful.

Alcohol may facilitate creativity by removing inhibitions, but simultaneously it also impairs motivation and cognitive function. To map this to the framework of Chapter 1, alcohol boosts the blue power ring, but weakens the pink and red ones making it difficult to call upon Captain Creativity. Benedek et al. found alcohol improved "creative problem-solving" or convergent thinking (as based on the RAT), but not divergent thinking (Alternative Uses Test) and proposed that alcohol may break down fixation (2017). In a similar study, Jarosz et al. looked at *moderate* alcohol intoxication and the RAT and found that alcohol-intoxicated individuals solved significantly more RAT triads and did so in less time (2012). This study also attributes this phenomenon to lowered inhibitions and lowered fixation.

As for *marijuana/cannabis* experimental studies, Weckowicz et al. (1975) found cannabis at low dose levels can improve performance on *both* convergent and divergent tests, and specifically divergent thinking as measured by the Unusual Uses/Alternative Uses Test. Like the alcohol studies, high

Figure 8.1 Four potential creativity–drug relationships as based on several experimental drug studies. In general, most of the studies use the Remote Associate Test as a measure of convergent thinking and variations of the Alternative Uses Test as a measure of divergent thinking.

doses of cannabis resulted in poorer performance on these same assessments. These researchers suggest that cannabis lowers inhibitions and thus results in more divergent production. A more recent similar study (Kowal et al., 2015) found that low doses of THC (tetrahydrocannabinol), the primary psychoactive compound in cannabis, had produced a non-statistically significant increase in fluency, flexibility, and originality of responses in the Alternative Uses Test. They also found that a high dose of THC significantly decreased performance.

Microdosing is the term for taking very low doses of a *psychedelic* substance, typically LSD (lysergic acid diethylamide) or psilocybin-containing mushrooms (Anderson et al., 2019). The few studies that were conducted found potential creative benefits. Anderson et al. found that increased creativity was the third most common self-reported microdosing benefit (2019). In a controlled experimental study, Prochazkova et al. found that both convergent and divergent-thinking performance was improved after a psychedelic truffle (psilocybin) microdose (2018). In this study, participants in the Netherlands were tested before and after ingesting a psilocybin microdose.

An older study (Harman et al., 1966) with a small sample size found that psychedelic agents (in this case mescaline—a hallucinogenic drug found in certain cacti plants comparable to LSD and psilocybin) increased creative problem-solving ability. Furthermore, the increased creative problem-solving ability continued for *weeks* after the session. This study included more objective creativity assessments like the Alternative Uses Test, as well as questionnaires, and a four-hour problem-solving session. The imagery presented in this paper via participant quotes about their experiences resonates with many of the topics discussed in this book: reduced inhibition, lateral thinking, fluency of ideas, divergent thinking, fantasy, increased motivation, and accessing random knowledge. David Nichols, expert in psychedelics, suggests that low doses of LSD could have a stimulant effect by activating *dopamine* pathways in the brain (Solon, 2016).

Dopamine

When you solve an insight problem or have a creative idea, you typically get a *dopamine* reward (at a very generalized level, this is why we enjoy comedy). Dopamine is a neurotransmitter chemical that your body naturally produces, and it is used to send messages between nerve cells in your brain. It gets released when your brain is sensing a reward or something that you enjoy and gives us a feeling of pleasure. Interestingly, dopamine may also help you *solve* problems too as it plays a role in the drive to be creative and make associations (Flaherty, 2005). Therefore, things that increase dopamine production have been found to increase your ability to make non-obvious connections and thus your ability to be creative.

There are several ways to increase dopamine production. *Exercise* increases dopamine and studies have shown it increases creativity (Steinberg et al., 1997; Latorre Román et al., 2018). Watching a funny movie increases dopamine (Isen et al., 1987). Marijuana and cocaine increase dopamine production and studies have shown they increase novel and uncommon association making (Block & Wittenborn, 2004; Hutten et al., 2019). There are also some foods that boost dopamine including bananas, avocados, almonds, and dark chocolate (which sound like the ingredients of a fantastic creativity smoothie). Although sugar doesn't directly increase dopamine, if you perceive receiving sugar as a *reward*, the rewarding process increases dopamine (Isen et al., 1987). *Tyrosine* is an amino acid that your body transforms into dopamine, and some studies have shown it improves

Figure 8.2 Old Dutch cheese showing tyrosine crystals (white crunchy spots).

creative thinking, specifically convergent thinking (Colzato et al., 2015). It is available for purchase as a supplement, but it also occurs naturally in some foods. As an example, *tyrosine crystals* are tiny crunchy amino acid crystals that form naturally (like geodes) on the insides of hard, aged cheeses like Romano, Parmigiano-Reggiano, and aged Dutch cheese. As cheese ages, the proteins break down and the tyrosine is released and forms crystalline structures in the "eyes" of the cheese. Those little crunchy umami nuggets are dopamine fuel (Cornish, 2017).

Many of the referenced drug–creativity studies in this chapter were conducted in the Netherlands perhaps due to a combination of their strong research institutes, expertise in creativity and design, and the government's tolerance of "soft" drugs. Although all four of these aforementioned drugs (caffeine, alcohol, cannabis, psilocybin) are available for consumption in the Netherlands, my Dutch creative "drug" of choice is *overjarige kaas* (really old Dutch cheese).

Now that we have explored what it means to be a creative person, as well as some research that may provide insights into how to be a *more* creative person, let's shift focus in Part II to what it means for a *thing* to be creative and theories of innovation.

References

Anderson, T., Petranker, R., Christopher, A., Rosenbaum, D., Weissman, C., Dinh-Williams, L.-A., Hui, K., & Hapke, E. (2019). Psychedelic microdosing benefits and challenges: An empirical codebook. *Harm Reduction Journal, 16*(43).

Benedek, M., Panzierer, L., Jauk, E., & Neubauer, A. C. (2017). Creativity on tap? Effects of alcohol intoxication on creative cognition. *Consciousness and Cognition: An International Journal, 56*, 128–134.

Biography.com Editors. (2014a, April 2). Pablo Picasso biography. *The Biography.com website*. A&E Television Networks.

Biography.com Editors. (2014b, April 2). Thomas Edison biography. *The Biography.com website*. A&E Television Networks.

Block, R. I., & Wittenborn, J. R. (2004). Marijuana effects on associative processes. *Psychopharmacology, 85*, 426–430.

Carson, S. H., Peterson, J. B., & Higgins, D. M. (2003). Decreased latent inhibition is associated with increased creative achievement in high-functioning individuals. *Journal of Personality and Social Psychology, 85*(3), 499–506.

Colzato, L. S., de Haan, A. M., & Hommel, B. (2015). Food for creativity: Tyrosine promotes deep thinking. *Psychological Research, 79*, 709–714.

Cornish, R. (2017, May 15). What are those weird, crunchy bits in cheese? *Good Food*.

Flaherty, A. W. (2005). Frontotemporal and dopaminergic control of idea generation and creative drive. *Journal of Comparative Neurology, 493*(1), 147–153.

Galloway, S. (2016, March 24). Why Aaron Sorkin Won't Dish on Leonardo DiCaprio and Ben Affleck in His Real-Life Gambling Drama 'Molly's Game'. *The Hollywood Reporter*.

Green, C. S., & Bavelier, D. (2003). Action video game modifies visual selective attention. *Nature, 423*(6939), 534–537.

Harman, W. W., McKim, R. H., Mogar, R. E., Fadiman, J., & Stolaroff, M. J. (1966). Psychedelic agents in creative problem-solving: A pilot study. *Psychological reports, 19*(1), 211–227.

Hedberg, M. (1999, January 5). *Mitch Hedberg: Comedy Central Special*. Comedy Central Television.

Hedberg, M. (2003, December 23). *Late Night with Conan O'Brien*. NBC Television.

Hutten, N., Steenbergen, L., Colzato, L. S., Hommel, B., Theunissen, E. L., Ramaekers, J. G., & Kuypers, K. (2019). Cocaine enhances figural, but impairs verbal 'flexible' divergent thinking. *European Neuropsychopharmacology, 29*(7), 813–824.

Isen, A. M., Daubman, K. A., & Nowicki, G. P. (1987). Positive affect facilitates creative problem solving. *Journal of Personality and Social Psychology, 52*(6), 1122–1131.

Jarosz, A. F., Colflesh, G. J., & Wiley, J. (2012). Uncorking the muse: Alcohol intoxication facilitates creative problem solving. *Consciousness and Cognition, 21*(1), 487–493.

Johnson, S. (2010). *Where good ideas come from: The natural history of innovation*. Riverhead Books.

Jones, N. (2018). How the college dropout schooled America: The public pedagogy of Kanye West. *Public Voices, 15*(2), 65–86.

Jonze, T. (2013, November 11). John Lennon's detention records up for auction. *The Guardian*.

Kowal, M. A., Hazekamp, A., Colzato, L. S., van Steenbergen, H., van der Wee, N. J. A., Durieux, J., Manai, M., & Hommel, B. (2015). Cannabis and creativity: Highly potent cannabis impairs divergent thinking in regular cannabis users. *Psychopharmacology, 232*(6), 1123–1134.

Latorre Román, P. Á., Vallejo, A. P., & Aguayo, B. B. (2018). Acute aerobic exercise enhances students' creativity. *Creativity Research Journal, 30*(3), 310–315.

Martindale, C. (1989). Personality, situation, and creativity. In J. A. Glover, R. R. Ronning, & C. R. Reynolds (Eds.), *Handbook of creativity* (pp. 211–232). Plenum Press.

Mendelsohn, G. A. (1976). Associative and attentional processes in creative performance. *Journal of Personality, 44*, 341–369.

Mitchell, D. C., Knight, C. A., Hockenberry, J., Teplansky, R., & Hartman, T. J. (2014). Beverage caffeine intakes in the U.S. *Food and Chemical Toxicology, 63*, 136–142.

Norwood, A. R. (2017). Lucille Ball. *National Women's History Museum*.

Prochazkova, L., Lippelt, D. P., Colzato, L. S., Kuchar, M., Sjoerds, Z., & Hommel, B. (2018). Exploring the effect of microdosing psychedelics on creativity in an open-label natural setting. *Psychopharmacology, 235*(12), 3401–3413.

Ritter, S. M., Abbing, J., & van Schie, H. T. (2018). Eye-closure enhances creative performance on divergent and convergent creativity tasks. *Frontiers in Psychology, 9*, 1315.

Segal, E. (2004). Incubation in insight problem solving. *Creativity Research Journal, 16*(1), 141–148.

Sellers, J., & Moss, B. (2016). *Learning with the labyrinth: Creating reflective space in higher education*. Palgrave Macmillan.

Solon, O. (2016, August 24). Under pressure, Silicon Valley workers turn to LSD microdosing. *Wired*.

Steinberg, H., Sykes, E. A., Moss, T., Lowery, S., LeBoutillier, N., & Dewey, A. (1997). Exercise enhances creativity independently of mood. *British Journal of Sports Medicine, 31*(3), 240–245.

Strauss, V. (2016, February 11). Was Albert Einstein really a bad student who failed math? *The Washington Post*.

Subramaniam, K., Kounios, J., Parrish, T. B., & Jung-Beeman, M. (2009). A brain mechanism for facilitation of insight by positive affect. *Journal of Cognitive Neuroscience, 21*(3), 415–432.

Weckowicz, T. E., Fedora, O., Mason, J., Radstaak, D., Bay, K. S., & Yonge, K. A. (1975). Effect of marijuana on divergent and convergent production cognitive tests. *Journal of Abnormal Psychology, 84*(4), 386–398.

Weiner, M. & Palmer, T. (Writers), & Hunter, T. (Director). (2007, October 4). Indian Summer. [Television series episode]. In *Mad Men*, AMC.

Zabelina, D. L., & Silvia, P. J. (2020). Percolating ideas: The effects of caffeine on creative thinking and problem solving. *Consciousness and Cognition, 79*, 102899.

Part II

Innovation, Play, and Humor

9

THREE REQUISITES OF INNOVATION,
UTILITY PATENTS, AND A TANNING
BOOTH TOASTER

In Part I, I discussed several theories of creativity through the lens of standardized creativity assessments such as the Alternatives Uses Test and the Torrance Test of Creative Thinking. Dr. Teresa Amabile presents another perspective on how to view a creative individual:

> Any identification of a thought process as creative must finally depend on the fruit of that process—a product or response. Similarly, even a clear specification of the personality traits that mark outstanding creative individuals would have to be validated against their work.

> (Amabile, 1982)

The best way to assess creativity is by looking at the *products* someone creates. I am using the term *product* in the general sense to mean output of any creative form (poetry, art, dance, architecture, mechanisms, music, theories, etc.) and not specifically manufactured goods. If one can produce things or ideas for things that others deem to be creative, it doesn't matter how well one performs on a convergent or divergent thinking assessment.

So, with this in mind, **what makes an idea a creative idea?** Generally, there are two main categories of criteria for creative ideas: novelty-based and multi-attribute-based (Dean et al., 2006). *Novelty-based* implies that ideas are creative based solely on originality or novelty and do not depend on any other factors (such as quality). *Multi-attribute-based* implies that creative ideas must be novel but must also possess additional *quality* attributes with the most common quality being *usefulness* (Dean et al., 2006). A multi-attribute approach is common in engineering as utility or usefulness is (at a minimum) equally valued to novelty (Shah et al., 2003). Other *quality* attributes sometimes include such things as: relevance, appropriateness, clarity, workability, feasibility, etc.

I think we can all agree that usefulness is often a good thing; however, when it is used to define *if* a concept is creative or not, things can get murky. In my research, I found *no* correlation between product concepts that people think are useful and those that people think are creative (Kudrowitz & Wallace, 2013). I want you to think about a few items and pretend that they didn't exist yet: Dip-n-Dots, a pogo stick, Dali's Lobster Telephone. Now I want you to imagine that someone asked you to rate only the *usefulness* of these ideas. So how *useful* are they? Now, what if I asked you to rate the *creativity* of those same ideas (again assuming they didn't exist yet). Usefulness is not required for an idea to be deemed *creative* (Runco & Charles, 1993; Christiaans, 2002; Kudrowitz & Wallace, 2013).

DOI: 10.4324/9781003276296-12

Novelty tends to be the most predictive factor of creativity, and, in my research, people are unable to separate ratings of novelty from ratings of creativity (Kudrowitz & Wallace, 2013). If I had to choose one additional attribute to define a creative idea to supplement novelty, it would be *relevance*. As an example, if I asked you to come up with a new concept for a camping backpack and you said: "Celery, celery, go go go! I'm an angry donkey wearing clogs!" That would be a highly *novel* response; however, it makes no sense... especially given the prompt. Novelty can only be creative within a context and *randomness* does not (usually) result in creativity.

Amabile again provides an alternative perspective to these attribute-based assessments and suggests that creativity cannot be determined objectively using metrics. She proposes the *Consensual Definition of Creativity*: "A product or response is creative to the extent that appropriate observers independently agree it is creative" (Amabile, 1982). In other words, instead of determining if an idea is creative by rating attributes like novelty, usefulness, etc., just straight up ask people who are familiar with the domain of work if the product is creative and to use their own subjective definition of creativity. This process of concept evaluation is what people would do in industry or during a design critique in academia—it is an ecologically valid way of measuring the creativity of a work and, indirectly, the creativity of the creator. By using product creation or idea generation as a measure of creativity of an individual "not only does the task itself mimic real-world performance but the assessment technique mimics real-world evaluations of creative work" (Amabile, 1982).

When we start to question the "usefulness" or "value" or "feasibility" of a creative concept, we are now venturing into the related domain of *innovation*. Innovation can be defined as a "novel application or combination of ideas and technology into marketable products or services" (Luecke & Katz, 2003). A similar distinction between creativity and innovation is as follows:

> Creativity is displayed when an individual develops a novel form of behavior or novel idea, regardless of its practical uptake and subsequent application [i.e., novelty-based]. Innovation means implementing a novel form of behavior or an idea in order to obtain a practical benefit which is then adopted by others [i.e., novel + value + feasible].
>
> (Bateson & Martin, 2013)

Innovation may be a buzzword, but it still represents a very important concept of *applied creativity* spanning across a variety of domains. It is often viewed as a business term, but it equally applies to engineering, design, and other creative disciplines. Typically, an innovative idea is one that is *novel, useful, and feasible.* This trio of criteria is referred to as a *NUF test* that is used as an early stage means of evaluating ideas (Gray et al., 2010). Figure 9.1 shows a few examples of toaster concepts with innovation ratings using this NUF assessment (Kudrowitz & Wallace, 2013).

Ideas with high novel and feasible scores, but low useful scores, are ones with an uncertain market (like the tanning bed toaster of Figure 9.1). Concepts in this domain include novelty items and *chindogu* (i.e., impractical objects, Chapter 10) (Patton & Bannerot, 2002). Ideas with high useful and feasible scores, but low novel scores are most likely existing things (such as the conveyor toaster of Figure 9.1). Lastly, ideas with high novel and useful scores, but low feasible scores, are non-attainable solutions (like the hand-crank toaster of Figure 9.1). Concepts in this domain can be called *chimera* (i.e., *pipe dream*) ideas. An innovative concept should score highly on all three of these areas (novel, useful, and feasible).

The NUF test is an adaptation of the process used to determine if something is patentable. The 1952 patent statue sets out three explicit conditions for patentability, specifically regarding *utility patents* (Klein, 1997). These *three tests of patentability* are that an invention must be *novel* (different from prior art in some manner), *useful* (provide some utility or improvement over existing means), and *non-obvious*. Non-obviousness is the most complicated to explain and test. It essentially means that a **p**erson **h**aving **o**rdinary **s**kill **i**n **t**he **a**rt/field of the invention (e.g., a *PHOSITA* for short or *POSA* for shorter) would not find the invention obvious. A fourth criterion outlined by the

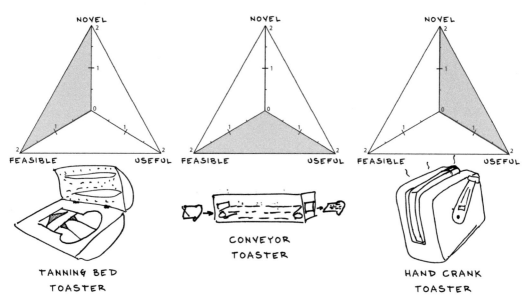

Figure 9.1 Three toaster concepts from Kudrowitz and Wallace (2013) showing ratings for novel, useful, and feasible.

United States Patent and Trademark Office (USPTO) is the "enablement" requirement in that the invention must be "adequately described or enabled for one of ordinary skill in the art to make and use the invention" (USPTO, 2016).

Between the years of 1790 and 1880, a patent required a three-dimensional physical model in addition to the written specification to demonstrate that the invention actually works or, in other words, it required a *reduction to practice*. These models were formerly displayed in the Patent Office in Washington DC for patent examiner reference and inventor inspiration. Many of these models are now in the care of the Smithsonian National Museum of American History (Hintz, 2018). In today's patent system, a physical model is no longer required.

> Reduction to practice may be an actual reduction [like these models] or a constructive reduction to practice which occurs when a patent application on the claimed invention is filed. [Given that patent language is required to enable a POSA to make the invention] The filing of a patent application *serves as* conception and constructive reduction to practice of the subject matter described in the application.
>
> (USPTO, 2020, italic and brackets added).

This is how *feasibility* enters the NUF test.

The NUF test and the tests of patentability are ideal when innovation is technical in nature and provides utility. However, I prefer using the broader criterion of *"value"* in place of *useful*. Usefulness is only *one* means of creating value. A concept can create value via aesthetic pleasure (like Dip-N-Dots!), a sentimental/emotional connection, or some meaningful personal connection (Sääksjärvi & Gonçalves, 2018). In engineering problems, value often comes primarily from usefulness, but this may not be the case with innovation across other domains. As examples, toys and games, artwork, recreational products, novelty goods, and immersive dining experiences can all be innovative, but may not innovate via "usefulness." Using the term "value" also jives with the Luecke and Katz (2003) definition evoking *"marketable* products or services." I should note that value can be measured in ways other than "marketability," such as a positive societal change.

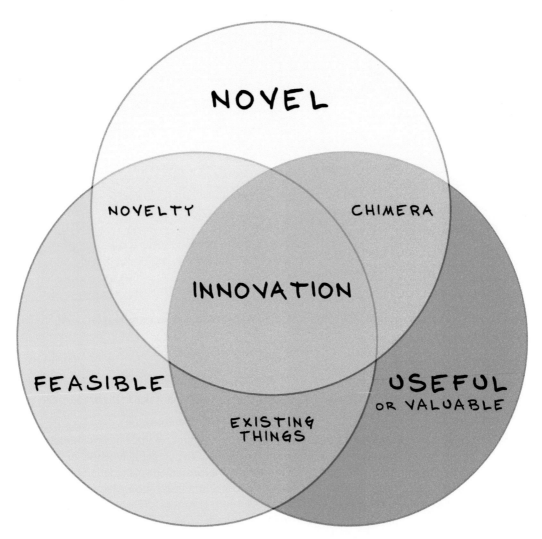

Figure 9.2 A Venn diagram of the elements of innovation: novel, feasible, and useful (or valuable, being a more inclusive criteria).

An idea can be deemed *creative* without having value, just as an idea can be deemed creative without being feasible. But to be *innovative*, an idea must be both valuable and feasible...*Or does it?*

The gray zone of questionable feasibility and questionable value is where interesting innovation is hiding. As I will discuss throughout Part II, sometimes we don't know what is feasible or what is not feasible. And in the process of developing an idea, you may invent a means of making something feasible. Value may also be ambiguous as sometimes people don't know what they want! Something that sounds like a great idea may turn out to not have public appeal, and, in contrast, something that may seem worthless, useless, or a joke at first may turn out to have value...like, say, a tanning bed toaster.

In Chapter 10, we will delve into this realm of questionable value and feasibility.

References

Amabile, T. M. (1982). Social-psychology of creativity - A consensual assessment technique. *Journal of Personality and Social Psychology, 43*(5), 997–1013.

Bateson, P., & Martin, P. (2013). *Play, playfulness, creativity and innovation.* Cambridge University Press.

Christiaans, H. H. (2002). Creativity as a design criterion. *Creativity Research Journal, 14*(1), 41–54.

Dean, D. L., Hender, J. M., Rodgers, T. L., & Santanen, E. L. (2006). Identifying quality, novel, and creative ideas: Constructs and scales for idea evaluation. *Journal of the Association for Information Systems, 7*(10), 646–698.

Gray, D., Brown, S., & Macanufo, J. (2010). *Gamestorming: A playbook for innovators, rulebreakers, and change-makers.* O'Reilly Media, Inc.

Hintz, E. S. (2018, June 18). *Patent models and prototypes on display.* Smithsonian National Museum of American History.

Klein, A. P. (1997). A funny thing happened to the non-obvious subject matter condition for patentability on its way to the federal circuit. *University of Baltimore Intellectual Property Law Journal, 19*(21).

Kudrowitz, B. M., & Wallace D. R. (2013). Assessing the quality of ideas from prolific, early-stage product ideation. *Journal of Engineering Design, 24*(2), 120–139.

Luecke, R., & Katz, R. (2003). *Managing creativity and innovation.* Harvard Business School Press.

Patton, A., & Bannerot, R. (2002, March 20–22). Chindogu: A problem solving strategy for transforming uselessness into fearlessness. *Proceedings of the 2002 Annual Conference of the ASEE Gulf Southwest Section,* Lafayette, LA, USA.

Runco, M. A., & Charles, R. E. (1993). Judgments of originality and appropriateness as predictors of creativity. *Personality and Individual Differences, 15*(5), 537–546.

Sääksjärvi, M., & Gonçalves, M. (2018). Creativity and meaning: Including meaning as a component of creative solutions. *Artificial Intelligence for Engineering Design, Analysis and Manufacturing, 32*(4), 365–379.

Shah, J. J., Vargas-Hernandez, N., & Smith, S. M. (2003). Metrics for measuring ideation effectiveness. *Design Studies, 24*(2), 111–134.

The United States Patent and Trademark Office (USPTO). (2016). *Patent FAQs.*

The United States Patent and Trademark Office (USPTO). (2020). 2138.05 Reduction to Practice [R-5]. *Manual of Patent Examining Procedure.*

10

SILLY IDEAS, SHITTY ROBOTS, AND POOP ICE CREAM

When I was in graduate school, I saw a flyer for an "unuseless" competition inspired by the Japanese concept of "*chindogu*." This term, literally translated to "unusual or curious tool/device," was coined by Kenji Kawakami (1995) to describe an invention that solves a problem but does so in such a convoluted manner that it minimizes any usefulness that it intended to create. As a result, it creates humor and intrigue. A few examples of chindogu from Kawakami's book are small umbrellas attached to shoes to keep them dry, and a toilet paper-dispensing hat for having tissues handy to blow your nose (1995). I submitted an entry into this competition with two other students: an anthropomorphic ketchup bottle that roller-skates on the table and poops ketchup onto your plate. It was deemed the most "unuseless."

Later versions of this *Catsup Crapper* (a.k.a. AuTomato or Ketchup Robot) circulated on the internet, and this device appeared on several television shows including Martha Stewart (at which she exclaimed "this is called poo-poo humor...I can*not* believe I have this on my show!" (Stewart, 2008)). We received countless emails asking where one can purchase a Catsup Crapper. What started out as an intentional joke, a chindogu, with little to no practical use, became something that people actually valued. As a more familiar example, *the selfie stick* was one of the 101 original unuseless concepts featured in the first book of chindogu (1995). Just nine years later, it was named one of the "Best Inventions" by *Time* magazine (2014) with an estimated global market value of US$1.41 billion in 2020 (Imarc Staff, 2020). Unfortunately, according to the 10 Tenets of Chindogu, tenet number five prohibits the sale of chindogu: "Chindogu are not tradable commodities. If you accept money for one, you surrender your purity. They must not even be sold. Even as a joke" (Sterling, 2013). The Catsup Crapper maintains its status as chindogu (*yay?*), but unfortunately the selfie stick has surrendered its purity to capitalism.

One study used chindogu in engineering design education to force students outside their comfort zone to "promote fearlessness in problem solving" (Patton & Bannerot, 2002). The idea is that engineering students are often taught to place emphasis on usefulness to such a degree that it stifles creativity. In this study, engineering students were required to intentionally ignore usefulness to challenge their worldview and biases in favor of making bold creative decisions. This is the same rationale behind *Hebocon*—the Japanese (now global) sumo-wresting-inspired robot competition in which the *worst* robots win. Hebocon derives from the Japanese word "heboi" meaning "poor quality" or "crappy." Like the Patton and Bannerot theory (2002), it's easier and less stressful to engage less technically skilled beginners in engineering concepts when the goal is to *not* succeed and have fun doing it (Ackerman, 2017). As *Adventure Time*'s Jake the Dog says: "Suckin' at something is

DOI: 10.4324/9781003276296-13

the first step towards being sorta good at something" (Ward et al., 2010). Chindogu and Hebocon are means of democratizing robotics and inspiring those who wouldn't typically build robots to take their first steps.

We can't discuss crappy robots without recognizing *Simone Giertz*, the inventor formerly known as "the queen of shitty robots." Her inventions solve problems, and, like chindogu, do so in a very crude and overly complicated manner. Some examples of her work include an alarm clock that slaps the user awake, a robot that feeds you popcorn, and a toothbrush helmet ("recommended by 0 out of 10 dentists") (Giertz, 2018). Aside from promoting innovation through humor, she is also a voice of the maker movement—democratizing robotics to be something that anyone can experiment with and not just engineers. This scrappy, playful approach to thinking about engineering and robotics allows for risk taking (Jenkins et al., 2020). Like Hebocon, Giertz makes it OK for prototypes to fail and not be perfect, and, furthermore, she celebrates it. As I will discuss in Chapters 22 and 32, we should not be afraid of failure: we should embrace it. This is how we learn. This is how we innovate.

The first filmed *intentionally* shitty robot is Charlie Chaplin's "eating machine" featured in the 1936 film, *Modern Times* (2010). In this scene, Chaplin's character "the Tramp" is fitted into a machine that rotates food in front of his mouth and then push-feeds the food off the circular conveyor (very much like Simone Giertz's "Head Orbit Device" (2018) or my own "Oreo Separating Machine" (Chin, 2013)). After some humorous demonstrations of the *Modern Times* eating machine, the observers declare to the inventors (via intertitle): "it's no good...it isn't practical" (Chaplin et al., 2010).

So why discuss chindogu, Hebocon, and shitty robots when one of the common requirements of innovation is *usefulness*? First, as mentioned, these are a low-stress, fun means of engaging novices and a broad audience with invention and technical creativity. But additionally, specifically related to the concept of innovation, **many things that were once deemed silly are now viewed**

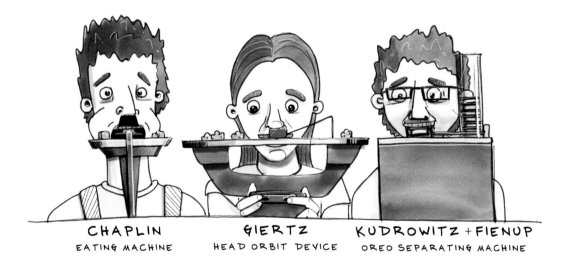

CHAPLIN
EATING MACHINE

GIERTZ
HEAD ORBIT DEVICE

KUDROWITZ + FIENUP
OREO SEPARATING MACHINE

Figure 10.1 Interpretations of select unuseless mechanical feeding machines from left to right: Charlie Chaplin's Eating Machine from *Modern Times* (2010), Simone Giertz's Head Orbit Device (2018), and Barry Kudrowitz and Bill Fienup's Oreo Separating Machine (Chin, 2013).

as innovative as I will illustrate throughout Part II. Even the McCormick reaper of Chapter 3 was ridiculed as a joke when it was first revealed. The *London Times* called it "a cross between an Astley chariot, a wheelbarrow, and a flying machine" (McCormick, 2018). This is also where humor and play come in. Those ideas that straddle the line of feasibility (hand-crank toaster) and/or value (tanning bed toaster) tend to also come with some degree of humor and/or playfulness.

Let's look at a poem by Shel Silverstein called "Somethin' New" from his book *Falling Up* (1996). This poem is intended to be a joke—showcasing silly attempts at innovation that intentionally lack value and/or feasibility. To avoid copyright infringement, I will summarize the "silly" ideas from the poem, but you are encouraged to find and read the original work. The poem includes four ideas: "paper umbrellas," "reusable gum," "mustard ice cream," and a "plug-bottom boat" (Silverstein, 1996). These product ideas are seemingly novel, but still "no one was willing to try it" or "taste it." The moral or punchline of the poem supports the definition of innovation as presented in Chapter 9: *innovation requires more than just being "something new" or something novel.* Novelty is *one* component, but if there is no value or feasibility, no one will want it, and it won't contribute to society.

Unlike chindogu, in which problem-solving is done in a convoluted, impractical, or extraneous manner, the examples in Silverstein's poem are intentionally trying to *not* solve problems and are intentionally trying to be contradictions. But contradictions can sometimes lead to creativity. One could read into these "silly" ideas to extract value and feasibility. For example, paper umbrellas exist and are generally impermeable to water if the paper is impregnated with wax or tung oil. These types of umbrellas have been used in China since the Han Dynasty and are a relatively inexpensive, lightweight, and an environmentally friendly means of crafting an umbrella (Jiang, 2021). "Reusable gum" could mean converting the remains of ABC (already been chewed) gum into a recycled gum polymer. This is exactly what British Designer Anna Bullus does with her company *Gumdrop* (Shaw, 2018), because it is a "pity to waste it" (Silverstein, 1996). Boats have drain plugs that are intended to be used for the exact purpose in the poem, except only when the boat is taken out of the water. Lastly, mustard ice cream is real. It was made popular by Chef Heston Blumenthal at his restaurant *The Fat Duck* (and in his eponymous cookbook) with the dish "Red Cabbage Gazpacho, Pommery Grain Mustard Ice Cream" (2009). At first, this dish may sound offensive or absurd as we associate mustard with more savory things like hot dogs, but when you break down the elements of the dish, it makes more sense. Gazpacho is a cold soup made with blended vegetables and/or fruit. Cabbage and cream appear together in a different cold vegetable soup, borscht. Cabbage and mustard are in the same brassica family. Making a cold mustard ice cream for a cold cabbage soup is a non-obvious connection that is surprising, playful, humorous, and innovative. Additionally, the pungency of the mustard is balanced by the richness of the cream (see Figure 10.2).

The purpose of me butchering all the fun and humor out of the Shel Silverstein poem and Heston Blumenthal's dish is to show how there can be nuggets of innovation in the seemingly (and intentionally) ridiculous, absurd, or even contradictory. **Things that seem silly at first may actually be innovative in the future.**

OK, let's push this ice cream "joke" even further. Let's say it wasn't *mustard* ice cream, but instead we were talking about *poop-smelling* ice cream?

Nathan for You is a television show that actively tries to push the boundaries of innovation while simultaneously parodying (the USD40 billion) management consulting industry (Arnold, 2014). In some manner, Nathan Fielder is to business plans as Simone Giertz is to robotics. The show

Figure 10.2 Visual analysis of Chef Heston Blumenthal's dish "Red Cabbage Gazpacho, Pommery Grain Mustard Ice Cream" (2009). Although the idea of mustard ice cream may seem unusual at first, it can be mapped back to a more familiar pairing.

features Nathan Fielder providing seemingly outlandish business consulting advice to small companies such as developing a poop-flavored soft serve as means of bringing in customers to a frozen yogurt store (spoiler…it worked) (Fielder, 2013). In another episode, Nathan Fielder proposes the idea of instead of hiring two maids to clean a house in two hours, one could hire a bus of 40 maids to clean a house in six minutes (Fielder, 2014). His ideas, like this one, are proposed as serious concepts to the contracting party, but are likely viewed as absurd to the home viewer. For the concepts on the show to work, his ideas need to straddle this innovation gray zone of value and/or feasibility (see Figure 10.3).

In *Nathan for You*, the ideas need to be just feasible or valuable enough for the client to agree to participate. This is the *"it's so crazy, it just might work"* trope. If the ideas were all clearly feasible, valuable, and novel, the premise may not be appropriate for *Comedy Central*. I'll get to humor in Part IV, but this pushing of the boundary is what leads to humor and sometimes innovation. Let's analyze the Bus-of-Maids concept. Although it's a *seemingly* ridiculous idea, this concept technically worked on the show: the client was pleased and impressed (even though it took 2 minutes and 16 seconds longer than planned) (Fielder, 2014). The concept is clearly novel, and the episode provided a test of feasibility and value. Instead of the innovation being a joke, the joke was actually innovation. As Albert Einstein said: "If at first the idea is not absurd, then there is no hope for it."

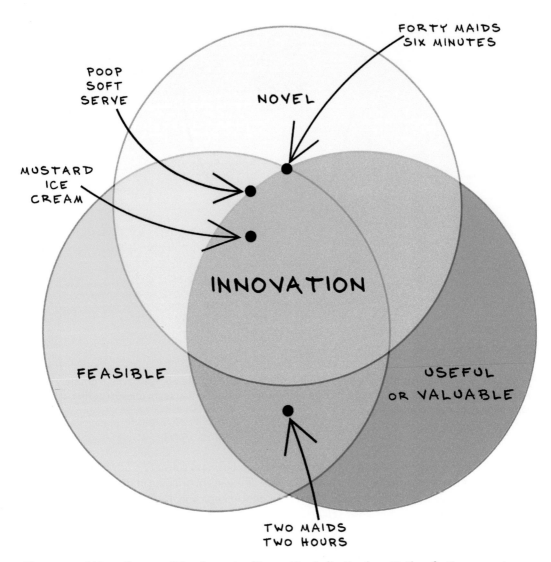

Figure 10.3 A Venn diagram of the elements of innovation indicating how *Nathan for You* concepts, Poop Soft Serve and a Bus-of-Maids (2013; 2014) straddle the border of innovation.

References

Ackerman, E. (2017, January 26). Hebocon: The best worst Robot competition. *IEEE Spectrum*.

Arnold, B. (2014, August 24). The insane business ideas on 'Nathan For You' have had mixed results. *Business Insider*.

Blumenthal, H. (2009). *The fat duck cookbook.* Bloomsbury USA.

Chaplin, C. et al. (2010). *Modern Times*. [film]. Criterion Collection.

Chin. R. (2013, March 6). Orobot: One Solution to your pesky Oreo cookie-from-crème problem. *Pioneer Press*.

Fielder, N. (Host). (2013, February 28). Yogurt shop/Pizzeria. *Nathan for You, 2*(3). Comedy Central.

Fielder, N. (Host). (2014, July 15). Pet store/maid service. *Nathan for You, 2*(3). Comedy Central.

Giertz, S. (2018). Why you should make useless things. *TED2018*.

Imarc Staff. (2020). Selfie stick market: Global industry trends, share, size, growth, opportunity and forecast 2021–2026. *Imarc*.

Jenkins, R., Hurley, M., Durall Gazulla, E., & Martin, S. (2020). A defense of (s)crappy Robots. 42-42. *Abstract from Constructionism*, Dublin, Ireland.

Jiang, F. (2021, October 2). *Traditional Chinese paper umbrellas: Origins and making.* China Highlights.

Kawakami, K. (1995). *101 Unuseless Japanese inventions*. W. W. Norton Company.

McCormick, R. (2018). *Memorial of Robert Mccormick: Being a brief history of his life, character and inventions, including the early history of the Mccormick reaper.* Franklin Classics.

Patton, A., & Bannerot, R. (2002, March 20–22). Chindogu: A problem solving strategy for transforming uselessness into fearlessness. *Proceedings of the 2002 Annual Conference of the ASEE Gulf Southwest Section,* Lafayette, LA, USA.

Shaw, D. (2018, March 6). World hacks: A surprising new afterlife for chewing gum. *BBC News.*

Silverstein, S. (1996). *Falling up.* HarperCollins.

Sterling, B. (2013, September 30). Design fiction: The ten Chindogu Tenets. *Wired.*

Stewart, M. (Host). (2008, February 15). Unuseless inventions. *Martha Stewart Show.* Fine Living Channel.

Time Staff. (2014, November 20). The 25 best inventions of 2014. *Time.*

Ward, P., & Williams, M. (Writers), & Leichliter, L. (Director). (2010, September 20). His hero. [Television series episode]. In K. Crews (Producer), *Adventure Time.* Cartoon Network.

11

FLAVORS OF INNOVATION, THE NONSTICK FRYING PAN, AND USB DRIVES

There are a few words that the general public tend to confuse when it comes to creativity and design: discovery, invention, and innovation.

Discovery is finding something unexpectedly or in the course of a search (e.g., the discovery of gravity, the moons of Jupiter, fire, DNA structure, photosynthesis). These items already existed in the world, and someone uncovered it. The discoverer didn't create anything new. Another way of saying this is that discovery "consists of seeing what everyone else has seen and thinking what no one else has thought" (Szent-Györgyi, 1957). Typically, one makes a new discovery through scientific exploration and research.

Invention is creating something that has not existed before (e.g., transistors, the printing press, the steam engine, gun powder, the water wheel). These items are human-made creations and are typically patentable. As a reminder, the three tests of patentability of an invention are that it must be *novel*, *useful*, and *non-obvious*, but it also must be *created by human*. The Supreme Court ruling on *Diamond v. Chakrabarty* of 1980 held that microorganisms created by human via genetic engineering *can* be protected by a patent. This case highlights the major difference between discovery and invention. Discovery is not patentable:

> The laws of nature, physical phenomena, and abstract ideas have been held not patentable. Thus, a new mineral discovered in the earth or a new plant found in the wild is not patentable subject matter. Likewise, Einstein could not patent his celebrated law that $E=mc^2$.; nor could Newton have patented the law of gravity. Such discoveries are 'manifestations of… nature, free to all men and reserved exclusively to none'.
>
> (*Diamond v. Chakrabarty*, 1980)

Invention often stems from engineering and applied science disciplines. There is a Sid Caesar joke about invention: "The guy who invented the wheel was an idiot. The guy who invented the other three, he was a genius" (France, 2014). Sid Caesar is hinting at the subtle difference between invention and innovation.

Innovation, as discussed in Chapters 9 and 10, is a "novel application or combination of ideas and technology into marketable products or services" (e.g., Dip n' Dots, Nintendo Switch, The Model T, Zip Car, The Walkman) (Luecke & Katz, 2003). These items are products or services that people can actually purchase and/or use that happen to utilize existing technologies. Aside from maybe inventors, people don't typically walk into a store and purchase a case of transistors or a bucket

DOI: 10.4324/9781003276296-14

of silicone, or (evoking Sid Caesar) a single wheel. *All innovation starts from inventions, but not all inventions become innovations.* There are many inventions (and related patents) that are never used, produced, or seen by others. If the invention stays in the inventor's basement, it can't be innovation. Innovation (unlike invention) requires an introduction to society or transformation into a marketable product or service (Garcia & Calantone, 2002). If *discovery* tends to be associated with sciences, and *invention* tends to be associated with engineering, *innovation* tends to be associated with design and business.

These three concepts all involve creativity and are connected: invention depends on discoveries and innovation depends on inventions. Let's look at an example of this creative progression (illustrated in Figure 11.1).

In 1886, Henri Moissan *discovered* elemental fluorine (Wisniak, 2002). Even though this element already existed in the world, it wasn't identified as a "new" element until this discovery. In 1938, DuPont chemist Roy Plunkett accidentally *invented* polytetrafluoroethylene (PTFE) or, as the general population refers to it, Teflon. Although Plunkett describes his invention as being an accidental discovery, he is the inventor of this human-made polymer. Plunkett was employed by DuPont at the time of the invention. DuPont patented the technology in 1941, registered it under the name Teflon in 1944 (Long, 2011), and later produced and sold granules of PTFE in 1946 (Thomas, 1998). Again, aside from maybe inventors, most people don't typically walk into a store and purchase a case of PTFE granules. In 1956, French engineer, Marc Grégoire created the first Teflon-coated nonstick pan in Europe and founded the company TEFAL (a contraction of Teflon and aluminum) to bring the product to the market as an *innovation* (Thomas, 1998). In the process of innovating the cookware market, he also happened to invent a process for bonding Teflon to aluminum. It is understandable that the general public confuses discovery, invention, and innovation as they are interrelated and quite difficult to separate.

DISCOVERY
ELEMENTAL FLOURINE
HENRI MOISSAN

INVENTION
"TEFLON"
ROY PLUNKETT

INNOVATION
NONSTICK PAN
MARC GREGOIRE

Figure 11.1 **The creative progression from discovery to invention to innovation as illustrated with fluorine used in polytetrafluoroethylene that was then used to make nonstick frying pans.**

To complicate matters further, innovation can be subdivided into different ways. Let's look at floppy disks. Floppies were the primary means of storing and transporting data for almost 25 years starting in 1971 when it was introduced to the market by IBM (Amankwah-Amoah, 2016). We then saw an emergence of a series of superior technologies (e.g., CD, DVD, flash memory). Specifically, around the year 2000, the USB drive appeared on the market that utilized a new type of flash memory technology. Compared with all prior storage technologies, it had higher capacity, it was smaller, it was faster, it was lighter, it was more reliable, it was more durable, and, in just a few years after market introduction, it was also less expensive (Amankwah-Amoah, 2016). There was no reason to continue to use floppy disks, especially as files and computer program sizes were increasing. The floppy disk became *obsolete*. There was a *radical innovation* via the introduction of the flash memory technology.

A similar term is sometimes used in this context: *disruptive innovation*. This term describes the process of when new entrants in a market challenge the incumbent firms. Disruptive innovation

> is not about technology alone, but rather the combination of technologies *and* business model innovation. *Radical innovations*, on the other hand, stem from the creation of new knowledge and the commercialization of completely novel ideas or products.
>
> (Hopp et al., 2018)

In this case, the USB flash drive was predominantly radical innovation as it was driven by technological advances. Netflix would be an example of disruptive innovation that involved some new technologies, but also business model innovation. Netflix began as a mail-order only rental model that served a different user group than those who would rent from Blockbuster.

> Only with the rise of technology, including eventually the ability to stream over the Internet, was Netflix able to grow its business and eventually offer on-demand movies and TV to a huge audience, conveniently and cost-effectively.
>
> (Hopp et al., 2018)

Returning to data storage, USB flash drives gradually improved since their introduction in 2000. These new features, benefits, or improvements to the existing technology in an existing market is *incremental innovation* (Garcia & Calantone, 2002). The USB flash drive became even smaller, faster, less expensive, and could hold more data. These are all examples of *technological incremental innovation*. USB drives also became more themed, more personalized, and with better visual and textile aesthetics. These are all examples of *aesthetic incremental innovation*: a transformation and manipulation of appearance or other sensory factors, including changes made to the materials, colors, proportions, textures, shape, sound, or ornamentation (Eisenman, 2013). All these incremental improvement examples are still using the same basic technology and means of storage. We are currently experiencing a radical change that will make all these USB drives obsolete. With cloud storage, we do not need to plug a miniature drive into our computers to share and store data.

There is one more creativity assessment that I intentionally neglected to mention until right now. The *Kirton Adaption-Innovation (or KAI) Inventory* looks at *style* of creativity as opposed to *degree* of creativity. Kirton's *Adaption-Innovation Theory* assumes everyone is creative and falls on a continuum between "adaptor" and "innovator" (1976). In this case, "adaptors" are more like incremental innovators who put effort into improving things and doing things better. They are systematic problem solvers—they are efficient and effective with their time. They tend to be "creative *within* the box." Thomas Edison, for example, would be more of an "adaptor." He was a highly prolific inventor with over 1,000 patents and followed a structured process for developing and improving new technologies (Smith, 2018).

But, hey, did he not *invent* the light bulb?! Was that not *radical*? Well, let me digress.

Technically, there were many earlier versions of incandescent lightbulbs, as early as 1808, which is roughly 70 years prior to Edison's *invention* in 1879 (Hargadon & Douglas, 2001). However, those earlier versions had critical flaws such as a short life, high current requirements, and/or they were too expensive (Smith, 2018). Edison's invention (one of his *many* related to lights) was specifically using carbon-coated bamboo as the filament. To revisit some of the concepts from Chapter 7 on inspiration, getting out into the world, and keeping a design notebook of interesting observations: Edison "had the idea of using bamboo from observing his fishing rod while on a field trip to watch an eclipse" (Smith, 2018). This in no way is trivializing his contribution to electric lighting, as that seemingly (and literally) tiny change solved many of the flaws of the prior art by allowing for low current, low cost, and long life. The entire first claim of one of Edison's first patents on the light bulb is simply: "an electric lamp for giving light by incandescence, consisting of a **filament of carbon** of high resistance, made as described, and secured to metallic wires, as set forth" (Edison, 1880). More importantly, Edison's success and innovation (I think *disruptive* innovation is the correct term here) was in "creating the first broadly successful commercial system of incandescent lighting" (Hargadon & Douglas, 2001). Edison did not invent the radical idea of using electricity to illuminate a filament in a bulb, nor did he invent generators or distribution systems for powering lights—he improved these technologies, brought them together, and created the system and means of bringing efficient electric lighting to society.

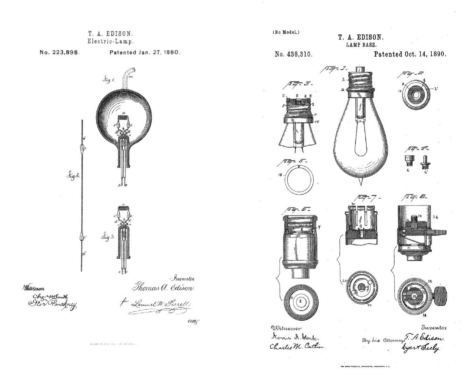

Figure 11.2 Two of Edison's patents related to the incandescent light bulb. One of the first Edison light patents (1880, left) claims the use of a carbon filament. A later patent (1890, right) claims the use of the conductive threaded base as a means to easily install bulbs. This is still the same mechanism we use today for screwing light bulbs into a socket!

On the opposite end of the KAI, are "innovators" who, in the context of this chapter, are more akin to "radical innovators." They are change makers; they have blue-sky ideas with a high failure rate. They tend to be creative "*outside* of the box" and try to do things differently as opposed to doing things better (Kirton, 1976). Albert Einstein, for example, would be more of an innovator on this continuum. Kirton emphasizes the importance of both types of personalities as well as the importance of both flavors of innovation (incremental and radical) for society (1976).

Between radical and incremental, we the people, tend to prefer incremental innovation. After all, what is there not to like? It is basically something that we already know, something that is familiar...but better! It's an electric incandescent light bulb, but it lasts much longer! It's a maid cleaning service, but it takes much less time! It's a frying pan, but it has a nonstick coating! This is the theory of *MAYA* or *Most Advanced Yet Acceptable*. People will find things most pleasing if they are both typical *and* novel (Hekkert et al., 2003). In the Hekkert et al. study, they found that car designs that people preferred most were those that had high scores for *both* novelty and typicality (2003). We like things to be familiar, but we also want them to be new and improved. It sounds like a contradiction, but what it comes down to is a *moderate* amount of innovation. In a similar study with chairs, participants preferred designs that fell somewhere right in the middle of a scale from typical to unique (Hung & Chen, 2012).

TYPICAL   MAYA   NOVEL
        MOST ADVANCED YET ACCEPTABLE

Figure 11.3 A series of floor lamps ranging from more typical to more novel. Lamps that would be considered "most advanced yet acceptable," and thus preferable, are ones that are both typical in some ways and novel in some ways (i.e., a moderate degree of novelty).

When we start to push that balance too much toward novelty (like mustard ice cream), we start to head into the domain of radical innovation and that is when the general non-novelty-seeking public begins to back away slowly into the bushes. In the next chapter, we will further explore radical innovation and why it's so scary (but good for us).

References

Amankwah-Amoah, J. (2016). Competing technologies, competing forces: The rise and fall of the floppy disk, 1971–2010. *Technological Forecasting and Social Change, 107*, 121–129.

Diamond v. Chakrabarty (1980) 447 U.S. 303.

Edison, T. A. (1880). Electric Lamp. U.S. Patent Application No. 223,898. Washington, DC: U.S. Patent and Trademark Office.

Edison, T. A. (1890). Lamp Base. U.S. Patent Application No. 438,310. Washington, DC: U.S. Patent and Trademark Office.

Eisenman, M. (2013). Understanding aesthetic innovation in the context of technological evolution. *Academy of Management Review, 38*(3), 332–351.

France, L. R. (2014, February 12). The words and comedy of Sid Caesar. *CNN*.

Garcia, R., & Calantone, R. (2002), A critical look at technological innovation typology and innovativeness terminology: A literature review. *Journal of Product Innovation Management, 19*, 110–132.

Hargadon, A. B., & Douglas, Y. (2001). When innovations meet institutions: Edison and the design of the electric light. *Administrative Science Quarterly, 46*(3), 476–501.

Hekkert, P., Snelders, D., & van Wieringen, P. C. (2003). 'Most advanced, yet acceptable': Typicality and novelty as joint predictors of aesthetic preference in industrial design. *British Journal of Psychology, 94*(1), 111–124.

Hopp, C., Antons, D., Kaminski, J., & Salge, T. O. (2018, April 9). What 40 years of research reveals about the difference between disruptive and radical innovation. *Harvard Business Review*.

Hung, W., & Chen, L. (2012). Effects of novelty and its dimensions on aesthetic preference in product design. *International Journal of Design, 6*(2), 81–90.

Kirton, M. J. (1976). Adaptors and innovators: A description and measure." *Journal of Applied Psychology, 61*, 622–629.

Long, T. (2011 April 6). April 6, 1938: Teflon, an invention that sticks. *Wired*.

Luecke, R., & Katz, R. (2003). *Managing creativity and innovation*. Harvard Business School Press.

Smith, N. (2018, October 1). *Engineering & Technology Magazine, 13*(9), 54–59.

Szent-Györgyi, A. (1957). *Bioenergetics*. Academic Press.

Thomas, P. (1998). The use of fluoropolymers for non-stick cooking utensils. *Surface Coatings International, 81*, 604–609.

Wisniak, J. (2002). Henri Moissan – The discoverer of fluorine. *Educación Química, 13*, 267–274.

12

RADICAL INNOVATION, WHISKEY-INFUSED LOTION, AND HIGH FASHION

On an episode of the television show *Parks and Recreation*, Aziz Ansari's character, Tom Haverford, convinces his coworkers to go to a "hot new bar" in town with the forewarning: "Just so you know, it's not your typical bar. They specialize in *molecular mixology*. It's kinda like an experimental new way to consume alcohol." To which Nick Offerman's character, Ron Swanson, responds, "son, there's no wrong way to consume alcohol." There is then an abrupt cut to Ron receiving a whiskey-infused lotion hand-massage and Tom inhaling an "aromasphere" cocktail. A frustrated and confused Ron declares that "*this* is the wrong way to consume alcohol" and asks if "this entire establishment is a practical joke of some kind" (King & Holland, 2013). This is reminiscent of another story about *Green Eggs and Ham*. "You do not like them. So you say," says Sam-I-Am, but "try them and you may" (Dr. Seuss, 1960).

Neophobia is the food science term for this reluctance to try new things (such as green eggs or whiskey lotion). Organisms have learned to approach novel foods with caution as some foods (such as green meat) are toxic, and experimentation could be fatal (Pliner & Salvy, 2006). Neophobia could be applied to any domain, but the term is most often used in academic research related to food. There is a history of neophobia specifically related to modernist or "molecular" cuisine like Ron Swanson's whiskey-infused lotion (Cifci et al., 2020). Neophobia is one of the reasons why innovation in the food industry has a high market failure rate (Barrena & Sánchez, 2013).

These are fictional food examples, but history has shown that radical concepts in general are feared, avoided, resisted, and ridiculed even if they provide substantial benefits. **Radical innovation is scary** (especially for neophobic people), **but it may also be good for us**. Below I briefly discuss seven interrelated reasons for neophobia using short examples from history.

Habits Are Hard to Break

IDEO, a design consultancy, provides insight into the phenomena of resisting radical change. In the early 2000s, IDEO was working on a redesign of a toothpaste tube cap that flipped open on a hinge as opposed to the traditional screw top. "Users kept trying to unscrew the cap even though they were told how it worked. The action was a well-ingrained habit that would probably be impossible to break" (Pethokoukis, 2006). Radical innovation involves changing the way you have always done something. We are creatures of *habit* and *tradition*. It is difficult for us to adapt new things when we have only known one way for our entire lives. In this case, the means in which you open and close your toothpaste cap is a relatively small part of your daily life. What happens when radical innovation has greater implications?

DOI: 10.4324/9781003276296-15

New Is Threatening

When the telephone was developed in 1876, telegraph was the primary means of communication, and Western Union held a near-monopoly status. Western Union released an internal memo stating that "the 'telephone' has too many shortcomings to be seriously considered as a means of communication. The device is inherently of no value to us" (Harris, 2012). Western Union already had a vast network of wires and poles across the country to simply update for this new technology, but they viewed this invention as *competition* as opposed to an opportunity. Radical innovation makes us put up our guards. When the next best thing emerges, it often means leaving the current technology behind, investing time and resources in learning new things, and developing new manufacturing processes, supply chains, and/or service structures. This is the *fear of (radical) change* at an industry scale. This same thing happens on a personal scale too. Think back to your music collection and the process of managing it through the shifts from records to 8-tracks to cassettes to CDs to digital MP3s to cloud services.

Radical Change Seems Impossible

When the first television was introduced, Lee de Forest (inventor of the amplifying vacuum tube that made television possible) said: "While theoretically and technically television may be feasible, commercially and financially I consider it an impossibility, a development of which we need waste little time dreaming" (de Forest, 1926). Marty Cooper, Motorola engineer and inventor of the first cell phone said: "Cellular phones will absolutely not replace local wire systems. Even if you project it beyond our lifetimes, it won't be cheap enough" (Grier, 1981). This is the nature of inventions. Inventors are not necessarily entrepreneurs, nor do they require an understanding of marketing and supply chain. "The creative people who came up with the ideas are not always the best equipped for testing and putting them into practice" (Bateson & Martin, 2013). Furthermore, when there is no precedent for a concept, bringing it to the public *seems impossible* even for the leading scientific minds of the time. As I mentioned in Chapter 10, radical innovation often starts in that gray zone of unknown feasibility and/or unknown value. Futurist and science-fiction writer, *Arthur C. Clarke*, devised three laws about the future. The first is that "when a distinguished but elderly scientist states that something is possible, [they are] almost certainly right. When [they state] that something is impossible, [they are] very probably wrong" (1962). In this case, Clarke was right, and de Forest and Cooper were wrong.

Current or Early Embodiments Require Future Thinking

When IBM released their first commercial computer (IBM 701) in 1953, it was the size of a room, weighed 20,516 pounds, and rented for US$12,000–18,000/month (which is ~US$125,000–180,000/month in 2021) (Weik, 1961). Thomas Watson Jr., the president of IBM at the time, shared with stockholders that they "expected to get orders for five machines" across the country (IBM FAQ, 2007). This quote has been mischaracterized and attributed to his father as saying, "I think there is a world market for maybe five computers." Although Watson Jr. underestimated the sales and "came home with orders for 18," this was a relatively modest prediction of the national market potential for computers (IBM FAQ, 2007). Between 1974 and 1977, Ken Olson, the president of Digital Equipment Corp, was quoted in different contexts as saying, "he couldn't see any need or any use for a computer in someone's home" (Ahl, 1980). Today, you likely have a couple of computers on your person at this very moment and many more in your home. Even though, *at the time*, computers were enormous and of prohibitive cost for most households, these statements from technology leaders show a slight lack of vision. Radical innovation typically starts as a scary looking, cost-prohibitive prototype, and prototypes rarely represent how a future product embodiment would look, function, or cost. This is very similar to the history of 3D printers, which were originally very large and expensive. Considering inflation, a 3D printer in 1987 would be roughly US$730,000 in 2021, and one can purchase desktop versions today for a few hundred USD (Miller, 2016). Even the McCormick reaper discussed in earlier chapters only sold *one unit* the first year because it was essentially a rough functional prototype and people were scared of it (McCormick, 2018). This is one of many reasons why industrial designers are so important when dealing with new technologies. They can interpret technologies into representations of concepts that consumers would want to use. They are visionaries and can think beyond current embodiments of prototypes or technology. They are aware that as technology advances, it will get smaller, more refined, more efficient, and less expensive.

"People Don't Know What They Want Until You Show It to Them"—Steve Jobs in Reinhardt (1998)

While we are talking about prototypes, when Harry Warner (one of the founding brothers of Warner Brothers Studios) was shown a prototype of the first Vitaphone synchronized film sound system in 1925, he was impressed that theaters would no longer require orchestras. But when prompted that it would also allow people to hear the actors talk, he wondered: "Who the hell wants to hear actors talk?" (Warner & Jennings, 1965). Well apparently, everyone did, as "talkies" had become the norm. This is an example of *latent needs* (i.e., desires you did not know you had). People *did* want to hear actors talk. Farmers *did* want machines to harvest their grain. People *did* want computers and televisions in their homes. However, it wasn't something that they knew they wanted *until they witnessed it*. Specifically, people need to experience the idea in a form that they can comprehend and assimilate into their life (e.g., a computer that is smaller than a room, a 3D printer that doesn't cost more than a house). This is again where designers come into the process. Designers can transform needs and technologies into representations (e.g., digital models, drawings, prototypes) that the public can understand, which allows for feedback on willingness to use or pay. Henry Ford is attributed with saying: "If I had asked people what they wanted, they would have said faster horses," however, there is no evidence of him saying this (Vlaskovits, 2011). In the same vein, Nathan Fielder said (actually on record): "No one knows how to ask for something that hasn't been invented yet" (2014).

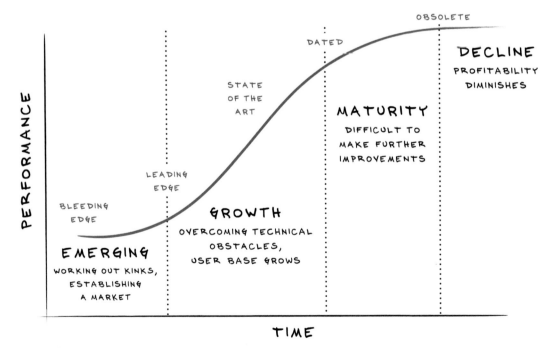

Figure 12.1 The Technology S-curve or Technology Life Cycle illustrating the stages in which a technology improves in performance over time.

Technology Needs Time to Catch Up

Radical innovation today will eventually become commonplace tomorrow. Things that were once viewed as ridiculous contraptions (such as the washing machine or mechanical reaper) are now simply a part of modern society. This is closely tied to the concept of the Technology *S-curve* or the *Technology Life Cycle.*

If you plot the performance of a specific technology over time, it will tend to form somewhat of an S-shape as shown in Figure 12.1 (Kovac & Dague, 1972; Roussel, 1984). The first phase involves experimentation, development, and market introduction. In this phase, there is little growth as developers are understanding both the technology and the market. This early stage of development goes by different names, including *market introduction phase, embryonic phase, infancy,* or *emerging phase.* Work in nanotechnology, as an example, is in this market intro phase. As technical obstacles are overcome and the user base grows, that technology then begins a *growth* or *expansion phase.* Personal computers, for example, are in a growth phase and they are rapidly changing every year. As the technology becomes well established and a few improvements can be made, the performance begins to plateau and the technology enters a *maturity stage.* Gasoline-powered automobile engines are in the maturity stage. Lastly, as profitability diminishes, technology is often replaced with a different technology, and this is the decline or retirement stage. VHS players are generally a retired technology.

The transitions of the S-curve are sometimes given names. For example, the beginning of the curve could be called *bleeding edge* technology; the initial performance growth can be called *leading edge* technology; the stable performance growth can be called *state of the art* technology; the decreasing performance growth can be called *dated* technology, and the final plateau can be called *obsolete* technology (Maxwell & Metz, 2021). Ideas sound wild/ridiculous/silly at the bleeding edge of the S-curve. Electricity in the home, automobiles, washing machines, and television were all wild concepts at first that gradually became luxuries for the wealthy and then eventually became commonplace things. Innovation "is the whim of an elite before it becomes a need of the public. The luxury of today is the necessity of tomorrow" (von Mises, 1953). Often the retirement of the technology is a result of the growth of a newer technology on a new S-curve overlapping in time in the same domain. This is illustrated in Figure 12.2.

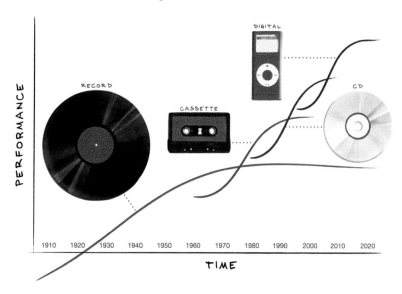

Figure 12.2 A brief history of select radical changes in music storage/playing from 1900 to 2020 illustrated with overlapping S-curves for records, cassettes, CDs, and digital MP3 players. The times are estimated, and the performance placement is somewhat subjective.

Trends Need Time to Catch On

If you have ever viewed a fashion runway show from a layman's perspective, you may have said, "who would possibly wear this stuff!" The answer is *you!*—just many years later when it becomes the norm and is regularly available at your local department store. *High fashion* is a form of radical innovation. This *trickle-down theory* of fashion is written into *The Devil Wears Prada* (based off the book by the same name), in which Meryl Streep portrays a New York fashion magazine editor (based on Anna Wintour). She delivers a monologue to the naive new assistant on how radical innovation eventually disseminates and normalizes. I'm going to break down a portion of this monologue and interrupt it with analysis:

> *you think this* [being the world of high fashion] *has nothing to do with you. You go to your closet and you select out, oh I don't know, that lumpy blue sweater...But what you don't know is that that sweater* [being the mature technology that is now commonplace] *is not just blue, it's not turquoise, it's not lapis, it's actually cerulean.* [aesthetic incremental innovation] *You're also blindly unaware of the fact that in 2002, Oscar de la Renta did a collection of cerulean gowns. And then I think it was Yves St Laurent, wasn't it, who showed cerulean military jackets?* [although these examples serve the chapter and movie well, they were fabricated by Streep (Miller, 2016)] *And then cerulean quickly showed up in the collections of eight different designers. Then it filtered down through the department stores and then trickled on down* [this is the "trickle-down theory" of fashion!] *into some tragic "casual corner" where you, no doubt, fished it out of some clearance bin. However, that blue represents millions of dollars and countless jobs* [this also applies to all services and consumer goods] *and so it's sort of comical how you think that you've made a choice that exempts you from the fashion industry when, in fact, you're wearing the sweater that was selected for you by the people in this room* [innovation of the past is commonplace today].
>
> (Frankel, 2006)

There are likely more than seven reasons for neophobia, but, for any case, neophobia can be overcome. To return to food-related research, there are generally three ways to overcome food neophobia: (1) *peer social facilitation* (e.g., role models, social media influencers), (2) *association with a known pleasure/preference* (e.g., bitter coffee with cream, spicy chili with sweet/salty), and (3) *repeat exposure* (i.e., the Sam-I-Am approach) (Rioux, 2019). Sam-I-Am's "try them and you may like them" philosophy was supported by academic research 40 years later:

> The neophobic's negative attitude toward an unfamiliar food ('I would not like them here or there!') may be ameliorated, but is not eliminated ('Say! I do! I do like them Sam I Am!'), once sensory information about the food is obtained ('Try them and you may like them!').
>
> (Dr. Seuss, 1960; Raudenbush & Frank, 1999)

The research on overcoming neophobia tends to focus specifically on children and vegetables, but these three general means (peer social facilitation, association with known preferences, and repeat exposure) can apply to adults overcoming the fear of radical change in any domain.

References

Ahl, D. (1980, April). Interview with Gordon Bell. *Creative Computing, 6*(4), 88–89.

Barrena, R., & Sánchez, M. (2013). Neophobia, personal consumer values and novel food acceptance. *Food Quality and Preference, 27*(1), 72–84.

Bateson, P., & Martin, P. (2013). *Play, playfulness, creativity, and innovation.* Cambridge University Press.

Cifci, I., Demirkol, S., Altunel, G. K., & Cifci, H. (2020). Overcoming the food neophobia towards science-based cooked food: The supplier perspective. *International Journal of Gastronomy and Food Science, 22*, 100280.

Clarke, A. C. (1962). *Profiles of the future: An inquiry into the limits of the possible.* Littlehampton Book Services Ltd.

De Forest, L. (1926, September 12). Television awaits scientific genius: Dr. Lee De Forest says a radical discovery in physics is needed for development of movies through the air. *New York Times.*

Dr. Seuss. (1960). *Green eggs and ham.* Random House.

Fielder, N. (Host). (2014, July 15). Pet store/maid service. *Nathan for You, 2*(3). Comedy Central.

Frankel. D. (Director). (2006). *The Devil Wears Prada* [Film]. Fox 2000 Pictures.

Grier, P. (1981, April 15). Really portable telephones: costly, but coming? *The Christian Science Monitor.*

Harris, J. A. (2012). Enterprising enterprises. In *Transformative Entrepreneurs* (pp. 121–130). Palgrave Macmillan.

IBM FAQ. (2007, April 10). IBM Archives. www.ibm.com/ibm/history

King, D. (Writer), & Holland, D. (Director). (2013, January 17). Two Parties. [Television series episode]. In A. Poehler (Producer), *Parks and Recreation*, NBC.

Kovac, F. J., & Dague M. F. (1972). Forecasting by product life cycle analysis. *Research Management, 15*(4), 66–72.

Maxwell, J., & Metz, K. (2021). How technology life cycles increase the financial position of the firm. *American Journal of Management, 21*(3), 1–8.

McCormick, R. (2018). *Memorial of Robert McCormick: Being a brief history of his life, character and inventions, including the early history of the McCormick reaper.* Franklin Classics.

Miller, A. (2016, August 1). The evolution of 3D printing: Past, present and future. *The 3D Printing Industry.*

Miller, J. (2016, June 29). How Meryl Streep terrified the Devil Wears Prada's screenwriter. *Vanity Fair.*

Pethokoukis, J. (2006, October 2). The deans of design. *US News and World Report.*

Pliner, P., & Salvy, S. J. (2006). Food neophobia in humans. In R. Shepherd, & M. Raats (Eds.), *The Psychology of Food Choice.* (pp. 75–92). CAB International.

Raudenbush, B., & Frank, R. A. (1999). Assessing food neophobia: The role of stimulus familiarity. *Appetite, 32*(2), 261–271.

Reinhardt, A. (1998, May 25). Steve Jobs: "There's sanity returning." *Businessweek.*

Rioux, C. (2019). Food Neophobia in childhood. In H. L. Meiselman (ed.), *Handbook of eating and drinking* (pp. 414–429). Springer Nature Switzerland AG.

Roussel, P. A. (1984). Technological maturity proves a valid and important concept. *Research Management, 27*(1), 29–34.

Vlaskovits, P. (2011, August 29). Henry ford, innovation, and that "Faster Horse" quote. *Harvard Business Review.*

Von Mises L. (1953). *Socialism: An economic and sociological analysis.* J. Cape.

Warner, J. L., & Jennings, D. S. (1965). *My first hundred years in Hollywood.* Random House.

Weik, M. H. (March 1961). IBM 701. *A third survey of domestic electronic digital computing systems* (No. 1115). Ballistic Research Laboratories.

13

QUESTIONING THE STATUS QUO, TABOO TOPICS, AND TOILETS

In the previous chapters, we discussed: what makes something innovative (Chapter 9), the "silly" gray areas surrounding innovation as far as feasibility, value, and usefulness (Chapter 10), why people prefer incremental innovation (Chapter 11), and, in contrast, why people are afraid of radical innovation (Chapter 12). Now, continuing with the poop theme of Chapter 10, in this chapter and the next, we will *plunge* into the history of toilets and toilet paper with case studies of innovation. All *rolled* into this, we will cover incremental and radical changes, the neophobia related to radical changes in bathroom practices, and the *straining* act of questioning of the status quo (and maybe some potty humor too).

Primitive forms of flushing toilets have been around for thousands of years. John Harington is credited with the first flushing toilet invention described in his 1596 book "A New Discourse of a Stale Subject called The Metamorphosis of Ajax" (Ajax is a pun with a "jakes" being a slang term for toilet) (2015). His book provides detailed instructions to "reform all unsavoury places of your houses" with instructions on how to construct a "jakes" in one's own home, complete with a part list and estimated cost as shown in Figure 13.1. Harington even constructed a functioning flushing toilet in his home as well as one for his godmother, Queen Elizabeth. Unfortunately, the book was written with deadpan humor and puns, and the concept was taken as a sensational and scandalous joke (Grist, 2020).

Jumping ahead two centuries to 1775, the first patented flushing toilet design was invented by a watchmaker, Alexander Cumming, published using the title: "A water-closet upon new construction" (Brown, 1882). This design featured an S-trap to keep sewer smells out of your dwelling and a sliding valve to release the bowl contents (Grist, 2020). A few years later in 1778, Joseph Bramah (who was most known for the invention of the hydraulic press) improved upon the Cumming toilet valve design (Brown, 1882). These early patented toilet concepts are very similar to the toilet technology we use today.

In the next 100 years, the use of flushing toilets in homes gradually increased, in part due to the industrial revolution in the 1820s, but also *maybe* due to the cesspits around people's houses, sewage in the streets and drinking water, cholera outbreaks, and the general stench within cities (Grist, 2020; Bailey, 2022). It took 350 years for the toilet to evolve from being a joke in a racy book, to a luxury of the wealthy, to (finally) a necessity of modern society (i.e., the *trickle-down* theory in Chapter 12).

This widespread popularization of having a flushing toilet in your own home was attributed to Thomas Crapper. Like Mr. Cumming, Mr. Crapper was also an inventor, and held several patents

DOI: 10.4324/9781003276296-16

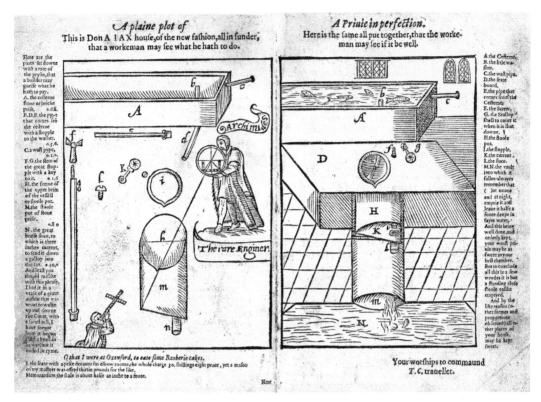

Figure 13.1 Illustrations on how to construct a flushing toilet from *A New Discourse of a Stale Subject called The Metamorphosis of Ajax* (1596). STC (2nd ed.) 12771.5, image 78462, used by permission of the Folger Shakespeare Library. Images are licensed under a Creative Commons Attribution-ShareAlike 4.0 International License (CC BY-SA 4.0).

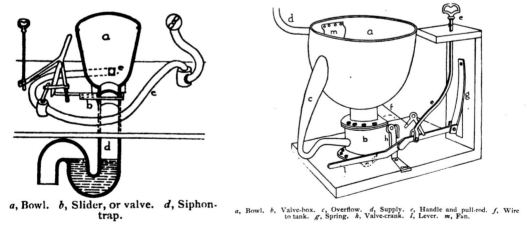

Figure 13.2 Images from Cumming's (1775) *British Patent* and Bramah's (1778) *British Patent* illustrating the first modern flushing toilet concepts. Reprinted patent images from Brown (1882).

related to toilets including the floating ball cock (that ball on a stick in your toilet tank that keeps your tank from overfilling), the U-bend trap (an improvement to Cumming's S-bend), and the man-hole cover (for people to access the sewer for maintenance for the first time ever) (Bailey, 2022). Those little innovations were just icing on his poop-empire cake.

Mr. Crapper's most significant achievement in the poop business was not an invention—he was the first to set up public showrooms to display toilets and toilet-related products (Bailey, 2022). This was incredibly risqué at the time. Discussing the idea of a toilet was taboo. Purchasing a toilet was taboo. Today, we can walk into any large hardware store and select a toilet from a shelf. We could probably even sit on it (clothed) in the store, and no one would look twice. Crapper's radical *movement* to have a toilet showroom, in addition to his technical toilet improvements, made him a plumbing sanitation pioneer and hero. He made it more acceptable to talk openly about pooping.

I just shared some examples of invention and innovation in toilet history up until 1880. Since then, however, there has been little radical change in the technology surrounding the way we poop at home. Today's toilet is generally the same toilet that people sat on back in 1880 with only incre-mental innovation (and some of those original toilets are still in use!). This is very similar to what Dr. Momen said about clothing dryers: They are "based on a technology that really hasn't changed much in about 30 years" (Roark, 2017). This makes me wonder: are we due for a change? Is there a better way? Let's *question the status quo*. Let's play *pretend* that we are in the future, and we are looking back at this primitive toilet technology. Let's analyze the flushing toilet objectively as if it were a device from another civilization.

Toilets are the primary contributor to water usage in homes, accounting for 30% of total usage in the United States (EPA, 2021). Every time you flush a toilet, assuming you have a standard model from the early 2000s, you use approximately 1.6 gallons of water, and it is most likely *potable* wa-ter (EPA, 2021). Some existing older models use up to 6 gallons (EPA, 2021), which is shockingly similar to the 7.5 gallons of water required for the very first flushing toilet prototype built by John Harington in 1592 (Bailey, 2022). All the toilet flushing water that we use daily is generally out of sight and out of mind in the hidden tank that quickly refills itself. But if you had to physically open two gallons of drinking water and dump it into the bowl every time you wanted to flush, you would question the process! This, however, is our norm, we are accustomed to the process, we take it for granted, and anything different would be radical. *Side note: If you regularly pee in the shower, you save approximately 580 gallons of water every year from not flushing the toilet. A family of four that pees in the shower saves 2,320 gallons of water a year!*

Aside from the environmental impact of current toilets, our bodies are not evolved to be in a sitting position while pooping. "We were not meant to sit on toilets. We were meant to squat in the field," says proctologist Michael Freilich (Time, 1979). Looking at our anatomy, while we are sitting, our puborectalis muscle (which is like a sling) physically chokes the rectum keeping feces inside (Demirbilek, 2011). When we are squatting, the puborectalis muscle relaxes and allows for easy feces elimination (a better pooping experience). Furthermore, when you are sitting, your rectum is at an angle (the "anorectal angle" as shown in Figure 13.3), but when squatting, the rectum is more of a straight line, also making it easier for feces elimination (Rad, 2002; Sikirov, 2003; Sandler & Peery, 2019). One study found that squatting vs. sitting is on average over twice as fast for a bowel movement and 2.5 times less difficult. Another study used radiology to take internal images of people while pooping using squatting vs. sitting toilets and found that in squatting, this anorectal angle is much larger and squatting produced more complete bowel evacuation when compared

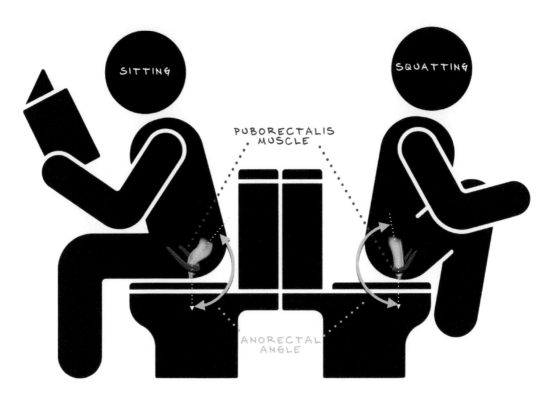

Figure 13.3 Illustrations of squatting and sitting showing the differences in the puborectalis muscle and the anorectal angle.

with sitting (Rad, 2002). Sitting to poop results in additional straining that can increase the occurrence of hemorrhoids, a condition that is uncommon in countries with squatting toilets (Sikirov, 2003; Sandler & Peery, 2019; Bailey, 2022).

In short, we are not meant to be *sitting* on toilets. We only do so because the original inventors didn't know the ideal pooping science. These first toilets were modeled after the most obvious comparable, chairs, including Mr. Crapper's finest model: a velvet-upholstered armchair toilet (Dupont & Bean, 1978). Sitting to poop was a sign of European achievement and civilization, and squatting was viewed as primitive and primordial (Demirbilek, 2011; Bailey, 2022). It's now part of the western tradition and expectations that a toilet should look like a chair with a hole, and we should therefore sit on it like we do a chair.

Solutions to these problems have existed for centuries. Waterless urinals and dry toilets are real options. For two-thirds of the world's population, squatting toilets are the norm (Demirbilek, 2011). Even the toilet's predecessor, the chamber pot, was essentially a squatting-based device. So why is western culture still stuck on this less efficient, less sustainable, and more expensive method?

If a new modern squatting, waterless toilet was available today at the same cost as a traditional toilet, how many people would adopt it? Installing a new toilet involves changing infrastructure. It involves explaining to your guests how to use your toilet. It involves learning a new way of doing something. In Chapter 12, you learned how people have issues with adapting to a new form of toothpaste cap. What happens when you change their toilet? The world needs a new John Harington or Thomas Crapper to *break the status quo* and nudge us into a brighter future of pooping.

Squatty Potty has entered the chat. Squatty Potty is the current leading incremental innovation toward changing the pooping experience. Squatty Potty is essentially a tiny stool that tucks under your toilet bowl that allows you to prop your legs up while pooping to get your anatomy into more of a squatting position (Sandler & Peery, 2019). As most westerners are not willing to remove their current toilets and replace them with a squatting toilet, this is a baby step in the right direction. It allows people to still use the old inefficient method at their discretion. It is also a relatively inexpensive solution for a process one engages in daily. Squatty Potty is today's Thomas Crapper. The company is making it acceptable to discuss pooping properly, but instead of using a showroom as a marketing venue, Squatty Potty talks about pooping on TV and internet commercials. Like John Harington, Squatty Potty uses play and dry humor as a means of making it acceptable to talk about this taboo topic. Squatty Potty attributed a 600% online sales increase and a 400% retail sales increase in 2015 to a specific commercial demonstrating the features of their product with an animatronic unicorn that poops rainbow soft-serve ice cream (Copeland, 2016). As discussed in the prior chapter, one of the three means of getting people to overcome neophobia is association with known preferences. In this case, who doesn't love unicorns, rainbows, and soft-serve ice cream? This is also incremental innovation and as discussed in Chapter 11, people love incremental innovation: it requires minimal investment with some improved results.

Let's move onto the bigger issue: toilet tissue.

References

Bailey J. (2022) Drawbacks with industrialization. Sanitary revolution offering technologies to improve public health. In *Inventive geniuses who changed the world* (pp. 107–116). Springer Nature.

Bramah, J. (1778). *British Patent-Reports, Vol XV, Vol. 1177.*

Brown, G. (1882, October 25–26). Water-closets [Paper presentation]. In G. C. Mason Jr. *Proceedings of the 16th annual convention of the American institute of architects.* 16th annual convention of the American institute of architects, Cincinnati, Ohio, United States (pp. 48–67). Committee on Library and Publications of the American Institute of Architects.

Copeland, L. (2016, July 21). *Meet the Mormon brothers who make adorable ads about disgusting things.* Washington Post.

Cumming, A. (1775). *British Patent-Reports, Vol XIV, Vol. 1105.*

Demirbilek, O. (2011). Alla Turca: Squatting for health and hygiene. In J. F. M. Molenbroek, J. Mantas, & R. De Bruin (Eds.), *A friendly rest room: Developing toilets of the future for disabled and elderly people* (pp. 271–280). IOS Press.

DuPont, H. L., & Bean, W. B. (1978). Sir John Harington, Thomas Crapper, and the Flush Toilet. *Southern Medical Journal, 71*(9), 1145–1147.

EPA -United States Environmental Protection Agency. (2021). *Residential toilets.* https://www.epa.gov/watersense/residential-toilets

Harington, J. (1596). *A new discourse of a stale subject, called the metamorphosis of Ajax.* STC (2nd ed.) 12771.5. printed by Richard Field, dwelling in the Black-friers. Used by permission of the Folger Shakespeare Library.

Harington, J. (2015). *A new discourse of a stale subject, called the metamorphosis of Ajax.* Ex-classics project. (Original work published 1596).

Grist, K. (2020, October 28). A flushing story. *Science Museum Group.*

Rad, S. (2002). Impact of ethnic habits on Defecographic measurements. *Archives of Iranian Medicine, 5*(2), 115–117.

Roark, C. (2017, July 6). Dryers of the future: How they dry faster without heat. *Knox News.*

Sandler, R. S., & Peery, A. F. (2019). Rethinking what we know about Hemorrhoids. *Clinical Gastroenterology and Hepatology: The Official Clinical Practice Journal of the American Gastroenterological Association, 17*(1), 8–15.

Sikirov D. (2003). Comparison of straining during defecation in three positions: Results and implications for human health. *Digestive Diseases and Sciences, 48*(7), 1201–1205.

Time Staff. (1979, January 8). Medicine: Carter's injury. *Time, 113*(2), 64.

14
QUESTIONING THE STATUS QUO, TABOO TOPICS, AND TOILET PAPER

The design of the automobile has changed *a lot* between 1880 and the present; toilet paper (TP), on the other hand, has not (see Figure 14.1). Aside from packaging, processing, and quality of paper, there hasn't been out of the box (or I should say, off the roll) thinking in the last 150 years.

This revelation appeared on *Seinfeld* when George states that "toilet paper hasn't changed in my lifetime, and probably wouldn't change in the next fifty thousand years" (David & Seinfeld, 1995). Jerry and Elaine disagree and argue that "toilet paper's changed… it's softer…more sheets per roll…comes in a variety of colors…" (David & Seinfeld, 1995). To kill this joke via dissection, George was likely implying that there hasn't been *radical* innovation in toilet paper, whereas Jerry and Elaine indirectly support his argument by listing only *incremental* changes in toilet paper. Our society is so advanced to the point that we can contact anyone in the world in seconds, we can land a spacecraft on a comet, and we can print artificial body parts, but the standard (western) practice of cleaning our bum is still a primitive wad of paper. This is just a few processing steps away from using leaves (and leaves are more environmentally friendly)!

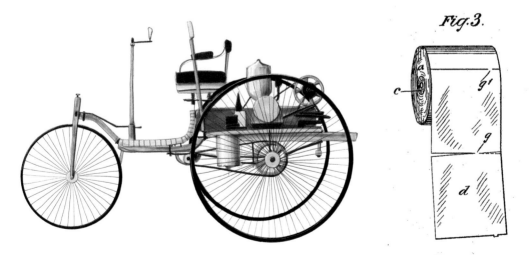

Figure 14.1 An illustration of the Benz Motorwagen (circa 1885), the first practical automobile manufactured by what is currently Mercedes-Benz, and an illustration from the US Patent Application for perforated toilet paper on a roll (Wheeler, 1891). Both products have existed for essentially the same amount of time.

DOI: 10.4324/9781003276296-17

If you somehow got poop on your arm (let's just say you were changing a diaper or picking up dog poop), few people, if any, would simply reach for some toilet paper, rub their arm a few times, and proceed to go on with their day. You would wash your poop-covered arm! Why doesn't the same apply to your bum? Is it because it happens to be further away from your nose? In any case, TP is not a great means of removing material. To quote *Parks and Recreation* again, a concerned Andy Dwyer played by Chris Pratt improvised this American quandary: "Sometimes when I wipe, I'll wipe and I'll wipe and I'll wipe... and I'll wipe. A hundred times. Still...poop. Still poop. It's like I'm wiping a Magic Marker or something" (Yang & Holland, 2012).

In addition to its hygienic flaw, TP is also not an environmentally friendly solution to the problem. Americans (literally) flush down the toilet somewhere between 140–160 rolls of toilet paper per person every year (British: 100–127 rolls; Australians: 88 rolls) (Skene & Vinyard, 2019; Stratton, 2021). Scientific American reported data to indicate Americans use 36.5 billion rolls of toilet paper per year, which equates to 15 million trees per year (EarthTalk, 2009). Producing TP also requires a significant amount of water (37 gallons/roll) and electricity (1.3 KWh/roll) (EarthTalk, 2009).

So, as I asked about toilets, *is there a better way?* We need to *question the status quo*. To do this, let's look back at the history of toilet paper because, at one point in time (just like toilets), toilet paper was a radical idea.

The first materials used for cleaning after pooping were sticks, leaves, grasses, moss, wool, fur, seashells, coconut shells, and snow when available (Ponti, 2020; Stratton, 2021). In ancient Rome, the public toilets were supplied with a *tersorium*, a sponge attached to the end of a stick soaked in vinegar or brine (McRobbie, 2009; Blakemore, 2020; Ponti, 2020). In Ancient Greece, they used small abrasive oval stones called *pessoi* (Blakemore, 2020). The first record of mass-produced toilet paper (made from rice) was in 1393 by the Chinese Hongwu Emperor (Blakemore, 2020; Ponti, 2020). In Colonial America, the common tool for wiping was corncobs (we really do put corn in everything!) until the 19th century, when newspapers became available (Adams, 1986; Stratton, 2021). Following newspapers, the Sears & Roebuck catalog and the Farmer's Almanac were the most popular form of "toilet paper." The Farmer's Almanac even came with a pre-drilled hole so it could be hung near the toilet in the outhouse (Ponti, 2020). A *latent need* for some magical product that could remove poop from bums was *lingering in the air* waiting for some inventor to develop a solution.

In 1857, it happened—the first form of toilet-specific tissue resembling that of today was developed in the United States by Joseph Gayetty of New York (Ponti, 2020, Stratton, 2021). "Gayetty's Medicated Paper, for the Water-Closet" was sold in boxes of 500 sheets for $0.50. They contained aloe and were marketed to cure sores and prevent piles (i.e., hemorrhoids) (McRobbie, 2009; Blakemore, 2020; Ponti, 2020; Stratton, 2021). In Gayetty's original advertisement (Figure 14.2), he calls out the absurdity of using newspaper: "individuals would not put printers' ink in their mouths...yet they have no hesitation in allowing themselves and children to...apply...that ink to the tenderest part of the body..." (1857). Gayetty, as inventor, was clearly immodest with his product; his "name was water-marked in each sheet" (Gayetty, 1857; Kravetz, 2004). The consumers, on the other hand, were more reserved with their purchases. If you were buying toilet paper, it meant that you had some medical issue. Unlike the free copy of the Sears & Roebuck catalog to hang in your outhouse, there was no disguising the intended purpose of a box of "Medicated Paper for the Water-Closet."

In 1890, the Scott Paper Company of Philadelphia introduced perforated toilet paper on a roll, and they quickly became the nation's leading producer of toilet paper (McRobbie, 2009, Rodriguez, 2009). At first, their toilet paper was sold through intermediaries, private labelers, hotels, and

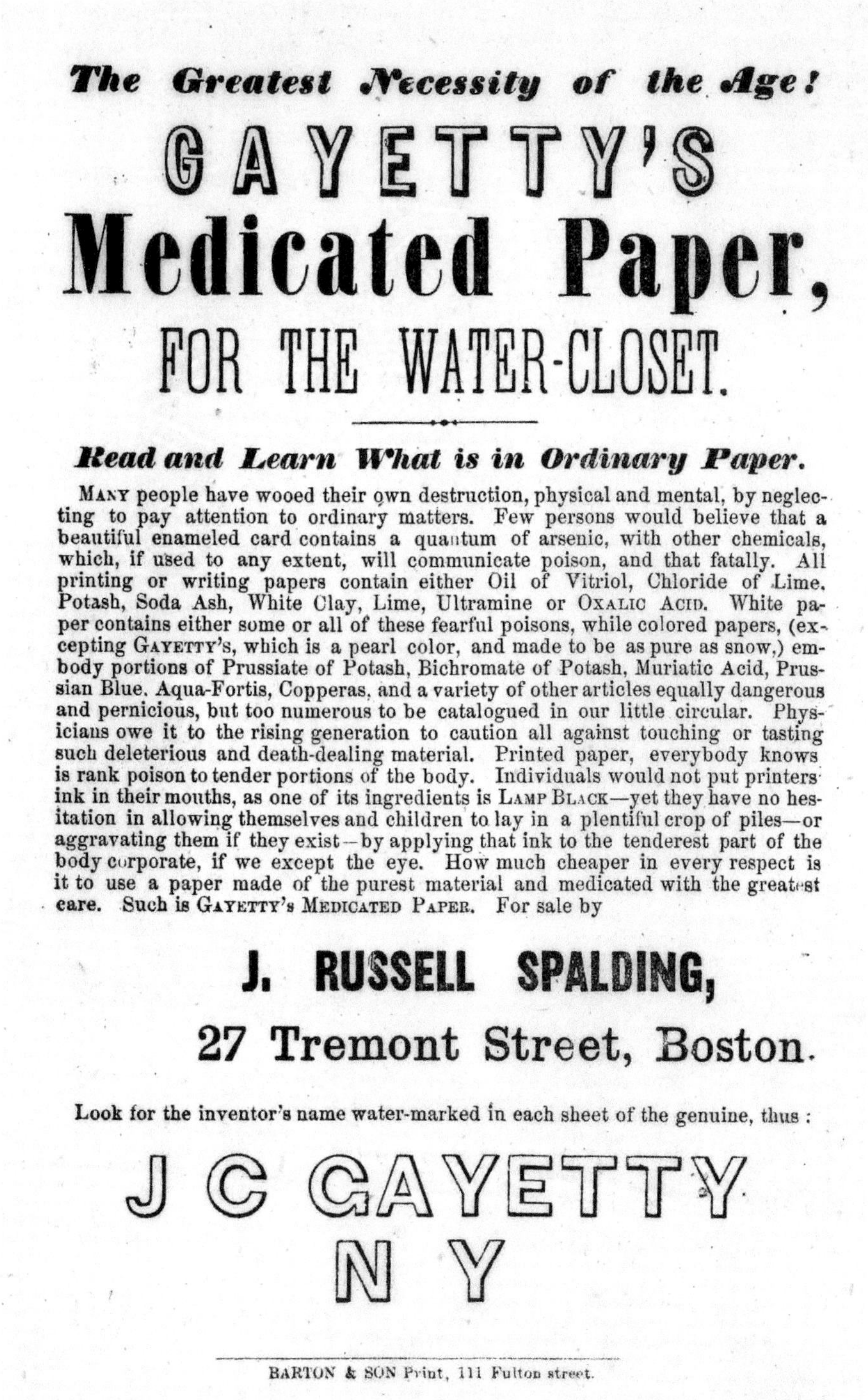

Figure 14.2 Gayetty's original printed advertisement for medicated paper for the water-closet (1857) (i.e., the first modern form of toilet paper). Retrieved from the Library of Congress. The library is not aware of any US copyright protection (see Title 17, U.S.C.).

drug stores as they did not want to be associated with this "unmentionable" and "lewd" product (McRobbie, 2009; Stratton, 2021). Consumers did not want to ask for it by name. It was a taboo subject, and so unlike Gayetty, the Scott Company did *not* put their name on the product until 1902 (Rodriguez, 2009). Even in the 1920s, some toilet paper was still marketed for therapeutic purposes, specifically hemorrhoids (Kravetz, 2004). It was hard to deny that the soft tissue was a better experience than newspaper and so the use of "therapeutic" paper slowly caught on. A shift in perspective from taboo medical product to luxurious necessity was attributed to some thoughtful ad campaigns in 1928 by a new TP brand, *Charmin* (Rodriguez, 2009). The adoption of TP as a standard part of western culture in the 1930s, however, was *in part* due to new indoor toilet and plumbing systems not being able to handle other wiping materials being flushed away (McRobbie, 2009; Rodriguez, 2009), and *in part* due to the updated Sears & Roebuck catalog being printing with colored pictures on coated, glossy, *non-absorbent* paper (Adams, 1986; Silverman, 2003).

The process took about *45–75 years* for the concept of toilet paper to catch on from its original inception as a therapeutic bathroom tissue. If we want to map this to an *S-curve* of Chapter 12, the *market introduction* of TP was in 1857 with Gayetty, the beginning of the *growth phase* was in 1890 with Scott Paper introducing the perforated toilet paper roll. Things ramped up around 1930 with Charmin's ads, the Sears & Roebuck catalog going glossy, and indoor plumbing requiring specialized paper. If you want to view this as multiple S-curves, this time also marks the *obsolescence* of using newspapers, corncobs, and catalogs as toilet paper. Toilet paper today is a *mature* technology with the types of improvements being mostly incremental (as pointed out in the aforementioned *Seinfeld* episode (1995)). We are heading for a radical change soon to make TP obsolete.

In the near future (as per Figure 14.3), our grandchildren are going to be saying: "Can you believe they used toilet paper XX years ago?" This is the joke from the 1993 film, *Demolition Man*. In this film, Sylvester Stallone's character John Spartan, a police officer, is cryogenically frozen

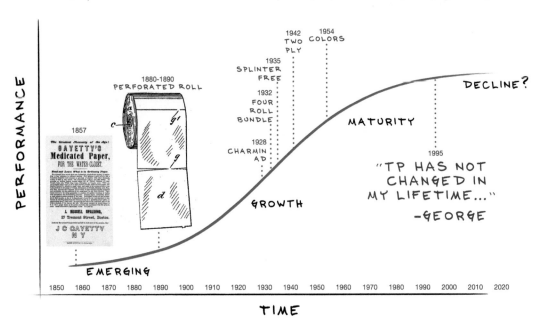

Figure 14.3 An S-curve of toilet paper showing the market introduction with Gayetty medicated paper (1857), and the beginning of the growth phase with perforated paper on a roll (Wheeler, 1891) followed by a series of incremental improvements. The *Seinfeld* quote (1995) exemplifies a state of technological maturity.

and reanimated in the future (Brambilla, 1993). After using the toilet of the future, the following (paraphrased) dialogue takes place with two future officers played by Sandra Bullock (Lenina Huxley) and Rob Schneider. Spartan discretely whispers to Huxley that he thinks they are out of toilet paper. Huxley, as somewhat of a historian, explains to the other officers how toilet paper was used in the 20th century. The officers laugh. An annoyed and confused Spartan then questions the shelf holding *three seashells* located where toilet paper is typically placed. The officers joke that he doesn't know how to "use the three seashells" (Brambilla, 1993). To put this in context, someone from Ancient Greece, accustomed to wiping with three round stones, would be equally confused by today's roll of toilet paper if they were cryogenically frozen in time and woke up today to a porcelain sitting-toilet.

Today, there are (objectively) better alternatives than toilet paper. One solution that addresses the "magic marker" problem, is wet wipes. We use these on babies, why not on adults too? In 2001, Kimberly Clark introduced premoistened toilet wipes as "the most significant category innovation since toilet paper first appeared in roll form in 1890," and others followed suit; however, these products were not well accepted in the market (Nelson, 2002). Furthermore, wet wipes are not environmentally friendly. Studies have found that both "flushable" and "non-flushable" wet wipes contribute to the microplastics in aquatic environments (Pantoja Munoz et al., 2018), and both are hard on plumbing and sewer systems (Hart, 2018, Harter et al., 2021).

There is another "futuristic" (and obvious) solution to this problem of bum-cleaning that is readily available: the bidet. Bidets were created in France in the 1600s (Hart, 2018) and are now very common throughout parts of Asia (specifically Japan), Latin America, and Europe—in 90% of homes in Spain, Italy, and Greece (Coles, 2017). Like most innovation, the bidet was first a luxury for the aristocracy before it became part of civilized life in France (Hart, 2018). Original bidets were a separate device that sat next to a toilet, but many bathrooms around the world were not built to support two separate water-based devices with space and plumbing. In 1980, *Toto* released the first "paperless toilet" in Japan which was a bidet *combined* with a toilet to accommodate for smaller bathroom spaces (Hart, 2018). The *Toto* also washed *and* dried your bottom (and warmed the seat). These combination bidets with washing and drying eliminated the need for toilet paper almost entirely. Combination bidets were also sold as "add-on bidets" to an existing toilet bowl with all the washing and drying mechanisms integrated into the seat. The company, *Tushy*, is taking the *Squatty Potty* approach and using clever ads, as well as minimal, low-cost modifications to bring about toilet behavior change (Coles, 2017, Hart, 2018). A *Tushy* bidet doesn't even replace the toilet seat, it just gets installed underneath an existing seat.

In the US, an average household may spend between US$123 (Statista, 2022) and US$182 (Anderer, 2020) on toilet paper each year. Regardless of which bidet you purchase, all options break-even within the lifetime of the product on savings in toilet paper costs alone. This does not include the additional savings in environmental impact of embedded water, electricity, and trees in each roll of TP not consumed. Also, while we have been discussing hemorrhoids (perhaps a bit too much in the book) resulting from sitting toilets, bidets have been shown to *prevent* hemorrhoids in those prone to them and relief to those who have them (Coles, 2017, Hart, 2018). Lastly, *on the whole*, can you really put a price tag on having an objectively (Oie & Kawai, 2021) cleaner bum?

Bidets are popular around the world, *but* not in North America (nor the UK, nor Australia) (Coles, 2017). A majority of Americans, 53% (Coles, 2017), and other western cultures think bidets are gross, shocking, disgusting, and uncivilized (Stratton, 2021). And oppositely, in parts of the world with bidets, they view the *lack* of bidets as gross, shocking, disgusting, and uncivilized (they are right). Once western culture catches up in bathroom technology, we are going to say, I can't believe we actually used toilet paper, just as we look back at Americans in 1900 and say I can't believe they used corncobs! Despite better, less expensive, more effective, more sustainable solutions (that are currently in use by a good portion of the world), flushing toilets and toilet paper are still the norm in western culture and there seems to be a reluctance to *make a move* to the next thing.

If you look at this through the lenses of Chapter 12 on why technology is not adopted, the majority of these reasons do not apply in this case. Bidets are an existing technology that has had time to mature and become affordable and move down from being a luxury. Bidets exist in many parts of the world already and so they should not feel like an impossible solution. In North America, the toilet is viewed as an item of utility that gets replaced when broken, and not something to upgrade (Coles, 2017), yet current bidet seat attachments make it easy to *assimilate*. Chapters 12 and 13, on toilets and toilet paper, introduce an additional rationale for the fear/slow adoption of radical change: *taboo takes time.* **When you don't talk about something, it's harder to change it** (e.g., we should "talk about Bruno" (Blake, 2022)).

The process took about *45–75 years* for the once-radical concept of toilet paper to replace corncobs, and it's taking even longer to phase it out for better technology. If you think about Mr. Crapper's toilet showroom, this was highly controversial at the time, but he created an opportunity to talk about flushing toilets and make change. The Squatty Potty commercials showing a pooping unicorn were racy and controversial, but they created space to discuss toilet behavior. As we talk about humor in Chapter 31, we will see how humor can be a means of discussing taboo topics with the goal of confronting issues and sparking change.

References

Adams, C. (1986, August 15). What did people use before toilet paper was invented? *The Straight Dope.*

Anderer, J. (2020, August 26). Average American spends over $11K on toilet paper over a lifetime — enough to buy a Rolex! *Study Finds.*

Blake, L. (2022, February 2). Yes, we do need to talk about Bruno. *Psychology Today.*

Blakemore, E. (2020, March 31). What did people do before toilet paper? *National Geographic.*

Brambilla. M. (Director). (1993). *Demolition Man* [Film]. Silver Pictures.

Coles, T. (2017, January 17). Let's be real: Americans are walking around with dirty anuses. *Vice.*

David, L., & Seinfeld, J. (Writers), & Ackerman A. (Director). (1995, May 11). The face painter. [Television series episode]. In L. David (Producer), *Seinfeld,* NBC.

EarthTalk Writers, Anonymous. (2009, December 16). Wipe or wash? Do bidets save forest and water resources? *Scientific American.*

Gayetty, J. C. (1857). *The greatest necessity of the age! Gayetty's medicated paper for the water-closet. Read and learn what is in ordinary paper...* J. C. Gayetty N. Y. Barton & son Print, 111 Fulton street n. d. New York. [Pdf] Retrieved from the Library of Congress. https://www.loc.gov/resource/rbpe.13400600/

Hart, M. T. (2018, March 18). The bidet's revival. *The Atlantic.*

Harter, T., Bernt, I., Winkler, S., & Hirn, U. (2021). Reduced dispersibility of flushable wet wipes after wet storage. *Scientific Reports, 11,* 7942.

Kravetz, R. E. (2004) Toilet tissue. *American Journal of Gastroenterology, 99*(7), 1212.

McRobbie, L. R. (2009, November 7). Toilet paper history: How America convinced the world to wipe. *Mental Floss.*

Nelson E. (2002, April 15). Moistened toilet paper wipes out after launch for Kimberly-Clark. *The Wall Street Journal.*

Oie, S., & Kawai, S. (2021). Microbial contamination of hands with or without the use of bidet toilets (electric toilet seats with water spray) after defecation. *Journal of Water & Health, 20*(1), 271–275.

Pantoja Munoz, L., Gonzalez Baez, A., McKinney, D., & Garelick, H. (2018). Characterisation of "flushable" and "non-flushable" commercial wet wipes using microRaman, FTIR spectroscopy and fluorescence microscopy: To flush or not to flush. *Environmental Science and Pollution Research, 25,* 20268–20279.

Ponti, C. (2020, April 15). All the ways we've wiped: The history of toilet paper and what came before. *History. com.*

Rodriguez, L. (2009, July 8). Why toilet paper belongs to America. *Mental Floss*.

Silverman, S. (2003). *Lindbergh's artificial heart*. Andrews McMeel Publishing.

Skene, J., & Vinyard, S. (2019, February). The issue with tissue: How Americans are flushing forests down the toilet. *NRDC, Natural Resources Defense Council*.

Statista Research Department (2022, January 13). U.S. household expenditure on cleansing, toilet tissue, paper towels. *Statista*.

Stratton, J. (2021). Coronavirus, the great toilet paper panic and civilisation. *Thesis Eleven, 165*(1), 145–168.

Wheeler, S. (1891). Wrapping or Toilet Paper Roll. U.S. Patent Application No. 459,516. Washington, DC: U.S. Patent and Trademark Office.

Yang, A. (Writer), & Holland, D. (Director). (2012, January 19). Campaign Ad (Outtakes). [Television series episode]. In A. Poehler (Producer), *Parks and Recreation*, NBC.

15

HINDSIGHT, TOOTHBRUSHES, AND SMART PHONES

In Chapters 13 and 14, we peeked back at the not-so-distant past. Through our "futuristic" eyes, some of these prior technologies seemed preposterous (e.g., it wasn't that long ago when the standard wiping technology was corncobs, and we kept a chamber pot underneath our bed). In this chapter, we are going to look at other not-so-distant past technologies through our futuristic lens and critically question some of our *current* technologies and practices.

Let's start with some products that had more serious ramifications than hygiene. During the 19th century, heroin and cocaine were often regarded as harmless and "helpful in everyday life" (Musto, 1991). "Heroin", coined by Bayer in 1898, was used as a cough syrup up until 1910 as shown in Figure 15.1 (Musto, 1991). Until 1900, one could find cocaine in Coca-Cola (the original energy drink!) and in toothache drops for an "instantaneous cure" (Boucher & Moeser, 1991; Musto, 1991).

From 1952–1956, Kent cigarettes used a form of asbestos (crocidolite—the form most strongly linked with mesothelioma) as their filters and advertised this feature as providing greater "health protection" (Longo et al., 1995). It is estimated that several hundred thousand people were put at

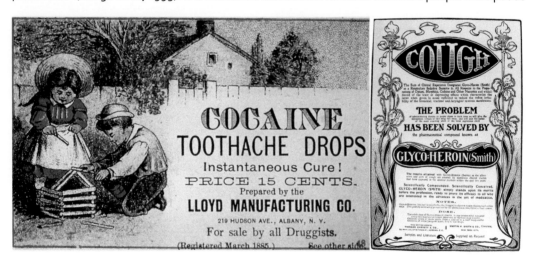

Figure 15.1 Original advertisements for Cocaine Toothache Drops (1885, retrieved from the National Library of Medicine, public domain) and Glyco-Heroin Cough Syrup (circa 1900, retrieved from wikimedia, public domain). Both advertisements indicate the product is for children with photos in the former and in text in the latter (for "the most capricious child...three years or more").

DOI: 10.4324/9781003276296-18

risk because of these filters (Longo et al., 1995). While we are discussing cigarettes and advertising, in the 1930s and 1940s, cigarettes were viewed as *healthy*, and a majority of physicians smoked. Advertisements often featured physicians smoking with unsupported claims of health benefits such as reducing cough and throat irritation (Gardner & Brandt, 2006).

With modern science and research, we know *now* that we probably should not give children heroin and cocaine if they are mildly inconvenienced, and we probably should not smoke asbestos-filtered cigarettes when we have a sore throat. The fun thing about research and science is that we keep learning new things! *What do you think we are consuming today that will be shocking to people in the near future?*

Up until the 1930s, people didn't have refrigerators. Someone would come to your house to deliver a block of ice to keep your perishables cold inside an insulated box. That ice was likely cut out of a frozen lake with a big saw during winter and then transported to be stored in an icehouse under straw to keep it from melting throughout the summer (like what they were doing in the opening scene of Disney's *Frozen*). Also, during this time, people didn't have washing machines. To wash clothes, one would use a washboard and washtub. This is not that long ago. What are our children are going to say they can't believe their parents did/used/didn't have? What are we doing now that people of the future are going to be justifying with: "*Hindsight is 20/20?*"

This is related to *hindsight bias* or the "I knew-it-all-along" phenomenon. Once you see a solution or a new technology, you can't unsee it. We tend to perceive these prior things as obvious (i.e., *Obviously*, we shouldn't have given children heroin! *Obviously*, we could have used soft paper on a roll instead of corncobs). Koestler (1964) describes this as:

> The discoveries of yesterday are the truisms of tomorrow, because we can add to our knowledge but cannot subtract from it. When two frames of reference have both become integrated into one it becomes difficult to imagine that previously they existed separately. The synthesis looks deceptively self-evident, and does not betray the imaginative effort needed to put its component parts together.

This is why non-obviousness (Chapter 9) is the most difficult of the three tests of patentability to explain and prove.

If you look back at the first toothbrushes in the United States, prior to 1938, they were made of wood or bone with boar hair bristles (Yu et al., 2013; Library of Congress, 2019). Most Americans didn't even brush their teeth until after World War 2, and, at that time, "between 90% and 95% of all children had untreated decaying teeth" (Fee & Brown, 2004). At least they had some powerful toothache medication for kids back then. Now that we have all this scientific data about the

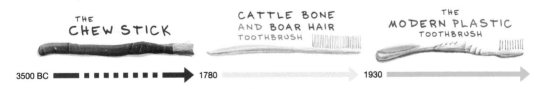

Figure 15.2 Chew sticks have been used since 3500 BC as a means of cleaning teeth and freshening the mouth (Yu et al., 2013). The end becomes bristle-like as it is chewed. In 1780, William Addis developed the toothbrush that is similar to the products today; however, it was originally made of cattle bone with boar hair bristles (Yu et al., 2013). In the 1930s, nylon was developed, and the modern plastic toothbrush became the norm, replacing animal bone and hair.

importance of brushing teeth and these super modern plastic injection-molded toothbrushes (with ultrasonic vibrations for better cleaning, bristle heads that tell you when they need replacing, a tongue massaging feature, and an over-molded silicone handle for better grip), that bone-and-animal-hair toothbrush from 1930 looks like a prehistoric tool found in a cave. But guess what?! Our supermodern toothbrush that we have in the bathroom *right now* is going to look like a prehistoric tool to our near-future society.

Chew sticks, the original tooth "brush" that is still in use in parts of the world (50% of Saudi Arabians, for example), seems primitive compared with these modern plastic toothbrushes; however, research has found the chewing stick to be equivalent and often *more* effective at plaque removal, both mechanical and chemical oral tissue cleansing, and gingival health when compared with the modern toothbrush (Malik et al., 2014). Research also now shows that your toothbrush is not actually that clean and might actually be contaminating your teeth. There is little public awareness that microorganisms from your mouth adhere to, reproduce, and thrive on toothbrush bristles regardless of where they are kept, and these microbes can be transmitted back into the mouth to cause diseases (Ankola et al., 2009; Asumang et al., 2019). For those who store their toothbrush exposed in the bathroom, a single flush of the toilet "releases millions of bacteria into the atmosphere" and "the most fertile breeding substrate in bathroom is the toothbrush" (Ankola et al., 2009).

Let's try to view this modern toothbrush from the perspective of someone from the future. A future person would say, "can you believe people would rub a plastic brush around in their mouth in the morning, then put it in a cup next to their sitting toilet and toilet paper, and, after a full day of exposure to toilet mist and microorganism growth, they would put the thing back into their mouth without even sterilizing it! And they were doing this all under the guise that they were cleaning their mouth. And then, after a few months, they would just throw the entire thing away and buy another one!"

If you look back at Ericsson's first "mobile" phone designed in 1956, it was essentially a heavy suitcase: "It weighed 40 kilos and...When mounted in a car, it cost almost as much as the car" (Staunstrup, 2022). This evolved to a slightly more portable suitcase, like the Ericsson Hotline Combi, with orange keys and black case. But the first truly mobile, "hand-held" phone was prototyped in 1973 by Marty Cooper while working at Motorola and then released to the public in 1983 as the Dynatac 8000X (Cheng, 2021). Although they were smaller than a suitcase, they were still referred to as "bricks" and retailed for USD 3,995 (in 1983 USD), which is close to USD11,000 in 2022 (Miller, 2009). It was a high price, but you could call someone from the car or from the beach! Again, radical innovation starts out scary ("Cellular phones will absolutely not replace local wire systems. Even if you project it beyond our lifetimes, it won't be cheap enough" (Grier, 1981), before it becomes a luxury, before it becomes a common everyday necessity.

If we look back at this original mobile phone from our future eyes, it looks like a joke. It required an entire briefcase of technology to function, it was *only* a phone, and yet still people thought it was impressive. Today, *most people* have a mobile phone (sometimes multiple phones), even 83% of people in developing countries without reliable access to clean water and electricity are likely to have access to a mobile phone as of 2018 (Klapper, 2019). And these phones can fit in our pocket! We can call anyone in the world. We can see the caller on video. We can look up information about any location in the world in seconds. We can play thousands of digital games. The phone can tell us the weather days in advance. It can record video. It will remind you to pick up milk at the store. It can even order the milk for you and tell you when it arrives at your house.

It's hard to imagine, but our current high-tech mobile device will also look like ancient technology in 50 years. It will be just like the briefcase phone and the bone-and-boar-hair toothbrush appears to us now. Future us will say, can you believe people actually carried around this phone the size of

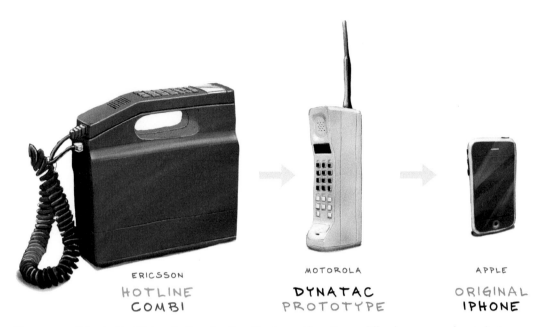

ERICSSON HOTLINE COMBI

MOTOROLA DYNATAC PROTOTYPE

APPLE ORIGINAL IPHONE

Figure 15.3 **Prior to the Motorola Dynatac 8000X released in 1983, mobile phones were large, heavy, and expensive like the Ericsson Hotline Combi. The prototype for the Dynatac 8000X was developed in 1973 by Marty Cooper (Cheng, 2021). The first Apple iPhone was released in 2007.**

a candy bar at all times and they kept all their personal information in it, and they would lose it, crack the screen, or drop it in their sitting toilet and all their information would be gone. When they wanted to contact someone, they had to remove it from their pocket, turn it on, unlock it, search for whom they wanted to call, touch a button, and then hold the thing up to their ear the entire time they were talking. And some people actually rode a bicycle or drove a car with a steering wheel (not an autonomous car!) while holding this device up to their ear. If they needed directions, they mounted the phone to their car with a clip that attached to an air-conditioning vent and alternated gaze between the road and the phone while driving!

Let's look at our technology and existence from an even wider perspective. Using a variation of Carl Sagan's (1975) 'Cosmic Calendar,' we can scale the entire 4.543-billion-year history of Earth down to one calendar year with Earth forming on January 1st. In this model, with each second of time corresponding to roughly 145 years, *Homo sapiens* appeared on December 31st...at roughly 11:30 p.m. Humans have only been around for 30 minutes of this scaled down Earth-year-of-existence. Let's zoom into the last second of time of this calendar (or approximately the past 145 years).

In this relatively short period of time, some radical changes occurred. Edison's light bulb was developed in 1879 and this was around the same time when electricity was first brought to people's homes (Hargadon & Douglas, 2001). This was not that long ago! In 1908, we had the first automobiles that were affordable and accessible to Americans (History.com, 2019). The first iPhone was released in 2007. *In just 100 years*, we went from not having electricity in homes, not knowing what a light bulb was, and not knowing what an automobile was, to having the internet and smart phones that can recognize faces, track our location, and connect us with anyone in the world.

What if we showed someone 100 years ago some of the technology from today? If I somehow could go back in time with my smart phone and I stopped a random person on the street to take a

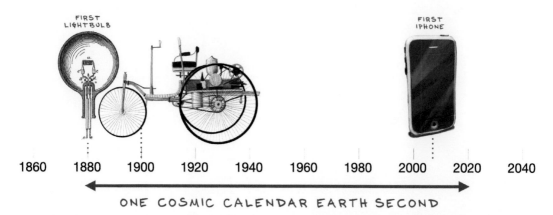

Figure 15.4 An illustration of a 'Cosmic Calendar' where Earth's existence is mapped to one calendar year, showing the last 'second' of time (or roughly 145 years). Edison's lightbulb (1880) using a carbon filament was developed in 1880. The first iPhone was released in 2007.

selfie, they would think I was a wizard (*You're a wizard, Barry!*). They would not be able to comprehend what they are looking at. They would not be able to understand how the technology worked. They would think that what I was showing them was a trick, or magic, or a miracle, or something alien from an advanced civilization, or from a higher being! This concept was presented on *Star Trek: The Next Generation* (Season 3, Episode 4) when Captain Picard tries to explain their advanced "god-like" powers/technologies to a less advanced civilization:

> suppose one of your cave-dwelling ancestors were to see you as you are today, what would she think?...Put yourself in her place...you have a power she lacks...she has never seen a bow... it doesn't exist in her world, to you, it's a simple tool. To her, it's magic.

(Manning & Beimler, 1989)

That is exactly what technology from just 50–100 years from now will be to us. If I showed you technology from the future, it would look like magic. I may even *appear* to be an alien or a god. The average person today would not be able to understand what they are seeing or experiencing.

In 1965, the Beatles met Elvis at his home in Los Angeles. It was the first time they had seen a television remote. Paul McCarthy recalled, "He was just aiming it at the TV, and the channels were changing and we go 'Whoa! He is indeed the mighty God. He can turn the channels without approaching the television set!'" (Woo, 2018). In 1877, Thomas Edison invented the phonograph or "speaking machine" that could "record and reproduce the human voice" (Buonanno, 2005). As this never existed before, it seemed like pure magic to the public. After this reveal, Edison was called the "The Wizard of Menlo Park" (Buonanno, 2005).

This phenomenon can be summarized nicely as: "Magic's just science that we don't understand yet." Arthur C. Clarke is given credit for this quote although the original source is not available. A variation on the wording happens to be his Third Law: "Any sufficiently advanced technology is indistinguishable from magic" (Clarke, 1962).

References

Ankola, A. V., Hebbal, M., & Eshwar, S. (2009). How clean is the toothbrush that cleans your tooth? *International Journal of Dental Hygiene, 7*(4), 237–240.

Asumang P., Inkabi, S. E., & Inkabi. S. (2019). Toothbrush bristles, a harbor of microbes and the risk of infection. *International Journal of Oral Health Science, 9*, 25–27.

Boucher, D. H., & Moeser, V. (1991). Cocaine and the coca plant. *Bioscience, 41*(2), 72.

Buonanno, J. F. (2005). *Thomas A. Edison: Wizard of Menlo Park, or ordinary thinker? A case study in the psychology of creativity* (Order No. 3202991). Available from ProQuest Dissertations & Theses Global.

Cheng, R. (2021, March 9). PTCellphone inventor reflects on pandemic-driven innovation -- and the first mobile call. *cnet.*

Clarke, A. C. (1962). *Profiles of the future: An inquiry into the limits of the possible.* Littlehampton Book Services Ltd.

Edison, T. A. (1880). Electric Lamp. U.S. Patent Application No. 223,898. Washington, DC: U.S. Patent and Trademark Office.

Fee, E., & Brown, T. M. (2004). Popularizing the toothbrush. *American Journal of Public Health, 94*, 721.

Gardner, M. N., & Brandt, A. M. (2006). "The doctors' choice is America's choice": The physician in US cigarette advertisements, 1930–1953. *American Journal of Public Health, 96*(2), 222–232.

Grier, P. (1981, April 15). Really portable telephones: Costly, but coming? *The Christian Science Monitor.*

Hargadon, A. B., & Douglas, Y. (2001). When innovations meet institutions: Edison and the design of the electric light. *Administrative Science Quarterly, 46*(3), 476–501.

History.com Editors. (2019, May 2). Model T. *A&E Television Networks.*

Klapper, L. (2019, April 10). Mobile phones are key to economic development. Are women missing out? *Brookings Institution.*

Koestler, A. (1964). *The act of creation.* Macmillan.

Library of Congress, Science Reference Section (2019, November 11). Who invented the toothbrush and when was it invented? *Library of Congress.*

Longo, W. E., Rigler, M. W., & Slade, J. (1995). Crocidolite asbestos fibers in smoke from original Kent cigarettes. *Cancer Research, 55*(11), 2232–2235.

Malik, A. S., Shaukat, M. S., Qureshi, A. A., & Abdur, R. (2014). Comparative effectiveness of chewing stick and toothbrush: A randomized clinical trial. *North American Journal of Medical Sciences, 6*(7), 333–337.

Manning, R., & Beimler, H. (Writers), & Wiemer, R. (Director). (1989, October 16). Who watches the watchers. [Television series episode]. In *Star trek: The next generation*, CBS.

Miller, S. (2009, June 20). Motorola executive helped spur cellphone revolution, oversaw ill-fated iridium project. *The Wall Street Journal.*

Musto, D. F. (1991). Opium, cocaine and marijuana in American history. *Scientific American, 265*(1), 40–47.

Sagan, C. (1975). Cosmic calendar. *Natural History, 84*(10), 70–73.

Staunstrup, P. (2022). Mobile phones – from luggables to pocket phones. *LM Ericsson and Centre for Business History.*

Woo, W. (2018, September 14). How Elvis introduced Paul McCartney to the remote control. *Wired.*

Yu, H. Y., Qian, L. M., & Zheng, J. (2013). *Dental biotribology.* Springer.

16

SCIENCE FICTION, SUPERHEROES, AND ALIENS

In 1917, Edgar Rice Burroughs published the book *A Princess of Mars*. The story begins with John Carter, a confederate veteran, who finds himself in a troubling situation and runs into a cave. This cave *magically* transports him to Mars where he encounters Martians. Now, because John Carter is accustomed to Earth's gravity, the weak gravity on Mars allows him to jump *super* high and punch *super* hard. John Carter suddenly has *super*powers, even though he has relatively normal powers back on Earth.

If this story sounds familiar, it is probably because it was a major influence on the story of *Superman* (Andrae, 1980). Superman came from a fictional planet larger than Earth and so when he found himself on Earth, he had superpowers *relative* to those of the Earthlings. The original Superman did not fly, and his original abilities were very similar to those of John Carter. He was strong and can jump really high (or as the radio show introduction would say): "Faster than a speeding bullet! More powerful than a locomotive! Able to leap tall buildings in a single bound!" (Beck, 1940) and nothing about flying. Superman's powers were intended to be based on a science. As per the creators:

> Scientific Explanation for Superman's Amazing Strength: Superman came to Earth from the planet Krypton, whose inhabitants evolved, after millions of years, to physical perfection! The smaller size of our planet, with its slighter gravity pull, assists Superman's tremendous muscles in the performance of miraculous feats of strength! Even upon our world today exist creatures possessing super-strength! The lowly ant can support weights hundreds of times its own. The grasshopper leaps what to man would be the equivalent of several city blocks! (Siegel & Shuster, 1939).

Super is relative.

On the topic of advanced alien lifeforms visiting Earth: the *Fermi paradox* is that given the high probability that there is other intelligent life in our galaxy much more advanced than our own, why have we not been visited by aliens or, as Enrico Fermi simply stated, "Where is everybody (Jones, 1985)?" One of the many interesting theoretical rationales is that these lifeforms simply can't communicate with us (Woodward, 2019). If these other civilizations are millions of years more evolved, it would be like us trying to introduce ourselves and communicate with a colony of ants. Advanced civilizations may be so physically and technologically advanced that they seem to be "Gods" to us, much like the *StarTrek* example in the prior chapter. Perhaps these visitors could move mountains, walk through walls, read minds, restructure matter, control lightning, etc.

DOI: 10.4324/9781003276296-19

Let's try to objectively think of our human selves as if we were John Carter being transported to another world. Are there things that we can do right now that could be viewed as "super" or "magic" to other hypothetical civilizations? As an example, our nose is so powerful that we can smell 2-isobutyl-3-methoxypyrazine, the molecule behind the green bell pepper scent, at 0.002 parts per *billion* in water (Rowe, 2000). That is a just a fraction of a drop in an Olympic swimming pool. Okay, maybe "Captain Bell Pepper" is not valuable enough to join the *Avengers*. When we get cut (superficially), our skin heals itself. This is a small-scale version of the abilities of *Marvel*'s Wolverine or Deadpool. We think it's impressive that bees can communicate with dancing (Riley et al., 2005) and rhinoceroses can communicate with poop (Marneweck et al., 2017), but it's no more impressive than humans being able to communicate by vibrating air with our mouth. We are super beings in many ways, we are just *normalized* to our powers.

There are some examples of things that we didn't know we were capable of, and so to most of us, they appear *super*. Joy Milne can *smell* Parkinson's disease. She can smell it a decade before a medical diagnosis, and she can distinguish if it is early or late stage. Her abilities were put to test in a scientific study in which she blindly and accurately identified those with and without the disease. In addition, she also identified (and accurately predicted) that one of the control subjects would later develop Parkinson's (Spiegel & Renken, 2020). Daniel Kish lost his eyesight at a young age, and he taught himself to use clicking noises to navigate (Sutter, 2001). He can echolocate similar to a bat or a whale. His ability is so strong, he can use his ears to ride a bike and to *reliably identify* objects in the environment. He has also taught over 500 blind children to do this too! Although Kish would prefer to be viewed as a "Batman" (Sutter, 2001), he is more similar in powers to the *Marvel* character *Daredevil*. Image is all in your brain and, as per the Matrix, *reality* is all in your brain too: "…'real' is simply electrical signals interpreted by your brain" (Wachowski, 1999). You can feed your visual cortex with inputs other than your eyes (or ears). You can also "see" via touch. A lollypop-like device covered in an array of electrodes can transmit a real-time image from a small wearable camera into an array of electric pulses you can feel on your tongue (Kendrick, 2009). Your brain will start to map the picture created via haptic sensations into a visual image and you can see and navigate the world without using your eyes.

Sometimes we don't always realize that human beings are getting more advanced in the same way we don't realize we are getting older. In 1921, Elizabeth Atkinson received the world record for the woman's one-mile-run with a time of 6:13.2 (Foster et al., 2014). The current world record, set in 2019, is held by Sifan Hassan of the Netherlands at 4:12.33 (Rowbottom, 2019). In less than a century, we have increased our speed by 33%. If Sifan Hassan ran in the 1920s, she would have looked like a superwoman next to Elizabeth Atkinson. In the 1896 Olympics, the men's high jump gold went to Ellery Clark at 1.81 m (Smythe, 2016). The current men's high jump record holder is Javier Sotomayor of Cuba with a jump of 2.45 m set in 1993. In just under a century, we are able to jump 35% higher. Javier Sotomayor would have looked like Superman next to Ellery Clark in 1896. We can do this with almost any Olympic sport. We all have superpowers relative to our prior selves and we just may need to visit another planet to realize it.

Just as if someone from 100 years ago saw our physical abilities today, they may have thought we had superpowers, if someone from 100 years ago saw the *technology* we were using to-day, they would have thought it was magic. There are hypotheticals portraying this concept on the cartoon series, *Rick and Morty*, in which scientist, inventor, and time/space traveler, Rick, utilizes technology and knowledge from more advanced societies and alternative dimensions (Harmon & Roiland, 2013; Brady, 2019). This is similar to the premise behind the "magical" powers of DC's *Green Lantern* ("power ring") as well as Marvel's *Thor* ("Mjölnir" hammer) in which technology of an advanced society empowers a hero. Similarly, *Wonder Woman* and *Black Panther* are from hidden places on Earth that have developed advanced technology that

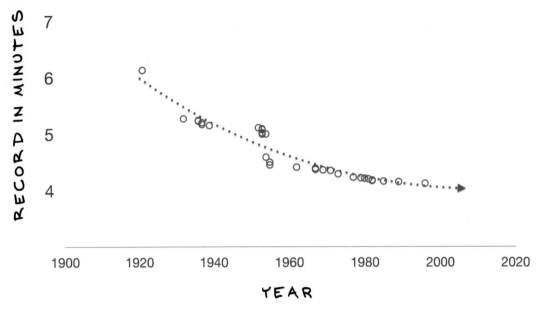

Figure 16.1 The progression of world records in the women's one-mile run. Data is taken from published world records and is also visualized in Foster et al. (2014). In less than a century, we have increased our speed by 33%.

was kept secret from the rest of the planet. Thor expressed this nicely: "Your ancestors called it magic, but you call it science. I come from a land where they are one and the same" (Branagh, 2011). This is a nice spin on: "any sufficiently advanced technology is indistinguishable from magic" (Clarke, 1962).

Many of the technologies of science fiction and superhero media today will be real in the future—even things like laser beam eyes, retractable claws, changing hair color on command, magic wands—in the same way, technology of sci-fi/superhero past is real today. Many of Jules Verne's futuristic ideas presented in his works of the mid-/late 1800s are now real: electric submarines, helicopters, news television, lunar modules, skywriting, videoconferencing, tasers, the jukebox, holograms, etc. Many futuristic gadgets in the original *Star Trek* are also now real: universal translators, tablet computers, a communicator badge, natural language queries, etc. Many (if not all) of the original *Batman* utility belt gadgets are real, including the portable self-ascending device (i.e., grappling hook gun). HAL from *2001: A Space Odyssey* is now real (being Alexa, Siri, and the like). Military drones from *Terminator* are now real. The self-lacing shoes from *Back to the Future 2* are now real (Rubin, 2015). The multi-touch digital screens and personalized advertising from *Minority Report* are now real. *Dick Tracy*'s watch phone that appeared in comics in 1946 is now real (Blakemore, 2015). The small headphones of *Fahrenheit 451* that go inside your ears to transmit music and talking sounds are now real. Even *Get Smart*'s shoe phone of 1965 is now real (Moses, 2009). In 1983, EPCOT (one of the theme parks located at the Walt Disney World Resort, Orlando) opened a ride called "Horizons" that transported guests into earlier predictions of the future (including those of Jules Verne) and then into a contemporary prediction of the future. Those predictions from 1983 included multi-screen video chatting, robotic farming, robotic vacuuming, and hydroponic vertical farming (Novak, 2013). All these predictions are now real.

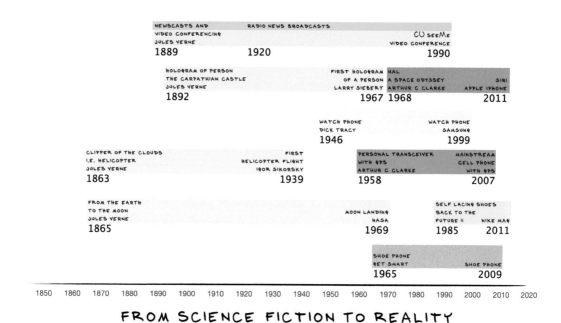

FROM SCIENCE FICTION TO REALITY

Figure 16.2 Examples of timelines for select published science fiction technology through appearance of the actual technology. The light blue lines follow science fiction concepts from Jules Verne, including the helicopter (Miller, 2014), newscasts and videoconferencing (Verne & Verne, 1889), holograms (Verne, 1892), and a moon landing (Verne, 1865). The red lines follow two of Arthur C. Clarke's concepts: mobile phones with GPS and voice-aware conversational AI (Anderson, 2019).

Let's look at some *super* technology that is not *exactly* real yet. We are currently developing variations of "telekinesis," using electroencephalogram (EEG) sensors to detect our brain's alpha waves to manipulate objects. The *Mindball* table game is an existing product using this technology to move a ball by turning on and off fans with our mind (Graham-Rowe, 2008). One can see how this technology could advance given the popularity of smart devices, drones, and internet of things. We may also be close to reading minds. Professor Brian Pasley found a way to map the sound profiles in brain activity when patients heard different words. He was then able to reliably send new words directly into patients minds without sound and have them "hear" it via Intracranial EEG (Pasley, 2012). This technology is in the early stages of development, but in years from now, something like this could transmit your thoughts to someone else or to your appliances or vehicle. These technologies are bringing us closer to the superpowers of *Marvel*'s Professor X or Jean Gray.

We can look at our superheroes on a spectrum of normal to futuristic abilities from both a technological perspective and a physical powers perspective (some superheroes rely on both technology and physical abilities, but they are separated in this mapping).

Here is an example of a progression of superhero powers ranging from normal human abilities to "super" human abilities:

- *Kickass* (an average person)
- *Batman/Black Widow* (a highly trained person)
- *Daredevil/Bullseye* (someone with a very enhanced yet feasible ability)
- *Wolverine* (someone with a highly enhanced ability that is currently not possible *yet*)
- *Wonder Woman* (someone with powers beyond human and seems magic or otherworldly).

Here is a progression of superhero technology, ranging from ones that are existing technology to ones that are future technology:

- *Green Arrow/Hawkeye*—bow and arrow (long existing technology)
- *Punisher*—guns (existing technology)
- *Batman*—rappelling gear, drones, smart devices, self-driving vehicles (modern technology)
- *Iron Man*—holograms, flying suit (Street, 2018), mind-controlled objects (believable, yet still distant/bleeding edge technology)
- *Green Lantern*—power ring (very distant technology that resembles magic).

One can visualize these technologies as phases on (and before) a technology S-curve in Figure 16.3.

Science fiction and superhero comic writers are *futurists*. They are making educated predictions about what technology will exist and, more specifically, what powers and abilities might be valuable to have in the future. They are great observers of the world. In a way, designers are trained to do this too. Designers study people's current means of doing things and make predictions in the form of non-existing services and technology to enhance people's current abilities. When you think about the process of invention—it starts with sparks in your mind, something that is unreal and fantasy. We then use stuff around us to create a thing that never existed before. This is *real* magic. In EPCOT's Horizons ride, they used the saying: "If you can dream it, you can do it" (Novak, 2013). In other words, we have the power to transform an image in our mind into a real thing (like a really slow version of *Green Lantern* powers).

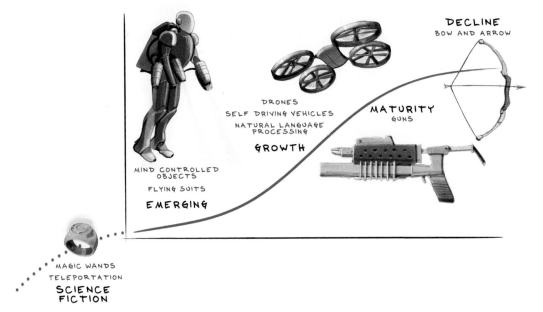

Figure 16.3 A Technology S-curve of some superhero-related technologies. A bow and arrow (like in *Green Arrow*) is a generally retired technology, guns (like in *Punisher*) are a mature technology, drones, and self-driving vehicles (like in *Batman*) are a growing technology, and flying suits (like in *Iron Man*) are an emerging technology. Magic wands and magic rings (like in *Green Lantern*) are not exactly on that curve yet, at least as they are presented in popular media, but like most science fiction, they may be on a curve soon!

References

Anderson, H. (2019, June 21). The fiction that predicted space travel. *BBC*.

Andrae, T. (1980). From menace to messiah: The prehistory of the superman in science fiction literature. *Discourse, 2*, 84–112.

Beck, J. (Presenter). (1940, February 12). *The Adventures of Superman* [Radio program]. WOR-AM.

Blakemore, E. (2015, March 9). How dick Tracy invented the smartwatch. *Smithsonian Magazine*.

Brady, M. (2019). *The science of Rick and Morty: The unofficial guide to earth's stupidest show*. Atria Books.

Branagh, K. (Director). (2011). *Thor [Motion picture]*. United States: Paramount Pictures Corporation.

Burroughs, E. R. (1917). *A princess of mars*. A. C. McClurg.

Clarke, A. C. (1962). *Profiles of the future: An inquiry into the limits of the possible*. Littlehampton Book Services Ltd.

Foster, C., de Koning, J. J., & Thiel, C. (2014). Evolutionary pattern of improved 1-mile running performance. *International Journal of Sports Physiology and Performance, 9*(4), 715–719.

Graham-Rowe, D. (2008). Let the mind games begin. *New Scientist, 197*(2647), 40–42.

Harmon, D., & Roiland J. (Executive Producers). (2013). *Rick and Morty* [TV series]. Adult Swim.

Jones, E. M. (1985, March). *"Where is everybody?": An account of Fermi's question*. (Publication No. LA-10311-MS). Los Alamos National Laboratory technical report.

Kendrick, M. (2009, August 13). Tasting the light: Device lets the blind "See" with their tongues. *Scientific American*.

Marneweck, C., Jürgens A., & Shrader A. M. (2017) Dung odours signal sex, age, territorial and oestrous state in white rhinos. *Proceedings of the Royal Society B, 284*(1846), 20162376.

Miller, R. (2014, June 1). How Jules Verne helped invent the helicopter. *Gizmodo*.

Moses, A. (2009, March 2). Aussie boffin cobbles together Get Smart shoe phone. *Sydney Morning Herald*.

Novak. M (2013, October 1). Happy birthday (and RIP) to Disney world's best ride ever. *Gizmodo*.

Pasley, B. N., David, S. V., Mesgarani, N., Flinker, A., Shamma, S. A., Crone, N. E., Knight, R. T., & Chang, E. F. (2012). Reconstructing speech from human auditory cortex. *PLoS biology, 10*(1), e1001251.

Riley, J., Greggers, U., Smith, A. D., Reynolds, D. R., & Menzel R. (2005). The flight paths of honeybees recruited by the waggle dance. *Nature, 435*, 205–207.

Rowbottom, M. (2019, July 12). Hassan breaks world mile record in Monaco with 4:12.33- IAAF Diamond League. *World Athletics*.

Rowe, D. (2000). More fizz for your buck: High-impact aroma chemicals. *Perfumer and Flavorist, 25*(5), 1–19.

Rubin, P. (2015, October 21). Back to the future's self-lacing Nikes are finally real. *Wired*.

Siegel, J., & Shuster, J. (1939). *Superman #1*. DC comics.

Smythe, S. (2016, July 30). Olympic history: Men's high jump. *Athletics Weekly*.

Spiegel, A., & Renken E., (2020, March 23). Her incredible sense of smell is helping scientists find new ways to diagnose disease. *NPR News*.

Street, F. (2018, July 23). Meet Britain's real-life iron man. *CNN*.

Sutter, J. D. (2001, November 9). Blind man uses his ears to see. *CNN*

Verne, J. (1865). *De la terre à la lune*. Pierre-Jules Hetzel.

Verne, J. (1892). *Le Château des Carpathes*. Pierre-Jules Hetzel.

Verne, J., & Verne, M. (1889). *In the Year 2889*. Feedbooks.

Wachowski, L., & Wachowski, L. (Directors). (1999). *The Matrix [Motion picture]*. United States: Warner Bros.

Woodward, A. (2019, October 9). A winner of this year's Nobel prize in physics is convinced we'll detect alien life in 100 years. Here are 13 reasons why we haven't made contact yet. *Business Insider*.

17

THE ADJACENT POSSIBLE, *THE SIMPSONS'* PREDICTIONS, AND *RICK AND MORTY*

In a 1958 essay (reprinted later in 1962), Arthur C. Clarke envisioned "the personal transceiver, so small and compact that every [person] carries one with no more inconvenience than a wristwatch." He further elaborates that

> we will be able to call a person anywhere on Earth...No one need ever again be lost, for a simple position- and direction-finding device could be incorporated in the receiver, based on the principle of today's radar navigational aids.

(Clarke, 1962)

As illustrated in Figure 16.2 in the prior chapter, this prediction was about 50 years before cell phones with GPS were mainstream. In the same essay, Clarke describes "the automobile of the future" in which

> you need merely tell it your destination – by dialing a code, or perhaps even verbally – and it will travel there by the most efficient route, after first checking with the highway information system for blockages and traffic jams.

(Clarke, 1962)

Technologically speaking, this autonomous vehicle system of interaction that Clarke is describing is available today.

Writers of science fiction and fantasy, such as Clarke, are not pulling ideas out of nowhere. They are basing it on something: A morsel from the present that they find interesting enough to expound upon in a thoughtful prediction about the future. They are experts in exploring the *adjacent possible* (Kauffman, 2000). As described by Steven Johnson, the adjacent possible is "a kind of shadow future, hovering on the edges of the present state of things, a map of all the ways in which the present can reinvent itself" (2010). In other words, everything imaginable is based on something that is already in existence. This can be framed as Arthur C. Clarke's second law: "The only way of discovering the limits of the possible is to venture a little way past them into the impossible" (1962). All our future technology falls in that adjacent possible gray zone that comes right before the emerging technology portion of the technology S-curve. Science fiction, fantasy, superhero, comic, and cartoon writers are often the ones dreaming of the future and creating these enticing predictions. They can be viewed as "tech nerds" who closely follow the bleeding edge technology and ask the question of what happens in the future when a bleeding edge technology is commonplace, affordable, more advanced, more ubiquitous, etc.

DOI: 10.4324/9781003276296-20

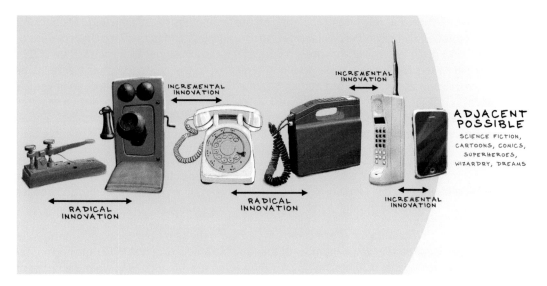

Figure 17.1 A simplified representation of the theory of the adjacent possible related to phones and long-distance communication. The jump from telegraph to telephone was a radical innovation as discussed in Chapter 12. There was another radical jump from corded phones to wireless phones.

Looking at Figure 16.2 in the prior chapter, it *appears* as if Jules Verne was a time traveler—predicting technologies over a century beforehand. Even though his predictive jumps in this chart were twice the time length as those of Clarke, Verne was also simply *playing* in the adjacent possible. He describes this in an interview:

> I have always made a point in my romances of basing my so-called inventions upon a groundwork of actual fact, and of using in their construction methods and materials which are not entirely beyond the pale of contemporary engineering skill and knowledge. Take, for instance, the case of the 'Nautilus.' This, when carefully considered, is a submarine mechanism about which there is nothing wholly extraordinary, nor beyond the bounds of actual scientific knowledge... the only point at which I have called in the aid of imagination is in the application of this force, and here I have purposely left a blank for the reader to form his own conclusion, a mere technical hiatus, as it were, quite capable of being filled in by a highly-trained and thoroughly practical mind.
>
> (Jones, 1904)

Verne took two modern (yet very much existing) technologies at the time (the submarine and electricity), combined them, and wrapped them in a narrative adventure.

> What may sometimes look like a daring imaginative leap into the future is, then, usually no more than the product of Verne's copious and compulsive note taking. As an avid reader of popular scientific, geographical or technological literature, he always had a ready store of recyclable information.
>
> (Unwin, 2000)

Following in the same *vein* as da Vinci, as described in Chapter 7, Verne "always took numerous notes out of every book, newspaper, magazine, or scientific report that [he] came across" (Belloc,

1895). Verne was also somewhat of a "tech nerd" similar to the writers of more contemporary forms of science fiction that rely on extrapolating on the technology of the time (e.g., *Minority Report* (Bleecker, 2009), *Black Panther* (Weisberger, 2018)). Verne attended the Paris Universal Exposition of 1867 like designers and sci-fi writers might attend the Consumer Electronics Show (CES), for inspiration. At *this* Expo, there were pavilions dedicated to the *new* concept of electricity as well as submarine vessels including one named *Nautilus* (Butcher, 1998). This dissection of Verne's "predictions" is not intended to devalue his work in any way; producing science fiction requires creativity and a working understanding and awareness of current science and technology as well strong storytelling skills. Verne is more of a master of storytelling within the adjacent possible than a prophet.

A more contemporary version of science fiction inspired by science fact is the gesture-based user interface concept presented in *Minority Report* (Spielberg, 2002) in which video, audio, and images are manipulated via motions through a pair of gloves.

> The idea for such a gestural interface came...in part from the film's technical consultant, John Underkoffler. Underkoffler was a member of the Tangible Media Group at M.I.T. and had participated along with a panel of luminaries in providing some speculations as to what the future of Minority Report might be experienced based on their insights and their extrapolations of the current trends in the technology world.
>
> (Bleecker, 2009)

A version of Underkoffler's prototype that allowed people to manipulate data with gloved hands was featured in the film (Merchant, 2018).

Does art imitate life or does life imitate art? It's probably both. Science fiction inspires artists, engineers, and designers just as artists, designers, and engineers inspire science fiction. **It is a dialog of sorts—a large-scale and long-term discussion between scientists, writers, and artists that gradually moves society forward.** In this example, "Minority Report shows how science fiction is shaped and informed by science fact. It also shows how science fact learns from and finds inspiration through the science of fiction" or in other words "fiction follows fact" and "fact follows fiction" (Bleecker, 2009).

Like in science fiction based-worlds, animated worlds are also not real. Part of the magic of cartoons and animation is that the characters and objects are capable of doing things that real people cannot. Even in watching cartoons, the viewer is open to more possibilities than they would be when watching real people. As a simple example, let's look at an illustration in one of Dr. Seuss's books, *Oh the Things You Can Think* (1975). In this book about endless possibilities and imagination, there is a visualization of a fanciful imaginary island place called "Da-Dake," depicting a seemingly *impossible* island composed of narrow concentric connected rings of land. In 2001, construction began on the Palm Islands, a series of manmade islands off the coast of Dubai, United Arab Emirates. This unique design allows all houses on the island to have beach front (and back) property. It also creates a unique experience of walking out into the middle of the ocean on a thin strip of land. These islands bear resemblance to the fantasy islands of Da-Dake as illustrated in Figure 17.2. In line with the message of this Dr. Seuss book, things that you think of may become real, but it starts with *trying* to think of these playful, wondrous, silly things.

Like Verne and Clarke, the *Simpsons'* writers have also been viewed as prophets as they often predict real world events such as: Homer proving the Higgs boson mass theory (15 years before it was discovered), Lady Gaga's Super Bowl half-time show performance details with flying entrance (five years beforehand), Roy of the magician duo Siegfried & Roy being attacked by his white tiger

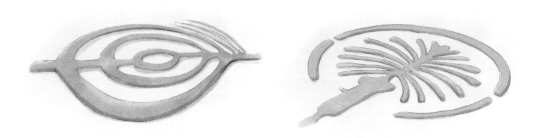

Figure 17.2 A generalized interpretation of the narrow-land-bridge island system of "Da-Dake" from "Oh the Things You Can Think" (Dr. Seuss, 1975) (left), and a generalized interpretation of the Palm Islands of Dubai (right). What was once considered a fanciful "thing that you can think" is now a thing that you can go see.

during a show (ten years beforehand), Bengt R. Holmstrom winning a Nobel Prize in Economics (six years beforehand), Disney buying 21st Century Fox (19 years beforehand), and the London's Shard skyscraper in the general location and form (14 years beforehand) (Locker, 2016; Murray, 2020). How many of these ideas are pure coincidence? How many are examples of the writers being futurists—accurately predicting the future? How many of these examples are the writers being thought leaders—creating ideas that inspire the public to act?

In a 1999 episode of *The Simpsons*, Homer creates a hybrid of a tomato plant and a tobacco plant called the "tomacco" to produce a nicotine-enhanced tomato fruit (Maxtone-Graham & Anderson, 1999). The tomacco plant was clearly an example of the latter in which Rob Baur, a fan of the show, grafted a tobacco root to a tomato stem and produced an edible "tomacco" fruit directly inspired by the episode (Philipkoski, 2003). The initial invention in the episode, however, was likely inspired by an illustrated Scientific American article in which a scientist presents the exact reverse procedure (grafting a tobacco plant onto a tomato root) to obtain nicotine-free tobacco (Robinson, 1959). The tomacco is an example of this back-and-forth dialog between scientists, artists, and writers from science fact to science fiction to science fact.

Perhaps the most discussed Simpson prediction occurred in a 2000 episode, "Bart to the Future" (Locker, 2016; Greaney & Marcantel, 2000). Bart sees a vision of the future in which his sister Lisa is the newly appointed president taking office following President Trump: "As you know, we've inherited quite a budget crunch from President Trump" (Greaney & Marcantel, 2000). This episode aired 17 years before Trump's presidency (off by 13 years). More recently, Vice President Kamala Harris' inauguration outfit is nearly identical to that worn by Lisa Simpson when she takes office (a dark purple suit jacket, with a lighter purple undershirt, a large pearl necklace, and large pearl earrings) (Greaney & Marcantel, 2000; White, 2021).

Many of the concepts presented on the show are simply examples of intelligent writers playing in the adjacent possible and making educated guesses about the future based on trends and nuggets of the present. As Bill Irwin, author of *The Simpsons and Philosophy*, said "Many jokes reach just beyond what is real, and that is a pretty good way of setting yourself up for things that may turn out to be real in the future" (2001). Irwin is describing the adjacent possible and how curious writers, when given the opportunity to make up hypothetical futures in an imaginary world where anything is possible, are able to make reasonable predictions. In this specific episode of *The Simpsons*, the story took place *in the future*.

When you have an animated world in which anything is possible *and* you can also travel forward in time, there is great potential for predicting radical innovation. *Futurama*, another Matt Groening television show, gets to play in this space all the time creating a world of technologies and social issues from the year 3000. *The Jetsons* aired in 1962 and took place in 2062 (Orlin, 2012). This plat-form allowed the writers of *The Jetsons* to imagine a future based on nuggets of information from the present. Rosie the Robot, for example, was the Jetsons' robotic maid and she is most often seen with a vacuum cleaner rolling on a set of caster wheels. This playful and humorous future that the writers imagined in which robots vacuumed the floor and could communicate with you became real when iRobot released the Roomba in 2002 (Todd, 2015).

Another mechanism for writers to introduce future technology in fiction is by creating *a character who is an inventor*. In the *Wallace and Gromit* stop motion animated short, *The Wrong Trousers*, Wallace invents a pair of mechanically actuated robotic trousers called "Techno Trousers" to as-sist him in taking his dog, Gromit, for walks (Park, 1993). The pants then get hijacked by an evil penguin in a plot to steal a diamond. This film won the Academy Award for Best Animated Short Film, but perhaps a greater honor is that it directly inspired the development of *actual* mechanical trousers to assist people with mobility problems—a technology with an estimated global market worth £40 billion (Hamill, 2018). Mechanical trousers are now also being used by soldiers to carry heavy loads long distances and by healthcare providers to lift and move patients. What started as a joke (Ha-ha, the pants walk you!) is now a serious and life-changing technology.

Another famous fictional inventor is Willy Wonka. In *Charlie and the Chocolate Factory*, this eccen-tric inventor of sweets develops an "impossible" ice cream that does not melt, even "without being in the refrigerator" (Dahl, 1964). Not only does this ice cream not melt, we also later learn that it can be served as "hot ice creams for cold days." Grandpa Joe explains to Charlie, "Of course it's impossible!... It's completely absurd! But Mr. Willy Wonka has done it!" (Dahl, 1964). Wonka also invented "sugar balloons that you can blow up to enormous sizes before you pop them with a pin and gobble them up" and Mr. Wonka's "most fascinating invention!"—gum that changes flavor as you chew it (Dahl, 1964). These "absurd" and "impossible" inventions are *all now real products*. You may notice that some ice cream sandwiches do not melt if left out of the refrigerator. These ice cream products contain a stabilizer such as guar gum or cellulose gum that keeps the ice cream from melting (Harris, 2014). More recently, scientists in Japan discovered that polyphenol liquid extracted from strawberries has a similar effect when used in ice cream (Nelson, 2017). Adding methylcellulose to ice cream allows you to actually make "ice" cream that you can serve hot, even for putting in hot drinks as per Wonka's suggestion (Santos et al., 2018). Edible helium-filled taf-fy-like balloons have been served to customers at *Alinea* since 2012 for them to pop (inhale the gas) and "gobble up" (Galarza, 2017). Some variations of flavor-changing gum are currently available on the market and a patent on flavor-changing gum was awarded to Kraft food in 2012 for a means of using microencapsulation of flavor liquids to be released at different times in the gum-chewing process (Liu, 2015). All of these "impossible" sweet ideas from 1964 are now possible and they are additional examples of the playful dialog between science fiction and science fact.

Now, if you have an animated universe unbound by the constraints of reality *and* you can also travel in time *and* a character is an inventor, then the writers have a free pass to play in the adja-cent possible whenever they want. *Rick and Morty* have just teleported into the room (Roiland & Harmon, 2013). *Rick and Morty* won the 2018 and 2020 Emmy for Outstanding Animated Program. The 2018 award was for the "Pickle Rick" episode in which Rick turns himself into a pickle to avoid family therapy. He later creates an organic mechatronic exoskeleton with brain-machine inter-face out of rats and roaches (Gao & Chun, 2017). Perhaps we are several years away from pickle transformation, but the material presented in this episode related to exoskeletons is closer to science fact than science fiction. Specifically, the concept of a brain-machine interface was demonstrated when scientists reliably created a "brain implant that allows monkeys to feed themselves [marshmallows] using a robotic arm just by thinking about it" (Hopkin, 2008). One intended use of this device is to allow paralyzed people to naturally operate prosthetic limbs. This is also another example of a technology that was presented first as a radical idea in superhero comics that is now real: Doctor Octopus' mind-controlled robotic arms in *The Amazing Spiderman* (Lee & Ditko, 1963). We should expect to see a variety of the radical ideas presented in *Rick and Morty* become reality in a few centuries from now (e.g., inter-dimensional cable, memory-saving device, dog translator, a self-aware butter-passing robot, etc.)

A RECIPE FOR FICTION THAT INSPIRES INNOVATION

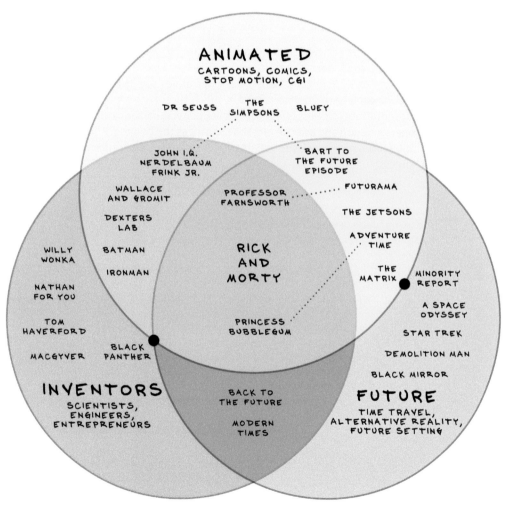

Figure 17.3 A Venn diagram illustrating types of fiction that tend to inspire future innovations with a plotting of some examples mentioned in this book. These three fiction categories include: (1) animated media such that the medium is not restricted to reality and creators can present content that does not exist and/or cannot actually exist yet, (2) inventors, scientists, engineers, or entrepreneurs as characters who are expected to create new things, and (3) the story takes place in a future time or alternative reality such that the content is required to represent a more advanced/future state of reality.

So how does all this map to creative design and innovation? One can craft speculative worlds based on cutting-edge technology to predict future technologies. This is called *science fiction prototyping*, future-casting, or world-building (Johnson, 2011). A related concept, *design fiction*, uses designed artifacts to imagine stories about future experiences and interactions in the same way science fiction writers use narrative to tell stories about the future (Bleecker, 2009). Unlike prototypes developed to illustrate how a concept could be manufactured, "design fiction objects are totems through which a larger story can be told, or imagined or expressed. They are like artifacts from someplace else, telling stories about other worlds... Design fiction works in the space between the arrogance of science fact, and the seriously playful imaginary of science fiction, making things that are both real and fake" (Bleecker, 2009). Like Underkoffler's gloves used in Minority Report, design fiction may be more similar in function to a storytelling prop than a prototype. As discussed in Chapter 12, industrial designers have the tools to transform bleeding edge technologies into representations (such as prototypes, props, and design fictions) that can look and function in such a way that the public can imagine how this could fit into their future life (when that technology becomes more affordable, more reliable, more feasible, smaller, etc.).

For the gesture-based user interface design concept, "the film [*Minority Report*] itself becomes an opportunity to explore an idea, share it publicly and realize it at least in part" (Bleecker, 2009). The film plays a similar role as Kickstarter videos. These narratives say "Hey society! Check out this thing that is almost possible! Are you interested in this future thing? A little more R&D can make it real." These presentations, stories, television shows, comics, cartoons, and movies initiate that dialog between science fiction and science fact that advances the boundary between adjacent possible and actual innovation. As you will see in Parts 3 and 4, these dialogs often come with and from both play and humor.

References

Belloc, M. A. (1895, February). Jules Verne at home. *Strand Magazine, 9.*

Bleecker, J. (2009, March). Design fiction: A short essay on design, science, fact and fiction. *Near Future Laboratory.*

Butcher, W. (1998). Introduction. In J. Verne (Ed.), *Twenty thousand leagues under the seas* (pp. ix–xxxi). Oxford World's Classics.

Clarke, A. C. (1962). *Profiles of the future: An inquiry into the limits of the possible.* Littlehampton Book Services Ltd.

Dahl, R. (1964). *Charlie and the chocolate factory.* George Allen & Unwin.

Dr. Seuss. (1975). *Oh, the thinks you can think!* Random House.

Galarza, D. (2017, May 25). Alinea's signature edible balloons have been ripped off. *Eater.*

Gao, J. (Writer), & Chun, A. (Director). (2017, August 6). Pickle rick. [Television series episode]. J. Roiland & D. Harmon (Producers), *Rick and Morty,* Adult Swim.

Greaney, D. (Writer), & Marcantel, M. (Director). (2000, March 19). Bart to the future. [Television series episode]. In M. Groening (Producer), *The Simpsons,* Fox.

Hamill, J. (2018, September 11). Scientists building real-life version of Wallace and Gromit's 'Wrong Trousers'. *Metro.*

Harris, J. (2014, July 28). Why a Walmart ice cream sandwich just won't melt. *Los Angeles Times.*

Hopkin, M. (2008). Monkeys move robotic arm using brain power. *Nature.*

Irwin, W. (2001). *The Simpsons and Philosophy: The D'oh! of Homer.* Open Court; Edition Unstated.

Johnson, B. D. (2011). *Science fiction prototyping: Designing the future with science fiction.* Morgan & Claypool Publishers.

Johnson, S. (2010). *Where good ideas come from: The natural history of innovation.* Riverhead Books.

Jones, G. (1904). Jules Verne at home. *Temple Bar, 129,* 664–670.

Kauffman S. A. (2000). *Investigations.* Oxford University Press.

Lee, S., & Ditko, S. (1963). *The Amazing Spiderman,* Volume 1, Number 3. Marvel Comics.

Liu, E. (2015, July 7). Flavor-changing chewing gum. *Discover Magazine.*

Locker, M. (2016, November 9). The all-seeing Simpsons predicted Donald Trump's presidency in 2000. *Time.*

Maxtone-Graham, I. (Writer), & Anderson, B. (Director). (1999, November 7). E-I-E-I-(Annoyed Grunt). [Television series episode]. In M. Groening (Producer), *The Simpsons,* Fox.

Merchant, B. (2018, November 28). Nike and Boeing are paying sci-fi writers to predict their futures. *OneZero.*

Murray, T. (2020, February 3). 18 times 'The Simpsons' accurately predicted the future. *Business Insider.*

Nelson, B. (2017, August 7). This Japanese ice cream will never melt — and it costs less than $5. *Business Insider.*

Orlin, J. (2012, January 1). It's 2012 already so where are all the Jetsons flying cars. *TechCrunch.*

Park, N. (1993). *The Wrong Trousers [Animated short film].* United Kingdom. BBC Enterprises.

Philipkoski, K. (2003, November 7). Simpsons plant seeds of invention. *Wired.*

Robinson, T. (1959). Alkaloids. *Scientific American, 201*(1), 113–123.

Roiland, J., & Harmon, D. (2013). *Rick and Morty [Animated Sitcom].* Adult Swim.

Santos, M., Gabriel, P., Mata, P., Fradinho, P., & Raymundo, A. (2018). Threading tradition—a path for innovation with methylcellulose threads. In R. Bonacho et al. (Eds.), *Experiencing Food, Designing Dialogues* (pp. 53–56). CRC Press.

Spielberg, S. (Director). (2002). *Minority Report [Motion picture].* United States: 20th Century Fox.

Todd, R. (2015, September 17). There might not have been an iRobot without Rosie the robot. *Fast Company.*

Unwin, T. (2000). Technology and progress in Jules Verne, or anticipation in reverse. *Journal of the Australasian Universities Language and Literature Association, 93*(1), 17–35.

Weisberger, M. (2018, April 17). The amazing tech in 'Black Panther' is more realistic than you think. *Livescience.*

White, A. (2021, January 21). Simpsons fans believe Lisa's presidential outfit 'predicted' Kamala Harris's inauguration ensemble. *Independent.*

Part III

Play, Creativity, and Innovation

18

DEFINING PLAY, PUPPIES, AND TOM SAWYER

What is play?

There are a variety of definitions of play that are often based in developmental psychology, but before we go to the obvious, let's start with the *mechanical engineering definition of play*. I realize this seems like the setup to a joke, but *play* is a real mechanical engineering term. This phenomenon is also called *backlash* and it describes a situation in a mechanism where there is lost motion or "wiggle room" between parts as shown in Figure 18.1 (Nordin & Gutman, 2002). In the engineering world, this is typically an undesirable occurrence (e.g., play in the gears of your bike, play in the steering wheel of your car). However, when viewed at a more abstracted level, this term describes the freedom of movement within given constraints. As we think about play in the context of creativity, this mechanical engineering definition is surprisingly appropriate: **Play is about freedom of movement within a given set of constraints.**

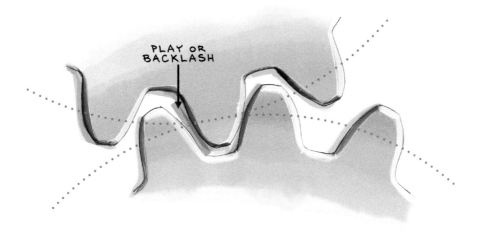

Figure 18.1 Gears showing mechanical play, slop, or "backlash."

To recall the activity from the Introduction, the Alternative Uses Test naturally included the constraint that all responses must involve the paperclip. You could bend it or straighten it or use it in

DOI: 10.4324/9781003276296-22

any context you wanted—there was "wiggle room" in the constraints that allowed you to play with the challenge. *Spoiler*: without that play, there is less room for creativity. Think about that same activity of generating alternative uses, but this time you are *not* allowed to modify the paperclip in anyway and it still must be used with paper. In Chapter 2, we discussed the game *Scribblenauts*: each challenge has a set of constraints, but you can use any tool that you can think of to solve the puzzle. The play and the resulting creativity emerge from this *slop*. When a challenge is too rigid, a creative person may be required to find their own slop to play in. This is related to Nobel laureate Max Delbrück's *Principle of Limited Sloppiness*:

> If you are too sloppy, then you never get reproducible results, and then you never can draw any conclusions; but if you are just a little sloppy, then when you see something startling, you say, 'Oh, my God, what did I do, what did I do different this time?' And…you nail it down.

(1979)

Let's briefly look to some traditional views of play. One of the great play researchers, Dr. Brian Sutton-Smith, describes *play* as "a primitive and paradoxical communication, schematic expression, and a succession of disequilibrial bipolar state, with their own rules, sequences, and climaxes" (1986). A rough translation of this is that play is a natural and fluctuating state of mind that involves its own rules and symbolic representations. For an even less academic definition, Oxford English Dictionary describes play as an "activity engaged in for enjoyment or recreation rather than for a serious or practical purpose" (2006). That's a good start, but there is a bit more to it than that.

Play is natural. It occurs in animals other than humans: dolphins, rats, elephants, monkeys, and dogs all play. Play has been recognized in mainly mammals and bird species, but also in some invertebrates such as spiders and octopi (Bateson & Martin, 2013). If you have spent time around dogs, specifically younger dogs, you may have witnessed something called a *play bow*. This is when a dog will seem to bow forward putting their head down and their tail in the air as illustrated in Figure 18.2. This is a means of communication from one dog to another to engage in play or resume playing (Bekoff, 1995). By doing this action, a dog is essentially saying "oh *hi*, do you want to engage in a fake fight with me? We can playfully attack each other, growl, show our teeth, chase each other around, but if one of us yelps, we have to stop. Is that *OK*?" And for the play to proceed, the other dog must return the play bow.

You, as a human, can actually give the play bow to a dog and the dog will understand what you are saying. One study found that humans giving a play bow to dogs had a 100% success rate in getting the dog to initiate play (Rooney et al., 2001). Other animals have play bows as well. Elephants have a form of play bow that is similar to dogs, but it takes much longer (O'Connell, 2021). Even birds, such as seagulls, play. A study found that young herring gulls play a game of catch with clams (Gamble & Cristol, 2002). After observing these gulls drop clams to break them on hard surfaces, they noticed that the younger gulls would drop the clam and then try to catch it before it hit the ground. The clams used in this game were not even consumed if they opened. The gulls would also play this game with inanimate objects and over soft sandy surfaces.

In a sense, humans have play bows too. Imagine a group of children in a room. If one child wants to initiate a game of tag with another child, they may make a facial expression combined with certain body motions that indicate that they are about to chase after them. If the other child doesn't start running in response (returning the bow), the game of tag will not happen. Clowns, mimes, magicians, and other entertainers also rely on a type of "play bow" to the audience to ask them to engage in some pretend scenario. For example, a performer may ask someone in the audience to come on stage, choose a card, take an imaginary balloon, or repeat a dance move. If the audience

Figure 18.2 The anatomy of a play bow for dogs.

member doesn't return the request, they are rejecting the invitation to play (and likely negatively impacting the show for the performer and the rest of the audience).

The American Academy of Pediatrics (AAP) states that play "is essential for helping children reach important social, emotional, and cognitive developmental milestones as well as helping them manage stress and become resilient" (Ginsburg et al., 2007). Adults *also* learn via play. A review of 142 laparoscopy studies found that "medical students and experienced laparoscopic surgeons with ongoing video game experience have superior laparoscopic skills for simulated tasks in terms of time to completion, improved efficiency and fewer errors when compared to non-gaming counterparts" (Ou et al., 2013). Play is how we learn major life skills as a child (*and* as an adult) in a *safe* context. "Engaging in play allows animals to experiment with new behaviors in a protected environment without dangerous consequences" (O'Connell, 2021). In the case of the dog, it helps develop their skills at hunting and fighting. In the case of the seagull, it helps them develop their foraging skills and diving reflexes. Play can also be a means of *catharsis* or emotional release (Sutton-Smith, 1997); it can be a means of both discharging *and* recharging energy (Lieberman, 1977). Even the United Nations recognizes how important play is for the development of a child. They drafted an article: "States Parties recognize the right of the child to rest and leisure, to engage in play and recreational activities appropriate to the age of the child and to participate freely in cultural life and the arts" (2013). The UN declared it a *right* for all children to play.

Perhaps one of the most interesting things about play is that it is a *state of mind during an activity and not the activity itself* (Brown, 2009). You can't say that Minecraft or table tennis or Cards Against Humanity is play. These are simply activities. The same activity can be viewed as work to one person and can be viewed as play to another. Furthermore, that activity can be viewed as play to a person on one day and not play to the same person on a different day. You can probably think of a few things that you enjoy doing that some people would not (e.g., vacuuming, sorting change, weeding a garden, waxing a car, processing data, etc.). There are young children who love raking leaves. They might enjoy the act of moving the leaves around to make a giant pile. And then, there are older children who might hate raking leaves and view it as a chore. You may be able to recall the first time you ever shoveled snow (or the first day of shoveling snow of the season)—you may have thought it was fun, and then there was likely an exponential decline in fun over time. You may enjoy picking apples, but if that happens to be your job or if you had to do it every day, you may not necessarily view apple picking as play.

In the Netherlands, there are recreational/educational public facilities across urban centers called *kinderboerderij*. This is Dutch for "children's farm," and it is a bit different from a "petting zoo." They were founded as a means of exposing urban children and adults to farming practices. There are over 300 of these farms in the Netherlands with 30 million visits annually (Siegal, 2017). Children go there to learn about growing food as well as engaging with and caring for farm animals (brushing goats, feeding chickens, cleaning stables, etc.). They have small child-sized rakes, shovels, and wheelbarrows for children **to collect poop from the fields**. And children love it! From experience, I had to convince my two-year-old to stop cleaning up goat poop when it was time to leave.

Mark Twain summarized this phenomenon as: "play and work are words used to describe the same activity under different circumstances" (Thomas, 1905). A great example of this is in his book *The Adventures of Tom Sawyer* (1876). Tom is *ordered* by Aunt Polly to whitewash the fence and he doesn't want to, so he *pretends* that he enjoys it. His friends come up and say, "Why, ain't that work?," to which Tom replies, "Well, maybe it is, and maybe it ain't." Intrigued, his friends then beg him for a turn ("Say, Tom, let me whitewash a little"), and on further refusal, they eventually pay Tom with gifts to participate in this whitewashing *activity*. "Tom was literally rolling in wealth... and the fence had three coats of whitewash on it! If he hadn't run out of whitewash he would have bankrupted every boy in the village" (Twain, 1876). **Play is a state of mind, not an activity.**

' AIN'T THAT WORK?'

Figure 18.3 True Williams's illustration of the whitewashing scene from Mark Twain's *The Adventures of Tom Sawyer* (1876).

In summary: (1) play is about freedom of movement within a given set of constraints; (2) it is a natural phenomenon that occurs in a variety of species; (3) it is a safe means of learning social, emotional, and cognitive developmental skills; (4) it is a state of mind and not the activity itself such that; and (5) it is possible to transform something that is typically viewed as work into something viewed as play (and vice versa). If the Dutch can find a way to transform cleaning up animal poop into play, we can probably find a way to make anything fun.

In the next few chapters, we will dig in deeper into the different types of play and the criteria that make something playful before we draw in connection lines to the world of creativity and innovation.

References

Bateson, P., & Martin, P. (2013). *Play, playfulness, creativity, and innovation.* Cambridge University Press.

Bekoff, M. (1995). Play signals as punctuation: The structure of social play in canids. *Behaviour, 132*(5–6), 419–429.

Brown, S. (2009). *Play: How it shapes the brain, opens the imagination, and invigorates the soul.* Avery.

Delbrück, M. (1979) *Interview with Max Delbrück* [Oral History]. Caltech Oral Histories.

Gamble, J. R., & Cristol, D. A. (2002). Drop-catch behaviour is play in herring gulls, Larus argentatus. *Animal Behaviour, 63*(2), 339–345.

Ginsburg, K. R. (2007). The importance of play in promoting healthy child development and maintaining strong parent-child bonds. *Pediatrics, 119*(1), 182–191.

Lieberman, J. N. (1977). *Playfulness: Its relationship to imagination and creativity* (A. J. Edwards, Ed.). Academic Press.

Nordin, M., & Gutman, P.-O. (2002). Controlling mechanical systems with backlash—a survey. *Automatica, 38*(10), 1633–1649.

O'Connell, C. (2021, August 1). Why animals play. *Scientific American, 325*(2), 48–55.

Ou, Y., McGlone, E. R., Camm, C. F., & Khan, O. A. (2013). Does playing video games improve laparoscopic skills? *International Journal of Surgery (London, England), 11*(5), 365–369.

Play. (2006). *In oxford English dictionary.* 3rd ed. Oxford University Press.

Rooney, N. J., Bradshaw, J. W. S., & Robinson, I. H. (2001). Do dogs respond to play signals given by humans? *Animal Behaviour, 61*(4), 715–722.

Siegal, N. (2017, March 21). The Dutch way: Tulips, windmills and barnyard animals. *The New York Times.*

Sutton-Smith, B. (1986). *Toys as culture.* Gardner Press.

Sutton-Smith, B. (1997). *The ambiguity of play.* Harvard University Press.

Thomas, A. E. (1905, November 26). Mark twain: A Humorist's confession. *The New York Times.*

Twain, M. (1876). *The adventures of tom sawyer.* American Publishing Company.

UN Committee on the Rights of the Child (CRC). (2013). *General comment No. 17 (2013) on the right of the child to rest, leisure, play, recreational activities, cultural life and the arts (art. 31).* Convention on the. Rights of the Child, CRC/C/GC/17.

19

PLAY TAXONOMIES, ADULT PLAY, AND JAKE THE DOG

In *Homo Ludens* (translated to "Man as a Player"), the Dutch historian Johan Huizinga claims there are two pure forms of play: "a contest for something" and "a representation of something" (1950). In other words, play can either be based in the form of a *challenge* or in the form of *fantasy*. These are perhaps the two most common forms of play that we associate with children's activities: games and pretend play. Challenge play can be physical or mental, luck or skill, individual or team-based, and includes activities like sports, juggling, crossword puzzles, and other games. In any of these activities, the playfulness stems from an element of challenge or mastery (like seagulls in Chapter 18 trying to catch clams before they hit the ground). Fantasy (pretend, symbolic, or make-believe) play includes playing with dolls or action figures, storytelling, pretending to be someone else, something else, or somewhere else, and pretending objects are other things. In any of these activities, the playfulness stems from an element of symbolism or fantasy (like the child with the cardboard box in the Introduction and on this book cover).

There are other activities that both children and adults do that are playful, but not necessarily based in a challenge or a fantasy. As you can see in Figure 19.2, after Huizinga, subsequent play classifications typically include *two* additional high-level categories: *creation/construction* and *sensory/sensorimotor.*

Sensory or sensorimotor play is called something different in almost every system of classification (e.g., manipulative play, exploratory play, object/body play), but always involves stimulating our senses: What does this feel like? What happens if I squeeze this? What does this taste like? I'm going to spin around really fast. I'm going to stick my hand in these beans (note: this is one of the small pleasures in life called out in the film, Amélie (Jeunet, 2001)). I'm going to put these beans in my nose. I'm going to now put these same beans in my mouth. I'm going to spin around really fast in the other direction!

The Caldecott-awarded children's picture book, *The Snowy Day*, features a series of examples of sensory play as it follows a young boy, Peter, through his neighborhood after the first snowfall of the season (Keats, 1962). In the book, Peter crunches the snow to make patterns, drags his feet to make tracks, drags a stick to make a line, hits a tree to make the snow fall, throws a snowball, makes a snowman, makes a snow angel, and slides down a hill. It is a beautiful collection of examples of childhood sensory play. Keats left out perhaps the most playful sensory winter activity for all ages: cracking thin shell ice underfoot on the sidewalk. This is very similar to the sensory pleasure of breaking the hard sugar crust of a crème brûlée (another small pleasure in life called out in the film, Amélie (Jeunet, 2001)). You may recall a scene from *Ratatouille* (Bird & Pinkava,

DOI: 10.4324/9781003276296-23

Figure 19.1 An example of sensory play in the cracking of the sugar layer on a crème brûlée as described in the film *Amélie* (Jeunet, 2001). This is a similar sensory experience to cracking thin ice sheets on the sidewalk under foot.

2007) where Remy (a rat) and his brother Emile are tasting food scraps. Remy instructs his brother on how to taste food and try different food combinations. Remy gets very excited about the possibilities of making infinite flavor combinations that no one has ever tried. In that scene, Emile did not view the experience as play, but Remy did. Not only is this an example of sensory play, it is also an example of how *play is a state of mind*. Sensory play is driven by a desire to explore our world, objects, and our body through our senses.

The last category of play (at least for this book) is *creation* or *construction play*. This is not just constructing physical things, but rather making anything, which includes structures, music, art, story, dance, etc. There might be some involved challenge, fantasy, or sensory element, but one can have creation play without any specific challenge or pretend scenario. Let's say for example that you are doodling with crayons or making up a song—the play is coming from the act of creation. You might be saying, "Aha! *This* is how play connects to creativity," but no, not exactly and not yet. All four types of play can be connected to creativity.

As you can see in Figure 19.2, scholars tend to dissect and name the categories of play in different ways. In general, there is some agreement (Smilansky, 1968; Garon et al., 2002; Kudrowitz & Wallace, 2009; Bulgarelli & Bianquin, 2017) on four main types of play: *challenge* (e.g., contest, rule play, mastery, competition) shown in pink; *fantasy* (e.g., representation, symbolic, simulation, make-believe, pretend) shown in red; *sensory* (e.g., practice, sensorimotor, vertigo, functional, movement, manipulative, body, object) shown in green; and *creation* (e.g., constructive, assembly, creative) shown in blue. Two of the most granular taxonomies (Hughes, 2002; Brown, 2009)

	HUIZINGA 1950	PIAGET 1945	CAILLOIS 1961	SMILANSKY 1968	GARON ET AL 1982	GOODSON & BRONSON 1997	HUGHES 2002	BROWN 2009	KUDROWITZ WALLACE 2009	BULGARELLI BIANQUIN 2017
CHALLENGE	CONTEST	RULES	COMPETITION / CHANCE	GAMES WITH RULES	GAMES WITH RULES	LEARNING	DEEP / MASTERY		CHALLENGE	RULES
FANTASY	REPRESENTATION	SYMBOLIC	SIMULATION	SYMBOLIC OR DRAMATIC	SYMBOLIC	MAKE BELIEVE	SYMBOLIC / DRAMATIC / SOCIODRAMATIC / ROLE PLAY / FANTASY / RECAPITULATIVE	PRETEND / STORYTELLING	FANTASY	SYMBOLIC
SENSORY	PRACTICE OR SENSORIMOTOR		VERTIGO	FUNCTIONAL	EXERCISE	ACTIVE MOVEMENT / MANIPULATIVE	LOCOMOTOR MOVEMENT / ROUGH AND TUMBLE / OBJECT / EXPLORATORY	BODY / OBJECT / ATTUNEMENT	SENSORY	PRACTICE
CREATION		CONSTRUCTIONAL *		CONSTRUCTIVE	ASSEMBLY	CREATIVE	CREATIVE / IMAGINATIVE / SOCIAL / COMMUNICATION	CREATIVE / SOCIAL	CONSTRUCTION	CONSTRUCTION

Figure 19.2 A selection of play taxonomies over time in chronological order of publication (Huizinga, 1950; Piaget, 1945; Caillois, 1961; Smilansky, 1968; Goodson & Bronson, 1997; Garon et al., 1997; Hughes, 2002; Brown, 2009; Kudrowitz & Wallace, 2009; Bulgarelli & Bianquin, 2017).

include an additional category of "social" play; however, any play can be made social or not social. This is more like a modifier.

Play isn't typically just one pure form—any activity may have elements of different play types. Jumping rope, for example, may have some elements of challenge play, but it may also have some sensory play. Building and playing with completed *Lego* sets, for example, may involve creation, challenge, and fantasy play. Building a snowman may involve all four types of play. One can view these four types of play as the vertices of a tetrahedron in which the edges consist of play that falls between two categories and the faces consist of play that combines three types of play. This classification visualization, shown in Figure 19.3, is what I call the "Play Pyramid," and any toy or activity can be placed somewhere inside (Kudrowitz & Wallace, 2009).

Jean Piaget, a Swiss philosopher and developmental psychologist, observed play in children from infancy to school age "and described the most prevalent types of play at each of those age levels" (Bergen, 2015). Three of the four play classifications fit nicely into Jean Piaget's *Stages of Cognitive Development* (1945). Play for infants tends to be primarily *sensory* with lots of sounds, textures, and colors. This aligns with Piaget's *Sensory-Motor* or *Practice Stage* (0–18 months) (1945). As children develop, they begin to create *fantasy* worlds and engage in pretend play (e.g., fake food, imaginary friends, cardboard box spaceships). This aligns with Piaget's *Pre-Operational Stage* of development in which children begin to develop language, but do not yet understand concrete logic (ages 2–7) (1945). For children ages 7–11, there will be more play specifically related to *challenge* and rules. This aligns with Piaget's third stage of development, the *Concrete Operational Stage*, in which children develop logical thinking processes (1945). Piaget's fourth stage, *Formal Operations* (from adolescence through adulthood) does not map to the Play Pyramid's fourth classification of *creation* play; however, Piaget does specifically call out "construction games" as a separate "class" of play (1945).

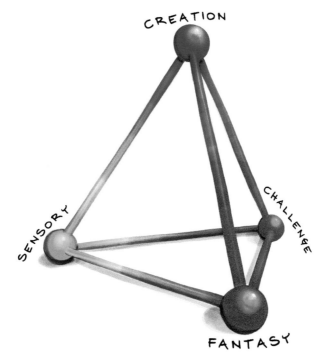

Figure 19.3 The Play Pyramid taxonomy of play types: challenge, fantasy, sensory, and creation (updated from Kudrowitz & Wallace, 2009).

As we become adults, we still play, but we tend to call it by different names: recreation, leisure, sports, adventure, outings, partying, experimentation. We, as adults, do use the term "play" when discussing games and sports (e.g., play tennis, play cards), but when adults do other playful things, we don't typically use the word "play." Perhaps this is because when we say "play," we sound childish. *And we don't want to sound childish, right?*

In the animated television series, *Bluey*, the *Stumpfest* episode is specifically devoted to the concept of adult play (Brumm & Jeffery, 2020). In this episode, Bluey's dad and friends gather to remove two tree stumps from the yard (*challenge play*). While they are removing one stump, the children convert the other stump into a nail salon (*fantasy play*). When it's time to remove the nail salon stump, Bluey questions why the adults can interrupt people while they are playing. Bluey's mother, Chilli, tries to explain that the children were actually interrupting the *adults* playing. "They're ripping out stumps, that's not playing," Bluey says. Chilli asks Bluey to watch the adults more closely and she sees the adults are engaging in play fighting and trying to remove the stump with tools. Play "just looks a bit different for grownups" (Brumm & Jeffery, 2020). When adults play, as opposed to children, the "toys" may be different, the degree of challenge may be different, the words we use to describe it may be different, but the elements are the same. Let's look at each of the four types of play and see what happens when we age from baby to child to adult.

Sensory play. As we get older, we try to push our limits and explore things differently with our senses. We have increased access to the world, which allows for more opportunities for sensory exploration. The play in squishing crinkle paper expands to the play of jumping into a pile of leaves or sticking your hand in a basket of dry beans. Putting different things in your mouth as a baby, leads to exploring new foods, and then, in some cases, to the *Ratatouille* example of trying new flavor combinations and wine pairings. The play of the playground swing leads to play on bigger carnival rides, which leads to the play on even bigger amusement park rides and roller coasters. Again, as we become adults, we don't necessarily call activities like wine tasting and roller coasters "play."

Fantasy play. As we get older, the fictional characters and worlds that we identify with become more grounded in reality and we relate to characters that are of a similar age. Very young children relate to cartoon animals and puppet monsters (e.g., Bluey, Elmo). Older children and teens relate to human children with magical or super abilities (e.g., Harry Potter, Spiderman). In adulthood, our fantasy characters include "old" talented special agents with no super abilities (e.g., James Bond, Indiana Jones). Young children tend to dress up and pretend play at any time, older children and teens may only dress up for specific events and Halloween. Adults, in some ways, never stop playing dress-up; we just stop *getting creative* with our dress-up. Every time we select the clothes, makeup, perfume, deodorant, and accessories to put on our body from our closet, we are wearing a form of costume. You may decide to wear something formal one day or you may decide to style your hair like some influencer. As RuPaul says "we're all born naked, and the rest is drag" (Winfrey, 2018). According to *Elephant and Piggie*, pretend play is "when you act like something you are not" and "Everyone pretends. Even grown-up people. All the time" (Willems, 2013).

Challenge play. Young children will find physical and mental challenges in copying a motion or mimicking a word. Simply balancing a block or putting a shape into the correct hole is challenge play to a young child. As we get older, we gain more knowledge, we refine our motor skills, and we are constantly desiring to find new challenges to master. If you think about ball games: rolling a ball leads to the game of catch, which leads to T-ball, which leads to baseball. If you think about puzzles, as we get older, we simply increase the overall number of pieces and decrease the size of each piece. We do still "play" ball and "play" board games as adults. So, it appears that when the activity is a game, it's OK to use the word "play" as an adult.

Creation play. Young children have limited motor skills and their creation play may be making crayon markings on a page. As we get older, both our gross and fine motor skills develop, we have access to more tools, and we can achieve a higher level of resolution. Focusing on *Lego* brand construction play, one can see a progression from *Duplo*, being large pieces with simple builds, to simple Lego sets, to more complicated Lego sets such as those in the *Ideas* and *Forma* lines, specifically targeted to adults (Bhattarai, 2020). In adulthood, although many adults still play with Lego (Giddings, 2014), we can now go into a machine shop and build with many different tools and materials. However, when we are working in a shop or in the kitchen or in a science lab, adults are not *typically* saying they are "playing."

Today, play is generally viewed as something only *children* do for fun and not something for adults. From the adult perspective, "play is usually regarded as a useless or, at best, inconsequential activity" (Lieberman, 1977). As you recall from Chapter 18, play is how we learn! Playtime, arts, and recess have been gradually cut back in schools to be replaced with study time as our educational system shifted focus to standardized tests (Sahlberg & Doyle, 2019). A CDC analysis of academic studies found consistently strong associations between academic performance and physical activity and *recess* during school time—specifically *all* studies found that time spent in recess had positive associations with "cognitive skills, attitudes, and academic behavior" (2010).

> While elementary schools are meeting the national guidance to provide at least 20 minutes of daily recess, there are still many that do not offer recess. Even for those that do, school recess practices can be stronger and more comprehensive.
>
> (Springboard, 2019)

Furthermore, as we progress through the educational system, once we are in high school and university, students engage in rote learning, copying notes off slides, and play is essentially nonexistent. "Even more important than the attitude of the preschool teacher is that of the elementary and high school teacher in not only tolerating but also encouraging playfulness in their classroom" (Lieberman, 1977). Society tells us that we shouldn't learn through play as we become an adult. As the *Little Prince* narrator explains:

> The grown-ups advised me to put away my drawings of boa constrictors, outside or inside, and apply myself instead to geography, history, arithmetic, and grammar. That is why I abandoned, at the age of six, a magnificent career as an artist.
>
> (de Saint-Exupéry, 1943)

Playwright George Bernard Shaw said, "We don't stop playing because we grow old; we grow old because we stop playing" (Bateson, 2015). Figuratively, this quote implies that you can stay "young at heart" if you continue to find play in life. Literally, there is some research to support this notion. "Higher frequency of playing games was associated with higher cognitive function at age 70" (Altschul & Deary, 2020). Another study found that a series of short physical play sessions with people ages 66–88 showed "statistically significant effects on all the test measures of elderly functional abilities (e.g., balancing, strength, mobility, agility, endurance)...and thereby achieve[d] remarkable collateral effect on their health" (Lund, 2015).

If we want to continue to be creative, we need to embrace play again (both adults and children). Adults, it's OK to have dress-up parties outside of Halloween. It's OK to have game nights. It's OK to watch cartoons. There is a history of famously creative individuals who happen to also be famously *playful* including: Wolfgang Amadeus Mozart, M.C. Escher, Alexander Fleming, and Richard Feynman (Bateson & Martin, 2013). Jake the Dog from *Adventure Time* embodies this notion of the child (or in this case, puppy) who never grew up. In one episode of *Adventure Time*, Jake's son, Kim Kil Whan, who conversely grew up a bit too fast, says that Jake "still lives the life of a child. I mean, it's his choice, but I really thought if he got a job and moved out of that tree house, it could have put some fire under him" (Ward et al., 2014).

Although this is fiction, it is a common sentiment about not conforming to the expectations of adults in society. And, even though Jake is still childish, he is one of the most creative characters on the show.

In Chapter 20, we will dissect the criteria that need to be present for an activity to be play and why an activity can be viewed as play to one person and as work to another—why Remy viewed flavor pairing as play, but Emile did not—why Bluey's dad viewed digging out a tree stump as play, but Bluey did not.

References

Altschul, D. M., & Deary, I. J. (2020). Playing analog games is associated with reduced declines in cognitive function: A 68-year longitudinal cohort study. *The Journals of Gerontology, B75*(3), 474–482.

Bateson, P. (2015). Playfulness and creativity. *Current Biology, 25*(1), R12–R16.

Bateson, P., & Martin, P. (2013). *Play, playfulness, creativity and innovation.* Cambridge University Press.

Bergen, D. (2015). Psychological approaches to the study of play. *American Journal of Play, 8*(1), 101–128.

Bhattarai, A. (2020, January 16). Lego sets its sights on a growing market: Stressed-out adults. *The Washington Post.*

Bird, B., & Pinkava, J. (Directors). (2007). *Ratatouille [Motion picture].* United States: Walt Disney Pictures.

Brown, S. (2009). *Play: How it shapes the brain, opens the imagination, and invigorates the soul.* Avery.

Brumm, J. (Writer), & Jeffery, R. (Director). (2020, March 22). Stumpfest [Television series episode]. In C. Aspinwall (Producer), *Bluey,* Ludo Studio.

Bulgarelli, D., & Bianquin, N. (2017). 3 Conceptual review of play. In S. Besio, D. Bulgarelli, & V. Stancheva-Popkostadinova (Eds.), *Play development in children with disabilities* (pp. 58–70). De Gruyter Open Poland.

Caillois, R. (1961). *Man, play and games.* The Free Press.

Centers for Disease Control and Prevention (CDC). (2010). *The association between school-based physical activity, including physical education, and academic performance.* Atlanta, GA: Centers for Disease Control and Prevention, US Department of Health and Human Services.

de Saint-Exupéry, A. (1943). *The little prince.* Harcourt Inc.

Garon, D., Chiasson, R., & Filion, R. (2002). *Le système ESAR. Guide d'analyse, de classification et d'organisation d'une collection de jeux et jouets.* Electre.

Giddings, S. (2014). Bright bricks, dark play: On the impossibility of studying LEGO. In M. J. Wolf (Ed.), *LEGO studies: Examining the building blocks of a transmedial phenomenon* (pp. 241–267). Taylor & Francis.

Goodson, B., & Bronson, M. (1997). *Which toy for which child a consumer's guide for selecting suitable toys for children: Ages birth through five.* [Technical Report]. U.S. Consumer Product Safety Commission.

Hughes, B. 2002. *A Playworker's taxonomy of play types.* PlayLink.

Huizinga, J. (1950). *Homo Ludens: A study of the play-element in culture.* Roy Publishers.

Jeunet, J-P. (Director). (2001). *Amélie [Motion picture].* France: UGC Fox Distribution.

Keats, E. J. (1962). *The snowy day.* Viking Press.

Kudrowitz, B. M., & Wallace, D. R. (2009). The play pyramid: A play classification and ideation tool for toy design. *International Journal of Arts and Technology, 3*(1), 36–56.

Lieberman, J. N. (1977). *Playfulness: Its relationship to imagination and creativity* (A. J. Edwards, Ed.). Academic Press.

Lund, H. H. (2015) Play for the elderly - effect studies of playful technology. In J. Zhou & G. Salvendy (Eds.), *Human aspects of it for the aged population. Design for everyday life* (pp. 500–511). Springer.

Piaget, J. (1945). *Play, dreams and imitation in childhood.* Taylor & Francis.

Sahlberg, P., & Doyle, W. (2019). *Let the children play: How more play will save our schools and help children thrive.* Oxford University Press.

Smilansky, S. (1968). *The effects of sociodramatic play on disadvantaged preschool children*. Wiley.

Springboard to Active Schools. (2019). *Keep recess in schools.* Atlanta, GA: Centers for Disease Control and Prevention, US Department of Health and Human Services.

Ward, P., Wolfhard, S., Muto, A., & Herpich, T. (Writers), & Han, B. H., & Salaff, A. (Directors). (2014, July 17). Ocarina. [Television series episode]. In Crews, K. (Producer), *Adventure Time*, Cartoon Network.

Willems, M. (2013). *An elephant and Piggie book: I'm a frog!* Hyperion Books for Children.

Winfrey, O. (2018). Oprah talks to RuPaul about life, liberty and the pursuit of fabulous. *O Magazine*.

20

THE CRITERIA FOR PLAY, FLOW, AND *BLUEY*

Play is difficult to define as it has historically been used to describe a variety of different activities and it is also studied across different academic disciplines. For the same reasons, there are many different sets of *play criteria* and some overlap (Spodek & Saracho, 1998). To not add an additional set of play criteria, I will simply elaborate on a few factors that influence one's state of mind during an activity viewed as play. In this chapter, I will discuss how play requires: *active engagement, intrinsic motivation,* and *pretense* or *internal reality*.

The first criterion for play is that the activity needs to be *actively engaging, enchanting,* or *captivating* (Huizinga, 1950; Garvey, 1990; Spodek & Saracho, 1998). This is the concept of *flow* by Mihaly Csikszentmihalyi (2008). Flow is that state you are in when you are fully engrossed in an activity and time seems to just fly by. For example, maybe you are playing a video game and you realize it's 4 am and you missed dinner. Or maybe you are building a bookshelf and you completely ignore someone calling your name multiple times. That is the state of flow. For any given activity, there is a challenge, or some degree of skills required. To be in a state of flow, your skillset needs to match

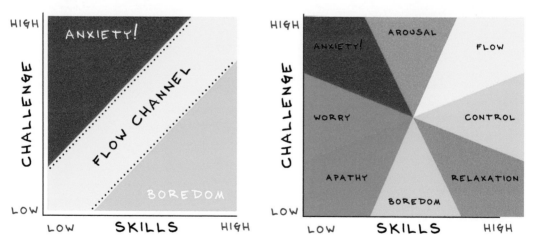

Figure 20.1 (Left) Representation of the original concept of flow as a channel that occurs when the challenge matches the skill set (Csikszentmihalyi, 2008), and (right) a visualization of a more recent model of flow that begins once both challenge and skill are above an average level for the actor. In this newer model, there are eight "channels" of experience, and flow only occurs at high challenge—high skill (Nakamura & Csikszentmihalyi, 2002).

DOI: 10.4324/9781003276296-24

the degree of challenge. If the challenge is too easy for you, you will be bored. If the challenge is too difficult, you are going to be anxious. As shown in Figure 20.1, there is always a sweet spot for the challenge to match your specific abilities for you to be fully engaged. The more you practice an activity, the better you will get at it, and the less of a challenge it will become. If you think about the example of raking leaves or shoveling snow, after doing it many times, not only has the novelty worn off, you are also no longer challenged by the task and it stops being engaging. Perhaps this sounds like a description of something you do in your daily life or at work.

The animated television series, *Bluey*, is full of interesting examples of play and parenting advice. Professor of Child Development, Marc de Rosnay says that this show "expresses something and demands something of the viewer that 1,000 developmental psychology or parenting books would struggle to do as well" (Fyfe, 2021). This is because the creator Joe Brumm "undertook an almost obsessive deep dive into the academic literature concerning play" and "…was actually mining the child development literature for script ideas and marrying those with his own family life" (Fyfe, 2021).

In the episode called "Keepy Uppy," Bluey and her younger sister, Bingo, are playing Keepy Uppy with a balloon (Brumm, 2018). After a while of hitting the balloon back and forth in the air without it falling to the ground, Bingo declares: "This is so easy now…I'm a Keepy Uppy Expert" to which Bluey adds "Yeah, but it's not as fun now, can you make it hard again?" The remainder of the episode involves their parents creatively *leveling up* the challenge to maintain the state of flow for the children and perhaps even surpassing it to the point of anxiety. Upon realizing this mistake, their father says "Did I make that a little too fun? It's a hard one to get right" (Brumm, 2018).

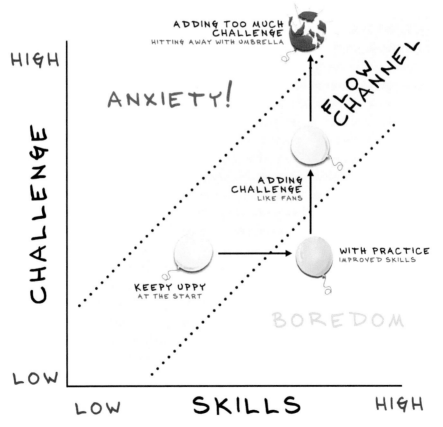

Figure 20.2 Visualization of the play progression in the "Keepy Uppy" episode of *Bluey* (Brumm, 2018) mapped onto a flow channel (Csikszentmihalyi, 2008).

Video games are extraordinarily good at keeping a player in the state of flow through the concept of *leveling up*. Most video games, by design, start out simple and gradually increase the challenge over time (like in this episode of *Bluey*). The video game always knows exactly how good the player is at any moment in time. When a level is successfully completed, the game knows the skills that have been mastered and raises the difficulty, keeping the player at the ideal level of challenge (i.e., in the state of flow).

Contrary to video games, teaching in a classroom setting is quite difficult as every student in the room has a different degree of mastery of skills. The instructor must then create content (in the form of activities and assignments) that engage a range of student abilities. This results in only a section of the class being in a state of flow, whereas some lower-skilled students will view the material as stressful, and some higher-skilled students will be bored. Perhaps there is a way our education system can learn from video game design.

In addition to being fully engaged in the activity, play requires some degree of *intrinsic motivation*, and it is voluntary (Huizinga, 1950; Caillois, 1961; Garvey, 1990; Spodek & Saracho, 1998; Bateson & Martin, 2013). This means that you are doing the activity because *you* want to do it and not because someone is making you do the activity. A closely related theme is that play is *process-focused* and not results-focused (Spodek & Saracho, 1998) (i.e., "it is not the marbles that matter, but the game" (Huizinga, 1950)). One must enjoy doing the activity itself for something to be viewed as play. If you are only doing the activity for the results (i.e., to win, for an award, for the reward, to say you did it, for the praise, etc.), then that activity is no longer play and starts to resemble work. If you ran a marathon just to say you ran a marathon, then running the marathon is not play. If you are gambling only to win money, gambling is not play. You may appreciate the results (e.g., winning, the reward), but you must *also* enjoy the activity for it to be play. If you think about the example of seagulls playing with clams in Chapter 18, the young gulls were not dropping clams to consume them for food, they were dropping them for the enjoyment of trying to catch them. *The activity itself is its own reward.*

Lego sets (and perhaps Lego in general) tend to be process-focused even though there is an "end goal." For most people, the play is in constructing the set (or whatever is being imagined). Although gratifying, the play is not *typically* driven by the desire to have a finished model on a shelf for display (and if it were the case, the activity may be more like work). An ethnographic study of play with Lego sets seems to confirm this:

> the pleasures of Lego do not end once the instructions in a particular set have been followed and the model depicted on the box is accurately realized. Generations of children have—just as the manufacturers intended—pulled apart the pristine model and begun again, making new vehicles, environments and creatures.

(Giddings, 2014)

One final requirement for play that I will discuss in this chapter, is *pretense* or *internal reality* (Huizinga, 1950; Caillois, 1961; Spodek & Saracho, 1998; Bateson & Martin, 2013). This is overt in pretend/fantasy play that we see in children engaged in dress-up or playing with action figures, but what is implied by *pretense* is a broader use of this term. You don't necessarily need to put on a costume to transform some activity into play (although it doesn't hurt!). Essentially, play involves a space that exists between internal and external reality. The activity operates in a separate dimension (or "temporary sphere of activity") with its own rules, and you are aware that it is not part of "real" life (Huizinga, 1950). This is in no way saying that play is unimportant or not valuable. Play is very important for development, learning, and enjoyment. However, in this play space, it is okay to mess up and fail because it won't have serious effects on the real world. "When the play activity becomes purposeful and dominated by the real properties of the stimulus, it loses its playful or ludic aspect" (Lieberman, 1977). In *professional games*, one may fail and lose their job or risk a salary decrease. In this case, the game (or *professional sport*) is closer to work than play; "with the increasing systematization and regimentation of sport, something of the pure play quality is inevitably lost" (Huizinga, 1950). Let's return to the *Bluey* example.

In their game of "Keepy Uppy," Bluey explains to her sister, Bingo, that the balloon must stay in the air, and it can't touch the ground. A very worried Bingo asks, "what happens if it touches the ground?" Their mother responds "Oh, nothing, Bingo. *It's just a game*" (Brumm, 2018). For Bingo to view the game as play, it can't have negative consequences on her real life (Huizinga, 1950).

In another *Bluey* episode called "Shadowlands (Brumm, 2018)," Bluey and her friends Snickers and Coco play a game called Shadowlands and they define the rules as such:

1: The cast shadows on the ground are "land" and the areas of the ground in the sun is the "sea."
2: You can only walk on "land" areas, and if you touch the "sea" then a crocodile will eat you.
3: The goal is to get to the picnic blanket.

Whenever things got difficult, Coco would suggest modifying or ignoring the rules that were set out from the start (walking on water, pretending the crocodiles are asleep, crocodile-proof shoes, etc.). "You can't just change the rules!" Bluey would exclaim. So, the children would ultimately uncover exciting and creative ways of playing *within* the rules. In the end, the children realize why they can't just change the rules as needed…"because the rules make it fun!" If they did break the rules or mess up "the whole play-world collapses" (Huizinga, 1950), but no one would actually be eaten by a crocodile, and life would continue as normal. Pretense (i.e., operating in a separate dimension with its own rules) is the differentiator between play and a simply enjoyable activity. Play takes place in a space where you can fail and not face lasting consequences (Huizinga, 1950). This is important as we start to discuss supportive environments for creativity and innovation.

Each of these individual criteria for play can be viewed as part of a spectrum (degree of engagement, internal vs. external motivation, internal vs. external reality). As every activity will fall somewhere between each of these extremes, the resulting overall playfulness will also fall somewhere on a spectrum or scale of play. Let's explore this play spectrum in Chapter 21.

References

Bateson, P., & Martin, P. (2013). *Play, playfulness, creativity, and innovation.* Cambridge University Press.

Brumm, J. (Writer/Director). (2018, October 3). Keepy Uppy. [Television series episode]. In C. Aspinwall (Producer), *Bluey,* Ludo Studio.

Brumm, J. (Writer/Director). (2018, October 5). Shadowlands [Television series episode]. In C. Aspinwall (Producer), *Bluey,* Ludo Studio.

Caillois, R. (1961). *Man, play and games.* The Free Press.

Csikszentmihalyi, M. (2008). *Flow: The psychology of optimal experience.* Harper Perennial Modern Classics.

Fyfe, M. (2021, May 10). Struggling with pre-schoolers? Take Bluey's lead, say experts. *The Sydney Morning Herald.*

Garvey, C. (1990). *Play.* Harvard University Press.

Giddings, S. (2014). Bright bricks, dark play: On the impossibility of studying LEGO. In M. J. Wolf (Ed.), *LEGO studies: Examining the building blocks of a transmedial phenomenon* (pp. 241–267). Taylor & Francis.

Huizinga, J. (1950). *Homo ludens: A study of the play-element in culture.* Roy Publishers.

Lieberman, J. N. (1977). *Playfulness: Its relationship to imagination and creativity* (A. J. Edwards, Ed.). Academic Press.

Nakamura, J., & Csikszentmihalyi, M. (2002). The concept of flow. In C. R. Snyder & S. J. Lopez (Eds.), *Handbook of positive psychology* (pp. 89–105). Oxford University Press.

Spodek, B., & Saracho, O. N. (1998). The challenge of educational play. In D. Bergen (Ed.), *Play as a medium for learning and development.* (pp. 11–28). Association for Childhood Education International.

21

WORK, MONTESSORI, AND TPS REPORT COVERSHEETS

On the playfulness scale, the opposite of play is *work*...but this statement requires some careful surgical dissection. Work has many meanings in the English language and there is only one meaning of work that is truly the opposite of play.

Work can mean *seriousness*, but that is not the opposite of play. If you have ever seen anyone play video games or a sport of any kind, you will know that seriousness and play are not opposites and often they go hand in hand (Huizinga, 1950). Mr. Rogers says

> play is often talked about as if it were a relief from serious learning. But for children, play is serious learning. At various times, play is a way to cope with life and to prepare for adulthood. Playing is a way to solve problems and to express feelings. In fact, play is the real work of childhood.
>
> (1995)

Similarly, work can also be a synonymous with *effort* (e.g., force times distance, "you better work" (RuPaul, 1992)), but one can put in a great deal of effort while playing and so effort is not the opposite of play.

Yet another definition of work is a job, career, or occupation, but one could be playful in one's job. The pioneers of early childhood education have made similar statements to that of Mr. Rogers regarding play being the *job* of children. *Frederick Fröbel* the founder of kindergarten says, "the play of children is not recreation; it means earnest work" (Fröbel & Hailmann, 1887). Similarly, *Maria Montessori* is often cited as saying "play is the work of the child" in the context of the Montessori method of early childhood education (1912). All the activities children do in the Montessori classroom from painting to sewing to sorting is called "work." In a Montessori classroom, the children may *seem* to be simply doing rote jobs such as chopping vegetables, ironing napkins, or washing a table. For example, the child

> must carry a mat to a table, lift the table onto the mat, fill a bucket to a specific level with water and add a specific amount of soap, carry the bucket and washing materials to the mat, put a sponge in the water, squeeze out the water with a taught squeezing motion, wipe the table from left to right (replicating the direction needed for writing), dry the table with a towel (from left to right), and so on.
>
> (Lillard, 2013)

Even though this seems like a rote job, the child is *choosing* to do this table washing activity on their own. And further, they may choose to do it over and over again. The child may enjoy the

DOI: 10.4324/9781003276296-25

process of mastering a skill. This is the concept of *flow* from Chapter 20—there are specific skills that a child requires to carry water, clean a surface, squeeze out a sponge and dry a table, and this can be a perfect challenge for the child until they *perfect* the challenge.

Lastly, work can mean a *chore* or a task that is required to be done that you don't want to do. This definition of work, a chore, is the opposite of play. To quote again from Mark Twain's *The Adventures of Tom Sawyer*: "Work consists of whatever a body is obliged to do. Play consists of whatever a body is not obliged to do" (1876). When kids rake leaves because they want to, then it *can* be play. When kids rake leaves and they do not want to, then it is work. Again, play is a state of mind not an activity.

Play and work are not a binary system and activities can fall "in-between." As early as first and second grade, children can characterize activities as being "in-between" work and play, and that activities have some elements of work and some elements of play (Wing, 1995). Furthermore, at this age, they can consistently identify the characteristics that make something play or work. Dr. Doris Bergen, expert of children's play and humor, describes a play continuum called *The Schema of Play and Learning*, which ranges from work to free play (Bergen, 1998).

Free Play, as described by Bergen (1998), has the greatest degree of internal control, internal reality (pretense), and internal motivation. *Work*, on the other hand/end, is an activity that is entirely externally motivated, based entirely in reality, results-driven, and not captivating.

Figure 21.1 Illustration of Doris Bergen's Schema of Play and Learning (1995).

The satire film, *Office Space* (Judge, 1999), captures the essence of work. The protagonist, Peter, loathes his job at a 1990s software company. When consultants are brought in to help downsize, Peter elaborates to them on why he doesn't care about his job: "When I make a mistake, I have eight different people coming by to tell me about it... my real motivation is... the fear of losing my job..." (i.e., *not pretense, serious impact on real world*). In response, the consultants ask, "what if you were offered some kind of stock option...?" (i.e., *results-focused, not process-focused*). Lastly, the consultants explain to the Vice President of the company, "... you haven't challenged him enough..." (i.e., *not actively engaged, not in a state of flow*) (Judge, 1999). This film explicitly calls out the absence of each of the criteria for play from Chapter 20 guaranteeing a score of 1 (work) for the protagonist on the play–work scale of Figure 21.1. A motif, and later a meme, that appears throughout this film as a physical embodiment of work is the "TPS report," specifically filling out the coversheets for the TPS reports, being a mindless required paperwork chore (Judge, 1999). Even though play and work are a mindset during an activity, most people would likely rate the process of filling out a TPS report coversheet as a 1 on the play scale.

Office Space is a satire, but it is based on some truths. There are similar things that we do in industry that often work against playfulness and creativity. For example, companies can base promotions or bonuses solely on results, as opposed to performance or creativity. In doing so, the message they are sending is that only the results matter and the activity itself is less important or praiseworthy. As creativity expert Teresa Amabile says: "money doesn't necessarily stop people from being creative, but in many situations, it doesn't help" (1998). If we want the person to feel empowered by doing the activity, we need to be praising the activity itself or making the activity more enjoyable. This is like the parenting philosophy of praising children for their good *efforts* as opposed to praising or rewarding outcomes: "Emphasizing effort gives a child a variable that they can control" (Bronson, 2007; Dweck, 2007). Sometimes when you reward a previously unrewarded activity, it can kill any preexisting intrinsic motivation and therefore make extrinsic motivation a requirement for that activity. This is called the *overjustification effect*. A classic study of this phenomena involved rewarding 3–5-year-old children for simply drawing with markers. Once the reward was removed, those children *used markers less often* than children who were not previously rewarded for the activity (Lepper et al., 1973).

In a classroom setting, grades and teacher approval may decrease interest in the actual content and activities (Lepper & Henderlong, 2000; Lillard, 2013). Too often in school, activities involve "do this assignment in this way, and, if you don't, you'll get *bad* grades." Grades are extrinsic motivation. Grades are results-focused. And grades try very much to impact the real world. Grades conflict with the requirements for an activity to be play. Try to recall a time in school or your career when a teacher or supervisor asked you to just explore a topic for fun and do *whatever* you *want to do* to get interested in something (like what you may see in a Montessori environment). "In both playful learning and Montessori education, the activities are intrinsically rewarding, and extrinsic rewards are not offered...the intrinsic reward of learning is an end in itself" (Lillard, 2013). Some industries are now adopting the Montessori-like practice of allowing a person to choose what they want to work on via *side project time*. One of the early pioneers of this practice is 3M, which began their *15% Time policy* in 1948, allowing employees to pursue personal projects with 15% of their paid time (Goetz, 2011). This process likely inspired Google's *20% Project* of a similar nature (Goetz, 2011). These types of agreements allow employees to engage in self-directed (internally motivated) work that should not impact their job if things don't work out (internal reality/pretense) with no required outcome (process-focused). The result should make their work fall somewhere closer to play on the work–play scale. Furthermore, it has shown to lead to some real innovation, such as the creation of Gmail, Google Earth, and 3M's Post-It notes (Goetz, 2011). Comedian and member of Monty Python, John Cleese, is quoted as saying: "If you want creative workers, give them enough time to play." This thread is woven throughout his academic journal article in which he connects both humor and play to creativity (Cleese, 1991). He specifically describes this concept of *side project time* to bring play into the workspace:

> You can't become playful and, therefore, creative if you're under your usual pressures...you have to create some space for yourself away from those demands...now creativity can happen, because play is possible when you're separated from everyday life.

> (Cleese, 1991)

So, I have a question for you. If you refer to the activity that we did in the Introduction, the Alternative Uses Test with a paper clip, where would you place *that* activity on the scale of work to play in Figure 21.1? I realize that I *asked* you to do the activity and we have been discussing the results as if they are important; however, I still want you to think about how you felt during the experience of doing the activity and place it somewhere on this continuum.

Decided?

I conducted a study that looked at the relationship between playfulness and creativity. I gave the same Alternative Uses Test that you completed to 106 employees (all patent awardees) of a large medical device company. Afterward, I asked them to rate the playfulness of the activity using the same scale of work to play (with a score of 1 being work and a score of 5 being play). As I mentioned in the Introduction, a way of scoring creativity in this test is by counting the number of responses. When I averaged the creativity scores from each work–play rating group, what I found was not surprising. The people who viewed the activity as work had *half* the number of ideas as the people

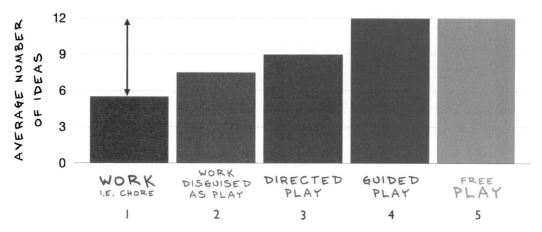

Figure 21.2 The relationship between number of ideas produced in the Alternative Uses Test and self-assessed rating of playfulness of the test from 106 scientists and engineers working at a medical device company (Kudrowitz et al., 2016). Those who viewed the test as play (i.e., rating a play score of 4 or 5) produced on average twice as many ideas as those who viewed the test as work (i.e., rating a work score of 1).

who viewed the activity as play. **When you view an activity as play, you are going to be more creative in that activity** (Kudrowitz et al., 2016). Additionally, in this study, we used another measure of creativity—a more *applied* measure—that this medical device company highly valued: *patents*. Those employees who viewed this specific activity as play had *five times as many patents as those who viewed the activity as work* (Kudrowitz et al., 2016).

So, where did this Alternative Uses Test fall on *your* work–play scale? If you didn't view it as play, that's OK, we will talk about that in Chapter 23.

In the words of the Oracle from the *Matrix*, the question that is "really going to bake your noodle" (Wachowski, 1999) is: are you more creative because you view the activity as play, *or* do you view the activity as playful because you are able to be creative with it. The answer to that question is not that critical for now. What matters is that the two items are strongly tied together. There are many other studies that have found similar results (Lieberman, 1965; Johnson, 1976; Russ & Grossman-McKee, 1990; Russ et al., 1999; Wyver & Spence, 1999; Bateson, 2015). Playing and playfulness have been found to correlate specifically with divergent thinking (Dansky & Silverman, 1973; Lieberman, 1977; Russ, 2003), as well as the Torrance Test of Creative Thinking (Berretta & Privette, 1990). Children who were allowed to play freely with everyday objects (like paper clips, a screwdriver, and a wooden board) generated significantly more nonstandard responses about the use of those objects than those children who simply watched adults using them (Dansky & Silverman, 1973). A related study found that children who played with objects (specifically, sticks and clamps) were more likely to solve a problem that required the use of those objects than children who did not have the opportunity to play with the objects beforehand (Sylva et al., 1976).

So, what exactly is happening when you are playing that leads you to be more creative?

References

Amabile, T. (1998). How to kill creativity. *Harvard Business Review.*

Bateson, P. (2015). Playfulness and creativity. *Current Biology, 25*(1), R12–R16.

Bergen, D. (1998). Using a schema for play and learning. In D. Bergen (Ed.), *Play as a medium for learning and development* (pp. 11–28). Association for Childhood Education International.

Berretta, S., & Privette, G. (1990). Influence of play on creative thinking. *Perceptual and Motor Skills, 71*, 659–666.

Bronson, P. (2007, February 9). How not to talk to your kids. *New Yorker Magazine.*

Cleese, J. (1991). And now for something completely different. *Management Review, 80*(5), 50.

Dansky, J. L., & Silverman, I. W. (1973). Effects of play on associative fluency in preschool-aged children. *Developmental Psychology, 9*(1), 38–43.

Dweck, C. (2007). *Mindset: The new psychology of success.* Ballantine Books.

Fröbel, F., & Hailmann, W. N. (1887). *The education of man.* D. Appleton and Co.

Goetz, K. (2011, February 1). How 3M gave everyone days off and created an innovation dynamo. *Fast Company.*

Huizinga, J. (1950). *Homo Ludens: A study of the play-element in culture.* Roy Publishers.

Johnson, J. E. (1976). Relations of divergent thinking and intelligence test scores with social and Nonsocial make-believe play of preschool children. *ETS Research Bulletin Series, 1*, i–16.

Judge, M. (Director). (1999). *Office Space [Motion picture].* United States: 20th Century Fox.

Kudrowitz, B., Alfalah, S., & Dippo, C. (2016). The Mary Poppins effect: Exploring a relationship between playfulness and creativity with the alternative uses test. *Proceedings - D and E 2016: 10th International Conference on Design and Emotion - Celebration and Contemplation*, 459–464.

Lepper, M. R., Greene, D., & Nisbett, R. E. (1973). Undermining children's intrinsic interest with extrinsic reward: A test of the "overjustification" hypothesis. *Journal of Personality and Social Psychology, 28*(1), 129–137.

Lepper, M. R., & Henderlong, J. (2000). Turning 'Play' into 'Work' and 'Work' into 'Play': 25 Years of research on intrinsic versus extrinsic motivation. In C. Sansone & J. M. Harackiewicz (Eds.), *Intrinsic and extrinsic motivation: The search for optimal motivation and performance* (pp. 257–307). Academic Press.

Lieberman, J. N. (1965). Playfulness and divergent thinking: An investigation of their relationship at the kindergarten level. *The Journal of Genetic Psychology, 107*(2), 219–224.

Lieberman, J. N. (1977). *Playfulness: Its relationship to imagination and creativity* (A. J. Edwards, Ed.). Academic Press.

Lillard, A. S. (2013). Playful learning and Montessori education. *American Journal of Play, 5*(2), 157–186.

Montessori, M. (1912). *The Montessori method*, Translated by A. E. George. Frederick A. Stokes Company.

Rogers, F. (1995). *You are special: Neighborly words of wisdom from mister Rogers.* Penguin Books.

RuPaul (1992). *Supermodel (you better work)/house of love.* Tommy Boy Music, LLC.

Russ, S. W. (2003). Play and creativity: Developmental issues. *Scandinavian Journal of Educational Research, 47*(3), 291–303.

Russ, S. W., & Grossman-McKee, A. (1990). Affective expression in children's fantasy play, primary process thinking on the Rorschach, and divergent thinking. *Journal of Personality Assessment, 54*(3–4), 756–771.

Russ, S. W., Robins, A. L., & Christiano, B. A. (1999). Pretend play: Longitudinal prediction of creativity and affect in fantasy in children. *Creativity Research Journal, 12*(2), 129–139.

Sylva, K., Bruner, J. S., &. Genova, P. (1976). The role of play in the problem-solving of children. In J. S. Bruner, A. Jolly, & K. Sylva (Eds.), *Play: Its role in development and evolution* (pp. 244–257). Penguin.

Twain, M. (1876). *The adventures of tom sawyer.* American Publishing Company.

Wachowski. L., & Wachowski, L. (Directors). (1999). *The Matrix [Motion picture].* United States: Warner Bros.

Wing, L. A. (1995). Play is not the work of the child: Young children's perceptions of work and play. *Early Childhood Research Quarterly, 10*(2), 223–247.

Wyver, S. R., & Spence, S. H. (1999). Play and divergent problem solving: Evidence supporting a reciprocal relationship. *Early Education and Development, 10*(4), 419–444.

22

PLAY–CREATIVITY CONNECTIONS, *THE LITTLE PRINCE*, AND POSITIVE AFFECT

Play allows us to escape reality. It is a safe bubble in which we pretend, imagine, and create. It allows us to say and do things that we don't typically say and do. It makes sense that multiple studies have found a connection between playing and creativity. This specific relationship is also the main topic of at least five (mostly academic) books (Lieberman, 1977; Russ, 1993; Bateson & Martin, 2013; Johnson, 2016; Resnick, 2018). In this chapter, I will discuss a few theories that help explain this relationship. I will use the criteria discussed in Chapter 20 of what makes something play (*active engagement, intrinsic motivation/process-focused,* and *pretense/internal reality*) as an organizational structure to identify the theoretical connections between play and creativity. I will also add two additional considerations: *positive affect*, which often accompanies play, and *spontaneity*, which some argue is a core criterion of play (Lieberman, 1977; Bateson & Martin, 2013). Figure 22.1 illustrates how these five concepts of play relate to the four requisites of creativity from Chapter 1.

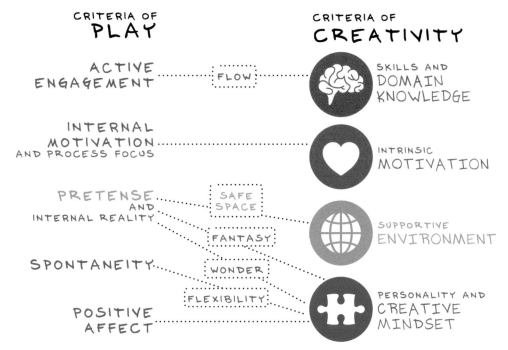

Figure 22.1 A theoretical mapping of some of the links between play and creativity.

DOI: 10.4324/9781003276296-26

Active Engagement

As shown in Figure 22.1, *flow* is often used to characterize a creative process just as it is used to characterize a playful activity. There is an entire book on this topic: *Creativity: Flow and the Psychology of Discovery and Invention* (Csikszentmihalyi, 2013). Flow occurs when the challenge meets the skill set of the individual. If the person does not have the proper skills or knowledge to perform the task, they are not going be in a state of flow and they will likely not view the activity as play. Play, like creativity, requires some level of familiarity with the subject matter and domain knowledge. This is related to the threshold hypothesis of Chapter 1: to be creative within a given domain, you need to have some familiarity with that domain. As you master a domain, you will find opportunities for creation and invention. From a play perspective, "Once the novel become familiar...the playful attitude of playfulness can set in" (Lieberman, 1977). This is perhaps why it's difficult to separate out the causal relationship between being fluent with the Alternative Uses Test and viewing that activity as play. Those who have significant cognitive skills and a collection of knowledge have a mastery that allows them to *both* play within the activity *and* be fluent in that activity.

Internal Motivation

Internal or *intrinsic motivation* is not just required for play, as described in Chapter 20, it is also one of the four requisites of creativity as described in Chapter 1 (Amabile, 1996; de Jesus et al., 2013). When you are intrinsically motivated to do an activity, you will be more persistent and dedicated in problem-solving and more likely to be creative. This is best summarized by Teresa Amabile's *Intrinsic Motivation Principle of Creativity* in that "people will be most creative when they feel motivated primarily by the interest, satisfaction, and challenge of the work itself—and not by external pressures" (Amabile, 1998). To not repeat content from Chapters 1 and 20, the transitive property suggests that because play requires intrinsic motivation and intrinsic motivation leads to creativity, play should therefore lead to creativity.

Pretense and Internal Reality

Pretense is connected to creativity in a few different contexts: it provides a safe space, it is fantasy, and it facilitates wonder.

Safe Space

Play requires a protected context and environment, just like creativity requires a supportive environment. Both play and creativity require "freedom from burdensome constraints and the availability of a stress-free (but not excessively relaxing) environment" (Bateson & Martin, 2013). John Cleese ties these domains together nicely:

> You cannot be playful if you're frightened that moving in some direction will be 'wrong.' You're either free to play or you're not. The best way to get the confidence to do that is to know that while you're being creative, nothing is wrong. There's no such thing as a mistake. Any drivel may lead to a breakthrough.

(1991)

As play is "not real," the activity is ***free from fear of failure***. In play, there are (generally) no real dangers and you can experiment and try things that you wouldn't normally do. *If it doesn't work out, it doesn't matter* because you are doing it for the process and for the experience, but not for the results (e.g., *side project time* discussed in Chapter 21). You may have heard the phrase "fail fast" and "fail often." Research suggests that more small failures lead to higher quality R&D output (Khanna et al., 2016) and "organizations learn more effectively from failures than successes" (Madsen & Desai, 2010). Even though some companies and instructors may not fully mean it when they say it, while in a play state, you can fail fast and often, and it doesn't matter. *This is how we learn as children, and it is also how we learn as adults.* Scientists throughout history who have produced many great works have also produced many additional bad works too (Begley & Ramo, 1993). When we fail, we learn what doesn't work, we learn what not to do, and we gain experience.

Failure is not binary: there is a spectrum of reasons for failure from preventable failures caused by negligence, deviance, or inattention, to complexity-related failures due to complicated processes, to intelligent failures that come from experimentation (Edmondson, 2011). We may learn from *all* failures, but the ones we should be encouraging are more of the latter variety. Industry and academia have simply made it too scary or risky to fail. We tend to only celebrate and report on the successes and then brush the failed attempts under the rug. When we hear success stories of inventions, we don't hear about the many unsuccessful attempts that are inevitable and part of the creative process. In highlighting only the success stories of famous creatives (e.g., Einstein, Curie, and Faraday), we may be inadvertently steering students away from math and science (Lin-Siegler et al., 2016).

The Phantom Tollbooth provides some good advice related to this. The protagonist, Milo, is advised by Princess Reason:

> You must never feel badly about making mistakes...as long as you take the trouble to learn from them. For you often learn more by being wrong for the right reasons than you do by being right for the wrong reasons.

> (Juster, 1961)

I often hear students say they don't want to take a drawing class because they are not good at drawing. That is exactly why you should take a class! *Jake the Dog* from *Adventure Time* said this best: "Suckin' at something is the first step towards being sorta good at something" (Ward et al., 2010).

Fantasy

When we engage in fantasy play, we are making up things, and that is inherently creative. Fantasy play is free from restrictions provided by reality. When you play, you are *pretending*, and that puts you in a domain where anything is possible. You can be *uninhibited in your thinking*, and uninhibited thinking can lead to creativity and discovery. In Chapter 17, I discussed the multiple reasons why cartoons and science fiction media allow for creativity. In essence, when things are not real, you can suggest anything and it's OK. At a deeper level, fantasy play is connected to a variety of cognitive creative processes including: divergent thinking, free association, fluidity of thinking, verbal fluency, transformation abilities, cognitive flexibility, shifting sets, and reordering information (Singer & Singer, 1976; Russ, 2003). Specifically, fantasy play is like divergent thinking in that it requires "breadth-of-attention deployment," which is the process of scanning your environment and memories in an associational manner (Russ, 2003). In fantasy play, one is collecting these memories, ideas, and stimuli, recombining them, and divorcing them from reality (Singer, 1973; Sherrod & Singer, 1989). Fantasy play allows us to loosen old associations (e.g., this paperclip is not just for holding paper, this box is not just for shipping things), which then allows for new non-obvious associations to be made (Dansky, 1980). It is understandable that children and adults who engage in more fantasy-based thoughts are more creative than those who do not (Lieberman, 1977; Russ, 2003).

Wonder

Play is how we learn, and so it makes sense that play and wonder (i.e., *curiosity*) go hand in hand. When we are playing, curiosity will lead to "what if?" questions, attempts in *doing things differently*, and *challenging assumptions* of the way things should be. In the paper clip Alternative Uses Test, there can be play in wondering about uses for that object that are not intended. This requires challenging assumptions of the obvious uses (breaking object permanence) just like a child does with a cardboard box. Children are great at challenging assumptions. It could be because children simply don't know what society expects of them and/or they do not come with the biases of prior experience, tradition, and habit. Children are therefore better at *questioning the status quo* than adults. That questioning sometimes comes in the form of asking "why?"... often aloud... and over and over again. John Locke said this best as: "There is frequently more to be learned from the unexpected questions of a child than the discourses of men, who talk in a road, according to the notions they have borrowed and the prejudices of their education" (Locke, 1693).

In *The Little Prince*, the child narrator draws a picture with colored pencils of a boa constrictor digesting an elephant (reinterpreted in Figure 22.2) that he titles "Drawing Number One" (de Saint-Exupéry, 1943). His drawing gets interpreted as a hat by the adults in the story. He then explains how he uses this drawing as somewhat of a creative barometer to evaluate if adults are wonderworthy.

> Whenever I encountered a grown-up who seemed to me at all enlightened, I would experiment on him with my drawing Number One, which I have always kept. I wanted to see if he really understood anything. But he would always answer, 'That's a hat.' Then I wouldn't talk about boa constrictors or jungles or stars. I would put myself on his level and talk about bridge and golf and politics and neckties. And my grown-up was glad to know such a reasonable person.
>
> (de Saint-Exupéry, 1943)

The little prince was giving people a version of the incomplete figures test (from the Torrance Test of Creative Thinking) to see if the person can think outside of the box, wonder, and provide a non-obvious response. If the person passed, they were deemed worthy of playing pretend and wondering together.

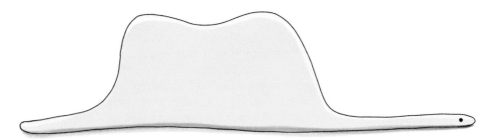

Figure 22.2 Interpretation of "Drawing Number One" from *The Little Prince* (de Saint-Exupéry, 1943). The little prince intends for his drawing to represent a "boa constrictor digesting an elephant" whereas adults see just a hat.

Spontaneity and Flexibility

Spontaneity (i.e., whim or unplanned action) is argued to be a hallmark of play (Lieberman, 1977; Bateson & Martin, 2013). In watching children play, they seem to pull ideas and thoughts from nowhere that take the play in unexpected and unpredictable directions. As you may recall from Chapter 6, flexibility (i.e., not being fixated) is one of the four components of the Torrance Test of Creative Thinking. Lieberman suggests that spontaneity and flexibility are essentially the same thing with spontaneity being internally motivated and flexibility being externally motivated (1977).

Guilford simply combines both words as a term to describe divergent thinking: *spontaneous flexibility* (1956).

To borrow an analogy that applies to both play and creativity, spontaneity

> operates like the whirl of the kaleidoscope. The bits and pieces of glass are the givens or familiar facts. The twist of the hand produces ever-different pictures with the same components. If we add to this the recombining of the components into unique and original patterns, we have spelled out the relationship between spontaneity and the creative product.
>
> (Lieberman, 1977)

Older individuals (i.e., adults), should have more "bits and pieces of glass" in their "kaleidoscope," and so the *potential* for spontaneous behavior should increase with age. Unfortunately, as we age, we tend to not bother playing with "kaleidoscopes" as they are not "age-appropriate."

The circles test in Chapter 5 and the Alternative Uses Test from the Introduction are both tests of "*spontaneous flexibility*." If we are playing during this activity, we are "breaking away from established patterns and combining actions or thoughts in new ways," which "is a powerful means of gaining new insights and opening up possibilities the had not previously been recognized" (Bateson & Martin, 2013). This is why children generate more alternative uses for an object when they have the opportunity to play with it first (Dansky & Silverman, 1973).

Positive Affect

Positive affect is not necessarily required for play, but it often occurs with play. *Affect* is any feeling or emotion distinct from cognition such as happiness, anxiety, sadness, and frustration (Russ, 2003). Lieberman describes the concept of "playfulness" (being a personality trait or state of mind) as requiring three elements: "physical, social, and cognitive spontaneity, manifest joy, and sense of humor" (Lieberman, 1977). Although "joy" may not be found in all types of play, Lieberman suggests that it is a requirement for a playful personality or state of mind. If being playful does not directly cause you to be creative, dedicating time to play as a means of catharsis, relaxation, and enjoyment could result in unexpected connections, realizations, epiphanies, and adventures.

Simply having fun and being in a state of positive affect arouses curiosity, reduces anxiety, and was shown to increase creative thought processes (Isen et al., 1985; Isen et al., 1987; Russ, 1993; Norman, 2005). Inducing positive affect states, for example by watching a comedy film, increases creative thinking ability (Isen et al., 1987). Isen et al. suggest that positive effect states increase one's tendency to make novel combinations of information and to see novel connections between divergent stimuli (1985, 1987). Additionally, Isen et al. found that positive affect improved convergent thinking as measured by the Remote Associates Test. It is suggested that positive affect cues positive memories and a large quantity of cognitive materials, which in turn diffuses focus (Chapter 8) and allows for non-obvious associations (Russ, 2003). In general, you are more likely to make insight connections and creatively solve problems if you are in a positive mood (Greene & Noice, 1988; Jausovec, 1989). A meta-analytic review of 72 studies on mood–creativity research concluded that positive mood enhances creativity (Davis, 2009). Specifically, Davis found a "strong relationship between positive mood and creative thinking or ideation" and there were no instances of increased creativity from negative moods (2009).

In summary, the elements of what makes an activity play can be individually linked to the elements that facilitate an individual's creative ability in the moment. In Chapter 23, we will step back and look at how one's play as a child might impact the creativity of that future adult.

References

Amabile, T. M. (1996). *Creativity in context: Update to "the social psychology of creativity."* Westview Press.

Amabile, T. (1998). How to kill creativity. *Harvard Business Review.*

Bateson, P., & Martin, P. (2013). *Play, playfulness, creativity and innovation.* Cambridge University Press.

Begley, S., & Ramo, J. C. (1993). The puzzle of genius. *Newsweek, 121*(26), 46–53.

Cleese, J. (1991). And now for something completely different. *Management Review, 80*(5), 50.

Csikszentmihalyi, M. (2013). *Creativity: Flow and the psychology of discovery and invention.* Harper Perennial.

Dansky, J. L. (1980). Make-believe: A mediator of the relationship between play and associative fluency. *Child Development, 51*(2), 576–579.

Dansky, J. L., & Silverman, I. W. (1973). Effects of play on associative fluency in preschool-aged children. *Developmental Psychology, 9*(1), 38–43.

Davis, M. A. (2009). Understanding the relationship between mood and creativity: A meta-analysis. *Organizational Behavior and Human Decision Processes, 108*(1), 25–38.

de Jesus, S. N., Rus, C. L., Lens, W., & Imaginário, S. (2013). Intrinsic motivation and creativity related to product: A meta-analysis of the studies published between 1990–2010. *Creativity Research Journal, 25*(1), 80–84.

de Saint-Exupéry, A. (1943). *The little prince.* Harcourt Inc.

Edmondson, A. C. (2011). Strategies for learning from failure. *Harvard Business Review, 89*(4), 48–55.

Greene, T. R., & Noice, H. (1988). Influence of positive affect upon creative thinking and problem solving in children. *Psychological Reports, 63*(3), 895–898.

Guilford, J. P. (1956). The structure of intellect. *Psychological Bulletin, 53*(4), 267–293.

Isen, A. M., Daubman, K. A., & Nowicki, G. P. (1987). Positive affect facilitates creative problem solving. *Journal of Personality and Social Psychology, 52*(6), 1122–1131.

Isen, A. M., Johnson, M. M., Mertz, E., & Robinson, G. F. (1985). The influence of positive affect on the unusualness of word associations. *Journal of Personality and Social Psychology, 48*(6), 1413–1426.

Jausovec, N. (1989). Affect in analogical transfer. *Creativity Research Journal, 2*(4), 255–266.

Johnson, S. (2016). *Wonderland: How play made the modern world.* Riverhead Books.

Juster, N. (1961). *The phantom tollbooth.* Random House.

Khanna, R., Guler, I., & Nerkar, A. (2016). Fail often, fail big, and fail fast? learning from small failures and R&D performance in the pharmaceutical industry. *Academy of Management Journal, 59*, 436–459.

Lieberman, J. N. (1977). *Playfulness: Its relationship to imagination and creativity* (A. J. Edwards, Ed.). Academic Press.

Lin-Siegler, X., Ahn, J. N., Chen, J., Fang, F.-F. A., & Luna-Lucero, M. (2016). Even Einstein struggled: Effects of learning about great scientists' struggles on high school students' motivation to learn science. *Journal of Educational Psychology, 108*(3), 314–328.

Locke, J. (1693). *Some thoughts concerning education.* A. and J. Churchill.

Madsen, P. M., & Desai, V. (2010). Failing to learn? The effects of failure and success on organizational learning in the global orbital launch vehicle industry. *Academy of Management Journal, 53*, 451–476.

Norman, D. (2005). *Emotional design: Why we love (or hate) everyday things.* Basic Books.

Resnick, M. (2018). *Lifelong kindergarten: Cultivating creativity through projects, passion, peers, and play.* The MIT Press.

Russ, S. W. (1993). *Affect and creativity: The role of affect and play in the creative process.* Lawrence Erlbaum Associates, Inc.

Sherrod, L., & Singer, J. (1989). The development of make-believe play. In J. H. Goldstein (Ed.), *Sports, games and play* (pp. 1–38). Erlbaum.

Singer, J. L. (1973). *The child's world of make-believe: Experimental studies of imaginative play.* Academic Press.

Singer, J. L., & Singer, D. G. (1976). Imaginative play and pretending in early childhood: Some experimental approaches. In A. Davids (Ed.), *Child personality and psychopathology* (Vol. 3, pp. 69–112). Wiley.

Ward, P., & Williams, M. (Writers), & Leichliter, L. (Director). (2010, September 20). His Hero. [Television series episode]. In Crews, K. (Producer), *Adventure Time*, Cartoon Network.

23

STEVE JOBS VS. MARY POPPINS,
KINDERGARTEN, AND SPINACH BROWNIES

In Chapter 22, we explored how play immediately inspires creativity, but there are also long-term creative benefits of play that could take years to develop. Several scholars including Plato, Kant, and Freud argued the importance of play as a child for a well-developed adult, but Herbert Spencer was the first to argue that play as a child leads to more creativity in adulthood (Spencer, 1872; Bateson & Martin, 2013). "Experiences gained during play can be used later in life and put together in novel ways to solve new problems" (Bateson & Martin, 2013).

Before *Fredrick Fröbel*'s invention of *kindergarten* in the 1830s, children under the age of seven did not attend school and were viewed as "small people" engaged in "useless activities" (Brosterman, 1997). Fröbel created this revolutionary movement to teach children through play. Like Montessori, these activities were often referred to as "work," but they were very playful. Fröbel developed a series of materials (objects and activities) that he referred to as "gifts" and "occupations." These begin with simple items (e.g., gift number 1: six colorful yarn balls) and gradually become more complex (e.g., gift number 14: weaving papers) (Brosterman, 1997). The gifts are intended to be used in different manners as the child develops. As an example: "The eight cubes of the third gift [shown in Figure 23.1] that children had just made into chairs and stoves in their mother's kitchens would now be laid in rows and expressed as 2x4 or 4+4" (Brosterman, 1997). "The final piece of this Fröbelian puzzle was a block of clay [shown in Figure 23.1 as the Twentieth Gift]. Malleable but solid, it could be shaped into virtually any form and thus allow for endless possibilities" (Kohlstedt, 2019).

These gifts inspired the work of some of the greatest creative minds in history. *Frank Lloyd Wright* explicitly credits the Fröbel gifts as the foundation for his architectural work (Brosterman, 1997). In *Inventing Kindergarten*, Brosterman provides uncanny side-by-side comparisons of how famous artists and designers (such as Paul Klee, Wassily Kandinsky, Walter Gropius of the Bauhaus, Le Corbusier, Buckminster Fuller, etc.) were inspired by their original Fröbel kindergarten gifts (1997). As an example, "the nineteenth gift [peas work, shown in Figure 23.1] provided the occasion for the first structural experiments of the architect R. Buckminster Fuller (1895–1983), which ultimately led to his invention of the geodesic dome" (Brosterman, 1997). In the same vein, but not explicitly linked to Fröbel, Watson and Crick developed their model of DNA by playing with a "children's toy"—a set of colorful balls (i.e., Fröbel's first gift) (Watson, 1981).

In short, the play you engage in as a child has great impact on you as a creative adult. Mr. Rogers said, "children's play is not just kids' stuff. Children's play is rather the stuff of most future inventions. Think how many people played about going to the moon before that was ever a reality. Let

DOI: 10.4324/9781003276296-27

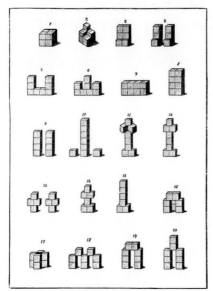

PLATE III.—THE THIRD GIFT.

PLATE XII.—THE TENTH GIFT.

PLATE XXI.—THE NINETEENTH GIFT.

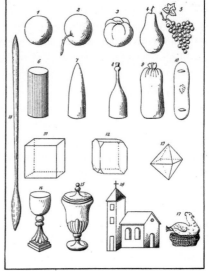

PLATE XXII.—THE TWENTIETH GIFT.

Figure 23.1 Examples of Fredrick Fröbel's gifts from Van Norstrand's *Royal gifts for the kindergarten* (1889). Retrieved from the Library of Congress, public domain. The third gift is a set of wooden blocks that the child may use to arrange into different configurations to represent different things as well as practice fine motor skills and learn basic math. The tenth gift is a grid-based drawing workbook, grid-based drawing slate, and pencil. This allows the child to practice drawing basic lines, shapes, and eventually to draw objects using a grid to help understand proportions. The nineteenth gift is a set of peas (or wax or cork) and wire (or sticks) for the child to create two- and three-dimensional geometric forms. The twentieth gift (the last gift) is modeling clay for the child to make simple geometric forms and eventually open-ended creations (Van Norstrand, 1889; Brosterman, 1997).

your imagination help you know the truth about your identity" (2005). There are a few studies to support this. Singer found that creative adults reported higher levels of childhood imaginative play than less creatively oriented adults (1973). One of my studies found a moderately strong relationship between the quantity of creation-related toys someone recalled enjoying as a child and their creativity scores as an adult (Johnson & Kudrowitz, 2015). If we want to be innovative, we need to continue to encourage play throughout our lives from childhood to the classroom, and into our occupational setting (Lieberman, 1977).

With the discussion in Chapters 20–22 on how important play is for creative production, you might be thinking: "If I don't view an activity as play and I want to (or am required to) be creative in that activity, what should I do?"

There are two paths here: the *Steve Jobs* approach and the *Mary Poppins* approach. This is a bit like Morpheus offering Neo a red pill and blue pill (Wachowski & Wachowski, 1999). One path is to get out of the Matrix and the other path is to stay and figure out how to make it work *(or...play)*.

In Steve Jobs' Stanford Commencement Speech in 2005, he said "your work is going to fill a large part of your life, and the only way to be truly satisfied is to do what you believe is great work. And the only way to do great work is to love what you do. If you haven't found it yet, keep looking. Don't settle" (Jobs, 2005). Making a small cognitive step here to tie this to play: *if you don't view an activity as play, you are not going to be creative with that activity*. Steve Jobs would suggest doing something else that you do love and naturally find to be joyful. Torrance suggested a similar theory: "The essence of the creative person is being in love with what one is doing" (Torrance, 1988).

An *alternative* view is provided by Disney's *Mary Poppins*: "...in every job that must be done, there is an element of fun. You find the fun, and—SNAP—the job's a game (Stevenson, 1964)!" Mary Poppins believes that one can find play in *any* activity. As play and work are a state of mind (as per Chapter 18) and are on a continuum (as per Chapter 21), in theory, any activity can be moved away from work and more toward play. The trick is figuring out how to find the play.

In the film, Mary Poppins suggests that the children play a game of tidying up the nursery. The children question if this is really a game, to which Mary Poppins replies that it is all about their point of view (Stevenson, 1964). In addition to reminding children that play is a state of mind, she is also suggesting that an activity that is typically viewed as a chore (e.g., cleaning the nursery) can be viewed as play with a change in perspective.

Aside from using magic to clean the house, there are a few things that the film suggests that transform a chore into a game. As Mary Poppins starts to clean the nursery, the first thing she does is close the dresser drawer with her bum. This act is captivating, process-focused, and imaginative. And, although it was probably added to the scene as a joke, it is an example of turning a rote task into something more playful. Another example, which gets the most attention in the musical number, is suggesting that the children sing while they work as robins do while feathering a nest. This message is in line with another Disney song: *Whistle While You Work*. Although the concept is catchy and will seemingly "move the job along," it is not about finding the fun in the activity itself: it is simply masking the activity with something else that you might enjoy (like literally making the medicine go down with sugar). This method is akin to hiding vegetables in dessert if you want children to eat more vegetables. I call this putting "*spinach in the brownies*." If we hide spinach in brownies, we are only making crappy brownies while simultaneously missing an opportunity to show children how delicious spinach could be.

Figure 23.2 There is a difference between masking an activity with some unrelated fun ("spinach in the brownies" or "Whistle While You Work") and finding the inherent fun within a given activity.

In school, you may recall playing some form of game to learn a concept (such as *Jeopardy* with historical facts). In this case, are you learning to enjoy history or are you just finding play value in the *Jeopardy*-style game (i.e., "making spinach brownies")? And if it is just about the game, are you playing to win or is it about the process itself? There are other ways to learn about history that could transform the *content* into the playful part. Coming from an engineering education, I often see *robot competitions* as a means of teaching mechanical design. If you want someone to find a passion for the subject matter, you have to find fun in the content itself and not hide the content in a game or competition (i.e., "making spinach brownies"). Not everyone is motivated to learn through competition. For example, at the University of Minnesota, the mechanical engineering department teaches engineering design in a slightly different manner. Their introductory design class is not about competition; it's about self-selected interests driving the learning process. Students are tasked to "design and construct an autonomous machine that does something interesting for 45 seconds" (Durfee, 2003). They can make a robot that does *anything the student wants* as long as it meets a few simple constraints (e.g., size, cost, microprocessor-controlled, safe, at least one moving part, no interaction with the operator while running). The students literally have *freedom of movement within given constraints* to play. If you attend the final event for this class, which is more of a *showcase* than a competition, you will see robots that chop vegetables, play guitar, shuffle cards, draw pictures, etc. In this case, the students are getting exposed to principles of robotics through a topic of *their own choosing* and the goal is not to win or have the best design or beat others. Instead, the primary goal is to learn through creating something that one is passionate about. This makes the activity of developing the robot more engaging for the students, and it also makes the final showcase much more engaging for a wider variety of attendees.

So, let's assume we want to take the Mary Poppins approach, in Chapter 24 we will discuss methods that we can employ to take an activity (perhaps a career obligation or a chore) and make it more playful.

References

Bateson, P., & Martin, P. (2013). *Play, playfulness, creativity and innovation.* Cambridge University Press.

Brosterman, N. (1997). *Inventing kindergarten.* Harry N. Abrams Inc.

Durfee, W. (2003). Mechatronics for the masses: A hands-on project for a large, introductory design class. *International Journal of Engineering Education, 19*(4), 593–596.

Jobs, S. (2005, June 12). *Stanford commencement address.* Stanford University.

Johnson, K., & Kudrowitz, B. (2015, November). A relationship between physical construction play as children and adult creativity scores. *IASDR InterPlay 2015.* Brisbane, Australia.

Kohlstedt, K. (Producer). (2019, April 9). Froebel's Gifts (Episode 349). [Audio podcast episode]. In *99% Invisible.* PRX.

Lieberman, J. N. (1977). *Playfulness: Its relationship to imagination and creativity* (A. J. Edwards, Ed.). Academic Press.

Rogers, F. (2005). *Life's journeys according to mister Rogers.* Hachette Books.

Singer, J. L. (1973). *The child's world of make-believe: Experimental studies of imaginative play.* Academic Press.

Spencer, H. (1872). *Principles of psychology* (2nd Edition). Appleton.

Stevenson, R. (Director). (1964). *Mary Poppins [Motion picture].* Walt Disney Productions.

Torrance, E. (1988). The nature of creativity as manifest in its testing. In R. Sternberg (Ed.), *The nature of creativity* (pp. 43–73). University Press.

Van Norstrand, F. P. (1889) *Royal gifts for the kindergarten, a manual for self instruction in Friedrich Froebel's principles of education; together with a collection of songs, games, and poems for the home, the kindergarten and the primary school.* Chicago, Standard Pub. Co.

Wachowski, L., & Wachowski, L. (Directors). (1999). *The Matrix [Motion picture].* United States: Warner Bros.

Watson, J. D. (1981). *The double helix: A personal account of the discovery of the structure of DNA.* Weidenfeld and Nicolson.

24
ADDING PLAY VALUE, *OVERCOOKED*, AND THE HOLLE BOLLE GIJS

To push an activity along the work–play scale, one must find a way of strengthening the three criteria of play discussed in Chapter 20.

Active Engagement, Intrinsic Motivation, and Pretense

Active Engagement

How can you make the activity more captivating? How can you adjust the challenge to match your skill set? Alternatively, can you build your skill set to match the challenge? This technique of adjusting for flow to keep things playful was discussed in Chapter 20 with the "Keepy Uppy" example of Figure 20.2. Let's explore this concept with some real examples.

Tiger Woods would "throw balls into the trees, have them drop randomly into the thick rough, and try to make par anyway because it was more fun" (Brown, 2009). This is how Woods added challenge to shift the activity back into a state of flow (and play). Jack White of *The White Stripes* intentionally adds challenge to his performances to keep them engaging for him such that they stay engaging for the audience. He moves his instruments farther apart on stage for each show to force him to run between instruments, he uses instruments that are difficult to stay in tune, and he makes up the set list in real time. "All these components force [him] to create" (Malloy, 2009). Timothy Parker (a.k.a. Gift of Gab) released the song Alphabet Aerobics in 1999 as a member of the duo *Blackalicious* (Breihan, 2021). Rap in general presents the challenge of creating meaningful lyrics that incorporate a rhyme scheme. In this song, Parker increases the challenge by writing the narrative entirely in alphabetical order while increasing the tempo throughout the song (Breihan, 2021). Mozart, who was known for his playfulness, allegedly

> composed a piece of music where, at one point, both hands were at the right end of the piano keyboard and a note had to be struck at the far left. The challenge was that nobody could play this. Whereupon Mozart, who was blessed with a rather long and pointy nose, demonstrated that while his hands were at the other side of the keyboard, he could, with his nose, strike the note.
>
> (Lieberman, 1977)

Theodore Geisel (Dr. Seuss) wrote *Green Eggs and Ham* based on a challenge from his publisher to create a compelling children's story using only 50 words (Haught-Tromp, 2017). These are all examples of the play concept of *self-handicapping* in which "animals actively seek and create unexpected situations in play" by "deliberately relaxing control over their movements or actively

DOI: 10.4324/9781003276296-28

putting themselves into disadvantageous positions and situations" (Spinka et al., 2001). This is done to increase the challenge, add play value, and, from a developmental perspective, is a means of self-training to prepare for unexpected situations in the future.

Intrinsic Motivation

How can you make the task more self-directed? Are there elements of the activity that you can control? Can you add elements that you can control? Can you remove elements that you cannot control? How can you make the task process-focused? Is there a way to minimize the emphasis on the results or outcomes? Amabile (1983) suggests that a good way to foster creativity at home is to *not* use a reward as the sole purpose to do a task, and to allow children the choice in *how* to perform a task (Russ, 1993). This relates to the illusion-of-choice parenting strategy of providing options on *how* to do a task, but not the option of doing the task (e.g., "do you want to put on your shirt first or your pants first?" vs. "can you please get dressed now?"). Connecting back to the Montessori environment, another option is allowing for the choice of *which* activities are done and in what order (Lillard, 2013). This provides some element of control, even if there may be rigidity within each activity. To evoke the Mary Poppins examples, can you do something else during the activity that makes it more enjoyable like watching movies while folding laundry or, as Mary suggests, sing and consume sugar.

Pretense

How can you add pretense? Can there be less pressure to succeed? Is there room for failure? Is there room to explore imaginative ways of doing the task that are not exactly the expected or traditional means? Can you dedicate some "safe space" or *side project time* to work without any risk of failure (Cleese, 1991; Goetz, 2011).

Examples of Adding Play Value

Let's look at an example of pushing an activity into the play domain that resulted in some serious innovation. In 1948, Mac (Maurice) and Dick (Richard) McDonald developed a system for their *McDonald's* restaurant to create food in "30 seconds, not 30 minutes" and innovated the modern fast-food industry (Hancock, 2016). The McDonald brothers took elements of assembly-line manufacturing, invented new technologies, and reframed the expectations of a restaurant (e.g., there was no indoor seating, there were only a handful of items on the menu, it was self-service, there were no plates or silverware to wash). To remind you briefly of Chapter 12, this was *radical* and seemed impossible and ridiculous at the time (e.g., "people are going to think we are crazy" (Hancock, 2016)). And, like most radical change, people did not understand the new model *at first* (e.g., "totally revolutionary and a complete disaster" (Hancock, 2016)). The element of this story that I want to focus on is the method that the brothers used to develop their "Speedee System" that is visualized in the film, *The Founder* (Hancock, 2016). They used play to design and develop their restaurant layout and service model:

> Mac and Dick had a tennis court behind their house, and they got…a couple of other operations people up there to draw out the whole floor plan with chalk, actual size, like a giant hopscotch. It must have looked funny as hell—those grown men pacing about and going through the motions of preparing hamburgers, french fries, and milk shakes. Anyhow, they got it all drawn, just so, and the architect was to come up the next day and copy the layout to scale for his plans.
>
> (Kroc, 1977)

If you watch the film (based on real accounts), all the employees were playing pretend "making pretend burgers and fries" (Hancock, 2016) for six hours (i.e., in a flow state).

This was *fantasy play*: everyone was pretending as if they were making real food in a real restaurant, and if they messed up, it didn't matter because it was not real.

This was *creation play*: the chalk allowed for quickly rearranging the entire play space, erasing and redrawing, testing, and iterating.

This was *challenge play*: "They do it over and over, hashing it out…" (Hancock, 2016) until they were able to solve the assembly-line puzzle to reduce the time it took to produce and deliver a pretend hamburger.

This is an example of using play to solve a lean manufacturing problem (something that is typically under the umbrella of industrial engineering). The McDonald brothers *gamified* industrial engineering and revolutionized the food service industry.

This specific type of play is the premise of a video game, *Overcooked*. In this cooperative game, a team of chefs must prepare ingredients, cook, clean, and deliver food within a set time in different kitchen layouts that contain a variety of obstacles. Overcooked is more than just a game about cutting tomatoes, the creators *found the fun* (as Mary Poppins would say) in industrial engineering, lean manufacturing, and assembly cell design, and turned it into a game. The kids and adults who play Overcooked don't realize how much they are learning about industrial engineering. The puzzles, which gradually get more difficult, are building a unique skill set related to spatial thinking. It also requires teamwork and clear communication. This game is such a strong example of gamifying team building skills. Studies have shown that one "can derive meaningful team process, performance, and communication measures and that the interactions with this video game meet the requirements of psychological fidelity of human-autonomy teaming (Bishop et al., 2020)." Other studies found that playing Overcooked "significantly increases cooperative behavior" (Zheng et al., 2021) and suggest using the game to prepare students for working in the food service industry, specifically because it builds collaborative problem-solving skills (Aleman & Nadolny, 2021).

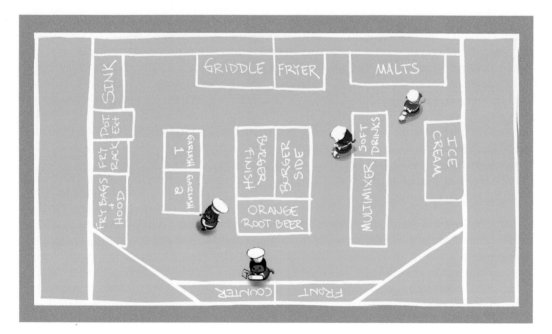

Figure 24.1 A representation of the McDonald brothers' chalk-drawn, tennis court prototype of the "Speedee System" overlaid with *Overcooked*-like characters.

As I discussed in Chapter 20, video games (and games in general) are very good at keeping play-ers in a state of flow and therefore have the potential to add play value. Deterding et al. (2011) defined the term *gamification* as "the use of game design elements in non-game contexts." It can span beyond simply adding a challenge, competition, or game play in an educational setting (i.e., Game Based Learning) (Caponetto et al., 2014). Gamification can also involve adding game fiction (e.g., narrative, fictional worlds, avatars) and social interaction (e.g., collaborative or corporative arrangements) (Sailer & Homer, 2020). Multiple surveys of studies have found there are generally positive effects of gamification, but with mixed results depending on the context, implementa-tion, and people involved (Hamari et al., 2014; Seaborn & Fels, 2015; Sailer & Homer, 2020). One meta-analysis of studies found specifically that "inclusion of game fiction and combining compe-tition with collaboration were particularly effective within gamification for fostering behavioral learning outcomes" (Sailer & Homer, 2020).

If you think about the Play Pyramid of Chapter 19, one can add game-like elements by adding any of challenge, fantasy, sensory, or creation types of play elements to an activity. The following are a few examples of transforming things that are typically viewed as chores and pushing them along the scale toward play and, in some cases, "gamifying" them. In these cases, designers have incorporated opportunities for play with the goal of making the activity more engaging, playful, and effective.

In 2009, DDB Stockholm, an ad agency, launched a Volkswagen campaign called "The Fun Theory," which featured a series of videos and a website that use play to motivate people to change lazy or irresponsible behaviors (Kim, 2015). In one of the videos online, you can see a set of subway stairs transformed into a piano to incentivize commuters to play their way upward instead of using the escalator: they reported a 66% increase in stairs usage (Kim, 2015). Simply designing each step to produce the next note of a musical scale allows for *sensory* play. It can allow for *creation* play if users choose to make songs, and, because of the three dimensionality, it also adds *challenge* to actually create music. Additionally, it's a giant piano made from stairs and that could be considered *fantasy* play. In any case, this design addition helps shift what is typically a chore (stair climbing) into play.

In 1959, *de Efteling* theme park in the Netherlands installed a collection of talking trash bins that are themed with characters from an old children's song: *Holle Bolle Gijs* (Wever et al., 2006). These characters can eat anything and are always hungry. In *de Efteling*, there are at least 10 members of the Gijzen family throughout the park (one of them is represented in Figure 24.2). The Holle Bolle Gijzen mouths are the openings for receiving trash. Their mouths are connected to a vacuum system that sucks in items that are brought to the opening. When you walk by, they call out for trash saying "Papier Hier!" (i.e., waste wanted, feed me your trash) and when you feed them trash, they say "Dank u wel" (thank you), "lekker" (delicious), and they may also burp or fart. By adding this themed playful experience (*sensory* and *fantasy*), the children run around the park and clean everything. The Holle Bolle Gijs have taken a chore—throwing away trash—and pushed it along the play scale turning it into something children *want* to do. The result is a clean theme park that benefits everyone. Donald Norman discusses this concept in his book, *Emotional Design*, by saying that "products and systems that make you feel good are easier to deal with and produce more harmonious results" (2003).

Figure 24.2 A representation of one of the *Holle Bolle Gijs* trash collectors at de Efteling theme park in the Netherlands.

Figure 24.3 An illustration of the fly in the urinal concept developed in the Netherlands in 1997 by Jos van Bedaf.

One final example comes from Schiphol Airport in the Netherlands in 1997. Jos van Bedaf, manager of the airport cleaning department, had the idea to add a decorative fly to the urinals with the hope of getting users to have a better aim (illustrated in Figure 24.3). With the installation of these urinals, the airport reported an 80% reduction in spillage, which was estimated as an 8% reduction in total bathroom cleaning costs (Krulwich, 2009; Evans-Pritchard, 2013). What happened here was that they took an activity that was a chore and simply added a *challenge*. This nudged the activity into a *flow* state, making it more engaging and effective. The concept of a toilet target quickly spread around the world, sometimes with different graphics, such as a rival sport team logo. There are also children's toys that use this same concept for potty training.

Lastly, you may not even need to change *anything* about the activity to make it play. Simply calling an activity "play" can make people behave differently. In one study (Glynn, 1994), students were assigned a task, and some were told the task was "play" and others were told the same task was "work." Those that were told the activity was play were more intrinsically motivated, broke rules, and were more organic in responses. The participants that were told the activity was "work" were results-orientated and focused primarily on formulating organized responses (Glynn, 1994). This study provides empirical support for the Tom Sawyer whitewashing story in Chapter 18. I also used this technique on you in the Introduction (*teehee*). I could have told you that we were going to take a short test of creativity (which is true), but instead, I said we were going to "*play a short game.*"

References

Aleman, E., & Nadolny, L. (2021). Integration of video games to support the FCS education food production standards. *Journal of Family & Consumer Sciences, 113*(2), 46–49.

Amabile, T. (1983). *The social psychology of creativity*. Spinger-Veclay.

Bishop J. et al. (2020). CHAOPT: A testbed for evaluating human-autonomy team collaboration using the video game overcooked! 2. *2020 Systems and Information Engineering Design Symposium (SIEDS)*, Charlottesville, VA, USA.

Breihan, T. (2021, June 25). Blackalicious rapper gift of gab dead at 50. *Stereogum*.

Brown, S. (2009). *Play: How it shapes the brain, opens the imagination, and invigorates the soul*. Avery.

Caponetto, I., Earp, J., & Ott, M. (2014, October). Gamification and education: A literature review. In *European conference on games based learning (Vol. 1, p. 50)*. Academic Conferences International Limited.

Cleese, J. (1991). And now for something completely different. *Management Review, 80(5)*, 50.

Deterding, S., Dixon, D., Khaled, R., & Nacke, L. (2011). From game design elements to gamefulness: defining "gamification". In *Proceedings of the 15th International Academic MindTrek Conference: Envisioning Future Media Environments (MindTrek '11)*. New York, NY, USA, 9–15.

Evans-Pritchard, B. (2013). Aiming to reduce cleaning costs. *Works That Work*.

Glynn, M. A. (1994). Effects of work task cues and play task cues on information processing, judgment, and motivation. *The Journal of Applied Psychology, 79(1)*, 34–45.

Goetz, K. (2011, February 1). *How 3M gave everyone days off and created an innovation dynamo*. Fast Company.

Hamari, J., Koivisto, J., & Sarsa, H. (2014, January). Does gamification work? A literature review of empirical studies on gamification. In *2014 47th Hawaii International Conference on System Sciences (pp. 3025–3034)*. IEEE.

Hancock, J. L. (Director). (2016). *The Founder [Motion picture]*. FilmNation Entertainment.

Haught-Tromp, C. (2017). The green eggs and ham hypothesis: How constraints facilitate creativity. *Psychology of Aesthetics, Creativity, and the Arts, 11(1)*, 10.

Kim, B. (2015). Gamification. *Library Technology Reports, 51(2)*, 10–18.

Kroc, R. (1977). *Grinding it out: The making of McDonald's*. St. Martin's Paperback.

Krulwich, R. (2009, December 19). There's a fly in my urinal. *Weekend Edition Saturday: NPR News*.

Lieberman, J. N. (1977). *Playfulness: Its relationship to imagination and creativity* (A. J. Edwards, Ed.). Academic Press.

Lillard, A. S. (2013). Playful learning and Montessori education. *American Journal of Play, 5(2)*, 157–186.

Malloy, E. (Director). (2009). *Under Great White Northern Lights*. [Motion picture]. Canada: Three Foot Giant.

Norman, D. (2003). *Emotional design: Why we love (or Hate) everyday things*. Basic Books.

Russ, S. W. (1993). *Affect and creativity: The role of affect and play in the creative process*. Lawrence Erlbaum Associates, Inc.

Sailer, M., & Homner, L. (2020). The gamification of learning: A meta-analysis. *Educational Psychology Review, 32(1)*, 77–112.

Seaborn, K., & Fels, D. I. (2015). Gamification in theory and action: A survey. *International Journal of Human-Computer Studies, 74*, 14–31.

Spinka, M., Newberry, R. C., & Bekoff, M. (2001). Mammalian play: Training for the unexpected. *The Quarterly Review of Biology, 76(2)*, 141–168.

Wever, R., Gutter, N., & Silvester, S. (2006). Prevention of littering through packaging design: A support tool for concept generation. In I. Horvath, I. & J. Duhovnik, (Eds.), *Proceedings of the 6th international symposium on tools and methods of competitive engineering (TMCE 2006)*, Ljubljana, Slovenia.

Zheng, W., Cao, S., Wang, Y., Yang, K., Chen, Y., & Song, G. (2021). The impact of social value orientation, game context and trust on cooperative behavior after cooperative video game play. *Psychological Reports, 124(3)*, 1353–1369.

Part IV

Humor, Creativity, and Innovation

25

TWO THEORIES (AND LARRYS) OF HUMOR,
THROWING SHADE, AND THROWING PIES

Now that we have explored play in depth and how it links to creativity and innovation, we will move into the domain of humor. Although it's not exactly the intended purpose of this book, play and humor have some connections with each other too. One of the three requirements of "playfulness" according to Lieberman (1977) is a sense of humor. In Chapter 4, we discussed wit and puns being a form of *playing* with words. Children use laughter as a cue to indicate to others that a situation is play (Cundall, 2007). It is theorized that the panting sounds that animals (including rats, dogs, and chimpanzees) produce during play is the origins of the "ha-ha" sound of laughter (Provine, 2000). Joking can sometimes be playful, and play can sometimes be funny. The overlap of a play–humor Venn diagram (see Afterword) is not insignificant, but *fun* is not the same thing as *funny*. Specifically, regarding the nature of this book, the individual relationships of play and humor with creativity and innovation is not necessarily through the same connective links.

In this Part, we will delve into the world of comedy, jokes, wit, improvisation, and all things humorous, starting first with an overview of different theories of humor. This chapter and the next will explore three of the most common theories that attempt to explain the essence of humor: the Release (or Psychoanalytical or Relief) Theory, the Superiority (or Social) Theory, and the Incongruity (or Cognitive) Theory (Attardo, 1994; Cundall, 2007). In this chapter, I am going to focus on the first two.

The Release Theory of Humor

This theory revolves around humor being a release of emotional energy or stress (i.e., *catharsis*) (Attardo, 1994). It is a means of relieving tensions related to fear, nervousness, and overwhelming or uncomfortable situations. This "release" laughter occurs regularly in general conversation... like *a lot*. Laughter researcher, Robert R. Provine, found that most laughter in conversation (over 80%) is *not* induced by witticism, jokes, funny stories, or anything resembling humor, but rather by banal statements in ordinary conversation such as, "Look, it's Andre" (1996). This laughter is a *social lubricant*. "People are 30 times more likely to laugh when they are in a social situation than when they are alone" (Provine, 1996). Just as jokes are often used as a means of reducing tension in certain situations, simple awkward laughter during normal conversation has been found to reduce tension and improve interaction (O'Donnell-Trujillo, & Adams, 1983; Meyer, 2000; Iivari et al., 2020). It is also a means of sharing playfulness, indicating a friendly intent, and strengthening social bonds (McGhee, 1979; Provine, 1996). While we are discussing the idea of a social lubricant, one study found that "laughter increases people's willingness to disclose [personal information about themself], but that they may not necessarily be aware that it is doing so" (Gray et al., 2015).

DOI: 10.4324/9781003276296-30

A related theory is that laughter began as a means of communication in prelingual times as it signaled good news that a threat was avoided (Keith-Spiegel, 1972). As an example, let's say you were a prehistoric hunter out in the woods with your tribe. And let's say you hear something in the distance and so you wander off to investigate. Now you happen to be a little nervous because you are alone and there could be *predators* nearby. Suddenly, a bush starts to rustle by your foot, and you jump back. Is it a venomous snake?

Nope. A tiny mouse scurries across the ground.

All that built-up stress is released in the form of a laugh because everything is OK and there is no real threat. This is the *"False Alarm Theory"* of humor and laughter (Ramachandran, 1998). In this example, laughter is not just anxiety-reducing and blood-pressure reducing (Eshg et al., 2017; Provine, 2000), it also serves a very specific communication function. That sound of laughter resonates across the woods for the rest of the tribe to hear. The tribe recognizes the sound and now knows that you are OK, and they also know your location. Perhaps the tribe also makes the laugh sound in response, and now you know that you have been heard. "Laughing is an ancient form of social signaling that is more akin to animal calls or bird songs than human speech" (Provine, 1996).

Figure 25.1 The False Alarm Theory of laughter suggests that we laugh as an emotional release from a situation that seemed to be initially threatening. The shadow cast on your bedroom wall was just your coat. The shaking bush was just a mouse.

This nervous and uncomfortable release humor has been increasingly exploited in popular culture. Larry David's *Curb Your Enthusiasm* is a paradigm of uncomfortable situational humor.

> In nearly every episode, Larry finds himself in sharp opposition to his social milieu. At times, this conflict is because of his failure—or refusal—to follow unwritten social guidelines, and at other times it is because someone else has not adhered to Larry's own conception of propriety.
>
> (Gillota, 2010)

There are many other popular shows and movies that make you laugh via an empathetic uncomfortable reaction toward a character or situation. Much of the work of Sacha Baron Cohen involves release humor in which his characters place others in uncomfortable situations. The humor of *Nathan for You*, from Chapter 10, is similar to that of Cohen's, involving lightly scripted and intentionally uncomfortable interactions with real people. Productions such as *The Office*, *Ziwe*, *I Think You Should Leave with Tim Robinson*, and some Ben Stiller films (e.g., *Meet the Parents*, *Something About Mary*) also play in this domain of humor. The writers create uncomfortable situations that set the viewer up for anxiety-releasing laughter. It would be an overstatement to say that awkward situations are the *only* reason these creative works are funny. Humor often involves a combination of factors and theories.

Specifically to *Curb Your Enthusiasm*, both the Release Theory *and* the Superiority Theory are critical to this style of humor.

The *Superiority Theory* of Humor

This is the evil one. In this theory, humor is believed to be a means to triumph over or make judgment of other people to highlight one's own superiority (Cundall, 2007). In short, we laugh at others' misfortunes and flaws to show that we are better. "We laugh because we are not the losers—at least not this time" (Kaufman et al., 2008). This theory suggests that at the heart of funny is someone or something being *criticized*.

The documentary *Paris is Burning* explores New York City drag culture in the 1980s (Livingston, 1990) and it introduces the concepts of "*reading*" and "*throwing shade*." "*Reading* is the real artform of insult" (Livingston, 1990); it is insult with imagination. *Throwing shade* is a more indirect, underhanded and refined level of reading. This concept of creative insults as sport was brought to the public as a regular *RuPaul's Drag Race* mini-challenge: "Reading is Fundamental." In this challenge, RuPaul declares that the "*library* is open" and the contestants take turns donning *reading* glasses as they attempt to throw shade at their opponents. Reading is a means of scrutinizing the competition and highlighting non-obvious flaws for improvement and, in a way, building community through critique. "One of the golden rules of reading [is] avoiding apparent 'fact.' If reading is masterful insult, then reading a queen for her size or race is seen as boring, insulting and deeply inadequate" (O'Halloran, 2017). As per Chapter 3, obvious connections are not creative or imaginative. Insult jokes are not new: scholars believe they have found the oldest recorded "your mama" joke inscribed onto a tablet from Babylon, circa 1500 BC (Streck & Wasserman, 2011).

The concept of a *roast* is similar in nature to a reading session. A roast is a celebration of a guest of honor, the *roastee*, which involves comedians, friends, and colleagues sharing insulting jokes at the roastee's expense. Since 1983, the *White House Correspondents' Dinner* took the form of roast of the sitting President and their administration (Stracqualursi & Hansler, 2018). The intent of a roast is a unique form of honor, and, as such, the jokes can't be *simply* insulting. In both a good read and a good roast

Figure 25.2 When the "library is open" on *RuPaul's Drag Race*, contestants don reading glasses to throw shade at their opponents.

> 'it's important to balance being insulting with being intelligent'…The best reads come from a place of love and familiarity…'reading isn't being nasty, it's being clever to someone you know quite well, so you can get away with it'
>
> (Maher, 2021)

Philosophers like Hobbes and Plato viewed humor as a vice and a display of *lack* of wisdom (Cundall, 2007). Until the 1860s, it was considered impolite to laugh in public in the United States as laughter was even then viewed as aggressive antipathy (Martin, 2007). In society today, however, it is acceptable to laugh at someone when they slip on a real or proverbial banana peel.

This goes by the German term *schadenfreude* (*schaden* meaning 'damage, harm' and *freude* meaning 'joy')—the inexplicable sense of joy in someone else's misfortune. Nelson Muntz on *The Simpsons* is the poster child of schadenfreude with his regular pointing and laughing at tragedy ("*Ha Hah!*"). An extreme version of this is the *diabolical, wicked,* or *maniacal laughter* of fictional evil villains (*muahahahhaa*) such as the Joker, the Wicked Witch of the West, Mr. Burns, Dr. Evil, Dr. Horrible, Ursula the Sea Witch, etc. The evil laugh of villains in fiction is a means of "marking, visually and aurally, the villain's moral corruption" and

> signaling that the villain is intrinsically motivated by the prospect of causing harm. Villains laugh when they do or plan evil things. In contrast, heroes laugh when they build or enjoy prosocial relationships. Malicious laughter thus shows audiences that they are right to hate the villain and to uphold the moral order implicit in the fiction.
>
> (Kjeldgaard-Christiansen, 2018)

In *Dr. Horrible's Sing-Along Blog*, Dr. Horrible sings, "if you're gonna get into the Evil League of Evil, you have to have a memorable laugh" (Whedon, 2008).

Humor, in the form of *humiliation*, can be viewed as a means in which society corrects deviant behavior (Attardo, 1994). Through this lens, the Nelson Muntz point-and-laugh might be him saying: "hey, please be more careful next time...you idiot." You may say that you don't do that Nelson Muntz thing and laugh when other people get hurt, and that it is just a fictional exaggeration. However, there is enough schadenfreude in society to fuel the entire comedy industry of *slapstick*.

The show *Funniest Home Videos*, as well as a good portion of the internet, consist of videos of people getting hurt or failing in unexpected ways (e.g., a person gets hit in crotch with a ball, a person accidentally breaks a phone, a wedding party falls off a dock). And sometimes failing in *expected* ways also leads to humor (e.g., *Jackass*). *The Three Stooges* exploited this form of humor as they intentionally and repetitively destroyed property and plans, while injuring themselves and others.

Studies have shown that men tend to prefer forms of hostile humor and slapstick comedy more than women (Terry & Ertel, 1974; Crawford & Gressley, 1991). *Wile E. Coyote and the Road Runner* is this form of humor for children. Chuck Jones created a strict set of rules that the animators must follow for all Road Runner and Coyote cartoons. Rule 2 is that "no outside force can harm the Coyote—only his own ineptitude or the failure of the Acme products" and Rule 7 is "the Coyote is always more humiliated than harmed by his failures" (Jones, 1999). These two rules ensure that the result of the injury results in humor. The Coyote's own poor decisions results in injury, but he is more humiliated rather than harmed.

There is a suggestion that this type of humor may be a viewed as "*inferiority*" instead of "superiority" in that we laugh not because we are better, but rather because we *relate*: we see our own failures and foibles in that of the characters (Solomon, 1992). We are all a Larry Fine and a Larry David deep inside.

Figure 25.3 Larry Fine and the other Stooges engage in slapstick comedy that is primarily explained by the Superiority or Inferiority (Solomon, 1992) Theory of humor. The humor of Larry David in *Curb Your Enthusiasm* can be described by theories of Superiority/Inferiority as well as the Release Theory.

In Yiddish and Jewish-American literature there are two relevant characters: *schlemiel* and *schlimazel*. The *schlemiel* is the fool who is "predestined for trouble" whose failures and unfortunate situations are a result of their own actions, while the *schlimazel* (i.e., a person with bad luck) "in contrast, suffers misfortunes through no fault of his own" (Gillota, 2010). The classic joke is that when the *schlemiel* inevitably spills his soup...it lands on the *schlimazel*. The Three Stooges, Larry David, and Wile E. Coyote often play *both* the schlemiel and the schlimazel—they "both attract... and cause... trouble in every episode" (Byers & Krieger, 2006).

So, you might be saying "how does getting poked in the eyes connect to creativity?" In *most* cases, it probably doesn't, *wise guy* (*nyuk nyuk nyuk*), but we will discuss some creativity connections to the Release Theory and Superiority Theory in Chapters 30 and 31. There is still one more major theory of humor.

References

Attardo, S. (1994). *Linguistic theories of humor.* Mouton de Gruyter.

Byers, M., & Krieger, R. (2006). Something old is new again?: Postmodern Jewishness in curb your enthusiasm, arrested development, and the O.C. In V. Brook (Ed.), *"You should see yourself": Jewish identity in postmodern American culture* (pp. 277–297). Rutgers University Press.

Cundall, M. K. (2007). Humor and the limits of incongruity. *Creativity Research Journal, 19*(2–3), 203–211.

Crawford, M., & Gressley, D. (1991). Creativity, caring, and context: Women's and men's accounts of humor preferences and practices. *Psychology of Women Quarterly, 15*(2), 217–231.

Eshg, Z. M., Ezzati, J., Nasiri, N., & Ghafouri, R. (2017). Effect of humor therapy on blood pressure of patients undergoing hemodialysis. *Journal of Research in Medical and Dental Science, 5*, 85–88.

Gillota, D. (2010). Negotiating Jewishness: Curb Your Enthusiasm and the schlemiel tradition. *Journal of Popular Film and Television, 38*(4), 152–161.

Gray, A., Parkinson, B., & Dunbar, R. (2015). Laughter's influence on the intimacy of self-disclosure. *Human Nature, 26*, 28–43.

Iivari, N., Kinnula, M., Kuure, L., & Keisanen, T. (2020). "Arseing around was Fun!" – humor as a resource in design and making. In *Proceedings of the 2020 CHI Conference on Human Factors in Computing Systems*. Association for Computing Machinery, New York, USA.

Jones, C. (1999). *Chuck amuck: The life and times of an animated cartoonist.* Farrar, Straus and Giroux.

Kaufman, S. B., Kozbelt, A., Bromley, M. L., & Miller, G. F. (2008). The role of creativity and humor in human mate selection. In G. Geher & G. Miller (Eds.), *Mating intelligence: Sex, relationships, and the mind's reproductive system* (pp. 227–262). Lawrence Erlbaum.

Keith-Spiegel, P. (1972). Early conceptions of humor: Varieties and issues. In J. H. Goldstein & P. E. McGhee (Eds.), *The psychology of humor* (pp. 4–39). Academic Press.

Kjeldgaard-Christiansen, J. (2018). Social signals and antisocial essences: The function of evil laughter in popular culture. *The Journal of Popular Culture, 51*(5), 1214–1233.

Lieberman, J. N. (1977). *Playfulness: Its relationship to imagination and creativity* (A. J. Edwards, Ed.). Academic Press.

Livingston, J. (Director). (1990). *Paris is Burning [Motion picture].* United States: Off White Productions.

Maher, A. (2021, November 10). A beginner's guide to throwing shade, according to Sydney's drag stars. *Timeout.*

Martin, R.A. (2007). *The psychology of humor: An integrative approach.* Elsevier Academic Press.

McGhee, P. E. (1979). *Humor: Its origin and development.* Freeman.

Meyer, J. C. (2000). Humor as a double-edged sword: Four functions of humor in communication. *Communication Theory, 10*(3), 310–331.

O'Donnell-Trujillo, N., & Katherine Adams, K. (1983). Heheh in conversation: Some coordinating accomplishments of laughter. *Western Journal of Speech Communication, 47*(2), 175–191.

O'Halloran K. (2017). RuPaul's Drag Race and the reconceptualisation of queer communities and publics. In N. Brennan & D. Gudelunas (Eds.), *RuPaul's Drag Race and the shifting visibility of drag culture* (pp. 213–228). Palgrave Macmillan.

Provine, R. R. (1996). Laughter. *American Scientist, 84*, 38–45.

Provine, R. R. (2000). *Laughter: A scientific investigation*. Viking.

Ramachandran V. S. (1998). The neurology and evolution of humor, laughter, and smiling: The false alarm theory. *Medical Hypotheses, 51*(4), 351–354.

Solomon, R. C. (1992). *Entertaining ideas: Popular philosophical essays (1970–1990)*. Prometheus Books.

Stracqualursi, V., & Hansler, J. (2018). Everything you need to know about the white house correspondents' dinner. *ABC News*.

Streck, M., & Wasserman, N. (2011). Dialogues and riddles: Three old Babylonian wisdom texts. *Iraq, 73*, 117–125.

Terry, R. I., & Ertel, S. I. (1974). Exploration of individual differences in preferences for humor. *Psychological Reports, 34*, 1031–1037.

Whedon, J. (Director). (2008). *Dr. Horrible's Sing-Along Blog [TV Miniseries]*. United States: Mutant Enemy.

26

THE INCONGRUITY THEORY OF HUMOR,
CARTOON CAPTIONS, AND THE EXCALIBUR TOILET BRUSH

In the academic world, humor is not the most funded research topic and so there are relatively few humor studies in general. Of these, the few experimental studies that attempt to link humor and creativity (shown in Figure 26.1) have all found positive correlations with varying degrees and significance. The consistent positive relationship in academic studies led some to conclude that that "humor seemed to be sufficiently integrated [with creativity] to be considered a subset of [creativity]" (Murdock & Ganim, 1993). However, it is likely that a collection of behind-the-scenes factors discussed in Chapter 1, including intelligence (Kellner & Benedek, 2017; Christensen et al., 2018), openness to experience (Sutu et al., 2021), and extroversion are shared variables that facilitate both humor and creativity (Howrigan & MacDonald, 2008). It is also hypothesized that humor evolved as an *indicator* of intelligence, creativity, and other valued personality traits for selecting a mate during initial social interactions (Miller, 2000; Howrigan & MacDonald, 2008).

AUTHORS	DATE	HUMOR ASSESSMENT	CREATIVITY ASSESSMENT
SMITH AND WHITE	1965	SELF SURVEY AND PEER RATING	WORD ASSOCIATION
TREADWELL	1970	CARTOON CAPTIONS AND SELF SURVEY	REMOTE ASSOCIATES TEST AND GESTALT TRANSFORMATION
BABAD	1974	CARTOON CAPTIONS, HUMOR APPRECIATION, AND PEER RATING	TORRENCE TEST OF CREATIVE THINKING
ROUFF	1975	EXPLAINING CARTOON HUMOR	REMOTE ASSOCIATES TEST
BRODZINSKY AND RUBIEN	1976	CARTOON CAPTIONS	REMOTE ASSOCIATES TEST
CLABBY	1980	CAMPAIGN SLOGAN CREATION	ALTERNATIVE USES TEST
HUMKE AND SCHAEFER	1996	MULTIDIMENSIONAL SENSE OF HUMOR SCALE	FRANCK DRAWING COMPLETION
SITTON AND PIERCE	2004	GEOGRAPHIC PUN GENERATION	REMOTE ASSOCIATES TEST
KUDROWITZ AND WALLACE	2010	CARTOON CAPTIONS	NEW PRODUCT IDEA GENERATION
KELLNER AND BENEDEK	2017	CARTOON CAPTIONS AND MULTIDIMENSIONAL SENSE OF HUMOR SCALE	ALTERNATIVE USES TEST

Figure 26.1 Experimental studies exploring the relationship between individual creative abilities and humor. All the listed studies found a positive correlation with varying degrees of correlation and significance.

DOI: 10.4324/9781003276296-31

In Figure 26.1, some of these studies attempt to correlate a general *sense of humor* with convergent or divergent thinking ability. A "sense of humor" assessment (such as the *multi-dimensional sense of humor scale*) can cover a wide variety of topics including the ability to comprehend jokes, ability to express humor, ability to appreciate humor, desire to seek out humor, memory of jokes, and tendency to use humor as a coping mechanism (Ruch, 1996). There is an important difference between humor *appreciation* and humor *production*. Specifically, appreciating jokes doesn't mean you are good at writing jokes. In the same way, there is a difference between the appreciation of creativity and being creative. There are only a few humor tests that focus on *humor production,* and it is the least studied area of humor (Turner, 1980). When talking about intentional cognitive-based humor production ability, we are referring to the quality simply called *wit* (Feingold & Mazzella, 1991). As discussed in Chapter 4, *wit* can be defined as the "creative aligning of concepts (i.e., *bisociation*)" across seemingly unrelated domains (Cundall, 2007). Wit is where the realms of humor and creativity overlap most clearly (O'Quin & Besemer, 1999).

Out of the 65 humor tests listed by Ruch (1998), the *cartoon caption test* or *cartoon punch line production test* is the only one that specifically tests humor production ability or wit. You may be familiar with this "activity" as the weekly *New Yorker Cartoon Caption Contest,* or in game form as the New Yorker Cartoon Caption board game. It also happens to be one of the only repeatedly used tests of humor production in academic studies. The first use of cartoon captions in an experimental study was actually as a *creativity assessment* and not specifically a test of humor production (Ziller et al., 1962).

Figure 26.2 is a *New Yorker* cartoon created by *Bob Mankoff*, cartoonist and former cartoon editor of *The New Yorker*. Let's try this "cartoon punch line production test" right now! First get in the right headspace: go for a walk outside, take a shower, and drink your dopamine smoothie (recipe in Chapter 8). Set a timer for three minutes and list as many captions as you can using the lines below the cartoon.

Figure 26.2 Bob Mankoff's cartoon from *The New Yorker* without a caption and a set of blank lines for your test of humor production ability (reproduced here with permission from Bob Mankoff). This is the same cartoon and humor production assessment used in the Kudrowitz & Wallace study (2010).

After speaking with Bob Mankoff about his cartoon in Figure 26.2, the original intent was for the suit to be a hazmat suit; however, some of the participants in the (pre-pandemic) study interpreted it as a spacesuit. In either interpretation, there is an *incongruity* that needs to be resolved: a person is wearing a specialized airtight suit in what appears to be a common, mundane office setting and someone else, perhaps a supervisor, is casually talking without wearing such a suit. How did you make sense of this incongruity? We will get to your responses, but, first, some theory.

The *Incongruity Theory* of Humor is a "cognitive" theory in that it attempts to explain humor with less attention to the emotional or social aspects. It is so closely related to creativity that its description could easily be used to describe the Associative Theory of Creativity from Chapter 3. The Incongruity Theory of Humor suggests that something is funny when there are "disjointed, ill-suited pairings of ideas or situations...that are divergent from habitual customs" (Keith-Spiegel, 1972). Specifically, something is funny when two things come together that are not expected to do so, but somehow make sense. As described in Chapters 3 and 4, Arthur Koestler developed a similar theory called *bisociation*, in which he emphasized how this is applicable to both humor and creativity. As a refresher, *bisociation* occurs when an idea or situation is perceived from two incompatible or disparate frames of reference at the same time (Koestler, 1964).

Let's look at examples of captions for this cartoon as a means of understanding the Incongruity Theory. I used this same cartoon in my own studies and so with hundreds of captions to evaluate, there were many with similar ideas. Figure 26.3 shows four similar captions with ratings of humor (Kudrowitz & Wallace, 2010).

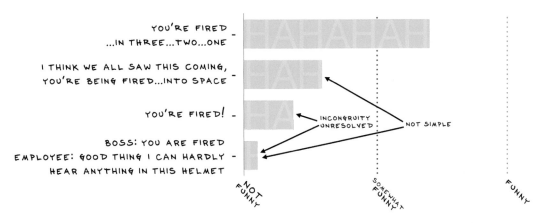

Figure 26.3 Four select captions with humor ratings for the cartoon in Figure 26.2 (Kudrowitz & Wallace, 2010). All four captions relate to being fired. The first two captions resolve the incongruity and have a higher average humor score than the last two which do not resolve the incongruity.

The first two captions in Figure 26.3 both resolve the incongruity through a non-obvious connection that links the out-of-place suit and the office setting (i.e., the person in the suit is getting *fired*). The word "fired" is the *bisociating link* that Koestler would say connects two intersecting mental "planes" (1964). "Fired" can be viewed from one frame of reference (e.g., person losing a job in an office setting) and simultaneously from a second frame of reference (e.g., person being launched into space requiring a special airtight suit). Humor theorists suggest that incongruity is a necessary condition for humor, but incongruity by itself is not sufficient as there are many incongruent occurrences that are not funny (Martin, 2007). Shultz proposed the *incongruity-resolution* model that states that *the incongruity must be resolved in order for humor to exist* (1974). Even though all four captions present the same idea of someone being fired, the first two captions have higher humor scores in the study than the last two, which do not resolve the incongruity. Without straying too far from the topic, *simplicity*, as discussed in Chapter 6, also plays an important role in humor just as it does in creativity. In this case, the responses that were shorter (i.e., the first and third) had higher humor scores than the same general caption presented in a longer form (i.e., the second and fourth). *Less is more.*

"Humor can be dissected, as a frog can, but the thing dies in the process and the innards are discouraging to any but the pure scientific mind" (White & White, 1941). And, as such, to thoroughly dissect incongruity-resolution humor and to make it only appealing to scientists, Jerry Suls (1972) formulated a flow chart called the "*Two-Stage Model for the Appreciation of Jokes and Cartoons.*" An interpretation of his model is illustrated in Figure 26.4.

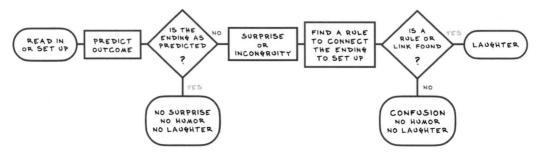

Figure 26.4 The two-stage model for the appreciation of jokes and cartoons adapted from Suls (1972).

Come join me as we "dissect" and "kill" (or should I say *de-preciate?*) a joke by walking through this joke appreciation model.

A joke begins with something called a *set-up* in a verbal or visual format. This set-up is the first part of a joke and it should not contain any incongruent elements. Here is a set-up to a joke:

Q: *Where does the general keep his armies?*

Your brain has already moved on to the second block of the flow chart and you are making predictions of what will follow given the information in the set-up. You may be thinking about forts, camps, army bases, tents, compounds, tanks, barracks, and perhaps other places where armies might be kept. This is a divergent thinking process, and you are building something like a mental *mind map* of things related to armies and generals.

Now, what happens next is that an ending or punchline is heard, read, or seen. If that ending is as predicted, for example:

Q: *Where does the general keep his armies?*

A: *In an army base!*

There is no surprise, no incongruity, and, thus, no laughter or humor. That is exactly what you were expecting, and it *generally (he he)* makes sense. If you did laugh, it may be because you were expecting an incongruity and there was none, making the lack of incongruity, the incongruity (but this is some meta-level stuff). Similarly, if you already knew the punchline to this joke, there may not be a surprise as the ending was already in your database. However, one study found that people find jokes funnier if they expect the punch line (Kenny, 1955).

Moving forward on the flow chart, if the ending is *not* as predicted, you, as the listener, will then search for a cognitive rule that will make sense of the incongruent information. For example:

Q: *Where does the general keep his armies?*

A: *In his sleevies!*

Your brain works much faster than you can read my explanations, so I'm going to try to rewind and replay your mental process in slow motion. The first thing that probably happened was you said "what are *sleevies*? This doesn't match any of the items in the database of places that generals would keep their troops. But wait a minute! *Sleevies* sounds like *armies* and arms go in sleeves..." At this point, your *Posterior Superior Temporal Sulcus* (the part of the brain we discussed in Chapter 3 that helps you make connections) is working hard with these incongruent bits to find a rule that makes sense of the ending. Perhaps you made the connection that we are using baby talk while describing a general keeping his *armies* in his *sleevies.* To use Koestler terms, the *bisociating link* is the word "armies" that can describe both military troops as well as what goes in the "*sleevies*" of your shirt. Once you made sense of the incongruity, your *Anterior Superior Temporal Sulcus* lights up, you have an *Aha! Moment*, and you laugh. In this case, your *Aha! Moment* is the same as a *Ha Ha Moment.* If you still don't understand the joke, then you are in that confusion block of the flow chart.

Humor can often be explained by a combination of these three main theories (Release, Superiority, and Incongruity). As an example, in one episode of the television show *Parks and Recreation*, Leslie Knope is running for City Council. Her campaign launch event was scheduled unintentionally in an ice-skating rink, and they didn't buy enough red carpet to fully cross the ice to their stage in the middle of the rink (Scully & Gates, 2012). The campaign team then slips and falls their entire way to the stage. On its own, without context, this is slapstick (Superiority Theory). Being that they were trying to make a bold entrance in front of a crowd of a hundred people, this social awkwardness adds to the humor (Release Theory). Lastly, the chosen entrance music, *Get on Your Feet* by Gloria Estefan, creates an unfortunate mismatch with the team not being able to physically get on their feet (Incongruity Theory).

This same process of joke appreciation from Figure 26.4 is applicable when you see *incremental innovation* for the first time. For example, if you look at Philippe Starck's *Excalibur* toilet brush (represented in Figure 26.5), you might say, "hey that doesn't look like the toilet brush I have at home. There is something different or incongruent about it." Most of the toilet brush is as expected (the set-up), but there is an element that is different from expected (a physical punchline). It has a bell guard on the handle in the style of a fencing épée or medieval jousting lance. When you make the connections that you hold a toilet brush in the same manner as you hold a lance and you fight toilet grime the same way you fight in battle, you resolve the incongruity. You get the joke and it's funny...but it also happens to be innovative! The guard protects your hand from dirty water just like a guard protects one's hand in battle. Philippe Starck made a non-obvious connection between sword fighting and cleaning a toilet and came up with a product that is humorous and innovative. Again, if you look at the Incongruity Theory of Humor and the Associative Theory of Creativity side by side, they say the same thing: *creativity/humor is about making non-obvious connections between seemingly unrelated things.*

Figure 26.5 An illustration of Philippe Starck's *Excalibur* toilet brush.

If you laugh at an idea or if someone else laughs at your idea, that may imply there was some non-obvious connection. That nugget of humor (*Haha!*) might actually be innovation (*Aha!*) in disguise (although there may be an 80% chance, it was just social lubricant). There are many examples throughout history (and in this book) that seemed to be a joke at first, but are now very real things (e.g., the mechanical reaper, a robotic vacuum, mechanical trousers, mustard ice cream, flavor-changing gum, edible balloons, submarines, hot ice cream, the flushing toilet, toilet paper, delivery drones, certain celebrities as president, man-made annular islands, digital books, wireless communication devices, tomacco plants, flying machines, flying cars, flying suits, movies with sound, a horseless carriage, 24-hour news, fast food restaurants, bacon pancakes, etc.).

References

Babad, E. Y. (1974). A multi-method approach to the assessment of humor: A critical look at humor tests. *Journal of Personality, 42*, 618–631.

Brodzinsky, D. M., & Rubien, J. (1976). Humor production as a function of sex of subject, creativity, and cartoon content. *Journal of Consulting and Clinical Psychology, 44*(4), 597–600.

Christensen, A. P., Silvia, P. J., Nusbaum, E. C., & Beaty, R. E. (2018). Clever people: Intelligence and humor production ability. *Psychology of Aesthetics, Creativity, and the Arts, 12*(2), 136–143.

Clabby, J. F. (1980). The wit: A personality Analysis. *Journal of Personality Assessment, 44*(3), 307–310.

Cundall, M. K. (2007). Humor and the limits of incongruity. *Creativity Research Journal, 19*(2–3), 203–211.

Feingold, A., & Mazzella, R. (1991). Psychometric intelligence and verbal humor ability. *Personality and Individual Differences, 12*(5), 427–435.

Howrigan, D. P., & MacDonald, K. B. (2008). Humor as a mental fitness indicator. *Evolutionary Psychology, 6*(4), 625–666.

Humke, C., & Schaefer, C. E. (1996). Sense of humor and creativity. *Perceptual and Motor Skills, 82*(2), 544–546.

Keith-Spiegel, P. (1972). Early conceptions of humor: Varieties and issues. In J. H. Goldstein & P. E. McGhee (Eds.), *The psychology of humor* (pp. 4–39). Academic Press.

Kellner, R., & Benedek, M. (2017). The role of creative potential and intelligence for humor production. *Psychology of Aesthetics, Creativity, and the Arts, 11*(1), 52–58.

Kenny, D. T. (1955). The contingency of humor appreciation on the stimulus-confirmation of joke-ending expectations. *Journal of Abnormal Psychology, 51*(3), 644–648.

Koestler, A. (1964). *The act of creation*. Macmillan.

Kudrowitz, B., & Wallace, D. (2010, October). Improvisational comedy and product design ideation: Making non-obvious connections between seemingly unrelated things. *International Conference on Design and Emotion*, Chicago, Illinois, USA.

Martin, R.A. (2007). *The psychology of humor: An integrative approach.* Elsevier Academic Press.

Miller, G. F. (2000). *The mating mind: How sexual choice shaped the evolution of human nature.* Doubleday.

Murdock, M. C., & Ganim, R. M. (1993). Creativity and humor: Integration and incongruity. *The Journal of Creative Behavior, 27*(1), 57–70.

O'Quin, K., & Besemer S. (1999). Creative products. In S. R. Pritzker & M. Runco (Eds.), *Encyclopedia of creativity* (pp. 267–278). Academic Press.

Rouff, L. L. (1975). Creativity and sense of humor. *Psychological Reports, 37*(3), 1022.

Ruch, W. (1996). Measurement approaches to the sense of humor: Introduction and overview. *International Journal of Humor Research, 9*(3–4), 239–250.

Scully, M. (Writer), & Gates, T. (Director). (2012, January 12). The Comeback Kid. [Television series episode]. In A. Poehler (Producer), *Parks and Recreation,* NBC.

Shultz, T. R. (1974). The role of incongruity and resolution in children's appreciation of cartoon humor. *Journal of Experimental Child Psychology, 45,* 100–105.

Sitton, S. C., & Pierce, E. R. (2004). Synesthesia, creativity and puns. *Psychological Reports, 95*(2), 577–580.

Smith, E. E., & White, H. L. (1965). Wit, creativity, and sarcasm. *Journal of Applied Psychology, 49,* 131–134.

Suls, J. M. (1972). A two-stage model for the appreciation of jokes and cartoons: An information-processing analysis. In J. H. Goldstein & P. E. McGhee (Eds.), *The psychology of humor* (pp. 81–100). Academic Press.

Sutu, A., Phetmisy, C. N., & Damian, R. I. (2021). Open to laugh: The role of openness to experience in humor production ability. *Psychology of Aesthetics, Creativity, and the Arts, 15*(3), 401–411.

Treadwell, Y. (1970). Humor and creativity. *Psychological Reports, 26*(1), 55–58.

Turner, R.G. (1980). Self-monitoring and humor production. *Journal of Personality, 48*(2), 163–172.

White, E. B., & White, K. S. (1941). *A subtreasury of American humor.* Coward-McCann.

Ziller, R. C., Behringer, R. D., & Goodchilds, J. D. (1962). Group creativity under conditions of success or failure and variations in group stability. *Journal of Applied Psychology, 46,* 43–49.

REMOTENESS OF ASSOCIATION,
GARTH'S SPEW CUP, AND *APPLES TO APPLES*

Both the Associative Theory of Creativity and the Incongruity Theory of Humor suggest that the *degree* of creativity or humor depends on the *remoteness of the association*. Humor depends on how much a punch line violates the recipient's expectations (Suls, 1972) or how much the perceived state of affairs diverges from the expected state (Nerhardt, 1970). Putting this in terms of creativity, "the more mutually remote the elements of the new combination, the more creative the process or solution" (Mednick, 1962). When the connections are too *obvious*, the output is not considered creative or funny. When the connections are too *distant*, such that they cannot be made (e.g., an *inside joke* that you are not in on), then the output is confusing.

In the movie *Wayne's World*, there is a scene in which a friend, Phil, is nauseous and Garth is concerned about him vomiting in his car. Garth proposes, "*if you're going to spew, spew into this*" and holds up a small paper cup (Spheeris, 1992). From an incongruity perspective, a container the size of a bucket would not be funny as it would be an expected and appropriately sized container for the situation. In this joke, the humor comes from the unexpected size of the container and that it won't hold nearly the appropriate volume of spew that is needed. A similar visual joke occurs in *This is Spinal Tap* (Reiner, 1984) in which a large Stonehenge set piece is intended to descend onto the stage

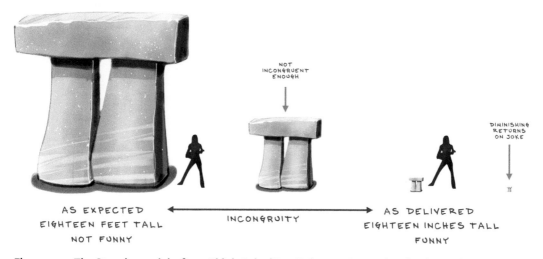

Figure 27.1 The Stonehenge joke from *This is Spinal Tap* (Reiner, 1984) as visualized as an incongruity of size difference between expectations (18 feet) and realization (18 inches).

DOI: 10.4324/9781003276296-32

during a rock concert, but, due to a drafting typo, a tiny Stonehenge model was produced and was lowered onto the stage. In both movies' jokes, the size of the object is unexpected and clearly does not fully meet the intended need.

If the spew container or Stonehenge model were *even smaller,* the joke would have diminishing returns to the point that it becomes somewhat of a different joke (e.g., the container cannot hold any spew at all; the Stonehenge model is not detectable from the audience). In both jokes, the spew container and Stonehenge model could get larger, but as it approaches the expected, appropriate size, it quickly loses humor as there is less of an incongruity. In both of these examples, it's possible to flip the joke in the opposite direction of size expectation and present an object that is *larger* than expected (although for differing reasons, an unexpected much smaller object may be more humorous than an unexpected much larger object). Figure 27.2 illustrates this concept of varying the size of Garth's spew container from *Wayne's World.*

There is some debate on the form of the relationship between degree of incongruity and humor. One theory is that the relationship is an inverted-*U* in which humor reaches a maximum at a moderate level of incongruity (Berlyne, 1972). Humor increases until some ideal level of divergence from expectations and, after which, further divergence will result in a decrease in humor. Another study found that as incongruity increases, the humor increases to some asymptotic value after which further increases do not result in a noticeable humor decrease (Deckers & Salais, 1983). Both models can be discussed using Figure 27.2 if we focus on only one side of the figure (one direction of incongruity). If we look only at the left side of the figure, as the container gets smaller and smaller diverging away from an expected bucket size container, the humor increases until some moderate level of incongruity (a small cup). If the size of the container decreases beyond this, the humor of the joke either diminishes (i.e., creating an inverted-U shape) or maintains at some level of humor (i.e., reaching some asymptotic value). This debated element is presented as the green zones in the figure.

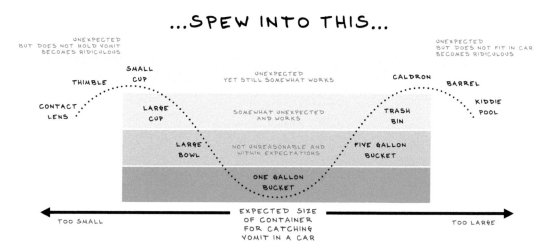

Figure 27.2 A graph of humor value on the *Y*-axis and variance from expectations on the *X*-axis. In this illustration, the *X*-axis is the size of the container offered to Phil for him to "spew" into from *Wayne's World* (Spheeris, 1992). As the incongruity or degree of variation from expectation grows, the humor potential increases up until some point of ideal incongruity. In the movie, a small cup was offered, which is unexpected. It is insufficient enough to be funny, but not overly insufficient. If the container was even smaller, the humor value may stay the same or may diminish.

The Incongruity Theory of Humor is often tested in a laboratory setting where subjects are tasked with lifting a series of weights. The incongruity between actual and expected weight is compared with the degree of humorous response (Nerhardt, 1970; Deckers & Kizer, 1975). These studies typically find a positive relationship between laughter and divergence from expectations—specifically "laughter decreased for the middle weights and increased for the very light or very heavy weights" (Nerhardt, 1970). This study can be presented using the same diagram of Figure 27.2 with the expected (moderate) weight being in the center and humor level increasing as the weight was either lighter or heavier than expected. A follow-up study in a real-world setting (passers-by lifting suitcases of varying weights at a train station in Stockholm) did *not* produce any laughter (Nerhardt, 2017), but this was explained in part by the setting not being an appropriate venue for laughter. Like in play, your environment has an impact on the appreciation and production of humor (Cundall, 2007).

Let's explore this phenomenon in the game of *Apples to Apples* (or equally *Cards Against Humanity*). This is a card game that involves strategically selecting a noun (person, place, thing, event) from a set of noun cards that can be described by a characteristic selected by the judge player for that round. For example, a player could be holding a hand of noun cards that includes things like "dirty diaper," "horror movies," and "pigeons." If the judge for this round reveals a characteristic card that reads "scary," the player would then select a noun card from their hand that they believe the judge would most appreciate being described as "scary."

This game is equal parts empathy and creativity. *Empathy* is important for creating successful products and services. Designers must understand their potential users—they need to tap into the emotional and physical needs and desires of their target audience. This typically involves extensive user research and observation. In the case of *Apples to Apples*, players who know each other well, have a deeper knowledge of each other's preferences, experiences, opinions, and, in this specific case, fears. In this example, when the judge reveals the "scary" adjective card, players must determine if the judge is most afraid of "dirty diapers," "horror movies," or "pigeons," and if they would prioritize an evocative response over an obvious response. In *Apples to Apples*, there is an underlying assumption that the responses should illicit humor via creative connections. As per the game instructions, "judges will often pick the most creative, humorous, or interesting response."

As we have discussed, for a response to be creative or funny, it needs to be unexpected yet still make sense, or in other words, the association must be distant enough to be non-obvious, but not so distant that it is confusing. In this example, when looking at a hand of noun cards, the player is searching for connections between these nouns and the characteristic word "scary" that is not too distant, but also not too obvious. A noun card that says "horror movies" might be too *obvious* of a connection and therefore not creative or funny. The noun card "pigeons" might be too distantly associated and therefore confusing. A noun like "Spice Girls" (i.e., Scary Spice) or "dirty diaper" may have a moderate degree of remoteness with the characteristic of "scary" to be deemed creative and/or humorous. Again, the inverted-U of humor and creativity reaches a maximum at a moderate level of incongruity (Berlyne, 1972). As shown in Figure 27.3, this maximum is the "Aha Zone" in which someone can easily have a moment of insight upon connecting two things.

As illustrated in Figure 27.3, a creative or humorous response will typically have a non-obvious connection that is neither too distant nor too obvious to the audience to result in an "Aha!" or "Haha!" moment. Relating this to joke theory in Chapter 26, if the receiver of a joke hears the punchline and either cannot make the connection back to the body of the joke or the punchline is obvious, then the joke will not be funny (Suls, 1972). Humor requires a moderate amount of cognitive challenge on the part of the receiver (Lieberman, 1977).

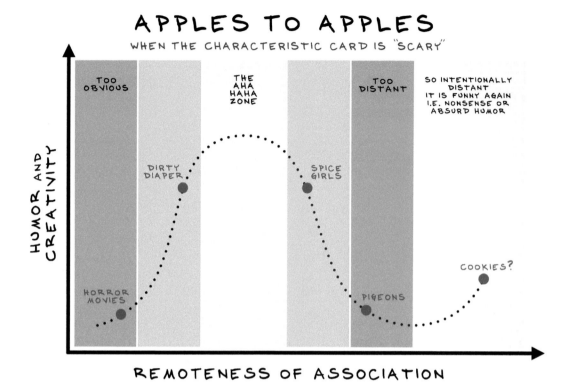

Figure 27.3 The inverted-U relationship between incongruity or remoteness of association and humor value, illustrated with an example from the game *Apples to Apples*. A noun like "horror movies" is too obvious of a connection to the characteristic of "scary." A noun like "pigeons" may be too distantly related to the characteristic of "scary" to form any clear association. The ideal response for humor is a noun with some moderate degree of incongruity or remoteness.

As for exceptions to the rule, it is possible for a very distant association or no connection at all to illicit humor (e.g., scary + cookie in Figure 27.3). *Nonsense, absurdist,* or *non-sequitur* humor seems to go in opposition to the incongruity-resolution model of humor. Viewing nonsense humor from the incongruity perspective, no rule or connector is present to make sense of the incongruity and the reader is left with a sense of confusion. Nonsense humor is only effective if it *pretends* to make sense (Koestler, 1964). This means that the creator must intentionally leave out the resolution with full understanding of what they are doing. To map this back to the game of *Apples to Apples*, if the player said they accidentally put down "cookies" as their noun card, it is less funny than if they seriously played the "cookies" card. *Monty Python*, Andy Kaufman, Tom Green, Tim and Eric, Gary Larson's *The Far Side*, *Mr. Show with Bob and David*, and Eric Andre are all examples of the range of nonsense or absurdist humor. There is a very fine line between confusing-disappointing and confusing-amusing, and the appreciation is dependent on the audience. Typically, individuals who are high in sensation seeking prefer nonsense humor to incongruity-resolution humor (Martin, 1998).

In *Dog Man,* a children's graphic novel series, Petey the World's Most Evil Cat, tries to explain to his clone "son," Li'l Petey, how jokes and the Incongruity Theory work (Pilkey, 2018).

> Jokes have a very specific structure. They are based on switching expectations. I'll give you an example: Knock knock (who's there?). Dwayne. (Dwayne who?) *Dwayne* the bathtub, I'm

dwowning. You were expecting someone named Dwayne. But I switched it around. That's why it's funny.

This is the Incongruity Theory as a knock-knock joke. The bisociating link is the word "Dwayne" being both a person's name and the word "drain" spoken with a rhotacism. Li'l Petey does not understand the joke and suggests that "it would have been funnier if a bathtub pooped on your head." Young children only require incongruity for humor and that the second stage of resolution is only crucial for adults (McGhee, 1971).

> In order to recognize something as surprising, incongruous, or novel, the individual would have to know what the expected or usual result or answer would be. That frame of reference is, of course, a function of developmental age and experiential exposure to facts and situations.
>
> (Lieberman, 1977)

As we age, we appreciate incongruity-resolution humor more and we appreciate nonsense humor less (Ruch et al., 1990).

To link this to creativity and innovation, we discussed the concept of *Most Advanced Yet Acceptable* in Chapter 11. People will find things most pleasing if they strike a balance between novel/unique/distant and typical/familiar/obvious (Hekkert et al., 2003). Just like good humor, we appreciate a *moderate* amount of cognitive challenge when it comes to creative things: too obvious is not creative and too distantly connected is confusing. In one of my studies (Ludden et al., 2012), we found that when people have difficulty understanding the presence of a novel feature or physical "punch line" in a product, the incongruity or surprise is deemed inappropriate and confusing, and it produces negative opinions about the product. On the other hand, people appreciate and enjoy appropriate incongruities that can somehow relate back to the nature of the product (e.g., incremental innovation). We will explore this phenomenon and ways of finding *appropriate* incongruities in Chapters 28 and 29.

References

Berlyne, D. E. (1972). Humor and its kin. In J. H. Goldstein & P. E. McGhee (Eds.), *The psychology of humor* (pp. 43–60). Academic Press.

Cundall, M. K. (2007). Humor and the limits of incongruity. *Creativity Research Journal, 19*(2–3), 203–211.

Deckers, L., & Kizer, P. (1975) Humor and the incongruity hypothesis. *The Journal of Psychology, 90*(2), 215–218.

Deckers, L., & Salais, D. (1983). Humor as a negatively accelerated function of the degree of incongruity. *Motivation and Emotion, 7*(4), 357–363.

Hekkert, P., Snelders, D., & van Wieringen, P. C. (2003). 'Most advanced, yet acceptable': Typicality and novelty as joint predictors of aesthetic preference in industrial design. *British Journal of Psychology, 94*(1), 111–124.

Koestler, A. (1964). *The act of creation.* Macmillan.

Lieberman, J. N. (1977). *Playfulness: Its relationship to imagination and creativity* (A. J. Edwards, Ed.). Academic Press.

Ludden, G. D., Kudrowitz, B. M., Schifferstein, H. N., & Hekkert, P. (2012). Surprise and humor in product design: Designing sensory metaphors in multiple modalities. *Humor: International Journal of Humor Research, 25*, 285–309.

Martin, R. A. (1998). Approaches to the sense of humor. In W. Ruch (Ed.), *The sense of humor: Explorations of a personality characteristic* (pp. 15–60). Mouton de Gruyter.

McGhee, P. E. (1971). Cognitive development and children's comprehension of humor. *Child Development, 42*(1), 123–138.

Mednick, S. A. (1962). The associative basis of the creative process. *Psychological Review, 69*, 220–232.

Nerhardt, G. (1970). Humor and inclination to laugh: Emotional reactions to stimuli of different divergence from a range of expectancy. *Scandinavian Journal of Psychology, 11*(3), 185–195.

Nerhardt, G. (2017). Incongruity and funniness: Towards a new descriptive model. In A. J. Chapman & H. Foot (Eds.), *Humor and Laughter* (pp. 55–62). Routledge.

Pilkey, D. (2018). *Dog man: Lord of the fleas.* Graphix.

Reiner, R. (Director). (1984). *This Is Spinal Tap [Motion picture].* United States: Embassy Pictures.

Ruch, W., McGhee, P. E., & Hehl, F.-J. (1990). Age differences in the enjoyment of incongruity-resolution and nonsense humor during adulthood. *Psychology and Aging, 5*(3), 348–355.

Spheeris, P. (Director). (1992). *Wayne's World [Motion picture].* United States: Paramount Pictures.

Suls, J. M. (1972). A two-stage model for the appreciation of jokes and cartoons: An information-processing analysis. In J. H. Goldstein & P. E. McGhee (Eds.), *The psychology of humor* (pp. 81–100). Academic Press.

28

METAPHORICAL THINKING, A FINGER TRAP
BIOPSY NEEDLE, AND SCAMPER

Both humor (in the context of the Incongruity Theory) and creativity (in the context of the Associative Theory) are variants of metaphoric thought. A metaphor links attributes from one conceptual domain with a different conceptual domain. "The creative act of the humorist consists in bringing about a momentary fusion between two habitually incompatible frames of reference" (Koestler, 1964). Whereas, the creative act, whether in poetry or science, depends on discovering analogies between two or more ideas previously thought unrelated (Martindale, 1999). More explicitly, Mednick refers to creative thinking process as "the forming of associative elements into new combinations which either meet specified requirements or are in some way useful" (1962).

In general, we enjoy metaphors and analogies because *they make complex concepts easier to understand*. We apparently love to do this with animals (and, yes, these are all real): hammerhead shark, tiger shark, shark mackerel, mackerel shark, kangaroo rat, rat kangaroo, bee hummingbird, hummingbird hawk-moth, elephant hawk-moth caterpillar, elephant shrew, elephant seal, tomato clownfish, pineapple, pineappleweed, pineapplefish, seahorse, giraffe seahorse, hedgehog seahorse, zebra seahorse, zebra turkeyfish, eel catfish, leopard catshark, tiger snake eel, oyster toadfish.

We make sense of new concepts and discoveries by comparing them with something we already know. How many times have you said, "it tastes like _____ but with _____," or "the movie was like _____ but with _____," or "the band sounds like _____ but with _____"? We enjoy finding interesting relationships as it makes new concepts easier to digest and explain to others.

Synectics is a creative process of using metaphorical thinking for "making the strange familiar, and making the familiar strange" (Prince, 1968). "The word Synectics, from the Greek, means 'the joining together of different and apparently irrelevant elements'" (Gordon, 1961). In this process, a problem is analyzed and generalized such that it can be compared via analogy to other models in the world (Prince, 1968). In viewing the problem from this new perspective, one can think of non-obvious solutions that may have been applied in different contexts. To reference an example in Chapter 3, the process of cutting down a field of wheat could be compared via analogy with the process of cutting hairs on someone's head (i.e., a field of wheat is like a head of hair). This shift in perspective could lead to applying solutions to the problem from another domain.

When we look at metaphorical thinking in design, we typically combine two concepts that have some overlapping element (like the Excalibur toilet brush of Chapter 26). Often the result comes

DOI: 10.4324/9781003276296-33

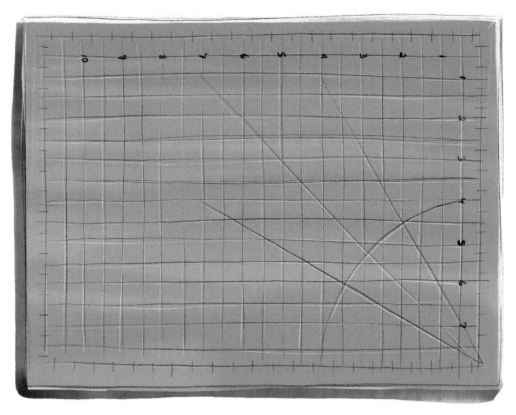

Figure 28.1 The Fred obsessive chef cutting board is a novelty product that provides both humor and incremental innovation. It is also an example of metaphorical thinking—comparing two things that are not typically connected. This wooden cutting board has etched lines like a crafting cutting mat for home cooks to have higher precision when cutting food.

across as humorous as it involves a non-obvious connection between seemingly unrelated things. In the product industry, this can describe *novelty products* (like the tanning bed toaster from Chapter 9) (Hatcher et al., 2018). *Fred* develops creative products based on associative and metaphorical thinking. One example of a Fred product is The Obsessive Chef Cutting Board in Figure 28.1. This is a wooden cutting board etched with a cutting mat pattern. The designer found a link (a rectangular flat cutting surface) that applies to a cutting board for food prep and also a crafting cutting mat. The joke is that the home cook typically does not need this degree of precision when preparing their *Mise en place*, but, like Garth's spew cup of Chapter 27, it still has *some* functionality and value.

There are a series of tools that facilitate making non-obvious connections and association making. In Chapter 2, I introduced the concept of a *mind map* as it pertained to divergent thinking. To refresh your memory, this is a tool developed by Tony Buzan as a means of organizing and visualizing one's thoughts in a nonlinear, network-structured representation (1974). It is not specifically a tool for humor production, but it is relevant to associative thinking. The technique was an attempt to break from the tendency to engage first in linear thinking. Since then, a growing body of research has developed on the effectiveness of mind mapping as a tool for different cognitive tasks. Mind mapping has shown to help with metaphorical thinking (Mento et al., 1999), studying/memory recall (Farrand et al., 2002), understanding of a subject matter (Abi-El-Mona & Adb-El-Khalick, 2008), and divergent thinking ability (Leeds & Kudrowitz, 2016).

In traditional mind mapping, you start with a central concept and branch outward in all directions. There is no specific process for connecting nodes to generate ideas. An *association map* (a variation on mind mapping) can be used to help a designer find non-obvious connections between a concept and seemingly unrelated things (Ludden et al., 2012). To begin, one starts with a concept in the center to be redesigned. Around this central concept are general attributes such as the environment or use location, the function, the use actions or motions, its name, etc. If the concept is a physical thing, it can include attributes like materials and form. Under each of these attributes, one then describes the concept in as simple terms as possible. The next step involves thinking of and listing other things that have similar attributes (*divergent thinking*). If the designer can incorporate properties of one of these "other things" back into the original concept, the result will be an incongruity that can be linked back to the product (*convergent thinking*). This incongruity could then produce a creative connection, a metaphor, a joke, a surprise, and/or a novelty product. Association mapping is essentially a structured mind map for incrementally innovating some concept by helping you find a non-obvious connection that is just a few nodes away from the original concept. *Witty people do this process naturally (and quickly) without using a tool or thinking about what they are doing.* This is the mechanism behind throwing good shade (Chapter 25) or excelling in a pun slam (Chapter 4). Figure 28.2 is an example of an association map for wireless earbuds.

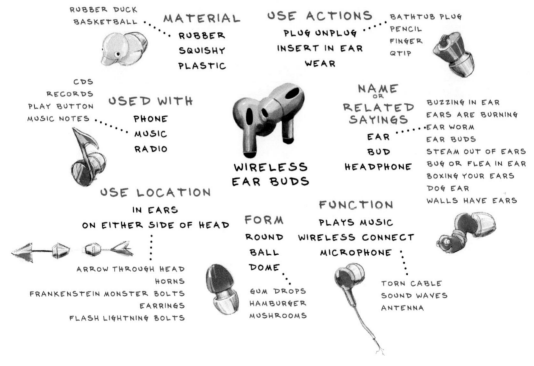

Figure 28.2 An association map for wireless earbuds. General attributes surround the central concept including use location, form, function, etc. Each attribute is described in simple terms, for example, the use location of ear buds is "in ears" or "on either side of the head." The designer then lists other things that also meet that attribute, for example, horns go on either side of the head. The designer then tries to incorporate something from these "other things" back into the original concept (in this case, wireless ear buds). Looking at this map, you can think of some novelty ear bud product ideas such as ear buds that make it look like an arrow is going through your head or ear buds that look like drain plugs.

Even though the product examples in Figure 28.2 seem to be more like silly jokes, some of these are real products. This tool can also be used for more serious functional ideation too. I was designing a coring endoscopic biopsy needle with a team of students, and we were trying to find a means of preserving the tissue histology inside the needle shaft (i.e., retrieving a clean plug of tissue). Through an association mapping process, biopsy needles were linked to finger traps. We designed a tiny, passive, internal flexure mechanism that opens when the needle is inserted and pinches shut when the needle is retracted (Figueredo et al., 2008). At some level, the idea is a "joke" because it is a little tiny finger trap for biopsies; however, it is also innovative, serious, and potentially patent worthy.

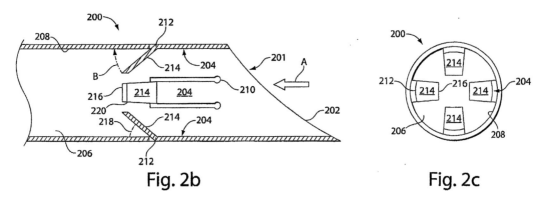

Fig. 2b   **Fig. 2c**

Figure 28.3   Figures from the coring endoscopic biopsy needle patent application (Figueredo et al., 2008) illustrating the finger trap-like mechanism.

TILMAG (Transformation idealer Lösungselemente mit Assoziationen und Gemeinsamkeiten) by Helmut Schlicksupp is an even more structured (German) technique that is in the same genre as association mapping (Silverstein et al., 2008). With this tool, instead of listing attributes of a product such as form, use motion, etc. This tool requires you to focus solely on the specific functional requirements or "ideal solution elements" of the central concept or problem. If we were talking about ear buds, this may include: wirelessly connected, produces sound, fits in or around the ears, self-powered, etc. Without going through the many steps involved in this process, the tool requires you to think of a collection of solutions: items/products/objects that meet two of the functional requirements at a time. For example, a hearing aid is self-powered and fits in or around the ears. The final step involves systematically trying to connect these seemingly unrelated items/solutions with the original idea in the same manner as one would link the items listed in an association map with the original idea.

Synectics, mind mapping, association mapping, and TILMAG are simply tools to provide a structured means of increasing the number of lateral connections one can make from a given starting point. They facilitate the first step in making a metaphorical connection for innovation and humor.

If a moderate amount of incongruity and MAYA (a balance of novel and typical) is important for both creativity and humor, then *SCAMPER* may also be a relevant tool for discussion. *SCAMPER* is a mnemonic for a set of creative techniques that are generally used for *incremental innovation*: Substitute, Combine, Adapt, Modify (or Magnify/Minify), Put to Other Uses, Eliminate, Reverse (or Rearrange) (Eberle, 1971). This tool is derived from a longer listing of techniques presented across three chapters of Osborn's book *Applied Imagination* (1953), which would have had a less effective

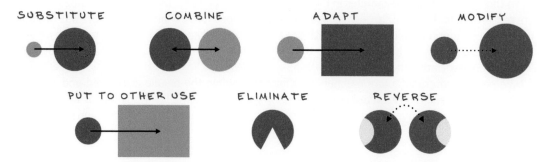

Figure 28.4 A graphical representation of the seven creative techniques of SCAMPER (Eberle, 1971). These methods can result in both humor and creativity. Four of the techniques (shown with green and pink elements) involve the intersection of two domains or concepts.

mnemonic: AMSAMSDRRC. These techniques all involve taking an existing familiar thing (like a product or a concept) and making some change to create a new thing.

We discussed Modifying as it pertains to humor in Chapter 27 (specific to minifying and magnifying Stonehenge and spew cups). We discussed Elimination (i.e., "less is more") in both creativity (Chapter 6) and humor (Chapter 26). In Chapter 17, we discussed an example of reversal that resulted in both humor and innovation: the *Simpsons* "tomacco" plant (a tomato plant grafted onto a tabaco root stem) was a reversal of a Scientific American study of the inverse grafting.

As you can see in Figure 28.4, Substitute, Combine, Adapt, and Put to Other Use all involve metaphorical thinking or the interaction of two difference references—taking something (a theme, technology, product, mechanism, context, etc.) and mapping it onto something else. The next chapter will focus on these four "SCAP" methods that are specific to connecting disparate domains.

References

Abi-El-Mona, I., & Adb-El-Khalick, F. (2008). The influence of mind mapping on eighth graders' science achievement. *School Science and Mathematics, 108*(7), 298–312.

Buzan, T. (1974). *Use your head*. BBC Books.

Eberle, B. (1971). *Scamper, games for imagination development*. D.O.K. Publishers.

Farrand, P., Hussain, F., & Hennessy, E. (2002). The efficacy of the 'mind map' study technique. *Medical education, 36*(5), 426–431.

Figueredo, S., Fienup, W. J., Kudrowitz, B., Wronski, J. A, Slocum, A. H., & Brugge, W. R. (2008). Biopsy Needle. U.S. Patent Application No. 20080300507. Washington, DC: U.S. Patent and Trademark Office.

Gordon, W. J. (1961). *Synectics: The development of creative capacity*. Harper and row.

Hatcher, G., Ion, W., MacLachlan, R., Wodehouse, A., Simpson, B., & Marlow, M. (2018). Applied humour in creative product design. In S. R. Luria, J. Baer, & J. C. Kaufman (Eds.), *Creativity and humour* (pp. 157–182). Elsevier.

Koestler, A. (1964). *The act of creation*. Macmillan.

Leeds, A., & Kudrowitz, B. (2016). Exploring how novel ideas are generated in mind maps. *Proceedings of the 4th International Conference on Design Creativity, ICDC 2016*, Atlanta, Georgia, USA.

Ludden, G. D., Kudrowitz, B. M., Schifferstein, H. N., & Hekkert, P. (2012). Surprise and humor in product design: Designing sensory metaphors in multiple modalities. *Humor: International Journal of Humor Research, 25*, 285–309.

Martindale, C. (1999). Biological bases of creativity. In R. Sternberg (Ed.), *Handbook of creativity* (pp. 137–152). University Press.

Mednick, S. A. (1962). The associative basis of the creative process. *Psychological Review, 69*, 220–232.

Mento, A. J., Martinelli, P., & Jones, R.M. (1999). Mind mapping in executive education: Applications and out-comes. *Journal of Management Development, 18*(4), 390–416.

Osborn, A. F. (1953). *Applied imagination: Principles and procedures of creative thinking.* Scribner.

Prince, G. M. (1968). The operational mechanism of synectics. *The Journal of Creative Behavior, 2*(1), 1–13.

Silverstein, D., Samuel, P., & DeCarlo, N. (2008). *The innovator's toolkit: 50+ techniques for predictable and sus-tainable organic growth.* Wiley.

29

CONNECTING DOMAINS, THE COMBINATION PIZZA HUT AND TACO BELL, AND TRIZ

According to the SCAMPER framework, there are four methods of connecting information across different domains for idea generation (Substitution, Combination, Adaptation, Put to Other Use). This section discusses these methods and how it relates to creativity and humor.

Substitution

Substitution is replacing a component of the original thing with something else. As a common example, we may find that we don't have a certain vegetable for a recipe and so we substitute a vegetable we have on hand. People with dietary restrictions may often use substitutes in their cooking to replace meat, dairy, eggs, gluten, etc. In a restaurant setting, we may see chefs doing more intentional versions of this creative technique with "*a play on*" something—for example, a "risotto" made with sunflower seeds instead of rice (Kudrowitz et al., 2014). In humor, this relates to *parody*. Five-time Grammy Award winning "Weird Al" Yankovic is well known as a musical parody artist. His artform typically involves taking a popular contemporary song and recreating the instrumental music, melody, rhyme scheme, and style of singing, while replacing the words for comedic effect. Parody, being a form of incremental innovation, is often easy to assimilate. In the case of music parody, the listener already knows most of the musical content, but the words are new. In the case of the "risotto" example, the diner is familiar with the preparation of the dish, but an ingredient is new.

Let's revisit *Nathan for You* (of Chapter 10) again acting as an intermediary between the worlds of humor and innovation. Nathan relies on parody for both humor and creativity when he develops the "Dumb Starbucks"—a Starbucks-like store that offers similar products, but with the word "dumb" as a prefix (Kemp et al., 2014). In innovation, we are often switching out components of some existing thing to create a new product or service. For example, in Chapter 11, we discussed Edison's lightbulb patent (1880), which was similar to prior art, but used carbon-coated bamboo as the filament as opposed to a metal filament. This *seemingly* simple substitution allowed light bulbs to be powered with low current, low cost, and longer life. I am emphasizing "seemingly" because doing substitution well is taxing as per accounts of the creative processes of both Weird Al and Edison.

Combine

According to Daniel Pink's "Reese's Peanut Butter Cup Theory of Innovation," "sometimes the most powerful ideas come from simply combining two existing ideas nobody else ever thought to unite. Most inventions and breakthroughs come from reassembling existing ideas in new ways" (2006).

DOI: 10.4324/9781003276296-34

Combining is also a successful practice for Taco Bell (soft shell + hard shell, Doritos + taco shell, Taco Bell + Pizza Hut, Taco Bell + KFC). Let's explore the Doritos taco shell example. As both Doritos and Taco Bell shells are corn-based hard tortillas, they have a strong connecting link, and the combination makes sense. The result should be an Aha! or Haha! moment. Alternatively, if Taco Bell crossed their shells with a different snack food (e.g., Cheetos), it may still be tasty, but the connection is weaker, and most observers would fall into the "confusion" block of the joke theory flow chart of Figure 26.4.

Product crossing works best when there is already some link (e.g., hard corn tortillas). In 2004, surfing brand Reef collaborated with Australian surfer Mick Fanning to release a pair of sandals that has a (patented) built-in bottle opener on the bottom of the sole. As of 2019, this sandal remains Reef's "all-time best seller product" (DeAcetis, 2019). This concept combines or crosses two items that are typically used on the beach.

There is an array of crossed cutlery products, which also happen to cross names too (i.e., *portmanteau*). The most common piece of crossed cutlery is the spork (spoon + fork), but there are others shown in Figure 29.1 as a Venn diagram. Most of these sound like jokes despite having existed and been sold for many years.

Figure 29.1 Crossing existing products is one means of creating incrementally innovative concepts (i.e., Combine from SCAMPER). This is an illustration of how often this occurs with some cutlery.

Tools like association mapping and TILMAG work by first finding connection links and that leads to uncovering a second item to cross/combine with the original concept. Another means of finding interesting connections is by *randomly* pairing things and then trying to find a link. This process is called *Brutethink* (Michalko, 2000) or *Random Stimuli*. In this process, a random word, object, or topic is presented, and one has to uncover a way of incorporating it back into some original idea or problem. I designed a game related to *Brutethink* called *Cross Products*. In this game, one player is the customer, and the other players are designers. Each designer has a handful of product cards. The customer flips over a product card from the deck and the designers have to find ways of combining attributes, elements, functionality, features, etc. from one of the products in their hand with that of the customer's product card. For example, if the customer's card was "pencil" and I wanted to use my "flowerpot" card, I could say, "a pencil that is made of compressed seeds and when you are done using it, you can plant it." If I wanted to use my toothbrush card, I could say, "a toothbrush that is impregnated with fluoride so when you chew it, you strengthen your teeth." After all ideas are pitched, the customer picks their favorite idea. This game can be played as an idea generation tool, and you don't necessarily need a deck of cards—you can write down a list of random products and exchange with others.

The tricky part of *Brutethink* or *Cross Products* is in trying to find an interesting connection without simply "*sporking*" the two concepts (e.g., a toothbrush with a pencil on the end). In order to get to the non-obvious interesting links, one needs to think deeper into both starting points. The *HIT (Heuristic Ideation Technique) Matrix* is a tool used for this purpose—to compare characteristics of two seemingly unrelated things to uncover some creative output. In the words of the creator of this tool:

> Most psychologists accept the definition of creative output (the ideas) as combinations of two or more concepts in the mind of the creator. If one could obtain all 'relevant' concepts that

Figure 29.2　Example cards from the *Cross Products* game.

apply to a product area, then, by definition, the set of all possible combinations of these concepts (the power set) would represent the total set of product ideas in that area given today's knowledge.

(Tauber, 1972)

To begin a HIT Matrix, take any two concepts and list characteristics or "factors" of each. This is what Tauber refers to as "decomposing" (1972). This is a divergent thinking task. Let's list some factors of a toothbrush: *thin flat handle, bristles, goes in mouth, cleans teeth, brushing motion, removes material, stores in bathroom, morning/evening routine, creates good breath, oral hygiene, foaming, plastic, used with paste*. And then let's list some factors of a pencil: *used to write, wood, graphite-filled, long thin rod, erases, able to be sharpened to reuse, tucked behind ear, used in school/work, people chew it, hexagon cross section, creates doodles, used with paper, consumed with use*. The factors of one item are placed across the top of a table and the factors of the other item are placed along the side of a table. Each cell of the table then represents a unique combination of characteristics from the two initial items. Now comes the convergent thinking part of the activity. This tool doesn't do all the creative work for you as you still need to find the connections. It does, however, allow you to look at the initial items as a set of characteristics as opposed to a fixed object. This is essentially a systematic structured process for the thought process that occurs when playing *Cross Products*. It is also the thought process that you go through when trying to link an item at the end of your Association Map or TILMAG matrix to the starting concept. In this specific HIT matrix, you can see how the idea for a fluoride-impregnated pencil could emerge in the cell "oral hygiene + people chew on it" or at least how the idea could more easily emerge than by saying "pencil + toothbrush."

Adaptation (or Put to Other Use)

Adaptation and Put to Other Use are inverse names for the same creativity technique of taking something from one domain and applying it in a different context. This process or phenomenon goes by a few different terms. *The Medici Effect* is a term used when someone brings ideas from one field into another (Johansson, 2006). It is named after the Medici family of Florence that funded creatives from a wide range of disciplines during the Renaissance. More specifically, this term is used when someone contributes to disruptive innovation in a field by bringing in their outside experience and knowledge. *Exaptation* is a term used to describe a biological trait evolving to serve a very different function than what it originally performed, such as bird feathers evolving first for temperature regulation but then later allowing for flight (Gould & Vrba, 1982). Stephen Johnson expounds on this term to describe taking technology from one domain and applying it in another domain (2010). In this context, there is an overlap with the Medici Effect description. *Biomimicry or biomimetics* is a third related term, but specific to adapting a process or mechanism found in nature to a problem or product at hand (Benyus, 1997; Vincent et al., 2006). If you recall Figure 15.4 illustrating Carl Sagan's 'Cosmic Calendar,' humans have only been around for 30 minutes of this scaled down Earth-year-of-existence, but nature has been working hard for "hours" experimenting and perfecting things before humans showed up. As an example of biomimicry, the nose of Japan's Shinkansen 500-Series (Bullet Train) was modeled after the beak of the kingfisher bird. When a fast train exits a tunnel, it creates a low-level sonic boom. In order to reduce this effect, the engineers needed a design that would allow for the train to move smoothly at high speeds across a change in resistance. One of the engineers working on this problem also happened to be an avid bird-watcher (i.e., the Medici Effect) and made the connection that kingfisher birds can dive into the water at high speeds (going from low resistance to high resistance) without making a splash (Benyus, 1997).

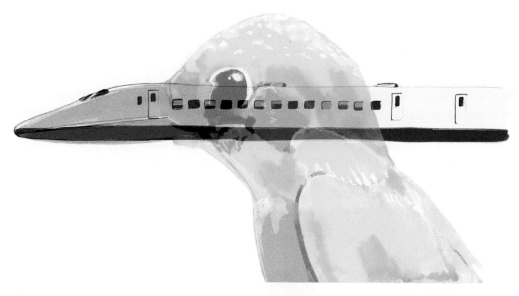

Figure 29.3 As an example of biomimicry, this is an illustration of the Shinkansen 500-Series train overlaid on the beak of the kingfisher bird. The form of the train nose was inspired by nature to eliminate the sonic boom created by the train exiting tunnels.

I was flipping through an IKEA catalog, and I saw an advertisement describing exaptation/Medici Effect:

> What started out as a door ended up as a bookcase. When our designers visited a door factory, they walked away with an idea for making furniture. Based on the door construction, they layered sheets of wood over a honeycomb core that's strong and lightweight with minimal wood content.

(2010)

The IKEA designers borrowed a process from a different industry and applied it to their own industry.

TRIZ (a Russian acronym that stands for "theory of inventive problem-solving") is a great tool for adaptation like this. It was developed by engineer and science fiction author (see Chapter 16), Genrich Altshuller. Working as a clerk in a patent office, Altshuller uncovered a series of generalizable patterns or rules that occurred across patentable inventions. He theorized that these manners in which technical problems have been solved in the past can be applied to solve new problems across different domains, industries, and sciences (i.e., adaptation) (1999). TRIZ starts with restructuring a problem as a contradiction among two or more elements or features. Contradictions and non-obvious modifications can naturally be tied back to the Incongruity Theory of Humor. One study actually used humorous cartoons to demonstrate and teach the principles of TRIZ (Likholetov & Aliukov, 2021). I will try to summarize the general process of TRIZ using this IKEA bookcase example.

With TRIZ, your contradiction must be between any 2 of a set of 39 factors (such as strength, weight, reliability, temperature, and complexity). These factors are arranged in a "contradiction matrix" such that you can take a contradiction between any two factors, and it points you to a selection of 40 inventive principles that have been used in prior inventions to solve similar contradictions. In this IKEA contradiction, we need an object (a bookcase) to be strong, but we don't want to increase the weight. The contradiction matrix for this pairing points to four inventive principles: Segmentation, Copying, Cheap short-living objects, and Composite materials. The inventive solution that IKEA adapted from the door industry was both Segmentation (honeycomb corrugation) as well as Composite materials (layered sheets of wood). In reality, the designers made the same non-obvious connection while physically exploring another domain. The TRIZ tool can be used to derive solutions like this by applying prior patent teachings without necessarily having to tour other industries.

Design heuristics is a younger, design-themed cousin of TRIZ that has also been shown to produce creative design solutions. This is a set of 77 strategies (akin to the TRIZ 40 inventive principles) that were derived from studying prior design solutions (as opposed to patents, like with TRIZ). A few examples from this set include "build user community," "make components attachable or detachable," and "use packaging as a functional component" (Daly et al., 2012). *BioTRIZ* is another younger TRIZ-like tool. This is a combination of biomimicry and TRIZ: it functions as a structured method of adaptation of nature to solve technical problems (Vincent et al., 2006).

One of the most famous historical examples of adaptation (and is also an example of combination) is *Gutenberg's Printing Press*. Gutenberg combined the movable type used in block/type printing in China (which was not well known in Europe at the time) with the screw-based press technology of a wine/olive press (which was not available in China) (Epstein, 2008). Gutenberg brought a technology from one culture and combined it with a technology of his culture to solve a problem. Although the printing press is now so old that it's mostly obsolete, I want you to try to imagine a time when all books were transcribed by hand. Let's say you were one of those people who transcribed books—it took you days to make one book copy. One day, you hear about Gutenberg who made a printing machine. You were able to see it in person. It was "hacked" from a wine press! This is a machine you were very familiar with and have only seen it in the context of pressing olives and grapes. You would never think of it being used in a context related to making books. But there it is...doing what you have been trained to do, yet in a tiny fraction of the time. There is a laugh in there somewhere. Perhaps an Aha! laugh (Incongruity Theory), but maybe also a nervous laugh as you think about your job being replaced by a machine (Release Theory).

Thomas Edison was fond of connecting domains as a creative method. He has said "Make it a habit to keep on the lookout for novel and interesting ideas that others have used successfully. Your idea needs to be original only in its adaptation to the problem you are working on" (Michalko, 2000). In the next chapter, we will dive deeper into the idea of "keeping on the lookout" and the humor of discovery.

References

Altshuller, G. S. (1999). *The innovation algorithm: TRIZ, systematic innovation and technical creativity*. Technical innovation center, Inc.

Benyus, J. M. (1997). *Biomimicry: Innovation inspired by nature*. Morrow.

Daly, S. R., Yilmaz, S., Christian, J. L., Seifert, C. M., & Gonzalez, R. (2012). Design heuristics in engineering concept generation. *Journal of Engineering Education, 101*(4), 601–629.

DeAcetis, J. (2019, July 31). Reef: How cushion bounce technology changed the game forever. *Forbes*.

Edison, T. A. (1880). Electric Lamp. U.S. Patent Application No. 223,898. Washington, DC: U.S. Patent and Trademark Office.

Epstein, J. (2008). The end of the Gutenberg era. *Library Trends, 57*(1), 8–16.

Gould, S. J., & Vrba, E. S. (1982). Exaptation—a missing term in the science of form. *Paleobiology, 8*(1), 4–15.

IKEA. (2010). *IKEA Catalogue 2011* (p. 84). Inter IKEA Systems B.V.

Johansson, F. (2006). *Medici effect: What you can learn from elephants and epidemics*. Harvard Business Press.

Johnson, S. (2010). *Where good ideas come from: The natural history of innovation*. Riverhead Books.

Kemp, D. J., Forsythe, L. M., & Jones, I. M. (2014). Parody in trademark law: Dumb Starbucks makes trademark law look dumb. *John Marshall Review of Intellectual Property Law, 14*(2), 145–198.

Kudrowitz, B., Oxborough, A., Choi, J., & Stover, E. (2014) The chef as designer: Classifying the techniques that chefs use in creating innovative dishes. In Y. K. Lim & K. Niedderer (Eds.), *Proceedings of the 2014 design research society conference* (pp. 127–146). Design Research Society.

Likholetov, V., & Aliukov, S. (2021). Humor is necessary for intensification learning creative technologies in engineering education. *International Journal of Engineering Education, 3*(1), 46–58.

Michalko, M. (2000). *Thinkertoys*. Gestión.

Pink, D. H. (2006). *A whole new mind: Why right-brainers will rule the future.* Penguin.

Tauber, E. M. (1972). Marketing notes and communications: Hit: Heuristic ideation technique—a systematic procedure for new product search. *Journal of Marketing, 36*(1), 58–61.

Vincent, J. F., Bogatyreva, O. A., Bogatyrev, N. R., Bowyer, A., & Pahl, A. K. (2006). Biomimetics: Its practice and theory. *Journal of the Royal Society Interface, 3*(9), 471–482.

30

THE HUMOR OF DISCOVERY, HIDDEN GORILLAS, AND *SEINFELD*

In Chapter 11, I discussed the differences between invention, innovation, and discovery and used the Albert Szent-Gyorgyi quote: "Discovery consists of seeing what everyone else has seen and thinking what no one else has thought" (1957). Just as there are Aha! or Haha! moments when you develop a new thing (invention/innovation), there are also Aha! or Haha! moments when you *discover* something that is already out there. When we think of technological discoveries, we think of observations in the physical sciences, but with humor, the discoveries are often observations in social science: life, society, humans, sex, childhood, culture, relationships etc. Chapters 26–29 attempt to connect creativity and innovation to the Incongruity Theory of Humor. This chapter and the next are reaching into the Release and Superiority Theories of Humor as we identify and call attention to our foibles as individuals and a society.

Humorists can question why people do things the way they do them. This involves observing people and making note of things that get overlooked, ignored, or are simply mundane. Those little quirks they notice are fodder for ideas or improvements in the way we do things. The act of dissecting culture and human behavior to question "something from the backwaters of life, an everyday phenomenon that is rarely noticed or discussed" is called *observational comedy* (Double, 2013). In the design/innovation world, it is simply a part of doing *user research*. In user research, one must objectively look at humans like an anthropologist or sociologist. One must divorce oneself from what is accepted as "normal" and question why we do the things we do; it is as if we were studying an alien society. There are many pop culture examples of aliens or God-like beings taking on the role of objectively questioning our human behavior (e.g., *The Humans: A Novel*, *3rd Rock from the Sun*, *Cone Heads*, *Monsters Inc*, *Thor.*). In one specific example from *The Good Place*, Michael, played by Ted Danson (who is not human), objectively analyzes the act of kissing: "Kissing is gross. You just mash your food holes together. It's not for that" (Schur et al., 2018). Nathan Pyle's comic strip *Strange Planet* is a celebration and dissection of human and societal idiosyncrasies illustrated through blobby blue aliens navigating mundane Earthly interactions. In a Valentine's Day themed comic, one alien shares a card depicting an arrow through a heart, "I drew a vital organ being wounded," and follows it with a bouquet of cut flowers, "also these are dying" (Pyle, 2019). Another cartoon holds a mirror to the strange act of tidying the house for company: "let us store irregular shapes inside shapes with flat surfaces...we own things but have hidden them" (Pyle, 2019). According to Pyle, "we [humans] would be pretty strange if someone were to observe us from the outside...We're observing another species from the outside, and we get a chance to see how quirky and yet lovable they are" (Dohms-Harter, 2020). This is how Aziz Ansari describes Jerry

DOI: 10.4324/9781003276296-35

Seinfeld: "You could stick him on some alien planet and he'd have the same brilliant, precise observations about how silly everything they do is" (Weiner, 2012).

When one makes an observation and it results in a "what's the deal with that?" response, that means a non-obvious discovery was made. This can be useful for humor, but maybe *also* for innovation. To revisit Sherlock Holmes from Chapter 3: "The world is full of obvious things which nobody by any chance ever observes" (Doyle, 2012). Observation is not easy, and designers have to practice to become good at it. People are naturally good at *seeing*, but that is not the same thing as *observing*. Let's take a three-question quiz. This is not a test of your drawing ability, but you will need to draw some things. For all of these, please don't cheat and look up images:

CAN YOU DRAW A LOBSTER FROM THE TOP VIEW?

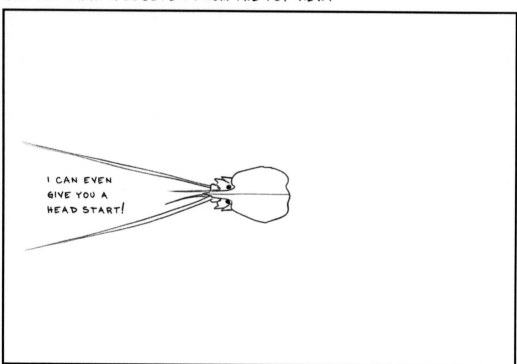

Figure 30.1 Observation Question 1: Can you draw a lobster from the top view?

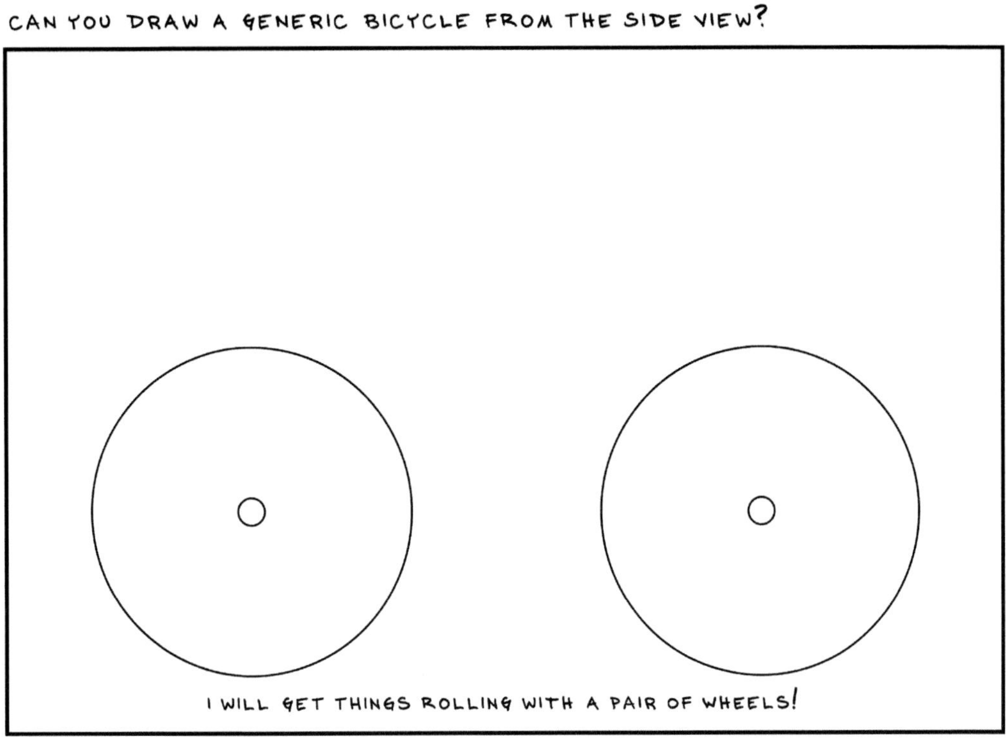

CAN YOU DRAW A GENERIC BICYCLE FROM THE SIDE VIEW?

I WILL GET THINGS ROLLING WITH A PAIR OF WHEELS!

Figure 30.2 Observation Question 2: Can you draw a generic bicycle from the side view?

CAN YOU DRAW THE HEADS SIDE OF THE US PENNY?

HERE IS A CHEAT SHEET OF THINGS THAT APPEAR SOMEWHERE ON THE FRONT OR BACK. YOU JUST NEED TO PUT THEM IN THE RIGHT PLACES!

THE DATE
'IN GOD WE TRUST'
'LIBERTY'
'ONE CENT'
'UNITED STATES OF AMERICA'

Figure 30.3 Observation Question 3: Can you draw the "heads" side of the U.S. one-cent coin (i.e., the penny)?

Let's see how you did.

For Question 1, my PhD adviser, David Wallace, would often ask his students to do this same activity in class. You have seen photos of lobsters before. You may have even consumed many of them, but have you really *observed* the lobster well enough to sketch the proportions correctly or include the important parts? Specifically, how many *legs* does the lobster have? Not including the claws, lobsters have eight legs! They also five tail fins.

For Question 2, The Bicycle Drawing Test was used by Piaget (1930) to assess a child's cognitive maturity and it has been used in a variety of different studies, including the ability to recall and reproduce a visualization of an object that is frequently encountered (Greenberg et al., 1994). I also use this test in my classes to see if students can recall an everyday object. After a minute, most students come to the realization that they don't actually know the geometry of a bike frame or how the seat, wheels, pedals, and handlebars mechanically connect to each other.

For Question 3, you have probably seen quite a few pennies before, but how well do you know the details? If you did not get these correct, you are not alone! In the original study that created this test, *no* participants were able to draw a penny from memory and "their attempts to do so were, for the most part, grossly inaccurate" even "when told what the features are" (Nickerson & Adams, 1979).

If you did get these three questions correct, congrats, Sherlock! For everyone else, these are examples of a phenomenon called *jamais vu* (French for "never seen") (Sno, 2000). Comedian George Carlin referred to this as "*Vuja de*"—"the strange feeling that, somehow, none of this has ever happened before" (Berger, 2014). Regardless of which expression we use, this phenomenon describes "when you feel and act as if an experience (or an object) is brand-new even if you have had it (or seen it) hundreds of times" (Sutton, 2002). We may see something regularly, but we don't notice any of the specific features until we are required to pay attention.

> Typically, the details of visual stimuli are not retained in memory-or at least they are not available from memory-unless there is some functional reason for them to be. In other words, what one is most likely to remember about the visual properties of objects is what one needs to remember in order to distinguish those objects in everyday life.
>
> (Nickerson & Adams, 1979).

People miss the little details when we are focusing on the big picture. If the little details are unimportant or unnecessary for our immediate goals, our mind filters them out.

The opposite happens too in which we miss the big picture because we are focusing too intently on the details. This is called *inattention* or *perceptual blindness*. The seminal study of this phenomenon involves subjects being asked to observe a video of people passing a ball and to count the number of times certain players make passes (Simons & Chabris, 1999). Halfway through the video, a person in a gorilla costume walks across the screen. After the video ends, the subject is asked how many passes were made *and then*...if they noticed a gorilla. *Half of the subjects did not see the gorilla*. A similar study was performed in which radiologists were asked to search for lung nodules in a set of CT scan images (Drew et al., 2013). These CT scans happened to also include an image of a gorilla. In this study, 83% of the radiologists missed the gorilla despite eye tracking indicating that they looked directly at it. The purpose of this study was to show that even experts can be so focused on searching for one thing that they miss something even more important (such as a gorilla in your lung). I can't try this experiment on you *now*, because I already explained the concept, however, I can ask if you noticed the gorilla inside the artificial heart patent of Figure 7.4.

One reason observation is difficult is because we have a hard time focusing on both the big picture and the little details simultaneously. And often we don't even know what we are supposed to be looking for. Magicians and pickpockets use this to their advantage with a combination of misdirection and sleight of hand to manipulate where someone is looking. Designers also use this "magic" to their advantage to create spaces and objects that direct a person to either ignore or pay attention to certain details. A nicer way of framing these intentional manipulations is as "*affordances.*" This concept was suggested first by Gibson: "the affordances of the environment are what it offers the animal, what it provides or furnishes, either for good or ill" (1979). The affordance concept was applied to design by Donald Norman in *The Psychology of Everyday Things* (1988) as the perceivable actionable properties of an object. These designed affordances are why Buddy the Elf couldn't resist pushing all the light-up buttons on the elevator (Favreau, 2003), why the painted (or milk) lines keep you on your side of the street when driving (Chapter 3), and how "Go Away Green" paint is used in Disney Theme Parks to divert attention from objects they do not want you to observe (Soto-Vásquez, 2021).

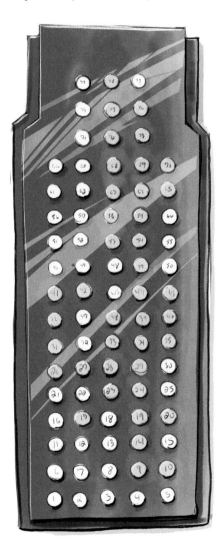

Figure 30.4 The elevator button scene from *Elf* (Favreau, 2003) is an example of how sometimes the designed affordances of objects make it difficult to resist their action potential.

Another equally important reason why observation is difficult is because we tend to not question the status quo or look at our daily routines from an objective/anthropological/sociological lens. However, observational humorists (like Mark Twain (Chapter 18), Mitch Hedberg (Chapter 8), Larry David (Chapter 25), Dave Chappelle, Paula Poundstone, George Carlin, Ellen DeGeneres, Hannibal Buress, Whoopi Goldberg, Bernie Mac, and Jerry Seinfeld) are experts at this. Douglas Coupland writes, "anybody can describe a pre-moistened towelette to you, but it takes a good observational comedian to tell you what, exactly, is the 'deal' with them" (Grassian, 2015). The trick to good observational comedy is also the trick to incremental innovation: MAYA, *Most Advanced Yet Acceptable*. It involves "recounting something that will hopefully be universally familiar, but that won't necessarily have been consciously noted by your audience. If it's too obvious an observation it won't be funny…and if it's too oblique then it won't hit home" (Herring & Caulfield, 2008). Director Judd Apatow called Jerry Seinfeld "the greatest observational comedian who ever lived" (Weiner, 2012). Let's look at some of Seinfeld's observations from his television sitcom and translate the discoveries into fodder for innovation.

"What's the deal with lampshades? I mean if it's a lamp, why do you want shade?" (Berg et al., 1997)

Thinking like a designer, is there an opportunity to redesign the lamp or the lightbulb such that it doesn't need a shade? Or perhaps we should rethink the concept of the lamp entirely. Technology has advanced significantly in lighting, yet we still have lamps that look the same as they did at the turn of the century. We now have plastic LED light bulbs that could be formed into any shape and yet we make them take the form of the original incandescent bulbs. I realize there are some practical reasons for this, but as discussed in Chapters 12–14, sometimes it is difficult to break tradition and question the status quo.

"I'm calling for my test results. Negative? Oh my God…What? Negative is good? Oh, yes of course! How stupid of me." (David & Cherones, 1993)

Thinking like a designer, is there an opportunity to rethink the way we share test results with patients? And speaking more generally, oftentimes scientists, doctors, engineers, and other professionals do not realize that the general population is not familiar with certain terms that are common language in the field. You may recall the first time you purchased a house, opened a retirement account, brought your laptop in for repair, did your taxes, brought your car in for service, purchased a nice bottle of wine, etc. Was there ever a time in those situations where you didn't understand terminology or felt "stupid"? Good user experience design should take this into account.

"You know the message you're sending out to the world with sweatpants?…'I give up. I can't compete in normal society. I'm miserable, so I might as well be comfortable'" (David & Cherones, 1993).

Thinking like a designer, is there an opportunity to create comfortable sweatpants that still appear professional? In 2014, *Betabrand* successfully crowdfunded for the development of the "Dress Pant Sweatpants," which is described on their website as:

> Boardroom Style, Bedroom Comfort…More than a pair of sweatpants, they're an experiment in sartorial subterfuge. At first glance, Dress Pant Sweatpants look like fine charcoal wool trousers. Which they are, except for the wool part…they look sophisticated — and feel slumped-on-the-couch comfy like your favorite pair of old sweats.

(2022)

What was once a joke, became less of a joke 20 years later, and is now a real product.

This process of transforming a "have you ever noticed?" or a "what's the deal with?" observation about society into a design prompt is what I call *Seinfeldian Design*. Comedians do the research and make the observations, but then leave the problem unresolved. One could argue they are doing the hard part. Former IBM CEO, Thomas J. Watson said, "the ability to ask the right question is more than half the battle of finding the answer" (Weiss, 2006). In any case, this is where designers can grab the baton. Koestler explains this as: "comic discovery is paradox stated—scientific discovery is paradox resolved" (1981).

References

Berg, A., Schaffer, J., & Mandel, D. (Writers), & Ackerman, A. (Director). (1997, September 25). The Butter Shave. [Television series episode]. In L. David & J. Seinfeld (Creators), *Seinfeld*, NBC.

Berger, W. (2014). *A more beautiful question: The power of inquiry to spark breakthrough ideas.* Bloomsbury Publishing USA.

David, L. (Writer), & Cherones, T. (Director). (1993, May 20). The Pilot. [Television series episode]. In L. David & J. Seinfeld (Creators), *Seinfeld*, NBC.

Dohms-Harter, E. (2020, June 18). Strange planet creator says comic strip celebrates humans. *Wisconsin Public Radio.*

Double, O. (2013). *Getting the joke: The inner workings of stand-up comedy.* A&C Black.

Doyle, A. C. (2012). *The hound of the Baskervilles.* Penguin Classics.

Drew, T., Võ, M. L. H., & Wolfe, J. M. (2013). The invisible gorilla strikes again: Sustained in attentional blindness in expert observers. *Psychological Science, 24*(9), 1848–1853.

Favreau, J. (Director). (2003). *Elf [Motion picture].* United States: New Line Cinema.

Gibson, J. J. (1979). *The ecological approach to visual perception.* Houghton Mifflin.

Grassian, D. (2015). *Hybrid fictions: American literature and generation X.* McFarland.

Gray Static Dress Pant Sweatpants. (2022). *Betabrand.* https://www.betabrand.com/gray-static-dress-pant-sweatpants

Greenberg, G. D., Rodriguez, N. M., & Sesta, J. J. (1994). Revised scoring, reliability, and validity investigations of Piaget's bicycle drawing test. *Assessment, 1*(1), 89–101.

Herring, R., & Caulfield, J. (2008, September 21). The comedian's toolbox. *The Guardian.*

Koestler, A. (1981). The three domains of creativity. In D. Dutton & M. Krausz (Eds.), *The concept of creativity in science and art* (pp. 1–17), Volume 6. Springer, Dordrecht.

Nickerson, R. S., & Adams, M. J. (1979). Long-term memory for a common object. *Cognitive Psychology, 11*(3), 287–307.

Norman, D. A. (1988). *The psychology of everyday things.* Basic Books.

Piaget, J. (1930). *The child's conception of physical causality.* Harcourt Brace & company.

Pyle, N. (2019). *Strange planet.* Morrow Gift.

Schur, M., Straessle, T., & Gersten, K. (Writers), & Robinson, J. A. (Director). (2018, January 11). Best Self. [Television series episode]. In M. Schur (Creator), *The Good Place*, NBC.

Simons, D. J., & Chabris, C. F. (1999). Gorillas in our midst: Sustained inattentional blindness for dynamic events. *Perception, 28*(9), 1059–1074.

Sno, H. N. (2000). Déjà vu and jamais vu. In G. E. Berrios & J. R. Hodges (Eds.), *Memory disorders in psychiatric practice* (pp. 338–347). Cambridge University Press.

Soto-Vásquez, A. D. (2021). Mediating the magic Kingdom: Instagram, fantasy, and identity. *Western Journal of Communication, 85*(5), 588–608.

Sutton, R. I. (2002). *Weird ideas that work: 11 1/2 practices for promoting, managing, and sustaining innovation.* Simon and Schuster.

Szent-Györgyi, A. (1957). *Bioenergetics.* Academic Press.

Weiner, J. (December 23, 2012). Jerry Seinfeld intends to die standing up. *The New York Times Magazine*, 24–31.

Weiss, J. J. (2006). *The quotable manager: Inspiration for business and life.* Gibbs Smith.

31

HOW COMEDY MAKES CHANGE, SATIRE, AND *SOUTH PARK*

In Chapter 12, I discussed radical innovation, neophobia, and how people tend to shy away from major change. Humor can be more than just a means of inventing new things; it can also be a mechanism for accepting change and calling attention to things that may need to be changed.

Here is a short segment of a joke from comedian Ali Wong from her Netflix special *Hard Knock Wife* (2018). *Note: In order to stay true to the joke, I am not censoring the one "potty word."*

> A lot of people like to ask me 'Ali, how on earth do you balance family and career?' Men never get asked that question. Because… they don't. My husband occasionally changes diapers, and when people hear that, confetti everywhere. When my baby girl was first born, I would do skin-on-skin contact every day to bond with her. She shit on my chest. Where's my confetti?
>
> (Wong & Karas, 2018)

Let's dissect the first part of this joke: "Men never get asked that question. Because… they don't." This is technically a very well-crafted joke. The punchline is a double meaning or a bisociation (see Chapter 4) on the phrase "they don't." Both meanings make sense and provide different insight. The joke represents two separate issues on the gender inequality of parenting: (1) society doesn't expect men to balance career and family and so *they don't* get asked the question; and (2) *they* (men) *don't* balance family and career in the first place and so the question doesn't get asked. Ali Wong was able to compress this complicated observation on the socially accepted gender inequities of parenting in the United States into nine words (again, less is more for *both* creativity and humor). Our society is full of gender inequality, and it is so strongly rooted in tradition and culture that we don't even realize it. But getting back to the joke… when Ali Wong tells the joke, the audience laughs. The moms laugh, the not-moms laugh. Everyone laughs. We laugh because we have an "Aha/Haha Moment" from the incongruity. We also realize how true and "shitty" gender inequality can be. This is an example of the Release Theory of Humor as we are addressing the uncomfortable-to-some topics of gender inequity… as well as a little (baby-sized-amount of) potty humor.

Now, if we removed the humor and you were just talking to someone in the street and they said, "hey, do you know that women sacrifice their careers for family more often than men do," there would be no laughter. There is no "haha" and there is no "aha!"

The power of humor is that it allows us to discuss uncomfortable things in a comfortable setting. Humor makes it OK and expected to laugh at our foibles, mistakes, cultural taboos, poor behavior, etc. Like play, humor can be that "spoonful of sugar" to help the medicine go down.

DOI: 10.4324/9781003276296-36

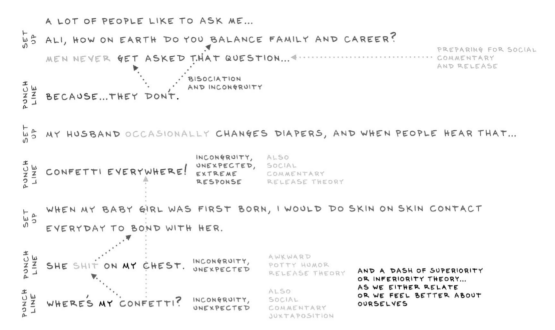

Figure 31.1 A dissection of Ali Wong's diaper-changing joke from her Netflix special, *Hard Knock Wife* (Wong & Karas, 2018).

> Humor give[s] [people] an open, rational attitude towards mistakes, it also gives them an openness to new experiences and ideas and to situations which can be interpreted in more than one way. That openness makes it easier for them to adapt to changes....
>
> (Morreall, 1991)

The humor is the "foot-in-the-door": "Jokes are uniquely designed to deliver messages...they sneak into consciousness past the barriers that normally defend against ways of thinking that threaten our comfort...we have to let comedians near the things we find uncomfortable or perhaps, even wrong" (Puschak, 2015).

Why would humor allow us to be more open to criticism? "Although there is not enough data to demonstrate that laughter is an all-around healing agent [i.e., laughter is the best medicine]... there exists sufficient evidence to suggest that laughter has some positive, quantifiable effects on certain aspects of health" (Mora-Ripoll, 2010) such as lowering the prevalence of cardiovascular disease (Hayashi et al., 2016), reducing anxiety, depression, and stress, and boosting immune system response (Martin, 2001; Kim et al., 2015). Laughter can also burn calories (Buchowski et al., 2014)! There is significant empirical support for the "clown therapy" popularized by *Dr. Patch Adams* and bringing humor back to clinical practice (2002). In summary, a well-developed sense of humor is positively related to someone's coping and adjustive ability and can help people navigate difficult or stressful situations (Saper, 1990; Abel, 2002). Mrs. Which in *A Wrinkle in Time* shared a similar sentiment (with some extra letters): "annd wee mussttn'tt looose ourr sensses of hummorr...the onnlly wway ttoo ccope withh ssometthingg ddeadly sseriouss iss ttoo ttry ttoo trreatt itt a llittlle lligghtly" (L'Engle, 1962).

Because of humor's unique ability to play with someone's adjustive ability, comedy can be used to raise awareness of social justice issues and create the social lubricant needed to facilitate these deep conversations. In two studies regarding issues of climate change and global poverty, comedic content resulted in greater engagement, awareness, and knowledge acquisition than the same content presented in non-comedic formats (Chattoo & Feldman, 2020). A related study found that comedy has significantly greater persuasive impact on support for refugees when compared with simply viewing the same content in traditional news format (Feldman & Chattoo, 2018).

It is not clear or likely that humor can persuade someone to change their views on a specific issue (Vidmar & Rokeach, 1974; Weinberger & Gulas, 1992; Nabi et al., 2007). Nabi et al., however, did find a few interesting relationships between humor and attitude change specifically, "respondents who find a message funny are also more likely to pay closer attention to the message" and "even if attitude change is not evidenced immediately… they may remember the message information thus allowing that information to increase its influence on attitudes after some time has passed" (2007).

We have just moved into the domain of *satire*. "Satire is a genre which necessarily sets out to critique and entertain" (Declercq, 2018). Although satire is usually humorous in its entertaining value, *the primary intent is criticism* about some issue, follies, abuses, shortcomings, vices, etc. Satire must do more than just make you laugh, which is essentially the slogan of the (satirical) *Ig Nobel Prize*: "first make people laugh…and then think" (Russell, 2014). Equally, satire can't simple be critique without the entertainment value. Like a good roast or read (Chapter 25), if the critique is not funny, it just comes across as mean. Let's look at some examples of how satire can make positive change.

In the medieval and Renaissance eras,

> *Jesters* and fools were able to say things that others could not. As in play, the context was protected. Their license to mock playfully meant that they could humorously dispense unwelcome truths and frank good sense. They could bring bad news to the king that no one else would dare deliver.
>
> (Bateson & Martin, 2013)

A portion of the role of the jester translates to the modern political cartoonists and news satire shows (e.g., *The Onion, Have I Got News for You, The Daily Show, The Colbert Report, SNL Weekend Update, Last Week Tonight*).

Politics needs humorists on the inside. This was the premise of the movie *Man of the Year* (2006) in which a TV comedian (played by Robin Williams) gets elected to office. As another example of the inspirational dialog between writers and artists that gradually move society forward (Chapter 17): comedian politicians became a reality three years later in 2009 with Minnesota's US Senator (and SNL writer/performer) Al Franken, in 2016 with Guatemalan President (and comedian) Jimmy Morales, and in 2019 with Ukrainian President (and comedian) Volodymyr Zelenskyy (Ryabinska, 2022). Politicians do not necessarily need to be overt humorists, but they should *have a sense of humor.* Just as Jerry Seinfeld spends hours dissecting the concept of a Pop Tart to find the best way of presenting an argument on it, humorists can also do that with serious topics. *Good humorists can take complex concepts and problems and make it understandable to the public such that they want to be engaged and know more.* This is beneficial in many fields, including politics, law, science, and education.

When accepting the Mark Twain Prize for American Humor, Jon Stewart said that the "fragility of leaders" and not the "fragility of audiences," is the real threat to comedy:

> When a society is under threat, comedians are the ones who get sent away first. Authoritarians are the threat to comedy, to art, to music, to thought, to poetry, to progress…what we have is

fragile and precious, and the way to guard against it isn't to change how audiences think, but to change how leaders lead.

(2022)

In other words, "dictators fear laughter more than bombs" (Koestler, 1979). *We need to be able to laugh at oneself if we want to be open to change and to different opinions.*

As per Chapter 17, this combination of comedy with *cartoons* allows you to create situations that never existed or can't exist and to exaggerate things as needed. There are many cartoons that are sending you morality messages under your radar via humor and satire. Dr. Seuss is most known as a children's book author and illustrator; however, he was also a political cartoonist and many of his books addressed societal and political issues.

> Seuss's concern about the rise of Hitler led him to leave the world of advertising and, initially, become a political cartoonist, and would later result in several books encouraging readers to challenge structures of power: *Yertle the Turtle*, published in 1958, and *The Sneetches*, published in 1961.

(West, 2016)

The Sneetches "has been invoked by different minority groups over the years as an allegory for discriminatory treatment by the majority against that group, with a particular focus on anti-Semitism and discrimination against African Americans" (Nicolas, 2013). *The Lorax* addressed concerns about the environment and consumerism. *How the Grinch Stole Christmas* also addresses consumerism, explicitly of the holiday season. *Horton Hears a Who!* addresses issues with anti-isolationism and equality: "A person is a person no matter how small" (1954). Out of all of Dr. Seuss's children's books, *The Butter Battle Book* (1984) is perhaps the most overt in its political message. This is an anti-war satirical depiction of an escalating arms-race with the threat of mutual assured destruction as a result of a trivial conflict related to buttered toast (Barone, 1993). Although "books like *Horton Hears a Who!* and *The Sneetches* can be used to promote tolerance, anti-bias, or anti-racism," a recent study illustrates how "racism spans across the entire Seuss collection" including "hundreds of racist political cartoons, comics, and advertisements for newspapers, magazines companies, and the United States government" (Ishizuka, 2019).

South Park producers, Trey Parker and Matt Stone, have a unique ability to generate episodes analyzing any current topic just days before air. They "have transformed this crudely animated collection of two-dimensional small-screen characters into one of contemporary television's freshest and most biting satirical takes on compelling social issues of the day" (Chidester, 2012). This is much like *SNL Weekend Update* and late-night shows that can quickly address the relevant topics of that week with humor. However, it's not just the timeliness of *South Park* that is unique to this show, it is that they push the envelope of what can be said/discussed on television (and in cartoons). Like Thomas Crapper and toilets, *if we don't talk about things, they can't change.*

Let's explore one example from the *South Park* video game, *The Fractured But Whole* (note: this title is a good example of bisociation and Release Theory). During character creation, you select the difficulty of the game with a sliding scale—a standard practice in most video games—however, in *this* game

> the easier the difficulty, the lighter your character's skin. Conversely, the harder the difficulty, the darker your character's skin. It means if you want to play *The Fractured But Whole* on a harder than normal difficulty, you have to play as a person of color. During the process, South Park stalwart Eric Cartman will comment: 'Don't worry, this doesn't affect combat. Just every

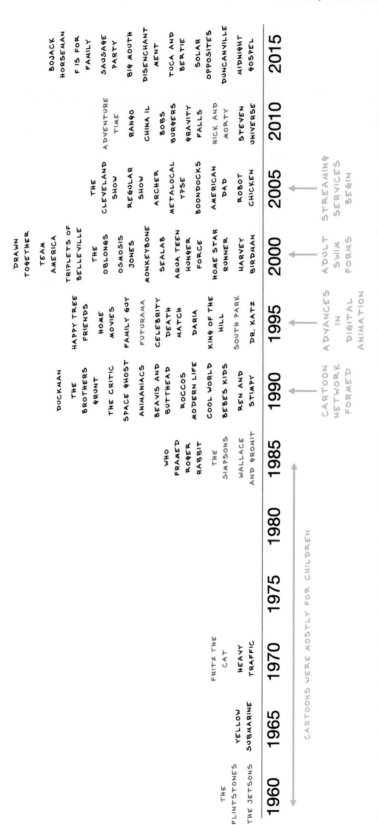

Figure 31.2 A semi-exhaustive timeline of animated cartoons in TV or film that are generally for adults or contain adult themes and are also primarily comedy. This list is limited to media primarily from the US. Prior to 1990, cartoons were primarily for children, and cartoons for adults were a novelty. Also, from 1950–1990, it was not financially feasible for most production companies to produce animation (Solomon, 1990). After the release of *Who Framed Roger Rabbit*, a survey in 1989 found that 42% of moviegoers wanted to see a cartoon before the feature (Solomon, 1990). Although interest likely existed since *The Flintstones*, the boom in animated comedy media for adults in the 1990s could be attributed to the formation of Cartoon Network and Adult Swim, advances in digital animation processes, and streaming services. References in pink are the ones discussed in this book.

other aspect of your whole life.'... the difficulty of the game affects the amount of money you receive, and the way other characters speak to you throughout the course of the game. It is, quite clearly, a social commentary on racism in modern society, and as far as video games go, a pretty effective one.

(Yin-Poole, 2017)

South Park (first aired in 1997) may seem controversial now compared with say, *The Simpsons* (first aired in 1989); and, likewise, *The Simpsons* was controversial compared with *The Flintstones* (first aired in 1960). And today, *The Flintstones* seems like Saturday Morning Cartoons for kids compared with *South Park*. You may not be aware that even *The Flintstones* was controversial at its time—it featured the first television couple to be shown sharing a bed and addressed issues like suicide and infertility (Bhami, 2020). *The Flintstones* was actually created for adults after it was found that "more than half of *Huckleberry Hound*'s audience comprised adults" (Newcomb, 2014).

Just as things that seem radical now will be commonplace in the future, what we think is controversial now in popular media (and cartoons) will not necessarily be the same things we think are controversial in the future. In 1972, Ralph Bakshi released the animated film *Fritz the Cat* based on R. Crumb's comic. It was the first animated film to present adult content, and it was also the first animated film to receive an "X" rating. In an interview, Bakshi says, "it was all a misunderstanding of me being too far ahead of the curve. Now they do as much on *The Simpsons* as I got an X rating for *Fritz the Cat*" (Epstein, 2006). The impact over time is that humor has advanced the discussion of what we can talk about in public. It shines a spotlight on issues, disturbs the status-quo, and acts as a bellwether or "the banana peel in the coal mine" (Stewart, 2022). In this sense, *humor indirectly fuels innovation*.

References

Abel, M. H. (2002). Humor, stress, and coping strategies. *Humor, 15*(4), 365–381.

Adams, P. (2002). Humour and love: the origination of clown therapy. *Postgraduate Medical Journal, 78*(922), 447–448.

Barone, D. (1993). "The Butter Battle Book": Engaging children's thoughts of war. *Children's Literature in Education, 24*(2), 123–135.

Bateson, P., & Martin, P. (2013). *Play, playfulness, creativity and innovation.* Cambridge University Press.

Bhami, A. (2020, September 13). The Flintstones cartoon: The top 10 big facts you might not know. *Icytales.*

Buchowski, M. S., Majchrzak, K. M., Blomquist, K., Chen, K. Y., Byrne, D. W., & Bachorowski, J.-A. (2014). "Energy expenditure of genuine laughter": Corrigendum. *International Journal of Obesity, 38*(12), 1582.

Chattoo, C. B., & Feldman, L. (2020). *A comedian and an activist walk into a bar: The serious role of comedy in social justice.* University of California Press.

Chidester, P. (2012). "Respect my authori-tah": South Park and the fragmentation/reification of whiteness. *Critical Studies in Media Communication, 29*(5), 403–420.

Declercq, D. (2018). A definition of satire (and why a definition matters). *The Journal of Aesthetics and Art Criticism, 76*(3), 319–330.

Dr. Seuss. (1954). *Horton Hears a Who!* Random House.

Dr. Seuss. (1984). *The butter battle book.* Random House.

Epstein, D. R. (2006, June 5). Ralph Bakshi interview. *UGO.com*

Feldman, L., & Borum Chattoo, C. (2019). Comedy as a route to social change: The effects of satire and news on persuasion about Syrian refugees. *Mass Communication and Society, 22*(3), 277–300.

Hayashi, K., Kawachi, I., Ohira, T., Kondo, K., Shirai, K., & Kondo, N. (2016). Laughter is the best medicine? A cross-sectional study of cardiovascular disease among older Japanese adults. *Journal of Epidemiology, 26*(10), 546–552.

Ishizuka, K. (2019). The cat is out of the bag: Orientalism, anti-blackness, and white supremacy in Dr. Seuss's children's books. *Research on Diversity in Youth Literature, 1*(2), 4.

Kim, S. H., Kim, Y. H., & Kim, H. J. (2015). Laughter and stress relief in cancer patients: a pilot study. *Evidence-Based Complementary and Alternative Medicine, 2015*, Article ID 864739.

Koestler, A. (1979). Humor arid Wit. *Encyclopaedia Britannica*, 15th ed. s.v.

L'Engle, M. (1962). *A wrinkle in time.* Farrar, Straus, and Giroux.

Martin, R. A. (2001). Humor, laughter, and physical health: methodological issues and research findings. *Psychological bulletin, 127*(4), 504.

Mora-Ripoll, R. (2010). The therapeutic value of laughter in medicine. *Alternative Therapies in Health & Medicine, 16*(6), 56–64.

Morreall, J. (1991). Humor and work. *Humor: International Journal of Humor Research, 4*(3/4), 359–373.

Nabi, R. L., Moyer-Gusé, E., & Byrne, S. (2007). All joking aside: A serious investigation into the persuasive effect of funny social issue messages. *Communication Monographs, 74*(1), 29–54.

Newcomb, H. (Ed.). (2014). *Encyclopedia of television.* Routledge.

Nicolas, P. (2013). The Sneetches as an allegory for the gay rights struggle: Three prisms. *New York Law School Law Review, 58*(3), 525.

Puschak, E. [TheeNerdwriter]. (2015, July 22). Louis C. K. Is A Moral Detective [Video]. *YouTube.* https://www.youtube.com/watch?v=pOO1AX7_jXw

Russell, C. (2014, September 23). *Ig Nobel prizes make you laugh, then think.* Scientific American.

Ryabinska, N. (2022). Politics as a joke: The case of Volodymyr Zelensky's comedy show in Ukraine. *Problems of Post-Communism, 69*(2), 179–191.

Saper, B. (1990). The therapeutic use of humor for psychiatric disturbances of adolescents and adults. *Psychiatric Quarterly, 61*(4), 261–272.

Solomon, C. (1990, May 25). That won't be all, folks, as cartoons make a comeback. *Los Angeles Times.*

Stewart, J. (2022, April 24). *Acceptance speech for the Mark Twain Prize for American Humor.* Kennedy Center, Washington D.C.

Vidmar, N., & Rokeach, M. (1974). Archie Bunker's bigotry: A study in selective perception and exposure. *Journal of Communication, 24*(1), 36–47.

Weinberger, M. G., & Gulas, C. S. (1992). The impact of humor in advertising: A review. *Journal of Advertising, 21*(4), 35–59.

West, M. I. (2016). Dr. Seuss's responses to Nazism: Historical allegories or political parables? *The Looking Glass: New Perspectives on Children's Literature, 19*(1). https://ojs.latrobe.edu.au/ojs/index.php/tlg/article/view/765

Wong, A. (Writer), & Karas, J. (Director). (2018, May 13). *Ali Wong: Hard Knock Wife* [Television Movie]. Netflix.

Yin-Poole, W. (2017, September 8). South Park: The fractured but whole's difficulty slider changes the colour of your skin. *Eurogamer.*

32

IMPROVISATION, YES AND... "BOOM! FREEZE! MICHAEL SCARN, FBI!"

Seinfeld takes a long time to perfect a joke. In his interview with *The New York Times*, Seinfeld discusses a *two-year process* of writing a joke related to Pop Tarts:

> I'm looking for the connective tissue that gives me that really tight smooth link, like a jigsaw puzzle link. And if it's too long, if it's just a split second too long, you will shave letters off words. You will count syllables. It's more like song writing.

(Woodward, 2012)

Coincidentally, the rigor of Weird Al's song writing is compared with that of chess and fine art with an eerie similarity in attention to grammatical precision:

> Weird Al approaches the composition of his music with something like the holy passion of Michelangelo painting the ceiling of the Sistine Chapel. Looking through the 'White & Nerdy' file felt like watching a supercomputer crunch through possible chess moves. Every single variable had to be considered, in every single line. The song begins with a simple sentence—'They see me mowing my front lawn'—and even here Yankovic agonized over 'lawn' versus 'yard' and 'my' versus 'the'.

(Anderson, 2021)

The comedy writer is *like a surgeon* (Weird Al reference intended): they have to choose their words carefully (especially when working with controversial topics). It is a creative artform to find the best possible wording to a joke (Koestler, 1964).

Improvisation (or "improv" for short) is a very different art form and means of creation; it is developing content (music, dance, comedy, speech, art, etc.) *in the moment*. Improvisational theater had its beginnings in the Commedia Dell'Arte in Italy in the 15th century in which performers had no scripts and were allowed to improvise around provided topics (Frances-White & Salinsky, 2008). This artform became popular in America in the 1950s with Viola Spolin—a drama teacher from Chicago, who developed a series of games and exercises to introduce children to the concept of theater (Sawyer, 1999). Her son, Paul Sils, used these games to create the first improvisational comedy group, the Compass Players, at the University of Chicago in 1955, which evolved into Second City (Sawyer, 1999). Many of Viola's games and exercises are published in her book, which is often viewed as the "Bible" of improvisational theater (Spolin, 1963).

DOI: 10.4324/9781003276296-37

Improv theater comes in two flavors: *short form* and *long form*. Short-form improv are short scenes that typically result from a predetermined game, structure, or idea often involving some audience suggestion (Spolin, 1963; Sawyer, 1999; Besser et al., 2013). Short-form improv is what you see on the television show *Whose Line Is It Anyway?.* Long-form improvisation builds on many of the skills and techniques of short form, but results in richer theatrical scenes or a series of scenes. Long-form improvisation also requires deeper plot and character development that is not necessarily critical to short form (Halpern et al., 1994; Besser et al., 2013). The "Harold" is a specific style of long-form improvisation in which the performers create a series of interwoven scenes starting from a single word (Halpern et al., 1994; Fotis, 2014). Whereas the improvised short-form scenes in *Whose Line Is It Anyway?* may each be a few minutes long, the long-form improv comedy of *Middleditch and Schwartz* on Netflix is a series of three hour-long shows. Regardless of how long the scene is, "being funny on demand requires complex analysis and creative restructuring of an immediate situation. It is problem solving behavior of the most elegant kind" (Derks, 1987). Another way of saying this is that "the person who is spontaneously humorous is, by the same token, spontaneously creative" (Goodchilds, 1972). I should note that not all improvisation is funny, nor should it be the primary intent. Jazz improvisation is not typically funny. We improvise in the kitchen. We improvise when painting. We improvise when arguing. *Almost all our life is improvised,* and it is not necessarily funny. However, both humor and creativity arise from non-obvious connections, and improvisation often results in making non-obvious connections.

Both improvisational comedy (short and long) and scripted comedy are creative processes (Hatcher et al, 2016), but there are two major differences between scripted comedy and improvisational comedy.

1)   Improvisation has a *short time scale for creation* whereas scripted does not.

2)   Improvisation often requires *real-time interaction with others* whereas scripted does not.

These are the same differentiating features between music composition and improvisational jazz, or even patent prosecution and patent litigation. Being a good comedy writer does not necessarily mean you are going to enjoy or do well in an improvisational comedy setting, just as there are creative people who do not enjoy or do well in team-based idea generation. *Short time scale for creation* and *real time interaction with others* are hallmarks of improvisational comedy, but they are also hallmarks of team-based idea generation, specifically *brainstorming*.

Time. In real-world projects, you do not have infinite time to come up with ideas: There may be a few days dedicated to idea generation or an exploration phase. There may only be a short block of time when a group of specific people can be present to generate ideas. There are also extreme examples of where creative ideas are needed instantaneously (e.g., the Apollo 13 example in Chapter 2). There is a benefit to be able to generate ideas under the constraint of a limited time frame.

Interaction. Some people work best on their own, but as I discussed in Chapters 7 and 29, innovation benefits from interaction with others. In a team setting, you can gain different perspectives, collect diverse bits of information, and make non-obvious connections that you would not necessarily make on your own. It allows everyone involved to get inspired and build on each other's ideas.

Combining these two factors, research suggests that the *earlier* you get *feedback from others* in a design process, the faster your ideas evolve and improve (Häggman et al., 2015). Both improvisation and *brainstorming* require you to share unfinished ideas as you generate them such that they can be improved and built upon by the team. This group interaction is an opportunity to take sparks of ideas that are *novel to the individual* and evolve/develop them such that they become *novel to a group*.

Team-based idea generation (such as brainstorming) and improvisational comedy have quite a lot in common. I wrote an entire dissertation on this (Kudrowitz, 2010). When you think of improvisation training, you may imagine corporate retreats, team bonding, and the improv training scene from *The Office* ("Boom! Freeze! Michael Scarn. FBI!" (Daniels et al., 2005)). Improv training can be helpful for improving teamwork and building communication. As an example, in The Office improv training satire, Michael Scott (or Scarn, being his recurring improv character name) ruins each scene by responding as an FBI agent busting into a room and "shooting" all the characters regardless of wherever the scene started. This is breaking most of the tenets of improvisation including not listening and reacting to your scene partners, *killing* the scene before it even starts, and (literally, Chapter 1 of Besser et al.), "if your character is holding a gun, don't extend your index finger and raise your thumb like the 'play guns' you made as a kid" (2013).

Figure 32.1 One of the first rules of improvisation related to object work is that you should pretend as if you are using the real objects as opposed to transforming your hands into the objects like Michal Scarn and his finger pistols (Besser et al., 2013).

There are many improv handbooks (Spolin, 1963; Halpern et al., 1994; Frances-White & Salinsky, 2008; Besser et al., 2013) and so I want to focus specifically on the intersection of improv training and creativity. At a deeper level, many of the short-form games used in improvisational training are designed to build the same skills that are useful for team-based idea generation, namely: listening and observing (Chapter 30), making non-obvious associations (Chapter 27), manipulating and building on ideas (Chapters 28–29), producing a large quantity of concepts (Chapter 5), deferring judgment (Chapter 12), encouraging wild ideas (Chapter 12), playing (Part III), and lowering inhibitions (Chapters 8 and 22). The success of the improvisation or team-based ideation depends on the participants feeling comfortable sharing ideas and building on ideas of others. There is a common practice in improv called "yes and..." (Halpern et al., 1994; Besser et al., 2013) that nicely summarizes the two main rules of brainstorming: *defer judgment* and *build on each other's ideas* (Osborn, 1963). As I have already discussed many of the other relationships between creativity and humor, I'm going to focus specifically on these two "*yes and*" factors as they pertain to both improvisation and team-based idea generation.

Deferring Judgment (*Yes!*)

There are a few reasons why judging may interfere with the creative process.

First, when we judge people's ideas in a group, *people become self-conscious,* and they shut down. In idea generation, if someone says, "that's not feasible" or "that's already been done" or "that's out of our budget" or "that's a dumb idea," the person who suggested the idea is no longer going to suggest any "out of the box" concepts. Furthermore, everyone else on the team is now going to be limiting and analyzing what they share as their own ideas may be treated with the same degree of criticism. One critical statement can create a filter on the entire team, reducing productivity and creativity. In improvisational theater and comedy, this is akin to a performer saying, "it's a great day here at the beach," and another performer on stage says, "we just did a beach scene, that's a bad idea."

A second reason why we should defer judgment is *time.* The team only has a short amount of time to develop a quantity of ideas. Similarly, in the improvisational theater context, there is only a limited amount of time to produce a narrative. In brainstorming, the goal is to generate as many ideas as possible and if your team spends time evaluating ideas (in a negative *or* positive manner), that is precious time taken from producing additional ideas. The team must use the limited time they have together to generate quantity. *We can evaluate later.*

A third reason why we should defer judgment is that we can *prematurely and unfairly judge ideas.* In an idea generation session or on stage, participants do not have access to all knowledge and

Figure 32.2 It is sometimes difficult to not critique ideas especially if they are silly or radical. Instead of tearing the idea apart (along with your teammate's confidence), try building onto the idea to make it better. This is useful in both brainstorming and in improvisational theater.

resources. They do not know what may actually *transform* into something innovative. As I discussed in Chapter 26, things that seem silly or impossible in the moment may actually be innovative in the future. Einstein said this too: "If at first, the idea is not absurd, then there is no hope for it." If we prejudge ideas before they have had an incubation period (Chapter 8), we may be throwing out the good stuff.

Building on Ideas (*And…*)

What makes team idea generation different from individual idea generation is that you have other minds to play with. If you are not listening and working with the concepts that are presented, you might as well be doing it alone. In brainstorming, if you are struggling to generate ideas, you can simply listen and build onto what you hear. Similarly, in the improvisational theater context, if you are on stage and you don't know what to say, you can listen and simply add onto what you just heard. In both contexts, when you add onto someone's idea, that person knows they have been heard and they feel empowered that someone is working with the material that they provided.

Hatcher et al. (2016, 2018) compares the long-form improv technique of "*heightening*" to the process of building on ideas. In long-form improv, once the scene is established, participants need to uncover the "unusual thing that makes the scene humorous. It is then the participants' mission to heighten that game thus heightening the humour" (Hatcher et al., 2016, 2018). In these studies, Hatcher et al. applies this improv technique to idea generation, which begins with designers identifying "'the unusual thing', or the feature that makes an idea innovative" and that feature is further developed by the group.

It took a long time for the callback, but 32 chapters later, I can now revisit the study mentioned in the Introduction. In that study, we had non-designers, professional product designers, engineers, students, and improvisational comedians generate new product ideas. The professional improvisational comedians were generating 20% more product ideas and *25% more creative product ideas than professional product designers* in time-limited challenges (Kudrowitz & Wallace, 2010). At the time, it seemed like a good opportunity for some more rigorous investigation to see if this could be a means of facilitating creativity in general. I began studying improv comedy. I was taking classes, but at a meta level, I was secretly studying how improvisation was taught. As improv appeared to be a teachable skill, I wanted to know if we can make *anyone* better at creative idea generation with improvisational training. The results were promising. I composed a workshop of short-form games (described in Chapter 36) to be administered prior to idea generation. In the first study, we found that groups of students increased their idea output by 37% by participating in an improv workshop prior to idea generation (Kudrowitz & Wallace, 2010). In a later study, we found that teams that participated in just a ten-minute improv workshop produced more ideas than teams that spent the same ten minutes relaxing outside before idea generation (Pilgrim-Rukavina & Kudrowitz, 2015).

Other researchers have made similar suggestions although not all with experimental studies. Gerber (2009) proposed several ways in which short-form improvisational games can reinforce the rules of brainstorming and that these games can be used as a mental warm-up similar to a warm-up used for physical sports. Medler and Magerko (2010) compare the practices of improvisation and role-playing in design, and suggest that improvisation is beneficial for group idea generation in generating novel ideas and improving group cohesion. Ludovice et al. (2010, 2013) illustrate ways in which improvisation can stimulate innovation in engineering design. Hatcher et al. (2018) demonstrate how improvisation tools can effectively be used to develop creative solutions by overcoming the common barriers of brainstorming sessions: fear of judgment, unequal contribution, premature rejection of ideas, idea fixation, and production blocking. Granholt and Martensen (2021) explore how improvisation can help facilitators in leading team-based design activities.

Nisula and Kianto (2018) explore how improvisational training can improve organizational creativity and not just individual creativity. Vera and Crossan (2005) show that improvisation skills can be taught and can have a positive effect on team innovative performance when combined with moderating factors. Even training in *musical* improvisation results in greater general creative ability when compared with musicians that were not trained in improvisation (Kleinmintz et al., 2014).

Lastly, even if improvisation training itself does not impact the cognitive processes and mechanisms for generating ideas, simply laughing and engaging with humorous content can indirectly facilitate creativity. In Chapter 22, we discussed how *positive affect* impacts creativity. One of the seminal studies used comedy as the means of producing positive affect (Isen et al., 1987). A similar study found that "adolescents who listened to [humor] performed significantly better on a creativity test than control groups" (Ziv, 1976). In general, teams that engage in jokes and laughter (not specifically improvisation) have greater team performance immediately and years later (Lehmann-Willenbrock & Allen, 2014). "When humor is encouraged in the workplace, creative thinking increases. And because humor also fosters an openness to novelty, there is an increased willingness to take risks to implement creative ideas" (Morreall, 1991).

In Part V, I will discuss how both play and humor can be incorporated into a creative design process in general. Specifically, Chapter 36 elaborates on the improv games that I use in my workshops to prepare teams for idea generation.

References

Anderson, S. (2021). The weirdly enduring appeal of Weird Al Yankovic. In S. Holt (Ed.), *The Best American Magazine Writing 2021* (pp. 411–435). Columbia University Press.

Besser, M., Roberts, I., & Walsh, M. (2013). *Upright Citizens Brigade comedy improvisation manual.* Comedy Council of Nicea LLC.

Daniels, G., & Celotta, J. (Writers), & Feig, P. (Director). (2005, November 22). E-Mail Surveillance. [Television series episode]. In G. Daniels (Creator), *The Office*, NBC.

Derks, P. L. (1987). Humor production: An examination of three models of creativity. *The Journal of Creative Behavior, 21*(4), 325–326.

Fotis, M. (2014). *Long form improvisation and American comedy: The Harold.* Springer.

Frances-White, D., & Salinsky, T. (2008). *The improv handbook.* Continuum

Gerber, E. (2009, April). Using improvisation to enhance the effectiveness of brainstorming. In *CHI '09: Proceedings of the SIGCHI Conference on Human Factors in Computing Systems* (pp. 97–104). Association for Computing Machinery.

Goodchilds, J.D. (1972). On being witty: Causes, correlates, and consequences. In J. H. Goldstein & P. E. McGhee (Eds.), *The psychology of humor: Theoretical perspectives and empirical issues* (pp. 173–193). Academic Press.

Granholt, M. F., & Martensen, M. (2021). Facilitate design through improv: The qualified eclectic. *Thinking Skills and Creativity, 40*, 100785.

Häggman, A., Tsai, G., Elsen, C., Honda, T., & Yang, M. C. (2015). Connections between the design tool, design attributes, and user preferences in early stage design. *Journal of Mechanical Design, 137*(7), 071408.

Halpern, C., Close, D., & Johnson, K. (1994). *Truth in comedy: The manual of improvisation.* Meriwether Publishing.

Hatcher, G., Ion, W, MacLachlan, R., Marlow, M., Simpson, B., & Wodehouse, A. (2018). Evolving improvised ideation from humour constructs: A new method for collaborative divergence. *Creativity and Innovation Management, 27*(1), 91–101.

Hatcher, G., Ion, W., MacLachlan, R., Wodehouse, A., Sheridan, M., & Simpson, B. (2016). Humour processes for creative engineering design. In D. Marjanović, et al. (Eds.), *DS 84: Proceedings of the DESIGN 2016 14th International Design Conference* (pp. 1025–1034). The Design Society, Glasgow.

Isen, A. M., Daubman, K. A., & Nowicki, G. P. (1987). Positive affect facilitates creative problem solving. *Journal of Personality and Social Psychology, 52*(6), 1122–1131.

Kleinmintz, O. M., Goldstein, P., Mayseless, N., Abecasis, D., & Shamay-Tsoory, S. G. (2014). Expertise in musical improvisation and creativity: The mediation of idea evaluation. *PloS one, 9*(7), e101568.

Koestler, A. (1964). *The act of creation.* Macmillan.

Kudrowitz, B. M. (2010). *Haha and aha!: Creativity, idea generation, improvisational humor, and product design.* (Doctoral dissertation, Massachusetts Institute of Technology).

Kudrowitz, B., & Wallace, D. (2010, October). Improvisational comedy and product design ideation: Making non-obvious connections between seemingly unrelated Things. *International Conference on Design and Emotion*, Chicago, Illinois, USA.

Lehmann-Willenbrock, N., & Allen, J. A. (2014). How fun are your meetings? Investigating the relationship between humor patterns in team interactions and team performance. *The Journal of Applied Psychology, 99*(6), 1278–1287.

Ludovice, P., Lefton, L., & Catrambone, R. (2010, June). Improvisation for engineering innovation. In *2010 Proceedings of the ASEE Annual Conference & Exposition* (pp. 16308–16325). American Society of Engineering Education.

Ludovice, P., Lefton, L., & Catrambone, R. (2013). Humorous improvisation tailored for technical innovation. In *Proceedings of the ASEE Southeast Section Conference.* American Society of Engineering Education.

Medler, B., & Magerko, B. (2010, April). The implications of improvisational acting and role-playing on design methodologies. In *CHI '10: Proceedings of the SIGCHI Conference on Human Factors in Computing Systems* (pp. 483–492). Association for Computing Machinery.

Morreall, J. (1991). Humor and work. *Humor: International Journal of Humor Research 4*(3/4), 359–373.

Nisula, A. M., & Kianto, A. (2018). Stimulating organisational creativity with theatrical improvisation. *Journal of Business Research, 85*, 484–493.

Osborn, A.F. (1963). *Applied imagination; principles and procedures of creative problem-solving.* Scribner.

Pilgrim-Rukavina, N., & Kudrowitz, B. (2015, November). Exploring the effects of warm-up games, criticism and group discussion on brainstorming productivity. *IASDR InterPlay 2015.* Brisbane, Australia.

Sawyer, R. K. (1999). Improvisation. In S.R. Pritzker & M. Runco (Eds), *Encyclopedia of creativity* (pp. 845–853). Academic Press.

Spolin, V. (1963). *Improvisation for the theater: A handbook of teaching and directing techniques.* Northwestern University Press.

Vera, D., & Crossan, M. (2005). Improvisation and innovative performance in teams. *Organization Science, 16*(3), 203–224.

Woodward, J. (2012, December 20). Jerry Seinfeld: How to write a joke. *The New York Times.*

Ziv, A. (1976). Facilitating effects of humor on creativity. *Journal of Educational Psychology, 68*(3), 318–322.

Part V

A Playful and Humorous Design Process

33
THINKING ABOUT DESIGN THINKING

What is design?

In one *very* narrow definition, design could refer simply to the look of something (e.g., I really like the design of that toaster). With the prevalent use of the word in this limited definition, the discipline takes on a myopic view to the general public as a field for people who make stuff look pretty. Although designers often call upon skills that facilitate the process of making something more aesthetically pleasing, design is not simply just about the aesthetics.

Design is a planning process for the creation of an entity. It is a process that can be taught and can be applied to many disciplines. It is not something that just applies to furniture, clothing, buildings, and graphics (and definitely not to simply the aesthetics of these things). Design is also not restricted to physical things! We can design a system, a service, or an experience. The world is getting more connected and complex such that designers of today are almost required to think at a systems and experiential level, and not simply at individual objects (Meyer & Norman, 2020). When one follows a design process, the result should be something that people want, meets a need, solves a problem, brings joy, and/or improves life. It just may happen that when something is designed well, it turns out to be aesthetically pleasing too.

"*Design thinking*" was originally the term used in research to distinguish the cognitive processes of designers from the more physical design processes (Tschimmel, 2012). Today, the term Design Thinking is used more broadly when we apply design methods or the design process to fields that are not traditionally design fields, such as healthcare or education. The term is also often used interchangeably with "*Human-Centered Design*" or "*User-Centered Design*" in that both "use the same range of methods and both have a common goal: the creation of a result that generates maximum added value for everyone involved in the project" (Burghardt et al., 2011). As you can see in Figure 33.1, there are many variations and definitions of what constitutes a human-centered, user-centered, or design thinking "design process," but they have some commonalities in their stages.

Let's explore some of the models in Figure 33.1. The Design Council originally proposed the *Double Diamond model* of design process in 2005, based on the divergence–convergence design model (Banathy, 1987) which has four phases: "discovery" (problem understanding with divergent thinking), "define" (using insights to converge on a problem), "develop" (diverging to exploring solutions for the clearly defined problem), and "deliver" (testing ideas and refining/down-selecting to the best concept) (Tschimmel, 2012). Design firm, IDEO, presents three stages of a design thinking

DOI: 10.4324/9781003276296-39

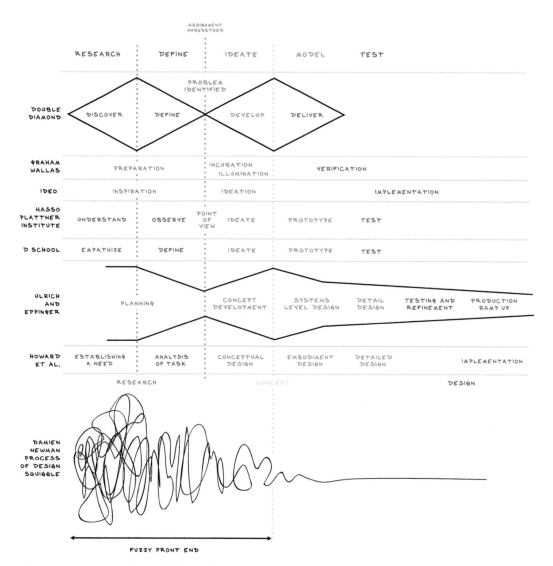

Figure 33.1 A comparison of different design process models. *The Process of Design Squiggle* by Damien Newman, thedesignsquiggle.com is included under a Creative Commons Attribution-No Derivative Works 3.0 United States License. The squiggle itself is unmodified and placed within the table. The "fuzzy front-end" text and arrow are not part of Newman's original work and refer to items in the table.

model: inspiration, ideation, and implementation (Brown & Katz, 2011). The Hasso Plattner Institute proposes a six-phase model (understand, observe, point of view, ideate, prototype, test), and they illustrate how the phases are iterative and loop back on each other (Plattner et al., 2009). The *d school* at Stanford presents a variation on this model with five iterative phases (empathize, define, ideate, prototype, test) (2009). When we focus specifically on engineering design or product development, the process lengthens as the stages of modeling deepen and expand into production (Howard et al., 2008; Ulrich & Eppinger, 2008). In any of these models, the early stages of the process can be referred to as the "*fuzzy front-end*" as they can incorporate ill-defined processes, uncertainty, and open-ended exploration (Almqvist, 2017). Damien Newman's (2010) "*Process of*

Figure 33.2 A general design process as well as the outline for the following chapters in Part V. Notice that the process involves iteration at each stage and across stages. End users and other stakeholders should be involved throughout the process, but are strongly involved in the first and last stages of research and testing.

design squiggle" creatively captures this "fuzzy front-end" in the early part of a design process and marks three phases of design (research, concept, design).

Figure 33.2 is not intended to declare one of the models to be best or correct, but rather a framework for structuring Part V. For this reason, I will also refer to this as "a" design process instead of "the" design process. Design processes typically start with some form of prompt or initiation (this is not in Figure 33.2). With an initial prompt, designers do research: market research, user research, site research, and scientific research. If we are following the Double Diamond model, this would be a divergent process. This research is then organized and used in refining and/or redefining a problem or original prompt (a convergent process). Once the problem, need, and project is understood, designers move into ideation (the portmanteau of idea generation). If you recall from Chapter 5, quantity leads to creativity and so this is another divergent process of exploring different ideas. Some of these ideas move forward and are modeled as drawings, prototypes, digital design representations, etc. Modeling is both a means of ideation and a means of testing (and so it bleeds into the phases on either side). Models of ideas are brought to stakeholders (potential users, manufacturers, clients, distributors, team members, etc.) for feedback and usability testing. That feedback is used to refine the idea or down-select from ideas (a convergent process). In engineering design, product development, and user experience design, these models are also tested for feasibility in addition to testing with users. Design is iterative. Within stages, research can lead to deeper research or other methods of research, ideas can lead to more ideas, and modeling can lead to additional, more refined modeling. Between stages, defining the problem can result in additional research needed; testing can send designers back to the ideation stage, and modeling can be used as idea generation.

In the domain of comedy, Yi et al. (2013) describe the creative design process and the process of humor formation as "twins" in that they share a similar mechanism starting with a "story" and ending with a surprising concept. In a related study, Hatcher et al. (2016) compare the Ulrich and Eppinger (2008) engineering design process to "the creation and/or performance processes of both long-form improvisation and long-form pre-planned (e.g., stand-up) comedy." In a later study, Hatcher et al. (2018) compares the *Upright Citizen's Brigade* improvisation model (Besser et al., 2013) to the Double Diamond design process. The improv model starts with building a wide variety of ideas (with "yes and") that make up the "base reality" of the scene and once the "creative idea" is selected, it gets "heightened" or built upon and refined (Hatcher et al., 2018).

In addition to humor and design process being "twins," Yi et al. also describe them as "partners," as they can influence each other: humor production requires a creative design process, and oppositely creative design process can utilize humor (2013). Similarly, playful things are created with a design process, and play can also be used in a design process. This was the topic of my master's thesis while working closely with Hasbro on Nerf and Supersoaker product development (Kudrowitz & Fienup, 2005). It is also what I teach in *Toy Product Design,* a course I developed at MIT with Bill Fienup and Professor David Wallace in 2005, and later at the University of Minnesota in 2011. In general, design process can be discovered working behind the scenes in a variety of fields or creative endeavors (like comedy and toys) once you start to look for it. Even in my studies of food design, we found that chefs were essentially following a design process when developing new dishes (Kudrowitz et al., 2014).

Hopefully after reading Parts 1–4, I have illustrated how and why both play and humor can spark creativity and foster innovation. In the next few chapters, I will discuss ways in which we can use humor and play throughout a design process (and not just during the fuzzy front-end). I'll use the high-level design process stages from Figure 33.2 as a structure. The process and methods discussed will have a playful and humorous flavor, but can be used in designing anything from medical devices to cruise ship experiences to toothpaste caps.

References

Almqvist, F. (2017). The fuzzy front-end and the forgotten back-end: User involvement in later development phases. *The Design Journal, 20*(sup1), S2524–S2533.

Banathy, B. H. (1987). Instructional systems design. In R. M. Gagne (Ed), *Instructional technology: Foundations* (pp. 85–112). Routledge.

Besser, M., Roberts, I., & Walsh, M. (2013). *Upright Citizens Brigade comedy improvisation manual.* Comedy Council of Nicea LLC.

Brown, T., & Katz, B. (2011). Change by design. *Journal of Product Innovation Management, 28*(3), 381–383.

Burghardt, M., Heckner, M., Kattenbeck, M., Schneidermeier, T., & Wolff, C. (2011). Design Thinking= Human-Centered Design? (Google Trans.). In Workshop-Proceedings der *Tagung Mensch & Computer 2011. überMEDIEN| ÜBERmorgen.* Universitätsverlag Chemnitz.

d.school (2009). *Bootcamp Bootleg* (pp. 1–5). Hasso Plattner: Institute of Design at Stanford. Retrieved from https://dschool.stanford.edu/resources/the-bootcamp-bootleg

Hatcher, G., Ion, W., MacLachlan, R., Marlow, M., Simpson, B., & Wodehouse, A. (2018). Evolving improvised ideation from humour constructs: A new method for collaborative divergence. *Creativity and Innovation Management, 27*(1), 91–101.

Hatcher, G., Ion, W., MacLachlan, R., Wodehouse, A., Sheridan, M., & Simpson, B. (2016). Humour processes for creative engineering design. In D. Marjanović, et al. (Eds.), *DS 84: Proceedings of the DESIGN 2016 14th International Design Conference* (pp. 1025–1034). The Design Society, Glasgow.

Howard, T. J., Culley, S. J., & Dekoninck, E. (2008). Describing the creative design process by the integration of engineering design and cognitive psychology literature. *Design Studies, 29*(2), 160–180.

Kudrowitz, B. M., & Fienup, W. J. (2005). *The exploration of concepts for projectile toys* (Master's thesis, Massachusetts Institute of Technology).

Kudrowitz, B., Oxborough, A., Choi, J., & Stover, E. (2014). The chef as designer: Classifying the techniques that chefs use in creating innovative dishes. In Y. K. Lim, & K. Niedderer (Eds.), *Proceedings of the 2014 Design Research Society Conference. Design Research Society* (pp. 127–146). Design Research Society/Umea Institute of Design.

Meyer, M. W., & Norman, D. (2020). Changing design education for the 21st century. *She Ji: The Journal of Design, Economics, and Innovation, 6*(1), 13–49.

Newman, D. (2010). The process of design squiggle. https://thedesignsquiggle.com/

Plattner, H., Meinel, C., & Weinberg, U. (2009). *Design-thinking.* Landsberg am Lech: Mi-Fachverlag.

Tschimmel, K. (2012). Design thinking as an effective Toolkit for Innovation. In *Proceedings of the XXIII ISPIM Conference: Action for Innovation: Innovating from Experience.* The International Society for Professional Innovation Management.

Ulrich, K., & Eppinger, S. (2008). *Product design and development.* McGraw Hill.

Wallas, G. (1926). *The art of thought.* Harcourt, Brace.

Yi, H., Nguyen, T. A., & Zeng, Y. (2013). Humour and creative design: Twins or partners? *Journal of Integrated Design and Process Science, 17*(4), 81–92.

34
RESEARCHING DESIGN RESEARCH

Design is not about the designer. Design is about other people. If you review Figures 33.1 and 33.2, the process begins and ends with the user. And sometimes the user is involved in the middle stages too (after all, this is "user-*centered* design").

I'm referring to this first stage simply as *research*, which is a bit less exciting than how other models refer to it: discovery, inspiration, understanding, empathizing, preparation, planning, establishing a need, etc. One way of categorizing this fuzzy front-end research is into two groups: *user-based research* and *content-based research*. Marketing literature (Sarstedt & Mooi, 2014) would refer to user-based research as "primary research" as it involves obtaining the information firsthand, and likewise, most of content-based research would be considered "secondary research" as it is secondhand information.

Content-based research can include literature review, internet searching, trade shows, visiting retail stores, speaking with experts, benchmarking, competitive shopping, exploring a site, trend research, etc. The field of product design requires market research in order to identify opportunities and to better understand the state of the art, but not all design fields have a "market." For example, architects do not do "market research," but they might conduct *site* or *field* research. A group of educators may not do "market research," but they would research alternative educational structures and collect data on enrollment history. Content-based research can also include collecting general knowledge about the subject. For example, if you are exploring the process of taking biopsies, you will need to become familiar with the biopsy process and this could include a review of medical literature.

In some large product companies, they pay their designers and engineers to go shopping... sometimes in other countries! Armed with a company credit card, their notebook, and a smart phone, these designers go on a mission for some combination of inspiration (e.g., "trend" shopping) and scoping the market competition (i.e., "comp" shopping). Their findings are then organized and presented to their design team to inform idea generation. In my classes, I ask students to engage in a similar process (without buying products) both in person and online. Aside from learning about the competition and trends, they also get to experience different retail environments and points of sale. They can gain insights into packaging considerations, and they can observe people shopping.

In user-based research, designers can uncover needs and insights by talking to, interacting with, and observing people. User-based research requires *empathy*. I've connected both humor and play to empathy in prior chapters. In Chapter 25, we discussed the Release Theory of Humor and how

DOI: 10.4324/9781003276296-40

CONTENT RESEARCH   USER RESEARCH

GENERAL	MARKET	ASK	OBSERVE	EXPERIENCE
LITERATURE REVIEW	BENCHMARKING	SURVEY	CONTEXTUAL INQUIRY	IMMERSION
INTERNET SEARCH	COMPETITIVE SHOPPING	INTERVIEW	CULTURAL PROBE	SHADOWING
PATENT SEARCH	TRADE SHOWS	FOCUS GROUP	DIARY STUDY	DAY IN THE LIFE
EXPERT CONSULTING	PRODUCT DISSECTION			EMPATHY TOOLS
FIELD TRIPS	RETAIL VISITS			BODYSTORMING
SITE VISITS	TREND FORECASTING			
TOURS				

Figure 34.1 An organization of different forms of design research. User testing is an important form of research, but it is not included in this diagram as it requires something to test with the user and that comes later in the process.

we can experience an uncomfortable empathetic reaction toward a character or situation. In Chapter 27, we discussed the game of *Scattergories*. In order to succeed, you not only need to select a noun card that has an appropriate remoteness of association, but you also need to empathize with the judge such that you choose a card that they would find most interesting. User research can be classified into three categories: **ask**, **observe**, and **experience** (Wallace, 2018).

Ask

When designers *ask*, they use tools like *surveys, interviews*, and *focus groups.* Just like with humor, creativity, and design, *less is more* in ask-based user research. I know that we all enjoy a lengthy survey now and then, but research suggests that you will get better data if the participants are not cognitively exhausted (Burchell & Marsh, 1992). This applies to interviewing too: the more the interviewee talks and the less the interviewer talks, the better. Again, design is not about the designer. The key to a good design interview is to get the interviewee to share *stories* that can later be mined for insights. Here are few tips (Grover et al., 2022):

- Ask *open-ended questions* (e.g., tell me about the last time you rode your bicycle).
- Be *neutral* (e.g., tell me about your backpack vs. what do you not like about your backpack).
- *Engage* with the interviewee (e.g., do not look down at a computer to take notes, try to record the meeting or have a scribe, use active or reflective listening).
- Make the interviewee feel *comfortable* (e.g., begin with introductions, try to build a rapport).

As an interviewer, one of the difficult skills to master is to embrace the awkward silence. Our natural tendency is to speak to fill silence, and an interviewer can use this to their advantage to extract details from their interviewee. We can learn a great deal about empathy and interviewing from *Mr. Rogers*:

> More and more I've come to understand that listening is one of the most important things we can do for one another. Whether the other be an adult or a child, our engagement in listening to who that person is can often be our greatest gift.

> (Rogers, 2003)

Mr. Rogers was comfortable with silence and just listening to guests and children speak—this silence would encourage visitors to open up more (Neville, 2018).

The opposite interviewing technique, perhaps inspired by childish wonder (Chapter 22), is "*The Five Whys.*" This was originally developed at Toyota Industries Corporation as a means of promoting problem-solving by getting to the root of a problem, but it could be a useful tool for interviews by encouraging interviewees to dig deeper on responses (Stull, 2018). There is a slight annoyance potential of this method as demonstrated by Li'l Petey in *Dog Man* (Pilkey, 2021):

> You need to get cleaned up! **Why**? Because I'm gonna be on TV! **Why**? Because Sarah is going to interview me! **Why**? Because she's doing a news story about former villains who have transformed their lives. **Why**? Because people like to watch stuff like that. **Why**? Because it makes them feel all warm and fuzzy! **Why**? Because it triggers dopamine responders...

Li'l Petey eventually gets to the root of the matter, but not without the repetitive probing.

The Theater of Public Policy (T2P2) is a Minnesotan improv troupe that has a unique format for their shows. Like many long-form improv shows, the performance starts with a suggestion from the audience. In the T2P2 model, the show begins with an interview in front of the audience with an expert on a given topic. During this interview, all the performers in the troupe are taking notes on stage (but not the interviewer, they are engaging with the expert). At the end of the short interview, the performers then put on an improvised performance based on the information presented during the interview. This model can take any dry topic or dry speaker at a conference and turn it into the most engaging subject matter—often the drier the speaker, the funnier the follow-up improvised show. Additionally, the audience is fully engaged in the interview because they know the content will come back during the performance. This is an excellent example of applying both humor and play to what is typically a humor-less and play-less part of a design process.

An issue with *ask* tools in general can be summarized with a few quotes from innovative leaders. Tom Kelley of IDEO said, "most customers are pretty good at comparing your current offerings with their current needs...but they're not so good at helping you plan for new-to-the-world services" (2005). Steve Jobs said, "a lot of times, people don't know what they want until you show it to them" (Reinhardt, 1998). And, as such, designers can also...

Observe

In Chapter 7, we discussed inspiration and how da Vinci encourages observation: "Go about, and constantly, as you go, observe, note and consider the circumstances and behavior of men." When designers *observe* people, sometimes we can extract interesting insights that would not come across when we just interview or survey them. Additionally, people don't necessarily behave the way in which they say or think they behave. The process of asking questions while *also* observing users in their natural context is called *contextual inquiry* (Beyer & Holtzblatt, 1999).

In Chapter 30, we discussed observational comedy with some examples from *Seinfeld* and *Strange Planet*. The skills required for good design observation are similar to those for being a good observational humorist. When conducting observation research, you put on your figurative deerstalker hat and become a design detective—a Seinfeldian Sherlock—deeply exploring individuals and society. Instead of repeating the content of Chapter 30, I will simply add a few examples of this being applied successfully.

Jonah Lehrer describes the invention of the Swiffer:

> One day, the designers were watching an elderly woman sweep some coffee grounds off the kitchen floor. She got out her hand broom and carefully brushed the grounds into a dustpan... After the woman was done sweeping, she wet a paper towel and wiped it over the linoleum, picking up the last bits of spilled coffee. Although everyone on the Continuum team had done the same thing countless times before [i.e., *jamais vu* or *vuja de*], this particular piece of dirty paper led to a revelation.

(Lehrer, 2012)

"The idea for Snake Light was born in 1989 when Bryan DeBlois, a designer for the company, was making home repairs and saw an electrician stuff a flashlight into his shirt so he could work with both hands" (Somerville, 1996).

Designers at Target added small tags sewn inside their fitted bedsheets to indicate which end is the top/bottom and which is the side (Shamsian, 2016). This seemingly simple and *seemingly* obvious innovation came about after observing people put on their bed sheets only to realize they need to rotate them, and then proceed to put it on again incorrectly. There is a nice nugget of observational-humor here ready to be transformed into a stand-up bit.

In all three of these examples, if you asked people in an interview about their process for cleaning up spills, repairing a sink, and putting on bedsheets, these insights are unlikely to arise without observing that physical interaction in the environment. This is the power of observation.

One major consideration in doing observational research (i.e., contextual inquiry) is the *observer effect*: the observation practice itself influences the thing being observed (Barnum, 2020). This is like trying to measure your bike tire air pressure without letting out any air. In an observational study, if you ask someone to load their dishwasher like they normally would (*and by the way don't mind me watching your every move and also the video camera*), that person is going to load their dishwasher like they never loaded a dishwasher before. Design tools to overcome this are journaling, diary studies, and *cultural probes*. A cultural probe is "a kind of gift" package that has "an assortment of maps, postcards, cameras, and booklets" and other materials "designed to provoke inspirational responses. Like astronomic or surgical probes", they are left behind with the users and "return fragmentary data over time" to the designers (Gaver et al., 1999). These tools are useful when you want to get insights into a local community or culture while reducing the observer effect. The process of creating the "gift box" is somewhat playful for the designer, and the process of using it is somewhat playful for the participants. Again, play is a state of mind, but referring to Chapter 20, this activity does afford play perhaps more so than filling out a questionnaire.

Figure 34.2 Target's labels sewn inside bedsheets to indicate top/bottom or side are a simple innovation that arose from user observation.

Experience

A designer knows that they are not the client or end user...*but they can* pretend *to be!* When designers *experience* a relevant situation themselves as if they were an end user, they can figuratively and sometimes literally put themselves in someone else's shoes to gain the empathy needed for understanding problems and uncovering opportunities. All experience tools require some degree of pretense, and perhaps, fantasy play.

A designer can physically take part and participate in whatever activity is being studied. For example, if we are exploring how school cafeterias prepare food, the designer can physically go to a school and prepare food in the cafeteria. This is called *immersion* and it can lead to a rich domain understanding, and can also foster interdisciplinary relationships (Hall et al., 2019). Now, if you cannot physically participate in the activity itself (surgery, as an example), but you can physically be present, designers can engage in *shadowing*. In this method,

> the researcher 'shadows' the target individual from the moment they begin their working day until they leave for home...shadowing can be done over consecutive or non-consecutive days for anything from a single day or shift up to a whole month. At the end of the shadowing period the researcher will have a rich, dense and comprehensive data set which gives a detailed, first-hand and multidimensional picture of the role, approach, philosophy and tasks of the person being studied.
>
> (McDonald, 2005)

A day in the life is a very specific subset of shadowing limited to just one day to create an intensive snapshot of a potential user or demographic (Rodgers & Milton, 2013).

To enhance immersion-based research, a designer could also use *empathy tools* or *capability simulators.* These are physical or digital devices that alter the abilities of the designer such that they can interact with a situation or product in a manner that mimics the intended user or demographic (Rodgers & Milton, 2013). Such tools could include a projector that mimics how people with dyslexia may view text or a worn apparatus that simulates hand tremor patterns. These tools can work across three major dimensions: agency (controlling the degree of freedom of movement or choice), perspective (the location of the designer relative to the user), and sensation (limiting mobility, perceptions, or physiological factors) (Pratte et al., 2021).

If designers are not physically able to be in the actual environment (e.g., the International Space Station), designers can pretend. *Bodystorming* is a method of physically recreating a situation and role-playing to help construct the same social or physical considerations (Oulasvirta et al., 2003; Schleicher et al., 2010). The tennis court scene in *The Founder* described in Chapter 24 is a great example of the power of bodystorming. It "permits immediate feedback for generated design ideas, and can provide a more accurate understanding of contextual factors... [and are] memorable and inspiring" (Oulasvirta et al., 2003). Children bodystorm all the time, but we simply call it "pretend play." *Bluey* (again serving as an overflowing fountain of examples for connecting play and creativity) has a bodystorming example in almost every episode. The children (and sometimes the adults too) create a simulated environment (e.g., a train station, a veterinary office, a restaurant, an operating room, a car, an airplane, a zoo) using materials that they have on hand. Like pretend play, bodystorming works well if you have a strong imagination and improvisational skills. It involves listening and building on ideas (i.e., *yes and*).

References

Barnum, C. M. (2020). *Usability testing essentials: ready, set... test!* Morgan Kaufmann.
Beyer, H., & Holtzblatt, K. (1999). Contextual design. *Interactions, 6*(1), 32–42.

Burchell, B., & Marsh, C. (1992). The effect of questionnaire length on survey response. *Quality and quantity, 26*(3), 233–244.

Gaver, B., Dunne, T., & Pacenti, E. (1999). Design: cultural probes. *Interactions, 6*(1), 21–29.

Grover, M., Lauff, C., & Wright, N. (2022). Developing design ethnography interviewing competencies for novices. *Proceedings of the ASEE Annual Conference and Exposition – Design in Engineering Education (DEED) Division*. American Society for Engineering Education.

Hall, K. W., Bradley, A. J., Hinrichs, U., Huron, S., Wood, J., Collins, C., & Carpendale, S. (2019). Design by immersion: A transdisciplinary approach to problem-driven visualizations. *IEEE Transactions on Visualization and Computer Graphics, 26*(1), 109–118.

Kelley, T. (2005). *The ten faces of innovation*. Currency.

Lehrer, J. (2012). *Imagine: How creativity works*. Houghton Mifflin Harcourt.

McDonald, S. (2005). Studying actions in context: A qualitative shadowing method for organizational research. *Qualitative Research, 5*(4), 455–473.

Neville, M. (Director). (2018). *Won't You Be My Neighbor? [Motion picture]*. United States: Tremolo Productions.

Oulasvirta, A., Kurvinen, E., & Kankainen, T. (2003). Understanding contexts by being there: Case studies in bodystorming. *Personal and Ubiquitous Computing, 7*(2), 125–134.

Pilkey, D. (2021). *Dog man: Mothering heights*. Graphix.

Pratte, S., Tang, A., & Oehlberg, L. (2021, February). Evoking empathy: A framework for describing empathy tools. In *TEI '21: Proceedings of the Fifteenth International Conference on Tangible, Embedded, and Embodied Interaction*. Association for Computing Machinery.

Reinhardt, A. (1998, May 25). Steve jobs: "There's sanity returning." *Businessweek*.

Rogers, F. (2003). *The world according to Mister Rogers: Important things to remember*. Hachette Books.

Rodgers, P. A., & Milton, A. (2013). *Research methods for product design*. Orion Publishing Group, Limited.

Sarstedt, M., & Mooi, E. (2014). *A concise guide to market research*. Springer.

Schleicher, D., Jones, P., & Kachur, O. (2010). Bodystorming as embodied designing. *Interactions, 17*(6), 47–51.

Shamsian, J. (2016). Designers have solved the biggest problem with bedsheets. *Insider*.

Somerville, S. (1996). Snake bite Market wars. *The Baltimore Sun*.

Stull, E. (2018). *UX fundamentals for non-UX professionals*. Berkeley, CA: Apress.

Wallace, D. (2018). *User-centric, Creative Design* [Lecture Notes]. MIT. web.mit.edu/2.744/.

35
HOW MIGHT WE... DEFINE HOW WE DEFINE OUR PROMPTS

The second stage of a design process depicted in Figure 33.2 can be referred to as "define." This stage is entangled with the "research" stage as illustrated by three of the models in Figure 33.1 simply combining research and define into one stage, and by the massive entanglement that makes up the front end of Newman's *The Process of Design Squiggle*. Part of this "fuzz" is a result of requiring some initial prompt or brief to begin research in the first place. That prompt gradually gets refined, defined, redefined, or clarified throughout the stages of research and definition. It is important that you are addressing the right problem before jumping into idea generation, which is why this definition stage is so critical. Former IBM CEO, Thomas J. Watson said, "the ability to ask the right question is more than half the battle of finding the answer" (Weiss, 2006). Einstein agrees: "The formulation of a problem is often more essential than its solution" (Einstein & Infeld, 1966). Design is more than just coming up with an elegant solution, design is equally about uncovering the problem.

[Why?]

Because we don't want to design something that is just a superficial "bandage" of a solution.

[Why?]

Because that is a waste of time and resources and doesn't actually get to the root of the problem.

[Why?]

Because if we invest in identifying the actual problem, we can save time and resources in the long run.

[Why?]

Because it will benefit more people in the end and that's what design is about!

[Why?]

Let's move on! (But you get my point on the Five Whys of Chapter 34.)

Define begins with *unpacking* (or downloading) and organizing (or synthesizing) the data collected during the research phase. From interviews and observations, you may have qualitative data from notes, recordings, photos, and videos. From surveys and literature review, you may have both qualitative and quantitative data. From market benchmarking, you may have a set of existing

DOI: 10.4324/9781003276296-41

alternative solutions and competition. There are many different tools to organize the collected data into a framework that is easy to assimilate and use in communication and idea generation. These tools often require some initial *affinity clustering* or visually grouping the bits of information into categories. Here are five organizational tools.

An *empathy map* can be used to organize information collected from user research to discuss and create a reflection of the intended user. In this process, individual bits of data (perhaps written on Post-It notes) are clustered into quadrants, for example, by what the users say, think, do, and feel (Gray et al., 2010; Tschimmel, 2012).

This unpacking into an empathy map is useful for having a team collectively craft and agree upon a *persona* (or *personas*) that represents the user group. Just like at the beginning of some first-person video games, crafting a persona is like creating a fictional character or avatar based on your real observations and experiences.

> Personas is a tool based on fictional characters, which helps to make the abstract idea of a group of users personal and human…[It] seeks to reveal deeper insights into the various kinds of experiences that users are having, with the objective of being an impulse for the generation of ideas about how to improve those experiences.
>
> (Tschimmel, 2012)

This can take the form of a photo or illustration with a biography.

"A *storyboard* is a series of images (drawings, illustrations or photographs), displayed in sequence, to visualize a process, service or event" (Tschimmel, 2012). "Where film and advertising industries use storyboards to provide a preview of the movie for production purposes, the product design storyboard helps the designer in understanding the product–user interaction in context, and over time" (Van der Lelie, 2006). The storyboard is useful across all the phases of design process, but, in this definition stage, it can be a tool for organizing and communicating the user research as a visual narrative of a user experience.

A *journey map* or *experience diagram* (perhaps a cousin of the storyboard) is also a graphical process representation of a user's experience. It is a means of organizing data collected from shadowing, immersion, observations, and interviews. A *customer journey map* (*CJM*), specific to retail and products, is

> a representation in a flowchart or other graphic format of the customer's experience as he or she interacts with your company in receiving its product or service…along the way, you are looking for the emotional highs and lows and the meaning the experience holds for the customer.
>
> (Liedtka, 2011)

These maps can then be used to identify opportunities for improvement and intervention. My biography and acknowledgments in the beginning of this book are presented in the form of a journey map.

A *2 × 2 matrix* is a tool for organizing, comparing, and communicating data by plotting it on any two dimensions (Both & Baggereor, 2009). The creation of a 2 × 2 is a bit like creating and solving a puzzle at the same time in that there is "freedom of movement" to create any organizational axes that helps to best visualize the data. You can change the axes and the content shifts. This tool is specifically useful in market research to plot the benchmarking of the state of the art (or *competitive landscape*). When working with product 2 × 2s, the *x*-axis is often "cost" from low to high. This tool can be used to identify a pattern and/or communicate a gap in the market for idea generation.

TIME SCALE vs QUANTIFICATION

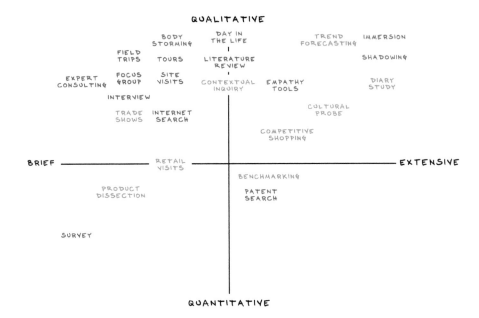

USER FOCUS vs ACQUISITION NATURE

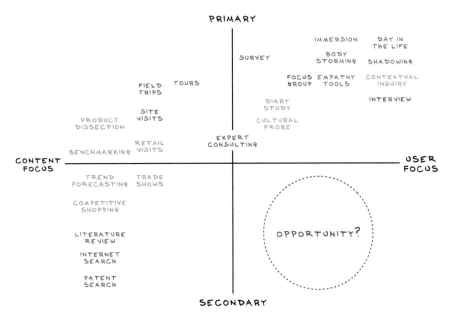

Figure 35.1 The 2 × 2 matrix is a versatile tool for organization and communication. These 2 x 2 figures plot the research methods described in Chapter 34 with the color-coding classification from Figure 34.1. Instead of research methods, a 2 × 2 could use existing products in a marketspace. A gap, such as the one in the figure, could indicate a market opportunity.

To further "fuzzy" up the front end, in addition to the phases of research and definition blurring and spiraling on each other, the internal definition processes (developing a persona, a journey map, an empathy map, etc.) influence each other and the order of creation is not necessarily linear. Furthermore, *prompts* can initiate at a variety of different breadths of scope. Four common starting points for design prompts are as follows.

- Starting with a *context* (such as rethinking the public restroom), research leads to uncovering a variety of needs, opportunities, and problems.
- Starting with a *problem*, *need*, or *opportunity* (such as "public restroom patrons don't wash hands"), research and idea generation leads to concepts for products, processes, and services.
- Starting with an *existing product*, *process*, or *service* (such as the automated soap dispenser), research and idea generation leads to new concepts for products, processes, and services.
- Starting with a *technology* (such as a microscopic peristaltic pump), research and idea generation lead to concepts for products, processes, and services incorporating that technology.

If your design process starts at the top of this list, it is a *market pull* situation, in which insights from user research drives the development of a solution. If your process starts at the bottom of this list, it is a *technology push* situation, in which a new technology drives development. An initial prompt can start from any of these locations (e.g., we need to redesign the automated soap dispenser), but research may pull you backward to redefine or reframe an initial prompt (e.g., actually, the real problem is the layout of the public restroom). A very playful phrase that captures this concept is that "[People] don't want quarter-inch [drill] bits. They want quarter-inch holes" (Leavitt, 1984). This is that loop-de-loop in Figure 33.2. Regardless of where you start in a design process, "successful innovations often require a combination of 'market pull' and 'technology push'" (LaZerte, 1989).

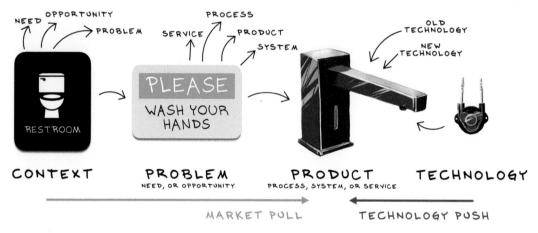

Figure 35.2 Initial prompts can be a general context, a problem/need/opportunity, a redesign of an existing product/process/service/system, or a new technology. Gender neutral toilet icon uncopyrighted by Sam Killermann.

There are also (well) structured and ill-structured prompts (Simon, 1973). These terms are used with some subjectivity, and they are fluid. For example, "generate ideas for bathroom products" is an *ill-structured* (or *blue sky* or *free form*) prompt in which there are no explicit constraints and the ideas generated could encompass a wide variety of concepts with no clear metrics of goodness (Bulter & Kline, 1998). "Design an aftermarket shower solution that creates the illusion of a large quantity of water while using less water than the average shower head" is a *structured* prompt as there are several clear requirements for any idea to be deemed viable. All ill-structured prompts will eventually become more and more structured as the problem and ideas converge and focus.

If you think about designing a new house, a general design vision gradually gets decomposed into smaller structured design decisions.

Framing (or *defining*) *the problem* is important for design. IDEO teaches a framework of translating the insights collected from the organized research data into *"How Might We (HMW) questions,"* which are prompts that begin with these words (Both & Baggereor, 2009). HMWs are used because they suggest

> that a solution is possible and because they offer you the chance to answer them in a variety of ways. A properly framed How Might We doesn't suggest a particular solution, but gives you the perfect frame for innovative thinking.
>
> (IDEO, 2022)

Whether you use the HMW format or not, the amount of constraint provided in the framing will impact idea generation.

This is where play comes in.

If I asked you to come up with a list of *any* ideas, it might be pretty stressful. There is no datum for what is good or creative, and it will result in very few creative ideas (Haught-Tromp, 2017). If you recall back to Chapter 9, creativity requires *relevance*, and if there is no prompt, it is difficult to assess what it is relevant to. One needs some minimal foundation or framework to be creative. On the other hand, I could ask you to come up with a list of ideas for *smartphone mounting systems that attach to a car dashboard that allow for one-handed loading and unloading and costs under 1 US dollar to manufacture with no more than three parts.* Now there are so many constraints that it is stressful in a different way and again will result in very few creative ideas. In this second prompt, the "freedom of movement within a given set of constraints" (Chapter 18) is limited. If we refer back to the concept of *flow* (Chapter 20), there exists an ideal level of challenge for a prompt for a maximum amount of creativity and play. With too few constraints, there is little to play with, and with too many constraints, there is not enough play. In my research, I found that around two constraints result in the maximum number of ideas. Let's test this theory with a little game:

List *any five things*:

1. _____
2. _____
3. _____
4. _____
5. _____

How fun was that on a scale of work to play (Figure 21.1)?

Now let's add one constraint.

List *any five snack foods:*

1. _____
2. _____
3. _____
4. _____
5. _____

How fun was that?

Now let's try *two* constraints.

List *any five snack foods that start with the letter P*:

     1._____
     2._____
     3._____
     4._____
     5._____

The constraints help make the challenge more interesting. If that last challenge feels familiar, it is likely because it is the same constraint level and format as the game of *Scattergories*.

We can also view what you just did as a creativity test! Did you think of any "P" snack foods other than potato chips, pretzels, popcorn, and peanuts? Were those the first things you thought of? To revisit Chapter 5, the first ideas you think of are often the same ideas the majority of people think of first. You need to push past that first handful of ideas in order to get to the more novel concepts that fewer people think of.

Framing of the prompt is critical in starting a design project to allow the participants to enjoy the challenge, but also to provide them with enough space to explore. Sometimes the designer, a client, or a senior manager believe they know what they want or what the problem is, but narrowing the scope too soon can restrict creativity. Even if one is provided with a constrained starting prompt, it may help to step backward and broaden the scope of the search. This process is called *boundary relaxation* (Maiden et al., 2010) or *abstraction laddering* (McKilligan & Creeger, 2018). Let's say for example we are using the HMW format, and our given challenge was: **how might we detect peanut proteins with a fork?** You can relax the boundary a little to expand the idea generation space. Perhaps a less constrained prompt would be: **how might consumers detect allergens in prepared foods?** With this prompt we can still generate ideas related to forks and peanut proteins, but we are not limiting ourselves to designing a utensil. If you relax the boundary too much, you get back to the low constraint problem: **how might we sense small particles?** And now ideas may be too distant from the actual problem at hand.

There is an idea generation technique that is almost the opposite of boundary relaxation, called *progressive revelation* (VanGundy, 1981). Let's say, for example, you actually do want to design a fork that detects peanut proteins, but you are open to exploring other ideas. You can start out by having your team generate ideas for the high-level prompt and gradually focus the prompt over time. This method of starting broad and then gradually moving to specifics is a good technique for interviewing too.

We tend to associate open-ended challenges with creativity, but creativity can come from constraints (or at least a couple of them). Just like deadlines, constraints add challenge and meaning and are necessary for play.

References

Both, T., & Baggereor, D. (2009). *Bootcamp bootleg*. Stanford d. school.

Butler, D. L., & Kline, M. A. (1998). Good versus creative solutions: A comparison of brainstorming, hierarchical, and perspective-changing heuristics. *Creativity Research Journal*, 11(4), 325–331.

Einstein, A., & Infeld, L. (1966). *Evolution of physics*. Simon and Schuster.

Gray, D., Brown, S., & Macanufo, J. (2010). *Gamestorming: A playbook for innovators, rulebreakers, and change-makers*. O'Reilly Media, Inc.

Haught-Tromp, C. (2017). The Green eggs and Ham hypothesis: How constraints facilitate creativity. *Psychology of Aesthetics, Creativity, and the Arts, 11*(1), 10.

IDEO (2022). *How Might We*. IDEO Design Kit. www.designkit.org/methods/3

LaZerte, J. D. (1989). Market pull/technology push. *Research-Technology Management, 32*(2), 25–29.

Leavitt, T. (1984). *The marketing imagination*. Free Press.

Liedtka, J. (2011). Learning to use design thinking tools for successful innovation. *Strategy & Leadership, 39*(5), 13–19.

Maiden, N., Jones, S., Karlsen, K., Neill, R., Zachos, K., & Milne, A. (2010, September). Requirements engineering as creative problem solving: A research agenda for idea finding. In *2010 18th IEEE International Requirements Engineering Conference* (pp. 57–66). IEEE.

McKilligan, S., & Creeger, S. L. (2018). Strategies to redefine the problem exploration space for design innovation. In *DS 93: Proceedings of the 20th International Conference on Engineering and Product Design Education* (pp. 318–325). The Design Society.

Simon, H. A. (1973). The structure of ill structured problems. *Artificial Intelligence, 4*(3–4), 181–201.

Tschimmel, K. (2012). Design thinking as an effective Toolkit for Innovation. In *ISPIM Conference Proceedings* (p. 1). The International Society for Professional Innovation Management (ISPIM).

Van der Lelie, C. (2006). The value of storyboards in the product design process. *Personal and Ubiquitous Computing, 10*(2), 159–162.

Van Gundy, A. (1981). *Techniques of structured problem solving*. Van Nostrand Reinhold.

Weiss, J. J. (2006). *The quotable manager: Inspiration for business and life*. Gibbs Smith.

36

AN IMPROV WARM-UP PROGRESSION FOR TEAM-BASED IDEA GENERATION

Warm-up games would typically be grouped with the ideation phase using the design process structure presented in Chapter 33. However, as humor and play are a major theme of this book, I am dedicating a separate chapter to share the improvisational games that I use in my workshops. As I discussed in Chapter 32, an improvisational warm-up prior to idea generation increases the total number of ideas produced in that session (Kudrowitz & Wallace, 2010). This is like stretching before engaging in a physical activity.

This chapter is written as a guide for you to conduct prior to your own idea generation sessions. These games would be classified as *short-form improvisation*, which are short scenes constructed from a predetermined game, structure, or idea (Spolin, 1963).

The order in which I present these games is important. In my years of facilitating this specific type of workshop, I found that you need to start out slow and (dare I say) not too playful, and then gracefully layer on skills, like in a video game. Some people are afraid of improvisation, public speaking, and sharing ideas. I typically reassure the entire group that although one goal of improvisation training is to make you *comfortable being uncomfortable*, we are going to start out with very simple games of pointing. Some people are also afraid to do improv because "they are not funny." Although humor is often a result of improvisation, the purpose of the training is not to be funny. You should not *try* to be funny in these games. Others may be concerned that they have not done improv before. I would then note that we improvise every day, *all the time*. Every conversation you have in life is improvised. None of that stuff is scripted. The main difference between real life and these improvised games is that real life is real, and so this should be *easier* as it doesn't matter at all. And, as you learned in Chapter 22, with pretense, comes play and creativity. These skills and games are not just helpful for creativity, but also for team dynamics, debating, presenting, critiquing, and making friends.

I found that a good size group for these warm-up games is 6 *or* 8, which incidentally, is the same suggested range for team-based idea generation. If the group is too small, there will not be enough energy and variety. If the team is too large, members will wait longer to participate in some games. The even numbers are helpful for games that require pairing off. In most games, the teams stand in a circle, facing each other.

I typically set a few ground rules before we start. The first rule is that people should keep their hands at their side or in front of them. Crossing your arms in front, hands in pockets, or hands behind the back gives off body language that you don't really want to participate, and others will be

DOI: 10.4324/9781003276296-42

less likely to engage with you. Hands out by your sides also keeps you ready to react. In some of the games, we are pointing at others on the team. As we are not trying to trick anyone, we should be very clear about who we are pointing to. This means looking at the person you are pointing at. Some facilitators teach a clapping-point that helps direct attention. I typically demonstrate a hands-together up-down pointing at chest level.

In this workshop, I focus on games that I feel are most strongly connected to team-based idea generation skills. Figure 36.1 shows which skills each game is intended to develop. I will try to provide credit and cite sources for games when applicable.

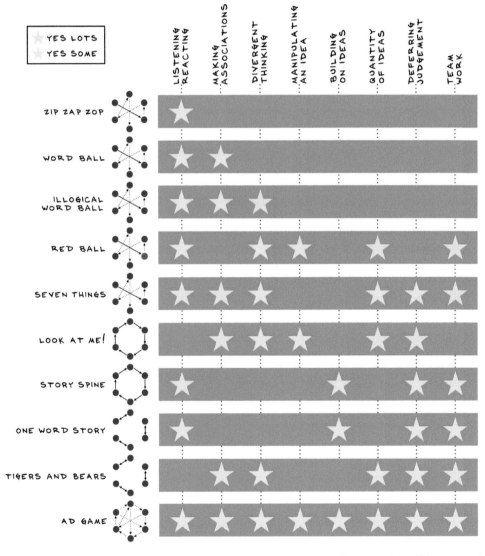

Figure 36.1 A progression of improvisational warm-up games that I use before team-based idea generation. The order of the games is intentionally chosen to start simple and gradually build skills. As shown in the diagrams, the first five games involve pointing around the circle to determine order, the next two use a rotation, the two after that use pairs, and finally, the team comes back together for the last game. I also note which skills are intended to be supported by each game with a silver and gold star rating.

Zip Zap Zop (McKnight and Scruggs, 2008)

This is a common improvisation game and it's easy to explain and play. One person in the circle points to someone else and says "zip." That person then points to someone else and says "zap." And that person then points to someone else and says "zop." This pattern continues: "zip zap zop zip zap zop…" Some play this game where if someone messes up, they are "out," but that is not the purpose. We should not be penalizing anyone for messing up. It's okay to mess up. This would be a very boring game if no one ever messed up. If you watch people play, the only time you hear laughter is when someone messes up (e.g., Release Theory + Superiority Theory). Generally, participants have no problem with this game as they don't need to be creative, they don't need to play pretend, and they just need to pay attention and react. After a few minutes of playing, everyone would have looked at each other in the eyes at least once, everyone hopefully would have smiled, and everyone is going to feel awake and ready for another game.

Word Ball (Faste, 1993; Koppett, 2002)

The goal of this game is to make quick *verbal associations*. It is a natural evolution from Zip Zap Zop as we are still listening, pointing, and reacting, but, in this game, we are also making simple associations. One player starts by tossing (pointing and saying) a word to another player in the circle. The receiver thinks of the first word or phrase that comes to mind and tosses that new word to yet another player. If you were listening to a group play this, it may sound something like: "shark—ocean—beach—volleyball—sports—Super Bowl—nachos—cheese…"

This is a bit like a team-based divergent thinking task in which the team is constructing one long mind map branch that never ends, and each person adds the next node. It is important to stress that this game should be played quickly. We don't want overthinking. *Under*thinking is the purpose of this game. We want players to feel comfortable saying the first thing that comes to mind, even if it is not interesting or clever. We are trying to break down the filtering process in a low-pressure environment. Again, there is no losing. If someone says something that is not connected or maybe they repeat a word, the team moves on. It's OK to mess up and we don't need to make someone feel badly about it. We are simply practicing rapid association-making.

Illogical Word Ball

This is a variation on the prior game with one small change—instead of saying a word that *is* related, players must say a word that has *no* relationship to the word they just heard. This is very difficult to do. Our brains want to build that mind map of logical associations upon receiving a certain prompt. In this game, you must force yourself to think of something that is *not* in that immediate mind map—you must force yourself to fly outside of that domain of obvious connections and pluck some random thought from the void. This game is getting us to practice diffusing focus (Chapter 8) and breaking fixation (Chapter 2). We are also priming the players for brute think (Chapter 29) or linking unrelated concepts. Although we are not explicitly doing that linking yet, if you are playing this game, you will find yourself trying to find a connection between the words.

Red Ball (Spolin, 1963; Fotis & O'Hara, 2015)

I play this game in three phases. In the first phase, an imaginary red ball is tossed between players in the group. The way the ball is tossed is important and follows a very specific format. The person holding the imaginary red ball looks at the person they intend to throw the ball to and says, "red ball?" Before this person is able to throw the ball, the receiver must acknowledge that they are ready to receive the ball by saying, "red ball," and also indicating readiness with their hands. At this point, player 1 can throw the ball to player 2. Player 2 now has the red ball and must pass it to another player using the same "red ball?"—wait for acknowledgment—"red ball" structure.

After several minutes of passing an imaginary ball, there is often at least one person that modifies the game a little (maybe they dribbled the ball first or maybe they made it larger or heavier). This is likely because it is no longer *flow* or play to them (Chapter 20). This is a sign that they are ready for phase two. I would now explicitly tell the players that the imaginary ball can take on any form, although for the sake of this game, we are still going to refer to it as a "red ball" even if it transforms into a bubble or a giant boulder or a frisbee or a puppy, it is still "red ball." Player 1 needs to convey how they are transforming the red ball with motions and sound. Again, they need to wait for the "red ball" acknowledgment from player 2 before they transfer it, such that player 2 can fully understand and embrace the new form being transferred to them. Once player 2 receives the red ball, it can be transformed again into a new form. As only one player has the red ball at any given time, this gives the other players time to think of possible ideas before it is their turn. Given the simplicity of a ball, it can be taken in infinite directions, as long as it is something that can be passed.

Once you see the team being comfortable with this process, it's time to make them uncomfortable again and move to phase three. I would pause the game and ask the person with the red ball to hold it for a second while I hand another player in the group an imaginary yellow ball. I'll then allow the game to start again, but with both a red ball and a yellow ball in play. After a while, I then add a green ball. At this point in the game, everyone is actively involved—either transforming a ball and looking for someone to receive it, receiving a ball, or waiting to receive a ball. This is a stressful and intense round for the players. There is no time to think of a concept until you receive a ball, and you are also simultaneously watching three balls being passed around the circle. *If a gorilla walked through the circle, players would not notice.* This maps to brainstorming in that participants must listen to ideas being shared around them, while simultaneously trying to think of their own idea to be shared.

7 *(or 5)* Things (Fotis & O'Hara, 2015)

This is an *ice breaker*: a game where the players learn more about each other. Admittedly, it's strange placing the ice breaker after people have played four games together, but if we did this game first, the responses would not be as strong. 7 Things begins with one player being asked to name 7 things for a given category (e.g., 7 things that are blue, 7 places you would want to visit, 7 movies you like, 7 favorite pizza toppings, etc.). As the player names 7 things, the rest of the team counts off in unison after each item, both verbally and with their fingers (pepperoni—*one*—mushrooms—*two*—olives—*three*...). When the player hits 7 items, the group cheers, and now the person who named 7 things gets to point at someone else and create a new category for this next person.

Aside from learning more about the other players on the team, there is a sense of team bonding, as the group must cheer each other on and count in unison. There is the goal of coming up with 7 things as fast as possible, so this is also a quantity exercise on the part of the person listing items and a deferring judgment exercise on the part of the other players.

Look at Me!

Discovery "consists of seeing what everyone else has seen and thinking what no one else has thought" (Szent-Gyorgyi, 1957). That is exactly what we are training ourselves to do with this game. Up until now, all the games involved players pointing at who should go next; however, this game is played in a circle and the turn moves clockwise. To begin, everyone on the team is making the exact same motion continuously and in unison. As an example, let's say we are all making a hammering motion with one hand overhead. One person starts and says, "look at me...I'm hammering a nail." The next person in the circle must view the same motion in a new way: "Look at me...I'm knocking on a door." This reframing of the motion continues perhaps making its way around the circle multiple times: "Look at me...I'm shaking my fist at those kids," "look at me I'm pumping my fist at a concert," "look at me I'm using a Shake Weight," "look at me I'm...". And if someone gets stuck and can't think of something new, it is that person's turn to change the motion for the entire team.

In a sense, this game is a physical movement version of the Alternative Uses Test and therefore divergent thinking. Just how divorcing the tack box from the tacks in the Candle Problem facilitates insight (Chapter 2), if you can divorce your action from your original intent in the motion, you are able to find different "uses" for the motion.

Story Spine (Koppett, 2002)

This game is a good example of "yes and..." in which the goal is to accept what someone says and build upon it. It also requires everyone on the team to be listening as you are creating something together. As with the prior game, the players are still in a circle and turns rotate clockwise as opposed to pointing. In this game, the team is going to tell a story, one line at a time, where each player adds the next line to the story. It can be stressful to ask players to develop plot and so this game provides a simple structure or "spine" to build a story around like *Mad Libs*. In this manner, the participant can be as detailed or brief as they feel comfortable. Each player adds the next line of the story using the following starting phrases:

- Once upon a time...
- And every day...
- But then one day...
- And because of that...
- And because of that... *(repeat as needed)*
- Until finally...
- And ever since that day...
- And the moral of the story is... *(optional)*.

A different person should start each round so players are always contributing differently. There is always some pressure on the last person to wrap up the story nicely and there is an unspoken desire for it to be funny. To reduce the pressure on this person, I ask the team to just applaud as soon as the last person finishes speaking. This also allows the facilitator to know when a team has finished a round. String of Pearls is a more advanced variation on this game (McKnight & Scruggs, 2008).

One Word Story (Koppett, 2002; McKnight & Scruggs, 2008; Fotis & O'Hara, 2015)

This game has similarities to *Story Spine* and could be performed as a team. I prefer to run this game in partners and so ideally the teams are composed of even numbers. In pairs, the players alternate saying words to form sentences. Like "Red Ball", I break this game into three or four phases to gradually increase the level of challenge.

In phase one, I ask the pairs to simply recite the alphabet alternating letters. This is a low-pressure means of getting the pairs familiar with the idea of speaking in this new manner. Once complete, we can move on to phase two, in which pairs are asked to pick up or point to an object in the room, and then describe the thing in full sentences using the alternating word manner. There is no specific request for creativity or humor, and so the focus is simply on trying to make coherent sentences with their partner. In phase three, we introduce the creative element. All pairs are given a very brief theme (e.g., a person + a place) and the pairs need to make up a story about the person + place using the same alternating word manner.

As you go through this process, you will note a few things. First, it is very difficult to only say one word at a time, and often people will try to slip in a bonus word (e.g., "is going", "is not", "full of"). Everyone has their own idea of where the story is going and typically it is not the same direction that the other person is thinking. This is why we play this game. Sometimes we must work together on a concept, and it means letting go of the direction you were planning to go. Just like in Story Spine, the resulting product is going to be something that neither of the individual players would have come up with on their own. It is going to be the unexpected result of true collaboration and real-time improvisation. *This game will be frustrating for some people, but those are the people who will benefit most from this type of activity.* Dr. Know-it-All (McKnight & Scruggs, 2008) is a fun variation of this game.

There is a phase four, but it is quite difficult. This involves the players saying…theeee…stoooory…aaaat…theeee…saaaaame…tiiiime. It helps if the players are staring at each other and speaking really slowly while elongating words. There is a bit of *Inception* meets *Ouiji* going on while playing this game in which players seem to influence each other on individual words.

Tigers and Bears

This is a simple game of listing as many things as you can in a short amount of time. It is based on a game called *Clams Are Great* by Jill Bernard. This game is played in pairs. Although it could go anywhere in the workshop, as we are already in pairs from the prior game, this is a natural continuation. The first step is for the pairs to determine who is the *tiger* and who is the *bear* in the relationship. The bear will go first, and they will have one minute to say as many reasons as possible that they can think of "why bears are great." We strive for quantity by having no wrong answers, including things that don't make sense or are not true. However, every response must be said in the format of "bears are great because…" It may sound like: "bears are great because they stand on two legs, bears are great because they catch fish, bears are great because they are from Chicago…" And, again, it doesn't have to be true: "bears are great because they shed their skin," or make sense: "bears are great because math." While the bear is listing ideas, the tigers are keeping count on their paws so the bear can see. After a minute, we switch roles, and the tigers say why tigers are great and the bears count on their paws. I would typically ask what the largest number of responses is for the bears and use that as a goal for the tiger round. As you may recall from Chapter 5, the first ideas you think of are often the same ideas the majority of people think of first. This game encourages everyone to get past those common responses and push themselves into the more novel tail.

The Ad Game (Koppett, 2002; McKnight & Scruggs, 2008; Fotis & O'Hara, 2015)

This is a modification of an original game by Del Close and Viola Spolin. I place this last in the warm-up as it applies all of the skills developed in the prior games and it is a great segue into brainstorming. In this game, the group pretends they are a design team developing a new product. They are provided a prop or everyday common object for which they need to imagine a new use that is not the actual intended use (i.e., removing object permanence).

The first part of this game is like *Look at Me* or the Alternative Uses Test, but with a physical item. This technique is used to generate ideas for what this new product concept could be. The group goes in a circle and each person suggests a novel product concept using the prop. They would pass the prop around and use the phrase, "look at what I just invented, it's a..." This is also similar to the game of *Props* on *Whose Line Is It Anyway?*.

After the team has exhausted ideas or the prop has made it around twice, the team decides which of the many ideas is the best concept. The team moves into a "yes and" activity that is a bit like Story Spine in which the best product concept is built upon by adding features and details. One person starts by reintroducing the product idea, and subsequent teammates agree with it and then add to it with a "yes and" statement.

Once the concept is fleshed out by the team, they need to develop a 30-second live commercial including a short jingle that presents their product idea using the prop. This allows the team to come together without a facilitator for a short amount of time to create something together using the skills they have been practicing. The workshop ends with a fun, brief performance.

At this point in time, the team should be ready for idea generation. Participants are also probably ready to sit down.

References

Faste, R. (1993). The use of improvisational drama exercised in engineering design education. In C. A. Fisher (Ed.), *ASME resource guide to innovation in engineering design*. American Society of Mechanical Engineers.

Fotis, M., & O'Hara, S. (2015). *The comedy improv handbook: A comprehensive guide to university improvisational comedy in theatre and performance*. Routledge.

Koppett, K. (2002). *Training using drama: Successful development techniques from theatre & improvisation*. Kogan Page Publishers.

Kudrowitz, B. & Wallace, D. (2010, October). Improvisational comedy and product design ideation: Making non-obvious connections between seemingly unrelated things. *International Conference on Design and Emotion*, Chicago, Illinois, USA.

McKnight, K. S., & Scruggs, M. (2008). *The Second City guide to improv in the classroom: Using improvisation to teach skills and boost learning*. John Wiley & Sons.

Spolin, V. (1963). *Improvisation for the theater: A handbook of teaching and directing techniques*. Northwestern University Press.

Szent-Györgyi, A. (1957). *Bioenergetics*. Academic Press.

37
IDEAS FOR IDEA GENERATION

There are many different idea generation techniques: Smith (1998) identified at least 172. Some books specifically present idea generation techniques as forms of play and games: *Lateral Thinking* (De Bono, 1970), *A Whack on the Side of the Head* (Van Oech, 1983), *Thinkertoys* (Michalko, 2000), and *Gamestorming* (Gray et al., 2010). Different techniques will have different advantages. For example, TRIZ and SCAMPER can result in *more useful ideas* than brainstorming, whereas brainstorming will result in *more novel ideas* than TRIZ and SCAMPER (Chulvi et al., 2013). Morphological Analysis (Chapter 6) and Design Heuristics (Chapter 29) produce *more elaborate, yet fewer ideas*, than individual brainstorming (Daly et al., 2016), which supports the arguments made in Chapter 6 on the inverse relationship between elaboration and other measures of creativity (Dippo & Kudrowitz, 2015).

Clearly, we have already covered many idea generation methods in prior chapters. We can present these methods using a 2 × 2 matrix in Figure 37.1.

This chapter will primarily discuss group-based ideation, specifically, *brainstorming*, as it is the most common (Lin et al., 2006) and most studied (Smith, 1998) idea generation technique. It is *so* common, that the term "brainstorm" has become synonymous with simply "idea generation" and some do not realize that brainstorming describes a very specific process. "*Brainstorming Sessions*" were first described by Alex Osborn in the final two chapters of his book, *Applied Imagination* (1953). It requires a *group* of people with *diverse perspectives* to sit together to generate a *large quantity of ideas* in a *short amount of time*. In prior chapters, we discussed the importance of quantity of ideas and how that is strongly correlated with creativity. So, in this chapter, I will spend a bit more time on discussing the value of groups before I describe the process.

Groups are Social

Steven Johnson presents an overview of major inventions from 1800 to 2010 and finds that "most commercial innovation during this period takes a collaborative form, with many individuals and firms contributing crucial tweaks and refinements to the product," as opposed to solo inventors having eureka moments (2010). Csikszentmihalyi and Sawyer (1995) further suggest that almost all (99%) of creative process takes place in stages that are predominately social. The original study of brainstorming (Osborn, 1953) found that a group model produced 44% more ideas than groups working individually. This difference was attributed to "social facilitation."

DOI: 10.4324/9781003276296-43

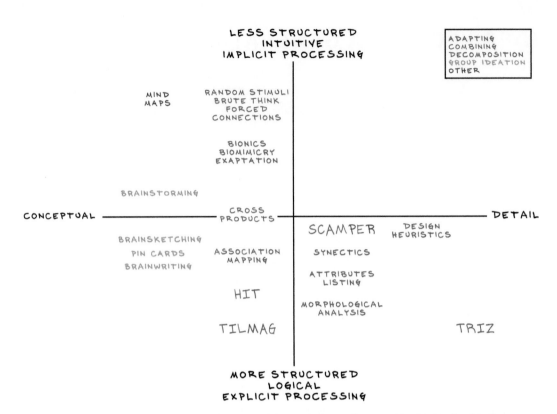

Figure 37.1 A 2 × 2 matrix presenting idea generation techniques discussed in this book. This figure incorporates technique classification from models presented in Asanuma et al. (2011) and Wang (2019). Techniques are also color-coded generally by where they appear in this book. The green techniques related to group-based ideation are discussed in this chapter.

Groups bring Diversity

As discussed in Chapter 8, a way to make non-obvious connections is to work with people that have different knowledge and perspectives. Diverse and multidisciplinary groups "are more effective in the pursuit of creativity, innovation and product development…and allow for rich combinations of otherwise disconnected pools of ideas" (Alves et al., 2007). "Cognitive diversity within a group is one of the primary bases for enhanced idea generation," but it requires strong group facilitation (Paulus, 2000).

I'm going to outline the way I structure a brainstorming session to keep it playful. Again, if partici-pants view an activity as play, they are likely going to be more creative in that activity (Kudrowitz et al., 2016).

A session starts at least two days prior to meeting (as per Osborn, 1979) by sharing the problem brief or How Might We statement. This allows for *incubation* time before ideation. As per Chapter 35, the prompt should be designed such that it is an *appropriate scope* to produce a good quantity of ideas. At the meeting, the participants are briefed on the process and rules. In Chapter 32, I discussed two of the rules of a brainstorming session: "judgement is ruled out" and "combina-tion and improvement are sought" (which also happen to be the components of *Yes And*) (Osborn, 1953). The theory behind these rules is that when we defer judgment, participants will be able to speak freely without the fear of being subjected to harassment. Like in play, brainstorming follows the rule of internal reality or pretense: It needs to be a *protected environment* to allow for play. "There should be nothing outrageous or risky in putting forward a novel idea" (Huizinga, 1950). Osborn has two additional rules that should be assumed at this point: encourage wild ideas (or "free-wheeling") and "quantity is wanted" (1953).

Participants are divided into groups or teams. I am using the word "group" in this chapter to be consistent with academic research, but I prefer the word "team." Osborn originally suggests that the ideal group size is between **5–10 participants** (1953) and then later suggests an optimal group size of 10 (including 5 internal core members and 5 guests) plus a *facilitator* and co-facilitator (1979). "Larger groups do provide more potential for exchange of a large number of ideas from a diverse group of individuals" (Paulus & Kenworthy, 2019). As such, there is a benefit to having more participants. However, "as group size increases the number of nonparticipators also increases [i.e., *social loafing*], resulting in a functional group size smaller than actual size" (Bray et al., 1978). From my experience, the ideal group size is either 6 *or* 8 plus a facilitator. The even number allows for partner warm-up activities. I prefer to have the group seated at a **round table** so everyone can clearly see and hear each other. The preferred setting involves the **table near a wall** such that ideas can be posted on the wall quickly for the entire group to see.

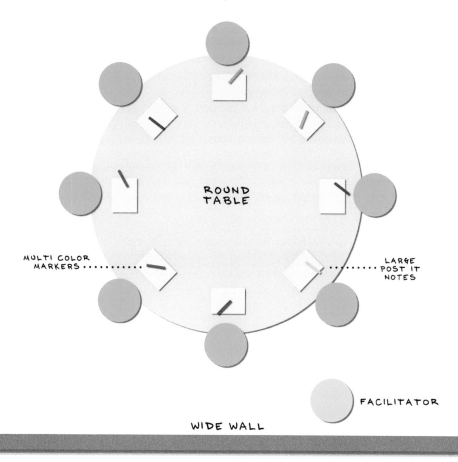

Figure 37.2 A group brainstorm setting with facilitator and round table arranged near a wall for posting ideas.

15	30	45	15	15	15

SHARE   NOMINAL   OVERVIEW   IMPROV   IDEATION   SORT   VOTE   DEBRIEF
PROMPT   IDEATION   WARMUP

Figure 37.3 A suggested timeline for a brainstorming session with times displayed in minutes.

As for time dedicated to the idea generation portion of brainstorming, we first need to understand the relationship between idea quality and idea quantity in groups (i.e., *the ideation function*). The *Bounded Ideation Theory (BIT)* describes the ideation function as a positive S-curve in which "the ratio of good ideas to total ideas may be smaller early on due to limited understanding of the task…, and then larger as understanding of the task increases…, and then smaller due to cognitive overload and physical exhaustion" (Briggs & Reinig, 2007). Brainstorming sessions are limited in time to avoid cognitive overload and physical exhaustion, but they need to be long enough to push past the obvious ideas. Osborn (1979) recommends *30–45 minutes* just for the idea generation portion of the brainstorming session. As shown in Figure 37.3, additional time is needed beforehand to explain the process and engage in warm-up activities, and then afterward, for processing the ideas. In my research, I have also found this to be an appropriate time frame.

Having a skilled and ***trained facilitator*** can have a major impact on the brainstorming session. One of the major criticisms of brainstorming is that individuals can generate more ideas working independently; however, a skilled facilitator allows groups to generate as many ideas as individuals working separately (Oxley et al., 1996). The facilitator can help frame the problem and break down the problem into separate prompts (Osborn, 1979). A good facilitator can shut down criticism effectively, push for quantity, introduce breaks as needed, and keep all participants engaged. Improv training is not just helpful for the participants in the session, it is also helpful for training the facilitator to run the session (Granholt & Martensen, 2021).

Osborn (1973) originally suggests that participants raise hands and simply vocalize ideas and a "secretary" takes notes. This is one of the major differences in how I conduct a session. ***Sketching ideas*** is important, even if we are talking about abstract concepts, and even if participants are "not good at drawing."

> In idea generation groups, sketches can stimulate creativity, especially in the immediate individual idea generation process, by providing new directions for idea generation in an individual generate-interpret cycle. And, sketches can provide a more integrated group process, by providing better access to the earlier ideas, especially in the shared parts of external memory.
>
> (Van der Lugt, 2005)

When we sketch, we remember (Meade et al., 2018). This is especially important at the end of a highly productive session: the visuals allow the participants to quickly parse through all the ideas when clustering and voting.

Each participant has a ***pad of large (6″ x 8″) unruled Post-It notes*** and a ***bold, colorful marker***. The large format paper and bold marker allow the participants to draw their ideas big enough such that others can see it from across the table and, later, on the wall. The post-it low-tack adhesive feature, allows the facilitator to *quickly* post the ideas on the wall and later allows for easy rearrangement (Isaksen et al., 1998). Each participant in the group should have a different color marker such that the group knows who created each idea. Every idea should go on its own page. This is a bit wasteful, but it allows participants to cluster and regroup ideas at the end. In addition to a large sketch, each page should have a ***short title***. The title is used so all participants can clearly refer to specific ideas. After a participant sketches and titles an idea, they hold it up to the group and give a **brief pitch**. The facilitator takes the page from the participant and places it on the wall.

Again, the goal is quantity. Many ideas will be silly but should not be immediately discarded as these fanciful ideas may lead to innovation (see Chapter 26). Popular culture often pokes fun of brainstorming as a means of generating not-so-great ideas. As a few examples: *Key & Peele*'s 'Gremlins 2' Brainstorm sketch ("Everybody here gets to design their own Gremlin" (2015)), *I Think You Should Leave with Tim Robinson*'s Focus Group sketch ("A good steering wheel that doesn't fly off while you're driving" (2019)), and *SNL*'s Black Eyed Peas sketch ("let's start by brainstorming answers to the question 'how's tonight going to be?'" (2022)). It's OK if many ideas seem silly, only a few of the many ideas will likely move forward, and that is all that is needed.

Some will naturally find ideation and sketching playful on its own. Generating ideas involves stepping outside of reality (i.e., pretending) and creating something that doesn't exist. There are also modifications and enhancements to brainstorming that a facilitator can incorporate to draw from both humor and play.

Rolestorming is a technique that allows participants to take on a different personality during ideation. This is like what children do in pretend play. The participant can view the prompt from a user's perspective or from the perspective of someone with different abilities or a different age. To further the pretend play, the facilitator can suggest rolestorming with *superheroes*, fictional characters, or famous people. With this technique, the group is not only viewing the prompt from a different perspective, they are also granted permission to play. If you refer to Chapter 22, play allows for wonder, flexible thinking, positive affect, etc. The facilitator should provide a set of cards with roles or fictional characters such that time can be spent on ideation on the prompt rather than for the roles.

Random Stimuli was discussed in Chapter 29 as a means of individual ideation, but it is also helpful for group-based ideation. This can be accomplished in a few ways. The facilitator can provide photos, magazine clippings, or *props* to the group. The prop method is similar to the Ad Game warm-up, but now applied to the prompt. "These objects… give players something to react to and start manipulating… [it] is the reason why design studios are typically filled with printed images, pages from magazines, material and product samples, and dozens of other seemingly random 2D and 3D props" (Backett, 2013).

At the end of ideation, I move into a very loosely inspired version of the *KJ Method.* This method was developed in the 1950s by Jiro Kawakita, an anthropologist who was searching for a way to organize an overwhelming quantity of data (Iba et al., 2017). The process requires taking pieces of information (or in this case, pages of ideas on a wall) and clustering them into groups by affinity. In my experience, I have found that a "*silent sort*" technique is an efficient means of doing a first pass on clustering. In this technique, no participants speak as they move ideas into clusters on the wall. If someone wants to rearrange clusters, they just do it. Another rule I offer is that no ideas should get stacked, even if the concepts are similar. Only after the ideas are roughly sorted, can the group discuss and then label the clusters. We label the clusters *after* the sorting such that ideas are not forced into categories, and it also allows for unexpected themes to emerge. Most participants view this activity as play as it is a giant puzzle with multiple solutions made up of pieces that the group created themselves.

The group then moves into a process called *multi-voting* in which each participant receives a certain number of votes (typically sticker dots) to place on individual ideas that they feel are worthy of pursuing for any number of reasons. At the end of the process, ideas with multiple votes reflect a group interest and should be further explored. I typically provide a strip of ten black dots such that they show up on any color paper; however, sometimes it is beneficial to use multiple colors to represent different qualities (such as novelty and feasibility). I also enforce a rule that participants cannot vote for their own ideas. They can, however, place multiple dots on the same idea. I inform participants that early votes bias later votes, specifically, "ideas that were the first to receive a vote [receive] almost twice as many votes as ideas that were not first to receive a vote" (Jedrzejewski, 2018). Participants also tend to view this activity as a game, especially if multiple color stickers are involved.

Issues with Brainstorming

A significant number of studies found that groups develop more ideas if they work individually or *nominally* (Diehl & Stroebe, 1987); however, one loses the benefit of bringing people together to inspire each other and make non-obvious connections. Some reasons why nominal idea generation produces more ideas than traditional brainstorming are as follows:

1) *Production blocking*—People can't generate ideas and listen to ideas at the same time.
2) *Evaluation apprehension*—People are afraid to share wild ideas as they may be critiqued.
3) *Free riding* or *social loafing*—Some people in a group will participate less as long as others are contributing.

Items 2 and 3 are generally reduced with an improv warm-up of Chapter 36, which is perhaps why some of my studies have found this results in an increase in the quantity of ideas (Kudrowitz & Wallace, 2010). Similarly, the Design Improv method (Hatcher et al., 2018) that incorporates the improv techniques *during* ideation is intended to overcome these issues of brainstorming. Production blocking, however, is not something that can be solved with improv alone as participants are not able to talk simultaneously. Furthermore, Diehl and Stroebe found that "production blocking accounted for most of the productivity loss of real brainstorming groups" (1987). A solution to all three of these brainstorming issues comes with shifting some or all the ideation from oral *and* visual to primarily visual.

Nominal Brainstorming Methods

"Hybrid Structure"—An obvious solution to these problems is to simply ask participants to generate ideas individually (or *nominally*) sometime before the group meets together. These early ideas become fodder for the group session. "Groups organized in the hybrid structure are able to generate more ideas, to generate better ideas, and to better discern the quality of the ideas they generate" (Girotra et al., 2010).

Brainwriting—To limit production blocking further and ensure all participants contribute, brain writing techniques can be used. Brain writing methods stem from German marketing consultant, Bernd Rohrbach, in the 1960s (Geschka, 1996). *Brainwriting 635* is one method in which six participants have a sheet of paper with a grid of three columns and six rows. Each person creates three ideas across the first row in five minutes. Every five minutes they rotate sheets, get inspired by the ideas on the sheet, and create three new or variant ideas in the next row (reminiscent of the game exquisite corpse). At the end of 30 minutes, the group has 108 ideas. *Pin Cards* is a variation on brainwriting (Geschka, 1996), but instead of passing a grid of ideas, participants work on notecards or Post-It notes. Like in the brainstorming model, participants put one idea on each card. These cards are then piled to the participants' right side on the table. When someone requires inspiration, they take a card from their left and then pass the new idea and the inspiration idea to their right. *Brainsketching* is a more graphical version of brainwriting. "During brainsketching, participants sketch ideas individually in short rounds. After each round they briefly share their ideas and switch papers. In the next round they use the ideas already present on the worksheet as a source of inspiration" (Van der Lugt, 2005).

Regardless of which ideation method you use, any method likely produces better ideas than no method at all (Chulvi et al., 2013)!

References

Alves, J., Marques, M. J., Saur, I., & Marques, P. (2007). Creativity and innovation through multidisciplinary and multisectoral cooperation. *Creativity and Innovation Management, 16*(1), 27–34.

Asanuma, T., Ujiie, Y., Sato, K., & Matsuoka, Y. (2011). Classification of idea generation methods for design based on multispace design model. *Bulletin of Japanese Society for the Science of Design, 58*(3), 11–20.

Backett, P. (2013). Getting serious about play. *Design Management Review, 24*(1), 12–19.

Bray, R. M., Kerr, N. L., & Atkin, R. S. (1978). Effects of group size, problem difficulty, and sex on group performance and member reactions. *Journal of Personality and Social Psychology, 36*(11), 1224–1240.

Briggs, R. O., & Reinig, B. A. (2007, January). Bounded ideation theory: A new model of the relationship between idea-quantity and idea-quality during ideation. In *2007 40th Annual Hawaii International Conference on System Sciences* (HICSS'07). IEEE.

Che, M., et al. (Writers), & Patrick, L., & Diva, M. (Directors). (2022, April 16). Lizzo. [Television series episode]. In L. Michaels (Creator), *Saturday Night Live*, NBC.

Chulvi, V., González-Cruz, M. C., Mulet, E., & Aguilar-Zambrano, J. (2013). Influence of the type of idea-generation method on the creativity of solutions. *Research in Engineering Design, 24*(1), 33–41.

Csikszentmihalyi, M., & Sawyer, K. (1995). Creative insight: The social dimension of a solitary moment. In R. J. Sternberg & J. E. Davidson (Eds.), *The nature of insight* (pp. 329–363). The MIT Press.

Daly, S. R., Seifert, C. M., Yilmaz, S., and Gonzalez, R. (2016). Comparing ideation techniques for beginning designers. *Journal of Mechanical Design, 138*(10), 101108.

De Bono, E. (1970). *Lateral thinking: A textbook of creativity.* Ward Lock Educational.

Diehl, M., & Stroebe, W. (1987). Productivity loss in brainstorming groups: Toward the solution of a riddle. *Journal of Personality and Social Psychology, 53*(3), 497–509.

Dippo, C., & Kudrowitz, B. (2015). The effects of elaboration in creativity tests as it pertains to overall scores and how it might prevent a person from thinking of creative ideas during the early stages of brainstorming and idea generation. *ASME Proceedings of the 27th International Conference on Design Theory and Methodology*, Boston, Massachusetts, USA.

Geschka, H. (1996). Creativity techniques in Germany. *Creativity and Innovation Management, 5*(2), 87–92.

Girotra, K., Terwiesch, C., & Ulrich, K. T. (2010). Idea generation and the quality of the best idea. *Management science, 56*(4), 591–605.

Granholt, M. F., & Martensen, M. (2021). Facilitate design through improv: The qualified eclectic. *Thinking Skills and Creativity, 40*, 100785.

Gray, D., Brown, S., & Macanufo, J. (2010). *Gamestorming: A playbook for innovators, rulebreakers, and change-makers.* O'Reilly Media, Inc.

Hatcher, G., Ion, W., MacLachlan, R., Marlow, M., Simpson, B., & Wodehouse, A. (2018). Evolving improvised ideation from humour constructs: A new method for collaborative divergence. *Creativity and Innovation Management, 27*(1), 91–101.

Huizinga, J. (1950). *Homo Ludens: A study of the play-element in culture.* Roy Publishers.

Iba, T., Yoshikawa, A., & Munakata, K. (2017, October). Philosophy and methodology of clustering in pattern mining: Japanese anthropologist Jiro Kawakita's KJ method. In *Proceedings of the 24th Conference on Pattern Languages of Programs.* The Hillside Group.

Isaksen, S. G., Dorval, K. B., & Treffinger, D. J. (1998). *Toolbox for creative problem solving.* Dubuque, IA: Kendall & Hunt.

Jedrzejewski, F. (2018). *Biases in Idea Screening: Exploring Gender Bias and First-Cast Vote Bias in the Process of Multivoting* [Master's Thesis]. Retrieved from the University of Minnesota Digital Conservancy. https://hdl.handle.net/11299/198965

Johnson, S. (2010). *Where good ideas come from: The natural history of innovation.* Riverhead Books.

Key, K.-M., & Peele, J. (Writers), & Atencio, P., & Benz, P. (Directors). (2015, August 26). Hollywood Sequel Doctor. [Television series episode]. In K.-M. Key, & J. Peele (Creators), *Key and Peele*, Comedy Central.

Kudrowitz, B., Alfalah, S., & Dippo, C. (2016). The Mary Poppins effect: Exploring a relationship between playfulness and creativity with the alternative uses test. *Proceedings - D and E 2016: 10th International Conference on Design and Emotion - Celebration and Contemplation* (pp. 459–464). Universidad de los Andes.

Kudrowitz, B. & Wallace, D. (2010, October). Improvisational comedy and product design ideation: Making non-obvious connections between seemingly unrelated things. *International Conference on Design and Emotion*, Chicago, Illinois, USA.

Lin, C., Hong, J., Hwang, M., & Lin, Y. (2006). A study of the applicability of idea generation techniques. In *Ponencia presentada a The American Creativity Association International Conference.* The American Creativity Association.

Meade, M. E., Wammes, J. D., & Fernandes, M. A. (2018). Drawing as an encoding tool: Memorial benefits in younger and older adults. *Experimental Aging Research, 44*(5), 369–396.

Michalko, M. (2000). *Thinkertoys.* Gestión.

Osborn, A. F. (1953). *Applied imagination: Principles and procedures of creative thinking.* Scribner.

Osborn, A. F. (1979). *Applied imagination: Principles and procedures of creative problem solving.* Scribner.

Oxley, N. L., Dzindolet, M. T., & Paulus, P. B. (1996). The effects of facilitators on the performance of brainstorming groups. *Journal of Social Behavior and Personality, 11*(4), 633–646.

Paulus, P. (2000). Groups, teams, and creativity: The creative potential of idea-generating groups. *Applied Psychology, 49*(2), 237–262.

Paulus, P. B., & Kenworthy, J. B. (2019). Effective brainstorming. In P. B. Paulus, & B. A. Nijstad (Eds.), *The Oxford handbook of group creativity and innovation* (pp. 287–386). Oxford University Press.

Robinson, T., Kanin, Z., & Solomon, J. (Writers), & Schaffer, A., & Mathias, A. (Directors). (2019, April 23). It's the Cigars You Smoke That Are Going to Give You Cancer. [Television series episode]. In T. Robinson, & Z. Kanin (Creators), *I Think You Should Leave w/ Tim Robinson*, Netflix.

Smith, G. F. (1998). Idea-generation techniques: A formulary of active ingredients. *The Journal of Creative Behavior, 32*(2), 107–134.

Van der Lugt, R. (2005). How sketching can affect the idea generation process in design group meetings. *Design Studies, 26*(2), 101–122.

Van Oech, R. (1983). *A whack on the side of the head.* Warner Book, Inc.

Wang, K. (2019). Towards a taxonomy of idea generation techniques. *Foundations of Management, 11*, 65–80.

38

MODELS OF TESTING AND TESTING OF MODELS

In Chapter 5, I introduced a Linus Pauling quote regarding the importance of the quantity of ideas: "you aren't going to have good ideas unless you have lots of ideas" (Richter, 1977). Now that we do have lots of ideas from a highly prolific brainstorming session, we need to hear the second-half of that quote: "... and some sort of principle of selection... as to what the ideas are that are apt to be good." This is why we model and test.

In Chapter 9, we discussed the criteria of what makes a concept innovative, and I introduced the NUF (Gray et al., 2010) or NVF (Novel, Valuable, Feasible) test in Figure 9.1. I like to use this same framework as a first-order screening of ideas (Kudrowitz & Wallace, 2013). We can also use this now as a framework for organizing the different forms of modeling and testing (see Figure 38.1).

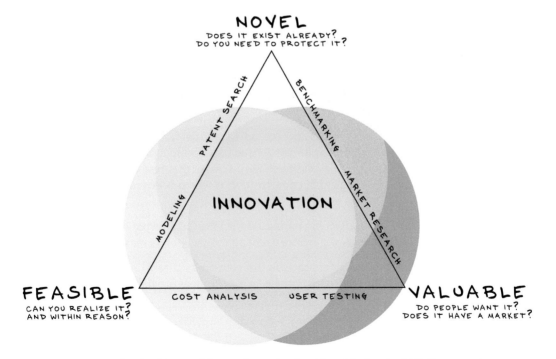

Figure 38.1 A Novel-Valuable-Feasible test for evaluating ideas (Kudrowitz & Wallace, 2013).

DOI: 10.4324/9781003276296-44

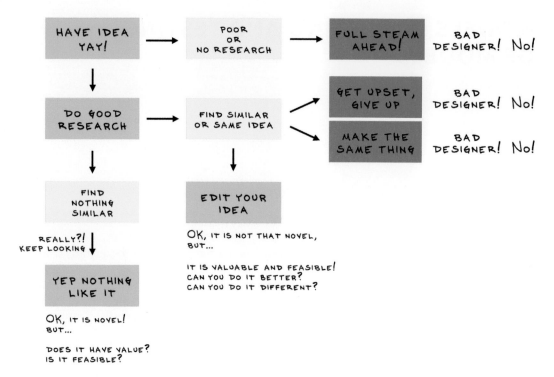

Figure 38.2 A high-level flow chart of testing for the novelty of an idea.

As for **novelty**, designers need to determine if a concept already exists or how different it may be from the state of the art. This can be done via benchmarking discussed in Chapters 34 and 35 and with tools like the *2 × 2 matrix* demonstrated in Figure 35.1. If *intellectual property* is important, designers may also need to conduct a patent search or explore copyright or trademark. If an idea does exist in some form, this is not *necessarily* a bad thing as feasibility and market have already been demonstrated. And, inversely, if an idea is truly novel, then value and feasibility have yet to be determined (see Figure 38.2).

As for **value** or **usefulness**, one will need to do more *market* and *user research* to test their ideas. If the concept is something that people will ultimately need to purchase, one will need to determine the *willingness-to-pay* as part of a value assessment. We discussed user research in Chapter 34, and most of that same content applies again, but now the user research needs to include *feedback* on ideas and *user testing*.

As for **feasibility**, this could be feasibility in producing the idea (i.e., a *proof of concept*), but also financial feasibility. This assessment may involve a cost analysis as well as making models.

With this information collected, designers can use this content as criteria in an idea comparison tool such as a Pugh Chart (Pugh, 1981) to determine "what the ideas are that are apt to be good."

PUGH CHART FOR A HEALTHY FRUIT ON THE GO

CHOOSE ONE IDEA AS THE
STANDARD TO COMPARE
ALL OTHER IDEAS
GIVE IT AN S RATING FOR EACH ROW
O HAS NEGATIVE CONNOTATION

PUT ALL TOP IDEAS ACROSS HERE
USING THE ACTUAL DRAWINGS IS HELPFUL
TRY TO KEEP IT TO UNDER TEN IDEAS
USE A PLUS IF BETTER, A MINUS IS WORSE, AN S IF SAME
COMPARE EACH IDEA TO THE STANDARD

YOUR EVALUATION CRITERIA
THIS ONE IS FOR FRUIT...
YOU SHOULD USE APPROPRIATE CRITERIA
LIKE NOVELTY, VALUE, FEASIBILITY, IMPACT,
OR WHATEVER YOU FEEL IS IMPORTANT
TRY TO KEEP THEM OBJECTIVE
I SUGGEST NO MORE THAN SEVEN

POSITIVE SIGN
MEANS BETTER
AND SO THIS MEANS
ORANGES COST LESS
THAN APPLES

COST PER UNIT WEIGHT 2X	S	+	−	+
HEALTHY GRAMS OF SUGAR PER UNIT WEIGHT 2X	S	S	−	S
EASE OF TRANSPORTATION 1X	S	−	−	S
TIME TO CONSUME 1X	S	S	S	−
INTEREST DO THIS LAST, IF USING IT AS VIEWS MAY CHANGE 1X	S	+	+	S

IF USING WEIGHTS
DETERMINE THEM BEFORE YOU
START FILLING OUT THE CHART

THE PURPOSE OF MAKING THIS IS PRIMARILY FOR THE THOUGHTFUL
COMPARISON OF EACH IDEA USING EACH CRITERIA,
BUT YOU CAN SUM IF YOU WANT TO SEE WHICH IDEAS CLEARLY STAND OUT

SUM?   O   2   4   1

Figure 38.3 An example of a version of a Pugh Chart, used to compare ideas based on specific criteria. This example compares fruit for the need of bringing a healthy snack on the go, but for your idea set, you want to use appropriate criteria such as novelty, feasibility, and value. As described in the figure, one idea is chosen as the standard and all other ideas are compared with that idea as either the same (S), better (+), or worse (−). The purpose is to critically consider each idea according to each of the important criteria in order to make a more informed decision.

Models of Testing Ideas

Models are informative representations of a concept for testing something. They can be physical or conceptual, and span a wide array of embodiments: drawings, digital renderings, physical prototypes, digital prototypes, scale models, analytical models, computer simulations, flowcharts, spreadsheets, storyboards, and performances. Designers do not typically consider drawings as "models" (Pei et al., 2011); however, as they are "informative representations of a concept," I will group them in the "modeling" bin of the design thinking phases of Figure 33.2.

In any modeling, the purpose is twofold (Lauff et al., 2018): first, the designer can use the model to learn more about the idea (which is helpful in refining the concept and making decisions). Second, the designer can use the model as a means of communicating the idea for feedback from users, partners, clients, managers, and other stakeholders (which, again, is helpful in refining the concept and making decisions). Let's explore three types of modeling: estimation, sketching, and physical modeling.

Estimation as (Conceptual) Modeling

The "*back-of-the-envelope*" calculation is a way to model feasibility with estimation. This requires some understanding of basic math and science as well as knowledge of some baseline values (e.g., a gallon of water weights approximately 8 lbs.). Before buying materials and investing time in prototyping, one can quickly estimate on paper if your hand-crank toaster (Chapter 9), for example, is actually feasible. If done well, this can approximate experimental results. For example, a 1970s commercial posed the question: "How many licks does it take to get to the Tootsie Roll center of a Tootsie Pop?" A *numerical simulation* found this to be approximately 130 licks, which was close to the results of an experimental study (Rowe et al., 2004). There is some inherent play value to this process. *Guesstimation* is a board game in which players try to get the closest to the actual value of something (like how many ping pong balls will fit in a car) using quick estimation. To practice estimation, I ask students to estimate how much they are paying per piece of popcorn when they go to the movie theater. As a more playful example, Figure 38.4 illustrates a back-of-the-envelope estimation to determine feasibility of the scene in *James and the Giant Peach* where 501 seagulls lift a giant peach (Dahl, 1961).

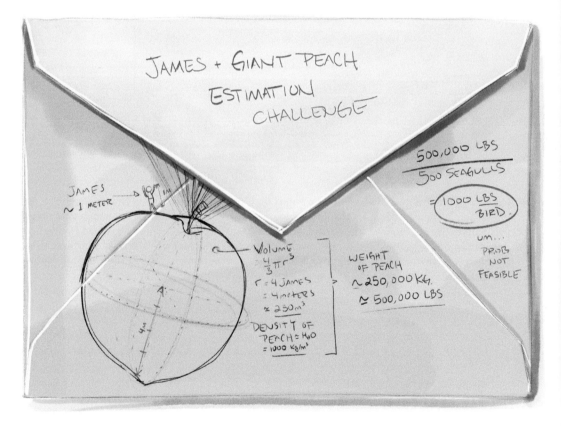

Figure 38.4 In *James and the Giant Peach* (Dahl, 1961), 501 seagulls lift James, his friends, and the giant peach. Starting with a simplified version of the illustration by Nancy Ekholm Burkert in the original publication, we can do a back-of-the-envelope calculation to determine that it is not feasible for this number of seagulls to lift the giant peach. Notice that I use rounded, simple numbers to approximate when possible.

Drawing as (Conceptual) Modeling

According to Huizinga, *sketching* and, perhaps more specifically, *doodling*, is play:

> It is known to everybody who, pencil in hand, has ever had to attend a tedious board meeting. Heedlessly, barely conscious of what we are doing, we play with lines and planes, curves, and masses, and from this abstracted doodling emerge fantastic arabesques, strange animal or human forms...it cannot be doubted that it is a play-function of low order akin to the child's playing in the first years of life....

> (1950)

The beauty of a sketch is that it is fast and costs almost nothing when compared with making physical models or simulations. You can also iterate directly onto the sketch. If you don't like something about the concept or the user wants something else, you can simply modify the drawing in real time. This is the *dialectics of sketching*: the thing you created provides some visual information that *inspires* you to iterate on your original work (Goldschmidt, 1991). The designer is having a conversation with themselves through their work. The wonderful creations throughout *Harold and the Purple Crayon* are an example of the dialectics of sketching: "the sandy beach [that Harold drew] reminded Harold of picnics. And the thought of picnics made him hungry [and so he drew a picnic]" (Johnson, 1955). There are a variety of games that use this ambiguity and flexibility of sketching as a creative play mechanic: exquisite corpse, picture consequences, Telephone Pictionary/*Telestrations*, Photoshop Tennis/Battle/Pong, etc. A version of this game also appears in an episode of *Bluey* where the children are encouraged to use their imagination and draw pictures. The children and adults then alternate creative drawings of how the adults are trying to escape from the children, and the children find creative ways of catching up with the adults. Eventually, the children draw their "dreamhouse car" with "11 burger shops...and 20 bedrooms, and 40 toilets...and a spa on the balcony" that later has rockets and parachutes (Brumm & Jeffery, 2020).

Doodling and brainstorming sketches are great for creativity and exploration. However, when moving from these forms of "*thinking sketches*" into those used for presentation and feedback (*explanative* and *persuasive sketches*), it is important to consider the quality of the drawing. In my

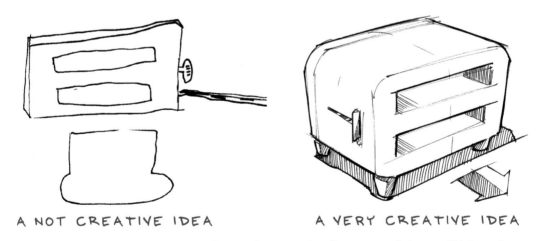

A NOT CREATIVE IDEA   A VERY CREATIVE IDEA

Figure 38.5 Toaster drawing examples from Kudrowitz and Wallace (2012) of a low- and high-quality sketch for a horizontal toaster concept. The concept presented as a high-quality sketch was 2.3 times more creative than the same idea presented with a low-quality sketch.

studies, I have found that higher quality drawings are perceived to be on average 2.3 times more creative than the *same* idea presented with a poor-quality drawing (Kudrowitz & Wallace, 2012).

Physical Modeling and Prototyping

Like sketching, Huizinga also suggests that the act of physical modeling has inherent play value: "A certain playfulness is by no means lacking in the process of creating and 'producing' a work of art… the play function is especially operative where mind and hand move most freely" (1950). When modeling, the designer is creating a representation of a future thing that doesn't exist yet: it is inherently pretend.

There are degrees of model refinement from quick and lo-fi, "sketch models," to refined and detailed alpha-prototypes that work and look like a real solution. In design, specifically industrial design and architecture, we tend to use the term "model" to describe a nonfunctional or roughly functional, physical, 3D representation of an idea. The term "prototype" is a specific form of advanced model that is functional, and closely resembles the actual product (Evans, 1992; Pei et al., 2011). When we start to think about the modeling of a process or service, our definitions need to broaden beyond physical embodiments.

Sketch modeling is a term used to describe low-fidelity physical models. It has some strong connections with terms like *tinkering, hacking, crafting, Frankenstein'ing, MacGyver'ing*, etc. Sketch modeling is taking 2D concepts and making them physical such that designers can get feedback, answer questions quickly, and "understand more fully the complex relationships between components, cavities, interfaces and form" (Evans, 1992; Pei et al., 2011). As the designer develops a model, the idea may evolve and, as such, modeling blurs into ideation (making it fuzzier).

Like with sketching, one of the benefits of sketch modeling is that it is also inexpensive and fast. Designers can use paper, cardboard, foam, and whatever materials are easily available. Figure 38.6 builds on the brainstorming workshop of Figure 37.3 to include sketch modeling. In this workshop, the group has a short amount of time, perhaps 45 minutes, to make a sketch model of their idea(s) using an assortment of common inexpensive materials like paper, tape, string, and cardboard as well as actual toys (Play Doh, crayons, balloons, pipe-cleaners, Lego, balls, googly eyes, etc.). Thomas Edison would support this model of testing ideas: "To invent, you need a good imagination and a pile of junk" (Hargadon & Sutton, 2000). Let's explore some famous examples of sketch models throughout history.

IDEO was in an early meeting with a medical device company to develop a nasal surgery tool when an engineer fashioned a "kindergarten-quality prototype" in five minutes:

> He picked up a whiteboard marker, a black plastic Kodak film canister, and an orange clothespin-like clip. He taped the canister to the whiteboard marker and attached the orange clip to the lid of the film canister. The result was an extremely crude model of the new surgical tool.
>
> (Kelley, 2005)

The surgeons immediately gave feedback that this was what they were looking for, and this crude model led to a real medical device. In another medical example, Dr. Willem Kolff created the first series of dialysis machine prototypes in the Netherlands using the limited resources available during World War II including: artificial sausage casings, fruit juice cans, and a Maytag washing machine (Kolff, 1990). Washing machine parts were also harvested to make the first prototype of the drain cleaning tool, Roto-Rooter (Peterson, 1988). If you recall back to Chapter 7, Leonardo da Vinci conducted research on flows in streams and rivers and made sketches of his fluid flow ideas in notebooks. He *also* made sketch models to test his ideas. The sketch in Figure 7.3 of how the aortic value may work was modeled with a glass container and grass seeds. "Leonardo used his simple glass model to simulate flow dynamics inside the aortic root, he conducted the first scientific flow visualization in the history of science about 400 years ahead of Osborne Reynolds' celebrated pipe flow visualization studies" (Gharib et al., 2002).

Testing of Models

As discussed in Chapter 32, the earlier you can receive feedback from others in a design process, the faster the concept evolves and improves (Häggman et al., 2015). When you bring a model to a user and ask for feedback, you are naturally asking that person to play pretend. The user is taking something that is not real yet and imagining what it would be like if it were real. The model becomes a toy; it is a thing to toy with, and it is also a pretend representation of something.

In addition to the model itself being pretend, the greater context and experience involving the model can also be pretend. We discussed *bodystorming* in Chapter 34 as a means of role-playing to understand an environment that one is not able to physically access. *Bodystorming* can also be used with a prototype to test and demonstrate how something would work, and it provides immediate feedback on ideas (Oulasvirta et al., 2003). Bodystorming becomes part of a user experience modeling process. In this context, modeling blurs into testing (making it fuzzier).

Sometimes your prototype is not able to function (*yet*) for several reasons, but you still desire feedback from users. Technology can also be faked for this stage of modeling and testing, or perhaps I should say: the designers and users "*play pretend*" together. This method of prototyping and testing is called *Wizard of Oz Prototyping*. When the functionality behind a product, app, or service is not fully implemented, the design team can "pull the strings behind the curtain," just like the *Wizard of Oz* (Bernsen et al., 1994). The user would then experience the concept as if it were functional in order to get feedback prior to costly and timely development.

Informance Design is a technique like bodystorming where designers roleplay in a performance using prototypes as props to demonstrate a concept or design solution to an audience. "Informances, like user testing are enactive and evaluative. Unlike user testing, they are intended to explore design ideas in ways that are generative rather than analytic" (Burns et al., 1994). The final portion of my design thinking workshop as shown in Figure 38.6 is an informance. The finale for my design classes (Toy Product Design & Product Innovation Lab) are productions called "PLAYsentations." At this event, the teams perform brief, five-minute theatrical skits with functional prototypes, props, costumes, sound effects, music, narration, etc. It is a form of informance design, and the audience can provide immediate feedback on the concepts.

At the end of Chapter 17, we discussed the concepts of *science fiction prototyping* (Johnson, 2011) and *Design Fiction* (Bleecker, 2009). These are using designed objects (like sketch models and prototypes) to demonstrate future experiences, but they also come with a richer narrative of a future world. With design fiction, informance, and bodystorming, the model is just one element of the demonstration of an encompassing experience that can be used to gather feedback. As we move into a future of experiences and integrated services and products, our modeling and prototyping

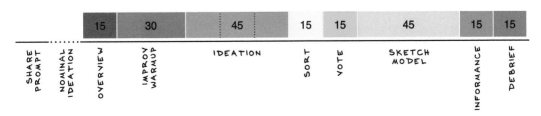

Figure 38.6 A suggested workshop that builds on the brainstorming session of Figure 37.3 to include sketch modeling and informance with times displayed in minutes.

will focus more on the experience of engaging with the objects, space, and system and less on the object itself (Buchenau & Suri, 2000).

At this point, I hope to have made my case on why play and humor are critical for creativity and innovation. To add one final rationale: improvisation, a sense of humor, and a sense of playfulness all seem to be helpful with *communication* throughout a design process. My research has found that stakeholders have a difficult time separating quality of presentation from quality of concept across most forms of design communication: oral idea pitches, visual drawings, lo-fi sketch models, and more refined prototypes (Kwon & Kudrowitz, 2018). All forms of testing (from taking a drawing to a user for feedback, to pretending with a partially functional Wizard of Oz prototype, to a more theatrical informance) benefit from designers having improvisation and role-playing skills (Medler & Magerko, 2010).

References

Bernsen, N. O., Dybkjær, H., & Dybkjær, L. (1994). Wizard of OZ prototyping: How and when. In *Proceedings of CCI Working Papers Cognitive Science/HCI*. Roskilde, Denmark.

Bleecker, J. (2009, March). *Design fiction: A short essay on design, science, fact and fiction.* Near Future Laboratory.

Brumm, J. (Writer), & Jeffery, R. (Director). (2020, April 6). Escape [Television series episode]. In C. Aspinwall (Producer), *Bluey*, Ludo Studio.

Buchenau, M., & Suri, J. F. (2000, August). Experience prototyping. In *DIS '00: Proceedings of the 3rd Conference on Designing Interactive Systems: Processes, Practices, Methods, and Techniques* (pp. 424–433). Association for Computing Machinery.

Burns, C., Dishman, E., Verplank, W., & Lassiter, B. (1994, April). Actors, hairdos & videotape—informance design. In *Conference Companion on Human Factors in Computing Systems* (pp. 119–120). Association for Computing Machinery.

Dahl, R. (1961). *James and the Giant Peach.* Alfred A. Knopf, Inc.

Evans, M. A. (1992). *Model or prototype which, when and why?* Loughborough's Institutional Repository.

Gharib, M., Kremers, D., Koochesfahani, M. & Kemp, M. (2002). Leonardo's vision of flow visualization. *Experiments in Fluids, 33,* 219–223.

Goldschmidt, G. (1991). The dialectics of sketching. *Creativity Research Journal, 4*(2), 123–143.

Gray, D., Brown, S., & Macanufo, J. (2010). *Gamestorming: A playbook for innovators, rulebreakers, and changemakers.* O'Reilly Media, Inc.

Häggman, A., Tsai, G., Elsen, C., Honda, T., & Yang, M. C. (2015). Connections between the design tool, design attributes, and user preferences in early stage design. *Journal of Mechanical Design, 137*(7), 071408.

Hargadon, A., & Sutton, R. I. (2000). Building an innovation factory. *Harvard Business Review, 78*(3), 157–157.

Huizinga, J. (1950). *Homo Ludens: A study of the play-element in culture.* Roy Publishers.

Johnson, B. D. (2011). *Science fiction prototyping: Designing the future with science fiction.* Morgan & Claypool Publishers.

Johnson, C. (1955). *Harold and the purple crayon.* Harper & Row.

Kelley, T. (2005). *The ten faces of innovation.* Currency.

Kolff, W. J. (1990). The invention of the artificial kidney. *The International Journal of Artificial Organs, 13*(6), 337–343.

Kudrowitz, B., Te, P., & Wallace, D. (2012). The influence of sketch quality on perception of product-idea creativity. *AI EDAM, 26*(3), 267–279.

Kudrowitz, B. M., & Wallace D. R. (2013). Assessing the quality of ideas from prolific, early-stage product ideation. *Journal of Engineering Design, 24*(2), 120–139.

Kwon, J., & Kudrowitz, B. (2018). Good idea! Or, good presentation? Examining the effect of presentation on perceived quality of concepts. *AI EDAM, 32*(4), 380–389.

Lauff, C. A., Kotys-Schwartz, D., & Rentschler, M. E. (2018). What is a prototype? What are the roles of prototypes in companies? *Journal of Mechanical Design, 140*(6), 061102.

Medler, B., & Magerko, B. (2010, April). The implications of improvisational acting and role-playing on design methodologies. In *CHI '10: Proceedings of the SIGCHI Conference on Human Factors in Computing Systems* (pp. 483–492). Association for Computing Machinery.

Oulasvirta, A., Kurvinen, E., & Kankainen, T. (2003). Understanding contexts by being there: Case studies in bodystorming. *Personal and Ubiquitous Computing, 7*(2), 125–134.

Pei, E., Campbell, I., & Evans, M. (2011). A taxonomic classification of visual design representations used by industrial designers and engineering designers. *The Design Journal, 14*(1), 64–91.

Peterson, E. G. (1988). *Roto-Rooter, 1935–1988* [thesis]. Michigan State University.

Pugh, S. (1981). Concept selection: A method that works. *Proceedings of International Conference on Engineering Design* (pp. 497–506). Edition Heurista, Zürich.

Richter, R. (1977). *Linus Pauling, Crusading Scientist*. [Radio broadcast]. WGBH-Boston.

Rowe, K. G., Harris, K. L., Schulze, K. D., Marshall, S. L., Pitenis, A. A., Uruena, J. M.,... & Sawyer, W. G. (2014). Lessons from the lollipop: Biotribology, tribocorrosion, and irregular surfaces. *Tribology Letters, 56*(2), 273–280.

Afterword

Thanks for joining me on this journey—linking together the domains of play, humor, creativity, innovation, and design. There was a lot covered throughout this book, and so I organized many of the topics discussed into a Venn diagram.

Figure 39.1 A Venn diagram classifying the topics in this book across the domains of play, humor, and creativity, innovation, and design.

I introduced this book with somewhat of a dystopian lens on society losing our creative abilities. I want to end with a spark of hope!

We all have the ability to be highly creative (well, at least 98% of us) according to Land and Jarman (1992). It is simply a matter of retaining those skills as we grow up. I have illustrated the numerous connections between these domains. If we can hang on to our playfulness and sense of humor, we can also retain our creative abilities as adults. And if you have lost your way, we can learn to develop our sense of humor (e.g., Part IV; Aaker & Bagdonas, 2021), and we can learn to be more playful (e.g., Part III). We can also learn to be more creative (e.g., Chapter 7).

Let's call back Captain Creativity. This book provides a foundation of *domain knowledge* related to creativity and design. You clearly have the *motivation* (e.g., you are reading the afterward!). Many of the tools related to play and humor throughout the book, as well as design process in general (e.g., Part V), can help develop your *creative mindset*. You are now also aware of what makes for an appropriate and supportive *environment* for creativity. When these four powers combine, you are ready to take on any challenge with creative fuel in your jetpack.

There are some interesting data points to suggest that we may be turning things around as a society regarding play and humor.

"A survey last year from the US industry's Toy Association found that 58% of adult respondents bought toys and games for themselves" (Gilblom, 2022). Additionally, these "kidults," as we are affectionately labeled by the toy industry, increased toy sales in the United States by 37% from 2019 to 2021. And with new demand, comes new supply! As per Figure 31.2, the market for cartoons for adults has grown significantly since 1990. During the pandemic, adults made up the majority of people playing Nintendo's popular Animal Crossing video game (Warren, 2020). Razor introduced the first adult-sized scooter, Lite-brite introduced a wall-sized adult version of their classic toy, and Lego introduced an entire line of kits for adults under their web category: "Adults Welcome" (Gilblom, 2022). In recent years, the market for adult play expanded so much that the annual Toy of the Year (TOTY) awards introduced a new category: Grown-Up Toy of the Year.

As for humor, a significant number of studies have explored humor in the workplace and found that employees report higher job satisfaction, job performance, and workgroup cohesion when their supervisors have a strong sense of humor (Decker, 1987; Romero & Cruthirds, 2006; Mesmer-Magnus et al., 2012). People are now taking humor seriously (Aaker & Bagdonas, 2021). Stanford added Humor: Serious Business as a course offering to their business majors. "We're living in a time when empathy, inclusivity and authenticity are important for all leaders. Humor is actually a secret weapon that can serve them well" (Purtill, 2021).

You may be thinking, "if we are being jocular and playful, aren't we just going to come up with silly ideas?" The answer is…not necessarily. And for many reasons as illustrated throughout this book:

- **When you view an activity as play, you are going to be more creative in that activity** (Chapters 21 and 23)
- When we play, we are **intrinsically motivated** and **fully engaged** in the activity—these are also core criteria for creativity (Chapters 1, 20, 21, 22, and 24)
- When we are playing, we are **uninhibited in our thinking**, and anything is possible—this state of **wonder** allows for discovery (Chapter 22)
- When we play, we are in a **safe, protected space free from failure**, and that facilitates creativity (Chapters 22 and 24)
- When we play, we are **thinking laterally, flexibly, and outside of the box**, and, in this state, we are more likely to make non-obvious connections (Chapters 2, 6, and 22)

- Play is how we *learn, develop new skills, and develop relationships*, and with new knowledge, inspiration, and networking comes increased creative capacity (Chapters 7 and 18)
- *Adding play value can make things more effective and engaging* (Chapter 24)
- Play and humor both lead to positive affect that then increases dopamine and has been found to increase creative abilities (Chapters 8 and 22)
- The play and humor of cartoons, science fiction, superheroes, and comics, is part of the dialog between artists, writers, and scientists that helps push society forward (Chapters 16 and 17)
- *Humor and creativity are both about making non-obvious connections between seemingly unrelated things* (Chapters 4, 26, 27, 28, and 29)
- Humor, in the form of *observational comedy, can shed light on our foibles* and things that society often overlooks or ignores (Chapters 25, 30, 31, and 34)
- Humor can make uncomfortable things more approachable, allow us to question the status-quo, and reduce the threat of radical change (Chapters 12, 13, 14, and 31)
- *Improvisation training* can increase idea production and there is a significant overlap in the skills required for improvisational comedy and team-based idea generation (Chapters 32 and 36)
- *There is an overlap in processes for developing comedy and design process* (Chapter 33)
- Playfulness, improvisational skills, role-playing, and *pretend play are useful skills throughout design process* (Part V)
- *Playful and silly ideas are an industry on their own* and that industry is growing!
- Lastly, *things that seem silly at first may actually be innovative in the future* (Chapters 10, 15, and 16): A Haha! may be an Aha! in disguise (Chapter 26)

You don't *need* play and humor to be creative and innovative, but it helps in every stage of design process from problem formation to ideation to modeling to testing. This is not an argument that the outcome of a design process should be a playful or funny thing. It may be the case that you are working on a very serious product or problem. My argument is that humor and play help facilitate the process of reaching creative and innovative solutions. Play and humor tend to be overlooked or viewed as childish, but they may be what is missing to rejuvenate innovation in our society.

To all of you artists, engineers, entrepreneurs, designers, students, teachers, healthcare workers, industry leaders, parents, community members, etc., this is your empirically supported, proverbial thumbs up to your Animal Crossing addiction, your Harry Potter Lego set purchase, your binge-watching Adventure Time, your trip to Disneyland without kids, and your overly excessive Halloween decorations. To you, *kidult*, I'm not just encouraging you to be sillier and more playful… it might actually be necessary to make the world a better place.

Now, go play.

References

Aaker, J., & Bagdonas, N. (2021). *Humor, seriously.* Currency.

Decker, W. H. (1987). Managerial humor and subordinate satisfaction. *Social Behavior and Personality: an International Journal, 15*(2), 225–232.

Gilblom, K. (2022, June 17). Adults who love toys? The toy industry loves them, too. *Bloomberg Businessweek.*

Land, G., & Jarman, B. (1992). *Breakpoint and beyond: Mastering the future today.* HarperCollins Publishers.

Mesmer-Magnus, J., Glew, D. J., & Viswesvaran, C. (2012). A meta-analysis of positive humor in the workplace. *Journal of Managerial Psychology, 27*(2), 155–190.

Purtill, C. (2021, March 6). How to laugh at work. *The New York Times.*

Romero, E. J., & Cruthirds, K. W. (2006). The use of humor in the workplace. *Academy of Management Perspectives, 20*(2), 58–69.

Warren, R. (2020, September 7). Animal crossing: New horizons mostly played by adults. *Gamerant.*

Index